PENGUIN BOOKS

Mind the Gaffe

Larry Trask was born in western New York State in 1944. In 1970 he
came to England and in 1983 he obtained his Ph.D. from the University of London. He taught at the University of Liverpool from 1979
to 1988; since then he has taught in the School of Cognitive and
Computing Sciences at the University of Sussex. His special interests
are historical linguistics, grammar and the Basque language. He is the
author of a number of books, including *A Dictionary of Grammatical
Terms in Linguistics, Language Change, Language: The Basics, The
Penguin Guide to Punctuation* and *The Penguin Dictionary of English
Grammar.*

Mind the Gaffe

The Penguin Guide to Common Errors in English

R. L. Trask

PENGUIN BOOKS

PENGUIN BOOKS

Published by the Penguin Group
Penguin Books Ltd, 80 Strand, London WC2R ORL, England
Penguin Putnam Inc., 375 Hudson Street, New York, New York 10014, USA
Penguin Books Australia Ltd, 250 Camberwell Road, Camberwell, Victoria 3124, Australia
Penguin Books Canada Ltd, 10 Alcorn Avenue, Toronto, Ontario, Canada M4V 3B2
Penguin Books India (P) Ltd, 11 Community Centre, Panchsheel Park, New Delhi – 110 017, India
Penguin Books (NZ) Ltd, Cnr Rosedale and Airborne Roads, Albany, Auckland, New Zealand
Penguin Books (South Africa) (Pty) Ltd, 24 Sturdee Avenue, Rosebank 2196, South Africa

Penguin Books Ltd, Registered Offices: 80 Strand, London WC2R ORL, England

www.penguin.com

First published as a Penguin hardback 2001
Published in paperback in Penguin Books 2002
11

Set in 8/11 pt Linotype ITC Stone Serif
Typeset by Rowland Phototypesetting Ltd, Bury St Edmunds, Suffolk
Printed in England by Clays Ltd, St Ives plc

ISBN-13: 978-0-14-051476-6

For my Jan

Contents

Acknowledgements

I am indebted to Jan Lock and to Martin Toseland, Myrna Blumberg, Emma Horton and the Penguin proofreaders for their valuable comments on a draft of this book, and to my linguistic colleagues at Sussex for assistance with certain vexed points. Any errors remain my own responsibility.

Introduction

As you know, English is spoken and written in a huge variety of forms. A Chicago taxi driver does not talk like a Surrey stockbroker. A student being interviewed for a job does not speak the way he speaks in the bar with his friends. The English in most national tabloid newspapers does not look like the English in most serious broadsheet newspapers, and neither looks quite like the English in a scientific journal.

All of these varieties of English are appropriate to their circumstances. However, there is one variety of English that occupies a rather special position everywhere in the English-speaking world. This variety is *standard written English*, sometimes also called *edited English*. Standard written English is the variety of English used in all careful writing, apart from certain styles of literature. It is the kind of English expected in student essays and dissertations, in business letters and reports, in non-fiction books, in serious newspapers, and in most other kinds of writing.

Unlike most other kinds of English, standard written English is strongly codified. That is, there is almost total agreement as to which forms and usages form part of it, and which do not. So, for example, *mischievous* is a standard spelling, but **mischievious* is not. (Throughout this book, an asterisk marks a form or usage which is not acceptable in standard written English.) Likewise, *this number of students* is standard, but **this amount of students* is not. Less obviously, perhaps, the sentence **Was any action decided to be taken?* is not accepted as part of the standard, while *Was any action taken?* is indisputably standard.

Mastery of standard written English is a requirement for many professions, and it is highly desirable in many others. But nobody comes naturally equipped with this mastery. Standard written English has to be acquired, usually by formal education. Sadly, however, in recent years schools in most English-speaking countries have pulled back from teaching this material. As a result, even university graduates with good degrees often find themselves with a command of standard English that is at best inadequate and at worst distressing. This is not a trivial problem, since a poor command of the conventions of standard English will often make a very bad impression on those who must read your writing.

Consider the following passage, which is taken from an expensively printed advertising brochure put out by a well-known chain of stores selling electrical goods, and which was meant to be written in standard English:

Micro Systems are defined by their amazingly compact size, so are ideal for places were space is at a premium . . . Many come with a built in timer and clock, mean their ideal for the bedroom and replacing the need for a radio alarm clock.

This passage contains at least six outright errors, and some of them, such as the use of *were* for *where*, are shocking to any reader with pretensions to literacy. It is hard to believe that a successful company paid somebody to write this passage, and that no one else in the company noticed anything wrong with it. Many readers will inevitably respond to such stuff by wondering 'If this is their idea of good English, what's their idea of a good product?'

Mastery of standard English is worth acquiring, and lack of it is a severe handicap. Recently I had to read a final-year dissertation written by a university undergraduate. In content, it was striking, even brilliant, and the student who wrote it showed a clear capacity for doing original research. However, she was virtually incapable of constructing a grammatical sentence in standard English, and her work, which should have been a pleasure to read, was in fact tedious, exasperating, annoying, and at times hard to follow – all because of her poor command of standard English. Regardless of her talent, she will never get an academic job with such inadequate English.

The purpose of this book is to help you with your written English. I hope your English is already better than what you saw in the dreadful example above. But all of us can learn ways of improving our writing. I myself, after thirty years of teaching and writing, am still learning ways of improving my written English.

Many other usage handbooks exist, but some of them are a little reluctant to lay down the law. They often tell the reader instead 'Well, some people prefer this, but other people prefer that.' I assume that you don't want to hear this. Instead, I expect, you want to read 'This is right, but that is wrong.' As far as possible, I'll try to say exactly that. This handbook adopts a much blunter tone than do most others. But sometimes it's just not possible to take such an uncompromising line. There are two reasons for this, a small one and a big one. .

First, the small one. Standard written English comes in two slightly different versions: the British version and the American version. Fortunately, the differences between the two versions are not great, except in vocabulary. This book is written by an American who works in Britain, and it covers most of the significant differences between the British standard and the American standard – in spelling, in punctuation, in grammar, and in the use of words. Naturally, you should try to stick consistently to one version or the other, since mixing British and American conventions will please nobody.

Second, the big reason. Every living language is constantly changing, and English is no exception – not even standard written English. Words and forms that were normal in standard English several generations ago, or several decades ago, may now be quaint, archaic or obsolete. Other words and forms that did not exist at all in standard English some time ago are now becoming accepted into the standard language, and may already have become fully accepted.

This may surprise you, but consider an example. Only a few generations ago, the construction illustrated by the example *My house is being painted* did not exist in standard English, and the only possible form for expressing this was *My house is painting* – a form which is impossible for us now. When, in the early nineteenth century, a few innovating writers began writing things like *My carriage is being repaired*, the conservative commentators of the day could not contain their fury. Veins bulging purply from their foreheads, they condemned the new form as 'illogical' and 'monstrous'. But their efforts were in vain. Eventually, all of the conservatives who objected to the new form died, and the old form died with them. Now we can only gape at this nineteenth-century brouhaha in astonishment, and wonder what all the fuss was about.

Things are no different today, except that the particular battles being fought are different. At every moment, including this moment, there exist very many forms which are either on the way out or on the way in, and this is where the difficulties lie. At what point can we safely say that a vanishing form is no longer part of the standard language, or that an emerging form is now uncontroversially part of the standard language? There are no simple answers to these questions, and every commentator must try to make the best judgement possible. Naturally, commentators do not always agree in these judgements, and different handbooks will offer conflicting advice on vexed points of this sort.

In this handbook, I have tried to err on the side of caution. If there appears to be a consensus among informed commentators, then I go along with that consensus. But, if the commentators are divided, I usually advise the reader to avoid the controversial form. That is, I advise you to refrain from using a form which will annoy the minority of readers with conservative tastes, and to choose instead a form that will annoy no one.

At the same time, though, I have no patience with those ignorant and silly beliefs about good English which have bedevilled us for so long. Such fetishes as insisting on *It's I*, not ending sentences with prepositions, and avoiding split infinitives are all dismissed as the nonsense they are.

This book deals only with written English. It has nothing to say about speech, and therefore nothing to say about pronunciation. If you want to check the pronunciation of a word, any good desk dictionary will provide it. But by far the best book for this purpose is J. C. Wells's *Longman Pronunciation Dictionary*, 2nd edition, 1999, London: Longman. This splendid book gives the current standard pronunciations of a vast number of words and proper names, in both British and American English.

Like most usage handbooks, this one offers some advice on good style. Much of this advice can be easily summarized here. Write simply, plainly and clearly. Use plain words and not fancy words – especially when you're not sure what the fancy words mean. Avoid vogue words and jargon. Plan your writing. Think about what you mean, and choose your words carefully. Don't just dump a pile of hackneyed phrases onto the page. If you're not sure about a spelling or a usage, look it up. Read what you've written. Edit it and polish it. Work hard to be sure that your meaning is so clear that no reader can possibly misunderstand you or be puzzled.

Unlike most other usage handbooks, this one goes on to venture some advice about content. I have chosen to exceed my brief here for good reasons. We live in an age when jargon-ridden, buzzword-laden, content-free writing surrounds us and almost drowns us. Advertising, junk mail, gushing celebrity pieces, the tracts distributed by assorted religious sects, all kinds of New Age dross, and the public statements of politicians and military men are just a few of the most obvious examples.

Much more subtle, but perhaps more insidious, is a style of academic writing which is now very prominent. This style seems to have started in France, but it is flourishing in American universities, and it is far from rare elsewhere. To this style I have, throughout the book, applied the label 'post-modernist' – perhaps unwisely, since I cannot tell the difference between post-modernism and post-structuralism, even though some people seem to think the difference is important.

What I am calling, wisely or not, post-modernist writing is frequently arrogant, sometimes strident, invariably pretentious, and, above all, almost always opaque. The goal of such writing appears to be nothing more than dazzling the hapless reader into stupefied and uncomprehending awe with an unending sequence of fancy words, usually inappropriate words, strung together in a way that makes no obvious sense at all. This stuff is produced by the yard, and it appears to captivate intelligent and well-educated people who really ought to know better. Instead of turning away from such prose in contempt and disgust, these readers devote their energies to turning out 'readings' of the masters. So far as I can tell, producing a 'reading' means wading painfully through the master's incomprehensible prose and then venturing a few guesses as to what the master might possibly have had in mind while consigning those opaque words to paper.

All this activity is a denial of what I understand by writing. If your readers cannot read your words and realize at once exactly what you mean, if they must struggle and agonize and argue and attempt 'readings' of your work, then you have failed as a writer. Of course, you may have succeeded in some other enterprise – I will offer no suggestion here as to what that might be – but you have certainly failed as a writer. Since I have no interest in seeing this industry expand further, I have thoughtfully provided a few clues to recognizing this stuff quickly, in the form of buzzwords which occur thickly in most post-modernist writing but hardly ever occur at all in good writing: things like 'privilege' (as a verb), 'hegemonic', 'linear' (as a term of abuse), 'hermeneutic' and 'transgress'.

As mentioned earlier, in this book I adopt the practice of prefixing an asterisk (*) to any form or example which I am presenting as wrong or unsatisfactory. But occasionally I use a pair of question marks (??) instead for an example of doubtful or borderline status. A word in boldface within an entry is a cross-reference to another entry.

Finally, note that this book uses the style of alphabetical order which ignores white spaces and hyphens. So, for example, **almanac** precedes **a lot of**, which precedes **alphabet**.

R. L. Trask

Mind the Gaffe

a, an Which form of the article should be used before a word beginning with *h*? If the *h* is silent, of course, then *an* must be used: *an honest man*, *an hour or two*. If the *h* is pronounced, and the first syllable is stressed, then only *a* is possible: *a history of Sussex* is right, while *✱an history of Sussex* is never acceptable.

The problems arise when the first syllable is unstresssed: should we write *a historical event* or *an historical event*? The second derives from the days when many people pronounced these words with no *h*: that is, they really said *an 'istorical event*, and so that's what they wrote. Today, though, almost everyone now pronounces an *h* in such words, and you are firmly advised to prefer *a historical event*: the other now looks strange or worse to most readers. The same goes for *a hotel*, which is better than *an hotel*.

Otherwise, the choice between *a* and *an* depends entirely on the pronunciation of the following item, not on its spelling. Write *a union*, because *union* is pronounced with an initial consonant sound (just like *a Yule log*), but write *an MP*, because *MP* is pronounced with an initial vowel sound (just like *an empty box*).

abattoir The word is so spelled, with one B and two Ts.

abbreviations An *abbreviation* is a short way of writing a word or phrase which could also be written out in full, using only letters of the alphabet and possibly full stops. Examples include *Dr* for *Doctor*, *lb.* for *pound(s)* and *e.g.* for *for example*. An abbreviation does not normally have a distinct pronunciation of its own. These properties distinguish abbreviations from **acronyms** and **initialisms** like *NATO* and *BBC*, from **clipped forms** like *gym* and *phone*, and from **symbols** like ✱ and *5*.

With only a few exceptions, it is poor style to use abbreviations in the body of your writing. The only abbreviations which are properly used in most writing are the following: *Mr, Mrs, Ms, Dr* (with surnames, though the middle two are only abbreviations by courtesy, since they abbreviate nothing), a few titles like *MP* and *QC*, *a.m.* and *p.m.*, and *A.D.* and *B.C.* (or their variants *C.E.* and *B.C.E.* (see **A.D.**).

You should write *for example*, not **e.g.*; *the second volume*, not **the 2nd vol.*; *the twentieth century*, not **the 20th cent.* or *C20; *miles per hour*, not *mph; *Professor Chomsky*, not **Prof. Chomsky*; and so on for other cases. It is far more important to make your writing easy to read than to save a few seconds in writing it.

One important exception arises in scientific writing, in which names of units are always abbreviated in a standard way, with no full stops and no plural-*s*: write *50 kg*, not **50 kilogrammes* or **50 kg.* or **50 kgs*.

Note that, when the abbreviation contains the first and last letters of the word, British usage favours no full stop, while American usage prefers the full stop: hence British *Mr* and *Dr* versus American *Mr.* and *Dr.*, for example.

See **Latin abbreviations**.

ability, capacity, capability Applied to a person, the first two mean about the same, but they don't behave grammatically in the same way. You have *an ability to do something*, but *a capacity for doing something*. As for the third, this is best used in the plural and with no material following: your *capabilities* are your abilities and your talents as a whole.

abjure, adjure To *abjure* something is to renounce it, especially under oath, to swear to have nothing more to do with it: *He abjured his homeland for ever*. To *adjure* somebody to do something is to entreat him earnestly to do it, or to make him swear to do it: *They adjured him to stay away from gambling*. The two should not be confused. If you have trouble with them, avoid them in favour of simpler words.

able Only a human being is *able* to do anything: *Jan will be able to join us after lunch*. It is poor style to write that an animal or a thing is able to do something, and very bad style to follow *able* with a passive. Do not write **This equation is able to be solved by computer*; write *This equation can be solved by computer*.

-able, -ible As a general rule, a word of English or French origin takes *-able* (*washable, portable*), while a word of Latin origin takes *-ible* (*audible*). But there are exceptions, and anyway this rule is unlikely to be of much use to you. Since *-able* is far more frequent than *-ible*, I list below the most frequent words ending in *-ible*. I omit rare, obsolete and technical words.

accessible
admissible
audible
collapsible
combustible
comestible
compatible
comprehensible
compressible
constructible
contemptible
controvertible
convertible
corruptible
credible
deducible
deductible
defensible
destructible
digestible
dirigible
discernible
dismissible
dispersible

divisible
edible
eligible
exhaustible
expansible
expressible
fallible
feasible
flexible
forcible
gullible
horrible
immersible
indelible
incorrigible
intelligible
invincible
irascible
legible
miscible
negligible
omissible
ostensible
perceptible

perfectible
permissible
plausible
possible
reducible
refrangible
reprehensible
repressible
resistible
responsible
reversible
risible
sensible
submergible
submersible
submissible
suggestible
suppressible
susceptible
tangible
terrible
transmissible
visible

Many of these form negatives. Their negatives are usually formed with *in-* (*inaudible, indigestible*), or with *im-* before *p* (*impermissible*), with *ir-* before *r* (*irresponsible*), or with *il-* before *l*. The exceptions are *unfeasible, unintelligible* and *unsusceptible*.

Other common words take -*able*, like *reliable, potable* and *comfortable*. A final *e* in the source word is usually dropped before the suffix (*love, lovable*), but the *e* is retained if the spelling would otherwise suggest the wrong pronunciation (*replace, replaceable*, not *✳replacable; pronounce, pronounceable*, not *✳pronouncable*). A short stem like *dye* may take either spelling: *dyable* or *dyeable*.

The derived nouns follow the same spelling: *accessibility* but *reliability*.

When in doubt, consult a good dictionary.

abolition, abolishment In most contexts, the noun derived from the verb *abolish* is *abolition*, but *abolishment* is sometimes preferred in legal and financial contexts. So, we write of the *abolition* of slavery but possibly of the *abolishment* of mortgage relief. But *abolition* is usually possible in any context.

aborigine, aboriginal The word *aborigine* is now widely considered offensive, and should be avoided. The alternative *aboriginal* is still accept-able, and is widely preferred in Australia. But this is an adjective, and, outside Australia, many readers will be annoyed to see it used as a noun (??*the aboriginals*). It is always safe, and recommended, to avoid both words and write *the indigenous people*, or something similar. When writing about a particular place, you are advised to write *native Australians*, *native Americans*, or whatever.

abridgement, abridgment Both are correct. British English strongly prefers *abridgement*, with the E; American usage is divided but slightly prefers *abridgment*.

abrogate, arrogate To *abrogate* something is to cancel it or annul it. You can abrogate a treaty or an agreement, but it is usually better to prefer an everyday word like *revoke* or *repeal*. To *arrogate* something is to claim it for oneself without justification, most often to claim powers or authority.

absence The phrase *in the absence of* is an example of **wordiness**. Don't write the clumsy ✳*in the absence of the latest figures*; write *without the latest figures*.

absorb, adsorb The word *absorb* is an everyday word meaning 'soak up', both literally and figuratively. The derived noun is *absorption*, and ✳*absorbtion* does not exist. But *adsorb* is a technical term in chemistry, meaning 'collect (molecules of gas or liquid) on the surface'.

abstinence The noun derived from *abstain* is *abstinence*, and there is no such word as ✳*abstination*.

abstract nouns See **nouniness**.

abuse, misuse, disabuse To *misuse* something is to use it wrongly. To *abuse* it is to misuse it so badly that you damage it. The noun form of the second is familiar to us from expressions like *child abuse*, and also *drug abuse*, which is odd, because it is not the drugs that are abused but the user's body. To *disabuse* somebody of an idea is to show her that that idea is wrong: *They will be quickly disabused of the notion that linguistics is an easy subject.*

academic The central sense of this adjective is 'pertaining to universities or to scholarly research', and the related noun *academic* means 'person who holds a teaching and research post in a university'. But the adjective now has a second sense: 'of no significance in the real world', as in *This discussion is purely academic*. Even academics use the term in this sense.

academic titles If you hold an academic title such as *Doctor* or *Professor*, you should use that title only within the context of a university, and even then only in formal contexts. In all other contexts, calling yourself *Dr Sylvia Horner* or signing yourself *Sylvia Horner, Ph.D.* is pretentious and will suggest to many readers that you are a shallow and ostentatious phony hoping to awe gullible people. Look at any serious book written by a real academic, and you will find the author's title buried in small print in the brief paragraph giving his or her background and credentials.

   Note, by the way, that the system of academic ranks and titles is very different in Britain and in the US, and that no British title corresponds very closely to any American one. The British titles, from lowest to highest, are as follows, with a few complications ignored: *lecturer, senior lecturer, principal lecturer* (only in some of the newer universities), *reader, professor*. The American titles are *assistant professor, associate professor,* (full) *professor*. In both countries, there is a cachet attached to holding a named chair (professorship).

accede To *accede* to something is to agree to it. The word is too pompous for everyday use: write *agree* or *consent* instead.

accent An *accent* is a particular way of pronouncing a language. It is important to realize that everybody has an accent: it is not possible to speak a language without using some accent or other. Accordingly, it is wrong to write things like *✳She spoke English without an accent*. If she is not a native speaker, and what you mean is that she had no trace of a *foreign* accent, then you can write *She spoke English like a native*. However, if she is a native speaker, then you must choose some more accurate wording, such as *She spoke English with an educated accent*.

accent marks See **diacritics**.

accentuate This verb means 'make prominent', 'put into relief': *This recording accentuates her Scottish accent*. The word does not mean 'aggravate', 'make more serious', and it should not be so used. Avoid writing things like *✳The shortage of spare parts has accentuated the RAF's problems*.

accept, except The word *accept* is a verb meaning 'agree to': *We have accepted their offer*. The word *except* is usually a preposition meaning 'other than', as in *Everyone is here except Brenda*, though it can also be a verb meaning 'exempt, exclude', as in *You will be excepted from this requirement*. Do not write the second when you mean the first.

accessible This word is applied to something which you can easily reach or get hold of. Recently, it has become a vogue word for *readable*. Prefer the plain word.

accessory The word is so spelled, with two Cs and two Ss. In the sense of 'person indirectly involved in a crime', the variant spelling *accessary* was formerly usual in Britain, but is now rather old-fashioned, and *accessory* is recommended for all senses.

accommodation The word is so spelled, with two Cs and two Ms. Do not write *✱acommodation* or *✱accomodation*.

accord, accordance When you do something *of your own accord*, you do it voluntarily, without being asked or instructed to do it. Note the preposition *of* here: *✱on your own accord* is not standard English. However, when you do something in obedience to instructions, you do it *in accordance with* those instructions.

accrue This is a problem word. The intransitive use is fine everywhere: *Interest has accrued from your investments*. The problem arises with the transitive use: *??You have so far accrued three weeks of holiday entitlement*. This use is unquestionably standard in American English, but it is borderline in British English. It is growing in frequency in Britain – and it is certainly normal in the university where I work – but, even though British dictionaries are now beginning to recognize it, it is perhaps best avoided by British writers, since it is far from generally accepted.

accurate, precise These words are not interchangeable. Something which is *accurate* is correct; the opposite is *inaccurate*, which means 'wrong to some extent'. But *precise* means 'correct to a very high degree of detail', and its opposite *imprecise* means 'lacking a sufficient degree of detail'. So, for example, if I try to explain the word *loris* as denoting 'a nocturnal primate', then I am accurate, since a loris is indeed a nocturnal primate, but I am rather imprecise, since there are several other kinds of nocturnal primates besides lorises, and my account fails to distinguish lorises from lemurs, bushbabies and aye-ayes.

Achilles heel The traditional form is *Achilles' heel*, with an apostrophe, and this form is still marginally preferred in American English. However, in British English, the spelling *Achilles heel* is now preferred by most authorities, and this form is gaining ground in the US.

Achilles tendon This is always so spelled, with no apostrophe.

acknowledgement, acknowledgment Both spellings are acceptable, but British English prefers *acknowledgement*, while American English prefers *acknowledgment*.

acoustics This word is singular when it denotes the scientific study of sound: *Acoustics is a branch of physics*. But it is plural when it denotes the sound qualities of a room or a building: *The acoustics in this hall are terrible*.

acquiesce When you *acquiesce in* something, you agree to go along with it without protest, even though you may not like it much. Note that acquiescence does not imply approval, but only a failure to protest. And note the preposition: we acquiesce *in* something, not *to* it or *with* it.

acronyms and initialisms When an organization has a long name, we frequently use a short form of that name obtained by taking the initial letters of the important words of the name. If the result can be pronounced as a word, we call it an *acronym*. Examples of acronyms include *NATO* for the *North Atlantic Treaty Organization* and *NASA* for the *National Aeronautics and Space Administration*. If the result cannot be pronounced as a word, but must be spelled out letter by letter, we call it an *initialism*. Examples of initialisms include *BBC* for the *British Broadcasting Corporation* and *RSPCA* for the *Royal Society for the Prevention of Cruelty to Animals*. Mixed cases are possible, such as *CD-ROM*. Initialisms are always written entirely in capital letters. In American English, the same is true of acronyms, while in Britain it is commonplace to see only a single initial capital used, as in *Nato* for *NATO*. This British style may look strange to other speakers of English, and should perhaps be avoided in work meant to be read outside Britain.

actual, actually These words should be used sparingly, and only when there is a clear contrast between the real state of affairs and some other state of affairs which is expected or hypothetical but not real. Write *In Japanese, the object comes before the verb*, and not ✻ *. . . before the actual verb*. An *actual verb* is no different from a *verb*, and *actual* does no work here. Likewise, write *The subjunctive does not exist in English*, not ✻ *. . . does not actually exist*. There is no difference between existing and actually existing. Whenever you find yourself writing *actual* or *actually*, check to see if the word can be eliminated without loss. Most of the time, it can.

acute, chronic An *acute* illness is one that comes on suddenly, is severe for a short time, but does not last long. A *chronic* illness is one that persists for a long time, possibly with symptoms that vary in severity. The word *chronic* may be safely extended to any kind of persistent problem: *chronic* *alcoholism, chronic indebtedness, chronic misbehaviour.* But the vernacular British use of *chronic* to mean 'acute' or 'severe', as in **London's chronic traffic problems*, is out of place in careful writing.

A.D., B.C., C.E., B.C.E., B.P. The familiar western calendar is of Christian origin, and it divides dates into *B.C.* (before Christ) and *A.D.* (which stands for Latin *anno domini* 'in the year of our Lord'). The first is always written after the date: *Caesar invaded Britain in 55 B.C.* But the second is traditionally written before a specific date, and this style is recommended: *Charlemagne was crowned emperor in A.D. 800.* However, it follows the name of a general period: *in the twelfth century A.D.* Note that both abbreviations are conventionally written in small capitals. If small capitals are not available, ordinary capitals will do as a substitute. The abbreviation *A.D.* may be omitted when the context makes it plain what is intended: *Roger Bacon died in 1292.* In fact, it is not usual to use *A.D.* with any date after 1000.

Non-Christians may prefer to avoid these Christian abbreviations by writing *B.C.E.* (before the common era) instead of *B.C.* and *C.E.* (of the common era) instead of *A.D.* This is always acceptable.

In the historical disciplines, the abbreviation *B.P.* (before the present) is commonly used for dates in the remote past: *There were people in the Americas no later than 13,000 B.P.* (this is about 11,000 B.C.). It is not usual to use *B.P.* dates for the last few thousand years, and these should never be used for dates within the *A.D.* period. And you should never mix *B.P.* dates with *B.C./A.D.* dates in the same passage, since doing so will greatly bewilder your readers.

All of these are usually written with full stops, as shown. The style omitting the full stops, as in *BC* and *AD*, is now preferred by some publishers but is not recommended.

adapt, adopt To *adapt* something is to modify it, often especially to make it suitable for a particular purpose: *Austen's* Pride and Prejudice *has been adapted for television.* To *adopt* something is to take it up: *We are adopting a new procedure for budget control.* The derived nouns are *adaptation* for the first, *adoption* for the second. Some people now use *adaption* in place of *adaptation*, but this is not recommended.

adapter, adaptor Some authorities advise writing *adapter* for a person who adapts something but *adaptor* for any kind of device. In practice, however, both forms are used indifferently in both senses. You can make the suggested distinction if you like, but few readers will notice or care.

adequate Something which is *adequate* is just enough for the purpose. Most of the time, the plainer word *enough* should be preferred. The word cannot easily be modified: *adequate enough* is a **pleonasm**, while *very adequate* and *more adequate* are illogical. There is nothing illogical about *more than adequate*, but why not just write *more than enough* instead?

adjacent, adjoining Things are *adjacent* when they are side by side: *We were sitting in adjacent seats*. But things are *adjoining* when they share a common boundary: *We had adjoining rooms in the hotel*. In many circumstances either word can be used. But note that *adjacent* does not mean 'near' or 'close', and wordings like *very adjacent* are therefore frowned on by careful writers. Write *very close* or *very near* instead. Note also the following difference in grammar: *Their land is adjacent to ours*, but *Their land adjoins ours*.

adjectives from names The surnames of certain famous people have given rise to derived adjectives, usually with the suffix *-ian*. Very often these adjectives can be coined at will: *Bloomfield* (the name of a famous linguist), *Bloomfieldian*; *Wellington* (a military commander), *Wellingtonian*; *Wagner* (a composer), *Wagnerian*. But names with certain spellings may cause difficulties, and with these you should be careful to use the established form, if one exists. For example, from *Shakespeare* we have either *Shakespearean* or *Shakespearian* (the first is preferred in the USA, while the second is often preferred in Britain); from *George Bernard Shaw* we have *Shavian*; from *Noam Chomsky* we have *Chomskyan* (which is widely preferred to *Chomskian*, though this last is also found).

By the way, note the different behaviour of the suffix *-esque*. The word *Wagnerian* means 'pertaining to Wagner or to his works', while *Wagneresque* means 'in the style of Wagner', 'reminiscent of Wagner'.

administer The verb related to *administration* is *administer*, as in *She administers the faculty office*. The dreadful verb *administrate* should not be used.

administration See **government**.

admit This verb traditionally takes either an object or a complement: *She admitted her mistakes*; *She admitted that she had lied*. Today the first use is often reinforced by *to*: *She admitted to her mistakes*. This form is now so common that it is recognized by most usage guides as permissible. However, the *to* here does no work, and you might consider sticking to the shorter traditional form.

There is also the expression *admit of*, which means 'leave room for': *This evidence admits of several interpretations*. This use is decidedly formal.

admittedly This is a word to be used with care, since it lends itself to unsubstantiated assertions. Consider an example: *The strong pound is admittedly hurting British exporters.* Who is making this admission? Why is he not identified? What evidence exists to back up the statement?

ad nauseam This Latin phrase is so spelled, and *ad nauseum* is wrong.

adopt See **adapt**.

adopted, adoptive A child taken in permanently by foster parents is *adopted*, but her new parents are *adoptive* parents, not *adopted* parents.

adverb placement When an English verb-form comes in two or more pieces (*will play*, *have been interpreted*), the most natural place to put an adverb is usually after the first element. Examples: *Sampras will surely play in the Davis Cup*; *The Easter Island inscriptions have never been interpreted*. Some writers, apparently out of confusion derived from stern warnings about the **split infinitive**, have the bad habit of moving the adverb to the front, producing awful things like *??Sampras surely will play in the Davis Cup* and *??The Easter Island inscriptions never have been interpreted*. Don't do this: it is terrible style.

adversary This word means 'enemy', and the common practice of using it to mean only 'opponent' in sporting contests is not to be encouraged.

adverse, averse These similar-looking adjectives have quite different meanings. The word *adverse* means 'contrary', 'unfavourable', 'hostile', and can be applied to a variety of non-human things, like decisions, circumstances, criticism, wind and weather. However, a person can never be described as *adverse*. Be careful with this rather formal word: its use can easily become pompous. Do not write *adverse weather conditions* when *bad weather* will do.

In contrast, *averse* means 'unwilling', 'disinclined', 'loath'; the word can be applied only to a person, and it must be followed by the preposition *to*. Example: *She was averse to gardening* ('She didn't want to do any gardening'). Faulty uses of this word include *She was averse to help out* (a verb is used where a noun is required), *She was averse from gardening* (the older style *averse from* is no longer regarded as standard English), and *She was averse to criticism* (the word does not mean 'hostile'). This word too should be used carefully: in most instances, *She disliked gardening* or *She hated gardening* is preferable to *She was averse to gardening*.

advertise This is the only possible spelling in all varieties of English: the spelling ✳*advertize* is never acceptable.

adviser, advisor Both spellings are standard, and both are widely used everywhere. You may use whichever you prefer, except when the word forms part of somebody's job title, in which case you must use the form preferred by the holder of the title. But the adjective is always *advisory*.

ae, oe, e A number of words and combining forms of Graeco-Latin origin are sometimes spelled with *ae* or *oe* and sometimes spelled with *e*. On the whole, British English is fonder of *ae* and *oe* than is American English, but the conventions are complex and unpredictable on both sides of the water. The most familiar such words are listed below, with comments on British and American usage.

	UK	US
(a)edile	*aedile* only	both
(a)egis	*aegis* only	both
(a)esthete	*aesthete* only	both; *ae-* preferred
(a)esthetic(s)	*aesthetic(s)* only	both; *ae-* preferred
(a)eon	*aeon* only	both; *eon* preferred
am(o)eba	*amoeba* only	both; *amoeba* preferred
anap(a)est	*anapaest* preferred	*anapest* only
an(a)emia, an(a)emic	*anaemia* only	*anemia* strongly preferred
an(a)esthetic	*anaesthetic* preferred	*anesthetic* preferred
aph(a)eresis	*aphaeresis* only	*apheresis* only
arch(a)eology	*archaeology* only	both; *archaeology* preferred
asaf(o)etida	*asafoetida* preferred	*asafetida* preferred
Caesar	*Caesar* only	*Caesar* only
C(a)esarean	*Caesarean* only	*Caesarean* preferred
c(a)esium	*caesium* only	*cesium* only
chim(a)era	*chimera* preferred	*chimera* only
di(a)eresis	*diaeresis* only	*dieresis* only
diarrh(o)ea	*diarrhoea* only	*diarrhea* only
encyclop(a)edia	both	*encyclopedia* strongly preferred
(o)esophagus	*oesophagus* only	*esophagus* only
(o)estrogen	*oestrogen* only	*estrogen* only
f(a)eces, f(a)ecal	*faeces* only	*feces* only

f(o)etid	*fetid* preferred	*fetid* only
f(o)etus, f(o)etal	both; *fetus* now preferred	*fetus, fetal* only
Gr(a)eco-	*Graeco-* only	*Greco-* only
gyn(a)ecology	*gynaecology* only	*gynecology* only
h(a)emoglobin	*haemoglobin* only	*hemoglobin* only
h(a)emophilia	*haemophilia* only	*hemophilia* only
h(a)emorrhage	*haemorrhage* only	*hemorrhage* only
h(a)emorrhoid	*haemorrhoid* only	*hemorrhoid* only
hom(o)eopathy	both; *homeo-* preferred	*homeopathy* only
Jud(a)eo-	*Judaeo-* only	*Judeo-* only
leuk(a)emia	*leukaemia* only	*leukemia* only
medi(a)eval	both	*medieval* strongly preferred
(o)enology	*oenology* only	*enology* preferred
(o)esophagus	*oesophagus* only	*esophagus* only
(o)estrogen	*oestrogen* only	*estrogen* only
p(a)ediatrics	*paediatrics* only	*pediatrics* only
p(a)edophile	*paedophile* only	*pedophile* only
p(a)ean	*paean* only	*paean* preferred
pal(a)eo-	*palaeo-* only	*paleo-* strongly preferred
p(a)edagogy	*pedagogy* only	*pedagogy* only
prim(a)eval	*primeval* preferred	*primeval* only

Formerly, it was the custom to write the digraphs *ae* and *oe* as ligatures: hence, *Cæsar* and *amœba*. This is no longer the custom, and you should avoid it, even though most word processors can produce these ligatures.

Note that names of ancient people and places are always written with *ae* and *oe* where these occurred: *Oedipus, Aeschylus, Boeotia, Aeolia, Aeneas, Aesop*, and so on.

aerate The word is so written: avoid the old-fashioned form *aërate*.

aerie See **eyrie**.

aeroplane, airplane Of these two forms, only *airplane* is acceptable in American English. In British English, the traditional form is *aeroplane*, and most authorities still recommend this for British usage. However, the issue is becoming academic, since, in practice, the alternatives *plane* and *aircraft* are commonly preferred – though note that the second of these, unlike the others, can be applied also to a glider, a helicopter, and certain other flying machines. All related words, such as *airport* and *aircrew*, take only *air-* in all varieties of English, and never *aero-*, with the single exception of the now little-used *aerodrome*.

a few See **few**.

affect, effect These two are often confused. Apart from one or two technical uses, the word *affect* is strictly a verb: *This won't affect our chances*. In contrast, *effect* is primarily a noun: *This will have no effect on our chances*. There is, however, a verb spelled *effect* and meaning 'bring about': *General Lee managed to effect the withdrawal of his troops*. But this last verb is rare, except perhaps in the expression *effect a change*.

affinity Affinity is mutual: except in chemistry, we cannot have an affinity in one direction. So, write *There is an affinity between the fauna of South America and that of Australia*, or *The South American fauna shows an affinity with that of Australia*. It is wrong to write *an affinity to* or *an affinity for*, except that the second is fine when it has its specialized technical sense in chemistry. In any case, do not copy the common practice of writing *have an affinity for* for 'like'. Write *She likes children*, not *She has an affinity for children*. The second form uses twice as many words and more than twice as many syllables in order to say the same thing badly.

affront, effrontery These are not interchangeable. An *affront* is a deliberate insult, while *effrontery* is insolence. Note that the first is a countable noun, while the second is not.

aficionado The word is so spelled, with only one F.

aforementioned, aforesaid These archaic words are still used in legal language, but they have no place in ordinary writing, where they sound ridiculous. Instead of *the aforementioned problem*, write *the problem mentioned above* or *the problem discussed above*, or something similar. It is still worse to write *as aforementioned*, which is not grammatical in any variety of English: write *as mentioned above*.

Afrikaans, Afrikaners The South African language is *Afrikaans*, with double A, while the Afrikaans-speaking people are *Afrikaners*, with single A.

afterward, afterwards The British form is *afterwards*, while the preferred American form is *afterward*.

ageing, aging The preferred British spelling is *ageing*; the preferred American one is *aging*. The British preference is unusual, since *staging, caging, paging, raging* and all other such words are spelled everywhere without the E.

agenda Though plural in Latin, this word is now strictly singular in English, and you should write *this agenda* and *these agendas*.

aggravate The original sense of this verb was 'cause (something) to become worse', as in *Be careful not to aggravate your injury*. For centuries, however, informal English has permitted the quite different sense of 'annoy', as in *??He was aggravated by the decision*. In formal writing, however, this second use will annoy many readers, and you are advised to avoid it. And you should not even consider using informal versions like *aggro* in careful writing.

aggressive Aggressiveness is an unattractive quality. It is unwise to label someone's efforts *aggressive* if you mean to be admiring, except perhaps in a contact sport like rugby. Prefer *vigorous* or *determined*.

agnostic, atheist An *atheist* denies the existence of God. An *agnostic* denies the possibility of knowing anything about any god who may exist. Both words should be applied accurately, if used at all. But that leaves us with no convenient word to label all those people who simply take no interest in religion at all and cannot be bothered to classify themselves. The usual stopgap here is *unbeliever*, which has the drawback of implying that religious belief is the norm, and which is also strangely formed (the expected form would be *non-believer*, which is little used).

ago *It is a year ago since we got married*. This is wrong: *ago* cannot combine with *since*. The reason for this is that *ago* can only be used in a statement about the past, while *since* can only be used in a statement about the present. Write either *It is a year since we got married* (a statement about the present moment) or *It was a year ago that we got married* (a statement about a time in the past).

agony This word denotes the most extreme kind of mental or physical suffering, and it should be reserved for cases in which it is appropriate. Do not devalue it by applying it to lesser degrees of suffering. Drivers stuck in a vast traffic jam may be hugely inconvenienced, uncomfortable and angry, but they are not experiencing agony.

agouti The name of the South American rodent is so spelled, and other spellings are best avoided.

agree (to) The verb *agree* behaves differently in British and American English. In American English, you can only *agree to* a settlement. In British English, you can either *agree to* a settlement or *agree* a settlement. This last is ungrammatical for Americans, and you might choose to avoid it if you are writing for American readers. Even in Britain, some conservative readers object to the use of *agree* without a preposition.

agreement Unlike most European languages, English has very little subject-verb agreement, but we still have enough to cause problems in writing.

One of the most frequent problems arises with subjects which are plural in form but singular (collective) in sense. Some cases are simple. For example, we all write (and say) *Five thousand pounds is too much money*, and never *. . . are too much money*, since the property of being too much money is clearly a property only of the total sum, and not of each pound individually.

By the same token, we should write *Five thousand NATO troops is too many for the task*, but many writers fall into the trap of noting that plural *-s* and of writing *. . . are too many*. And, of course, we should likewise write *Five thousand NATO troops is not enough to keep the peace*, but this time even more writers find the plural irresistible and write *. . . are not enough*. This is perhaps not a bad error, but careful writers would nevertheless be wise to avoid it. Write *Five thousand NATO troops are to be withdrawn* (since being withdrawn is a property of every one of those soldiers individually), but write *is* when you are speaking of some characteristic of the entire group only.

Here is another example of this error, from a lottery advertisement: *Three correct numbers win you £1000*. Clearly you get the money only if you have a total of three correct numbers, and not just one of them, and so the verb should be *wins*. And another, from a bank advertisement: *Fewer withdrawals mean more interest*. Once again, the greater interest results only from withdrawing money less often, and it is not a consequence of each individual withdrawal, so the verb should be *means*.

With periods of time, things can get a little complicated. Clearly we must write *Six weeks is a long time*, and not *. . . are a long time*, since the property of being a long time belongs only to the total time elapsed. However, we may write either *Ten years has elapsed* (since the entire period has elapsed) or *Ten years have elapsed* (since each individual year has also elapsed). In contrast, we must write *The last ten years has seen the Internet become a feature of everyday life*. Here it would be wrong to write *have seen*, since the phenomenon under discussion belongs to the whole period of ten years, and not to each year separately.

The following example, commenting on a comparison of two maps, illustrates another slip that is easy to make: *The general shape of the coasts are the same.* Here the verb should be *is*, agreeing with *shape*, but the writer has inadvertently used *are*, agreeing with *coasts*, which is not the subject. This can happen to anyone, and the only cure is to read what you have written.

A more serious problem arises in cases like the following: should we write *It may be you who is challenged* or *It may be you who are challenged*? That is, should the verb agree with *who* or with *you*? Opinions differ here, and both styles can be defended, but my advice is to choose the second. After all, in formal writing, probably nobody would prefer *It is I who is not ready*, even though informal English uses *It's me who's not ready*.

Yet another common error is illustrated by the following: *What she preferred were the plastic playing cards*. This is wrong, because the subject is *what she preferred*, which is grammatically singular, and so the required form is this: *What she preferred was the plastic playing cards*.

See also **one of the** for another common error.

agree with You can *agree with* a proposition, or with a person who declares a proposition. But you cannot agree with a state of affairs: you can only *approve of* it, or not. So, for example, you cannot write *I don't agree with the bombing of Serbia*: the standard form is *I don't approve of the bombing of Serbia*.

Aida The name of Verdi's opera is usually so written, and not as *Aïda*.

AIDS As most people know, this acronym stands for *acquired immune* (or *immuno-*) *deficiency syndrome*. AIDS is not strictly a disease, but only a medical condition. It does not kill anybody by itself, but, by destroying the victim's immune system, it leaves him vulnerable to any disease which may come along, such as pneumonia. Strictly, then, a victim dies of AIDS-related diseases, not of AIDS itself.

airplane See **aeroplane**.

akimbo When you have your arms *akimbo*, you have your hands on your hips with your elbows sticking out. It is impossible to have your legs akimbo: the word does not mean 'sprawling open', or anything of the sort. And do not write *a kimbo*.

albeit This quaint and archaic word has been undergoing a surprising revival. It sounds pretentious and silly, and it should not be used. Write *but*, *although* or *though* instead. Write *She is bright though careless*, not *She is bright albeit careless*. And it is even worse to follow the word with a complete sentence, as in this example: *The Basques are suspicious of outsiders, albeit* *they are wonderfully hospitable once they know you.* This is scarcely English at all. The word *albeit* is avoided by good writers, but loved by bad writers who foolishly believe that pretentious words make bad writing good.

Albuquerque Both the place in Spain and the place in New Mexico spell their names this way.

alga, algae The singular is *alga*; the plural is *algae*. Avoid errors like *✻a Caribbean algae*.

Algonquian, Algonkian, Algonquin, Algonkin For the family of native North American languages, specialists prefer *Algonquian* to *Algonkian*. But the Ojibwa dialect of the St Lawrence valley is *Algonquin*, or less usually *Algonkin*. The park in Ontario is *Algonquin Park*. The former club in New York is the *Algonkin Club*.

alibi The legal term *alibi* is a plea by an accused that he cannot have committed a crime because he was somewhere else at the time; it derives from Latin *alibi* 'elsewhere'. It is perfectly in order to write *The police were forced to release the suspect because he had an alibi*, meaning that the suspect could prove he was not at the scene of the crime. But the colloquial use of *alibi* to mean 'excuse' or 'pretext' is out of place in formal writing, while its use to mean 'opinion' or 'judgement' is diabolical.

all, all of In general, prefer *all* to *all of*: write *all my children, all the victims, all the money, all the way*. The variant *all of* is acceptable in some, but not all, cases, particularly with things that can be counted, as in *all of my children*, but why bother with the useless extra word?

Allegany, Allegheny The spelling is *Allegheny* for the river, the mountain range, the county in Pennsylvania, the national forest, the reservoir and the Indian reservation, but *Allegany* for the county and the town in New York and for the state park. Don't ask me why.

allege The word is so spelled, and *✻alledge* is wrong. The form *alleged* is much used by journalists, who are usually careful to avoid pre-judging an issue; they write, for example, of an *alleged assault*, rather than of an *assault*. But it is easy to overdo this. Write *He was charged with assault*, and then go on to speak of *the alleged assault*, but do not write *✻He was charged with alleged assault*. There is no crime called 'alleged assault'.

Note also that *allegedly* does not mean 'reportedly'. If you are repeating a report, write *The police have reportedly made an arrest*, not *✻The police have allegedly made an arrest*.

allergic This is a medical term: when you are *allergic* to some substance, you become ill if you swallow it, breathe it or touch it. Do not use *be allergic to* to mean 'dislike': things like *I am allergic to religiosity* are not standard English. If you want something stronger than *dislike*, you can write *I have an aversion to religiosity*.

all right Standard usage requires the form *all right* in all functions, and the one-word spelling *alright* is not at present accepted in formal writing in any circumstance, in spite of such familiar cases as *It'll Be Alright on the Night* (the title of a popular television show). This is perhaps illogical, since it might seem more orderly to make a written distinction between pairs like *These answers are all right* (all of these answers are correct) and *These answers are alright* (these answers are satisfactory). Perhaps in another generation or so this useful distinction will become accepted as standard, as has already happened with cases like *all ready* and *already*. But this has not happened yet, and you should avoid *alright* in formal writing. Oh, and don't even think of trying Mick Jagger's famous *awright*.

all together See **altogether**.

allude See **refer**.

allusion See **delusion**, **refer**.

almanac The word is so spelled, and *almanack* is wrong, except in the names of certain almanacs which favour this archaic spelling.

a lot of The expressions *a lot of* and *lots of* are normal in colloquial English, but they are still regarded by most writers as too informal for careful writing. Write *a great deal of research*, not *a lot of research*. And be sure to avoid the common error *alot of*.

alphabet An *alphabet* is a particular kind of writing system, one in which each character represents a single speech sound, a consonant or a vowel – at least in principle. But not all writing systems are alphabetic in nature, and it is wrong to write of *the Chinese alphabet* or *the Japanese alphabet*, since neither of these languages is normally written in an alphabetic script.

alphabetical order It may surprise you to learn that there is more than one way of putting things into alphabetical order, but, in fact, at least two rather different systems are in use. The first system looks only at the letters, and it ignores white spaces and hyphens. This is the system used in this book, in which, for example, **almanac** comes before **a lot of**, which comes before **alphabet**. The second system treats a white space, and sometimes also a hyphen, as a break. In this system, **a lot of** would come after **a** and before **abattoir**. When using an alphabetized reference work, you should check to see which system is being used, since otherwise you may fail to find what you're looking for. See also the problem with *Mc* in **Scottish and Irish names**.

already In contrast to what happens in many other European languages, English does not readily allow *already* with a simple past-tense verb-form other than *was/were*. Avoid writing things like *Chomsky already realized this in 1955*. Write instead *Chomsky had already realized this by 1955* or *Chomsky was already aware of this in 1955*.

Alsatian The other name for a German shepherd dog is *Alsatian*, not *Alsation*.

also The word *also* should not be used to mean 'and'. It is bad style to write *She has several children to support, also an invalid mother*. Write *and* instead. Moreover, it is widely considered to be poor style to start a sentence with *also*. Avoid things like this: *The European army facing Sultan Bayezit had no acknowledged leader. Also, their tactics were foolish*. Prefer *Moreover, . . .* or *Their tactics were also foolish*. But note that a phrase beginning with *also* can be moved to the beginning of the sentence without difficulty: *Also in the last eight is Kournikova*.

altar, alter The ceremonial centre of a church is an *altar*, while *alter* is a verb meaning 'modify', 'change'.

alternative, alternate The word *alternative* denotes a choice, particularly one which is expressly contrasted with one or more other choices. In origin, it means 'other of two', but this restricted sense is no longer usual in standard English, and it is perfectly acceptable in all but the most moss-encrusted circles to write *There are several alternatives to closure of the school*. But note that, in such constructions, the word must be followed by *to*, and not by any other preposition.

But the word should not be used too freely. Often 'other' or 'different' will do the job perfectly well: why write *??an alternative plan* when *another plan* will do? And do not combine *other* with *alternative*: *There is another alternative* says nothing that is not said by *There is an alternative*.

In recent years, this word has acquired a new sense of 'non-standard', 'not mainstream'. A good example is *alternative medicine*, now established as the label for a collection of practices which, whatever their merits, are neither underpinned by scientific understanding nor validated by careful testing. Again, though, you should not use the word thoughtlessly when a plainer word like 'unconventional' will carry your meaning.

Sometimes confused with *alternative* is *alternate*, which, as an adjective, means 'off and on', 'occurring by turns'. *She has alternate Thursdays off* means she has every second Thursday off. The common mistake is to write *alternate* where *alternative* is intended, especially when -*ly* is added: *✱The Russians wanted a port in the Mediterranean or, alternately, on the Indian Ocean* is wrong, and *alternatively* is required.

altogether, all together The spelling *all together* is only appropriate when the intended sense is indeed 'all of them together', as in *They arrived all together*. In all other senses, the required spelling is *altogether*, as in *This is altogether distressing, Our costs come to £7000 altogether*, and the somewhat jocular *Helen Mirren appeared on the London stage in the altogether*.

aluminium, aluminum The British form is *aluminium*; the American form is *aluminum*. The American form is conservative; the British one results from a capricious alteration.

alumnus, alumna Each of these words denotes a graduate of an educational institution, but there is a sex difference. A man is an *alumnus* (plural *alumni*), while a woman is an *alumna* (plural *alumnae*). A group of mixed sex are *alumni*. And there is no such word as *✱alumnis*.

a.m., p.m. These abbreviations are usually written *a.m.* and *p.m.* in Britain. In the US, they are written A.M. and P.M., with small capitals, or often AM and PM, with no points. Note that *12.30 a.m.* is half an hour after midnight, while *12.30 p.m.* is half an hour after noon. Things like *✱in the early hours of the a.m.* are poor style; prefer *in the early hours of the morning*.

ambidextrous See **dexterous**.

ambiguous comparative In a comparative construction, it is easy to write something which is seriously ambiguous. Here is a genuine example: *✱The Liberal Democrats get on better with Labour than the Tories*. This might mean either *The Liberal Democrats get on better with Labour than with the Tories* or *The Liberal Democrats get on better with Labour than the Tories do*. You must spell out what you mean, since otherwise your reader is helpless.

amend, emend When you *amend* a text, you change it, usually for the better – perhaps by polishing it or by correcting it. When you *emend* a text, you simply correct the mistakes, without attempting any other improvements. In philology, *emend* has a specialist sense: the editor of a text emends it by proposing corrections for apparent errors or omissions.

America, American In English, the name *America* means *the United States of America*, and usually nothing else whatever. In Britain, this is the ordinary name for the USA, while in the USA it is chiefly confined to formal and jingoistic contexts like patriotic songs and political speeches. The everyday American term is *the States*, though this is too informal for most careful writing, where *the US* or *the USA* is recommended.

Likewise, the adjective *American* means 'pertaining to the US', and the noun *American* means 'citizen of the US'.

The two continents of North and South America may be referred to collectively as *the Americas*, or, in some contexts, as *the western hemisphere* or *the New World*. Only in certain historical contexts can *America* be applied to the two continents together, as in *Columbus discovered America* (Columbus never set foot on any part of today's USA).

Latin Americans often perceive the English use of *America* and *American* as offensive, but it is not. There is no more reason to object to the English use than there is to object to the Latin American use of *yanqui* (= 'Yankee') for any American, a use which certainly surprises southern Americans.

See also **South America**.

American/British differences As the preface explains, there are just two versions of standard written English: the American one and the British one. Everybody else usually tries to conform to one standard or the other. The differences in spelling, in punctuation, in grammar and in the use of words – which are significant, but not as great as is sometimes supposed – are mostly explained in this book. The differences in vocabulary are another matter.

British/American differences in vocabulary run to thousands of words, phrases and expressions. Many of these merely represent different choices: US *liquor store*, UK *off-licence*; US *fall*, UK *autumn*; US *faucet*, UK *tap*; US *median*, UK *central reservation* (on a freeway or motorway); US *cookbook*, UK *cookery book*. A few are more complicated: US *first floor*, UK *ground floor* (UK *first floor* equals US *second floor*, and so on); US *school* (any educational institution, including a university), UK *school* (educational institution below university level). In some cases, one variety has a word for which the other simply has no equivalent: as far as I know, US *moving violation* 'offence committed while a car is being driven' has no UK equivalent, and UK *chat up* 'talk flirtatiously to (a person) in the hope of seducing him or her' has no

US equivalent. In other cases, the world is simply divided up differently: US *elementary school* does not match either UK *infant school* or UK *junior school*, but overlaps both. In still other cases, a word denotes something that does not exist on the other side of the Atlantic: US *major leagues* 'highest level of professional baseball' and UK *register office* 'municipal office where births, deaths and marriages are recorded and civil marriages are performed' are two examples.

But these vocabulary differences are not merely trans-Atlantic. Every English-speaking country and region has its own local words, which may be little known elsewhere. Examples are New Zealand *pa* 'village', South African *robot* 'traffic light', Caribbean *duppy* 'ghost', Australian *ziff* 'beard', Nigerian *chop house* 'restaurant serving local food' and Scottish *shoogly* 'wobbly'. These local forms may or may not be regarded locally as part of the standard language.

There exist several books listing British/American differences in vocabulary. For other varieties of English, resources are scarcer, though you may be lucky enough to find something. The only advice I can give you is this: if you are writing for an international readership, try to keep your use of local words to a minimum. Admittedly, this is not very helpful advice, since you probably don't know which of the tens of thousands of familiar words are not used outside your own country.

Meanwhile, the increasing globalization of English is perhaps beginning to iron out these regional differences. When I arrived in Britain, more than thirty years ago, nobody over here knew the American *rain check*. Today almost everyone in Britain understands this, and a few people even use it. At the same time, I find on my visits home that the British *van* has now displaced the American *panel truck*, the only word I knew when I left the States.

There is one special point to be considered: the citing of proper names from one variety when writing in the other variety. The rule of thumb is to retain the original spelling. So, for example, the name of the American psychologist B. F. Skinner's book *Verbal Behavior* must be so written even when you are writing in British English: changing this to *Verbal Behaviour is no more acceptable than is changing *Pittsburgh* to *Pittsborough* to match the form preferred in England. Likewise, I advise British writers to retain *the US Department of Defense* and American writers to retain *the Ministry of Defence*. These are names, and names should not be tampered with, even though some other handbooks will give you contrary advice.

See **subjunctive**.

American English The usual label for the varieties of English used in the United States, or sometimes for one of the two recognized versions of **standard English**, the one used in the US and elsewhere. American English is by no means homogeneous, though it is much less varied than is the English of Britain, merely because English-speakers have settled most of the US so recently and so rapidly. See also **British English**.

amiable, amicable An *amiable* person is good-natured and easy to get along with. The word is commonly applied only to people, though occasionally we find it extended to occasions, as in *an amiable conversation*. But *amicable* is not applied to people at all; instead, it is applied to human interactions and their outcomes, as in *an amicable settlement* (of a dispute) and *an amicable relationship*. The meaning here is 'friendly', 'good-natured', 'without rancour'.

amid, amidst Both forms are standard. Both were common a century ago, but today *amid* is overwhelmingly more frequent than *amidst*, which appears to be dying out. I recomend writing *amid*, unless you specifically want to cultivate a formal or old-fashioned tone.

amok, amuck The spelling *run amok* is much more usual, and is recommended. The version *amock* is regarded by most authorities as wrong.

among, amongst Both are acceptable, but the shorter *among* is far commoner and is recommended. The longer form now sounds a little fusty.

amoral, immoral An *amoral* person is one who does not understand the difference between right and wrong. An *immoral* person understands the difference but does wrong anyway. Do not write *amoral* when you mean *immoral*.

amount, number We use *amount* with things that cannot be counted, but *number* with things that can be counted: *this amount of money* but *this number of students*. Avoid the common error of using *amount* where *number* is required: *a large number of votes*, not *a large amount of votes*. The distinction is pointless, but it is established, and failing to make it will annoy many readers.

ampersand The ampersand, &, which represents the word *and*, should never be used in writing for any purpose at all, except in citing the name of a firm of which it forms an official part. You can cite a publisher as *John Compton & Sons* if that is the way the publishing house writes its name, but in all other circumstances you should write out the word *and*. Similarly, you should never use a plus sign or any other squiggle in place of *and*.

amuck See **amok**.

analogous The word is so spelled, and *analagous* is wrong.

analogy The word is so spelled, with two As, and *anology* is wrong.

anciently This rare adverb means 'a long time ago', 'in ancient times', as in *Celtic languages were anciently spoken across most of Europe*. The word is a favourite of mine, but I have yet to find a copy-editor who shares my enthusiasm for it. Perhaps we could start a campaign.

ancillary The word is so spelled, and *anciliary* is wrong.

and It is not wrong to begin a sentence with *and*. Often this can be quite effective. But use it sparingly: doing it too often will make your prose irritating. See also **missing *and***.

Andalucía, Andalusia Opinion is divided as to whether the Spanish spelling or the familiar English version is preferable. You may use either.

anemone The name of the flower is so spelled, and so is the name of the *sea anemone* (an animal). The misspelling *anenome* is curiously frequent, but must be avoided.

angle brackets See **brackets**.

annex, annexe The verb is *annex*: a country can *annex* territory, but it cannot *annexe* it. The noun meaning 'extension to a building' is *annexe* in British English but usually *annex* in American English.

annihilate When you *annihilate* something, you destroy it utterly, leaving nothing behind. It is therefore a **pleonasm** to write things like *It was totally annihilated*. There is no partial annihilation.

anorexia, bulimia These are two different eating disorders. A sufferer from *anorexia* fails to eat and gradually starves. A sufferer from *bulimia* stuffs herself but then forces herself to vomit.

antagonist See **protagonist**.

Antarctic See **Arctic**.

antenna This has two plurals. An insect's feelers are its *antennae*, while radio and TV receivers are *antennas*.

Anthony, Antony The male given name is almost always *Anthony*. But we write *Mark Antony* for the Roman statesman and *Antony and Cleopatra* for the Shakespeare play.

anti- This is a prefix, and it should be written as one. Write *antisocial*, not
✱*anti social*. A hyphen is not necessary unless the result would be hard on
the eye without it, as in an *anti-inflammatory* drug. Moreover, do not use
this word-forming prefix as a substitute for *opposed to*: write *He is fiercely
opposed to drugs*, not ✱*He is fiercely anti-drugs*. This prefix means 'against'; do
not confuse it with the unrelated prefix *ante-*, meaning 'before', as in *ante-
natal* and *ante-bellum*.

anticipate This word divides the authorities. It is long established in the
sense of 'foresee and take suitable action to deal with': *He anticipated his
opponent's every move; We were anticipating the price drop when we sold our
shares*. It is also established in the sense of 'mention (something) before its
proper time', as in *He anticipated my punchline*, and in the now uncommon
sense of 'make use of (something) before you have it', as in *He anticipated
his salary when he bought that car*. No problem so far.

However, for about two centuries the word has also been used in the sense
of 'expect': *We anticipate a fall in share prices; We anticipate that our investment
will start to pay off this year*. This sense is now so well established that it can
hardly be regarded as wrong, yet a number of conservative speakers still
object to it, and some usage handbooks condemn it, while others are
resigned to it. My advice is to avoid *anticipate* in this sense and to write
expect instead. What on earth is the point of writing a fancy four-syllable
word when a plain two-syllable word will do the job perfectly well? Prefer
We expect a fall in share prices.

Finally, the word has acquired yet another sense: 'look forward to'.
Example: *She was eagerly anticipating her lover's return*. Oddly, this sense
seems to attract less ire than the last one. Even so, bear in mind that *look
forward to* is available and effective.

Note that *anticipate* can never be followed by a *to*-infinitive: ✱*The ruling
is anticipated to be overturned* is wrong.

antimony, antinomy The metal is *antimony*, while the contradiction is
an *antinomy*.

Antony See **Anthony**.

anxious Once upon a time this word meant only 'nervous', 'uneasy',
'worried'. It still does in examples like *She is anxious about her exam results*.
However, for a very long time it has been used in the quite different sense
of 'eager', and *She is anxious to see you* is commonly taken as meaning the
same as *She is eager to see you*. Most authorities accept this newer sense as
standard, though a few do not. For the conservative minority, *She is anxious*

to get started implies that she is worried that the hour is growing too late to go ahead, and it carries an implication of nervousness or distress, rather than the unbridled enthusiasm expressed by *She is eager to get started*. If you prefer, you may confine *anxious* to this older sense, and use only *eager* in the other, but the great majority of careful writers do not do this.

any This word may take either singular or plural agreement. You may write either *Any of these books is fine* or *Any of these books are fine*, depending on just what you mean. And you may write *This book is not very helpful, but neither is any of the others* or ... *but neither are any of the others*, depending upon taste.

any (other) ??*This jigsaw is more difficult than any puzzle I have ever done.* This is illogical. Prefer ... *than any other puzzle I have ever done*, since *any puzzle I have ever done* clearly includes the puzzle under discussion.

any more This is always written as two words; the spelling *anymore is never acceptable in British English, though it is now widely accepted in American English. Avoid things like *They don't like him anymore than they did before or *She doesn't live here anymore*. However, even in American English, it is obligatory to write *any more* when the expression quantifies a following noun, as in *We don't have any more wine*. The version *anymore wine* is never acceptable in any variety of English.

anyone, any one These are sometimes confused, as in the wrong example *I would be happy with anyone of them*. If this troubles you, bear in mind that *anyone* is an exact synonym of *anybody*, and so *anyone* can only ever be used where *anybody* can be used – as it clearly cannot in my example.

anyplace This is a strictly American equivalent for *anywhere*. Even in American English, it is generally regarded as too informal for careful writing.

any rate See **at any rate**.

anyway, any way This is one word when it means 'regardless', but two words when it means 'in any manner'. So, we write *Do it anyway* ('Do it regardless') but *Do it any way you like*.

apex The plural is usually *apices* in mathematical and scientific work, but *apexes* otherwise.

apodeictic, apodictic Both spellings of this unusual word are in use. The authorities disagree in their recommendations, but the shorter form is perhaps more frequent.

apostasy The word is so spelled, and *apostacy is wrong.

apostrophe When you add an apostrophe or an apostrophe-*s* to a word to make a possessive, there are several rules to be followed. First, the thing that comes before the apostrophe must be a real word of English. Second, it must be the *right* word for the occasion. Third, the result must match what we would say in careful speech.

So, for example, it is impossible to write *ladie's shoes* or *childrens' clothes*, because there are no such words as *ladie* and *childrens*, and it is impossible to write *at each others' throats*, because there is no such item as *each others*.

For those shoes, the required form in most circumstances is *ladies' shoes*, which means 'shoes for ladies'. Compare this with *that lady's shoes*, which means 'the shoes of that lady'.

Finally, with words that already end in *s*, choose the form that matches speech. Nobody would say *an actress' performance*, and so you shouldn't write this either: write instead *an actress's performance*. On the other hand, *Ulysses' journeys* sounds better to most of us than *??Ulysses's journeys*, and so you will probably prefer to write the first.

See also **contractions**.

apostrophes in names Especially in Britain, but not only there, there is unpredictable variation in the use of apostrophes in proper names. Below are some famous names with their standard spellings.

All Saints' Day (1 November)
All Souls College (Oxford)
America's Cup (yachting trophy)
Barclays (British bank)
Bloomingdale's (New York department store)
Boots (British chain of chemists)
Brands Hatch (British racing circuit)
Christies International *but* Christie's Europe (auction houses; don't ask me why)
Christ's College (Cambridge)
Consumers' Association (publisher of *Which?* magazine in Britain)
Dillons (British bookshop chain, now defunct)
Diners Club (American credit-card firm)
Earl's Court *or* Earls Court (district of London) (the first is traditional, the second perhaps now more usual)
Golders Green (district of London)

Goldsmiths' College (London)
Guy's Hospital (London)
Hamleys (British toyshops)
Harrods (London department store)
Jane's (guides to warships and aircraft)
Kings Canyon (US national park)
King's College (Cambridge)
King's College (London)
King's Cross (London district and rail station)
King's Lynn (Norfolk)
King's Road (in Chelsea, London, but not necessarily elsewhere)
Land's End (in Cornwall)
Lloyd's of London (insurance firm)
Lloyds TSB (British bank)
Lord's (cricket ground)
Macy's (New York department store)
McDonald's (fast-food chain)
Moody's (US credit-rating agency)
Philips (electronics firm)
Phillips (US oil company)
Princes Street (in Edinburgh)
Queens (borough of New York)
Queen's College (Oxford)
Queen's College (London)
Queens' College (Cambridge)
Queen's University (Belfast)
Regent's Park (in London)
Reuters (news agency)
St Andrews (Scottish town, university and golf course)
Sadler's Wells (London theatre)
Sears Roebuck (US mail-order firm)
Sotheby's (auction house)
Tattersalls (British bloodstock agency)
Trades Union Congress (British labour organization)

Appalachians The name is so spelled, and *Appalatians* is wrong.

apparently, evidently The second of these is stronger than the first: *Apparently she's a good worker* means 'I gather that she's a good worker' or 'I'm told that she's a good worker', while *Evidently she's a good worker* means 'It seems clear that she's a good worker'.

appeal In British English you can only *appeal against* a decision. In American English you can *appeal* a decision, though the other form is also acceptable.

appositives An *appositive* is a noun phrase which immediately follows another and denotes the same thing. In most cases, an appositive is not required to identify the person or thing under discussion (that is, in grammatical terminology it is *non-restrictive*), and so it must be set off by a pair of commas. Example: *The Archbishop of Canterbury, Dr George Carey, will address us tonight*. Here the appositive *Dr George Carey* is in no way required: it could have been omitted without disturbing the sentence, and its presence does no more than provide extra information. Check this: *The Archbishop of Canterbury will address us tonight*. Omitting the commas here is wrong: *The Archbishop of Canterbury Dr George Carey will address us tonight* is not standard English.

But there exists a second type of appositive, one which really is required to identify the person or thing being spoken of. Such a *restrictive* appositive must not be set off by commas. Example: *The linguist Noam Chomsky will address us tonight*. Here the appositive *Noam Chomsky* is an essential part of the sentence, and so it must not be set off by commas: clearly *The linguist will address us tonight* is not what is intended.

See also **preposed appositives**.

appraise, apprise To *appraise* something is to estimate its value: *I'm having an art dealer in to appraise these paintings*. To *apprise* is to inform: *We have apprised him of the facts*. The common error is to use *appraise* where *apprise* is required. But who needs *apprise* anyway? Just write *inform* or *tell*.

approximately This word is not wrong, but remember that we also have *about* and *roughly*, which are shorter.

Arab, Arabic, Arabia, Arabian An *Arab* is a member of an ethnic group now predominant in much of the Middle East and North Africa. The language of most Arabs, and of some others, is *Arabic*, and we also write of *Arabic literature* and *the Arabic alphabet*, and, for historical reasons, of *Arabic numerals* (our familiar numerals like *1*, *2*, *3*). *Arabia* is a geographical region lying between the Red Sea and the Persian Gulf, today occupied largely, though not entirely, by the country of *Saudi Arabia*, whose citizens are *Saudis*, not *Arabians*.

The adjective *Arabian* is largely confined to geographical use: *the Arabian peninsula*, *the Arabian desert*. But it can also be applied to folklore and mythology, most famously in the title *The Arabian Nights*.

Arabic names These cause great difficulties, for several reasons. To begin with, an archaic form of Arabic called *classical Arabic* enjoys enormous prestige in the Arab world, and this is still used for most publication – rather as though the French and the Italians were to use Latin for publication. At the same time, the local varieties of modern Arabic which are the mother tongues of Arabic-speakers differ greatly from classical Arabic, and also from one another. Some of them are not even mutually comprehensible.

As a result, an Arabic name will typically be pronounced in one way in classical Arabic, but in a different way in Cairo, and in yet other ways in Damascus or Riyadh or Tunis. The result of putting the name into the roman alphabet will therefore vary according to the original form selected, and it will vary further because there exists no recognized single system for transliterating either Arabic spelling or Arabic pronunciation into English, at least for everyday purposes (scholars have their own systems, but these require a blizzard of diacritics). As a final complication, some famous Arabic names, like *Cairo*, *Mecca* and *Damascus*, have established English forms which may not correspond at all closely to *any* Arabic version.

This is why we encounter such bewildering variation as that exhibited by the name of the Libyan head of state, whose surname may be written as *Gaddafi* or as *Qaddafi* or as something else, while his given name may likewise surface as *Moamar* or as *Muammer* or as something else.

In the face of all this, there is little advice I can offer. If an established English form exists, use it. If an Arabic-speaker himself is known to prefer a particular English version of his name, use that. Beyond this, you are on your own.

One final complication. Not all Arabs have surnames of the familiar western sort. Some do, while others have only a string of given names, perhaps followed by an epithet or by a place name indicating the place of origin of the name-bearer or of his family. And there may also be a title, usually preposed, such as *Sheikh*.

Aran, Arran The island off Donegal in Ireland is *Aran*. The island in the Firth of Clyde is *Arran*. The islands off Galway in Ireland are the *Aran Islands*.

arbiter, arbitrator, mediator An *arbiter* is an umpire, a neutral person who makes decisions in a contest between players or teams. An arbiter's decision is final. An *arbitrator* is a person who decides between the claims of rival sides in a dispute, such as a labour dispute. An arbitrator's decision is also final. A *mediator* is a person who tries to persuade opposing sides to reach agreement, with some blend of coaxing and arm-twisting. A mediator makes no decisions.

arch- This is a prefix and must be written as one. Write *arch-enemy*, not ✳*arch enemy*.

Arctic, Antarctic The words are so spelled, with a medial C, and ✳*Artic* and ✳*Antartic* are wrong. Both normally get initial capitals, but we write *arctic* in the sense of 'frigid', as in *arctic weather*.

Argentina, Argentine, **Argentinian** The country is properly called *Argentina*, and not ✳*the Argentine*. A person or a thing from Argentina is *Argentinian*, not ✳*Argentine*.

argument Even though the verb is *argue*, the noun is *argument*, and the spelling ✳*arguement* is never acceptable.

aria There seems to be a widespread perception that an aria can only be sung by a woman. This is not so: an aria can be sung either by a man or by a woman. An aria is simply a vocal solo with orchestral accompaniment, forming part of a larger musical composition, most often an opera.

armory, armoury A place for storing weapons or for training in the use of weapons is an *armoury* in British English but an *armory* in American English. However, the less usual name for 'heraldry' is *armory* in all varieties.

Arran See **Aran**.

artefact, artifact The preferred British spelling is *artefact*; the preferred American one is *artifact*. The word denotes an object created by human workmanship, such as a tool or a carving, and it is most usual among archaeologists. It cannot be applied to anything else: bones, fossils and teeth are not artefacts merely because they are old.

   The word has acquired a second sense of 'a spurious result caused by extraneous factors', especially in experimental work: *The observed correlations are an artefact of the faulty procedure*. This usage is now acceptable in formal writing. However, the word does not mean 'unpleasant consequence', and you should not write things like ✳*The rise in violent crime is an artefact of growing poverty*.

articulate The derived noun is *articulateness*, not ✳*articulacy*.

artiste This pretentious word is now almost obsolete, except as an insult: it commonly means 'fraud pretending to be an artist', a usage delicately underlined by its enduring popularity as a label for a (female) stripper. Don't use it, unless you mean to be insulting.

Aryan The ancient Indians and Persians applied this name to themselves. It means 'noble'. It was formerly applied by European linguists to the whole vast **Indo-European** family of languages, which includes English, but no longer. Today, linguists apply the label *Indo-Aryan* (not *Aryan*) to the subgroup of this family which includes Hindi, Urdu, Panjabi, Bengali and Gujarati, among others. Otherwise, the word should be avoided, since its misuse by the Nazis has made it widely offensive.

as See **like, as**.

ascertain This is only a fancy way of saying *find out*, and the simpler expression should usually be preferred, since the long word is rather pompous. If you need a formal verb to express 'find out definitely and precisely', use *establish*: *The police established that the murder had been committed before midnight.*

as of This stiff business expression is best avoided in most writing; use *on*, *since* or *from* instead, as required.

aspire You *aspire to* something; you do not *✳aspire for* something, even though you *wish for* it, *hope for* it or *work for* it. Write *She aspires to a career on the stage*, not *✳She aspires for a career on the stage*. This verb is normally followed by a noun, and you are advised to avoid following it with a verb: write *She aspires to a professorship*, and not *??She aspires to be a professor*, which will annoy many readers.

as plus verb As a general rule, a finite verb-form in English must have an overt grammatical subject. But an exception occurs after the word *as*, especially (though not only) when this is followed by a passive or by an auxiliary plus a passive. Here are some examples: *as was noted above, . . . ; as can be seen from the graph, . . . ; as sometimes occurs in such cases, . . .* It is wrong to write *✳as it was noted above, . . . ; ✳as it can be seen from the graph, . . . ; ✳as it sometimes occurs in such cases, . . .* Foreign learners of English should particularly note this, but even native speakers sometimes get it wrong.

assignment, assignation An *assignment* is a task assigned to somebody, or the act of assigning the task. An *assignation* is a secret meeting, especially between lovers trying to conceal their affair.

assume, presume Both of these mean 'suppose', and their meanings often overlap. But there is a subtle distinction. To *assume* something is to take it for granted as the basis of a discussion or an argument, without offering any evidence for it. This may be done purely in order to explore the consequences of the assumption. To *presume* something is to suppose it is so because we have no good reason to suppose otherwise.

Of course, *presume* alone has a second sense of 'be overly bold', 'take something upon oneself without permission', as in *We are presuming upon his hospitality*.

asterisk Since I've encountered the same error twice in the last week, I guess I'd better mention it. The name of the little star used in printing (✳) is the *asterisk*, and not the ✳*asterix*. The French cartoon character is *Asterix*, but that's as far as it goes.

asterism See **constellation**.

as to These words are usually unnecessary. Write *the reason we are doing this*, not ✳*the reason as to why we are doing this*, and likewise with other question words.

as well This is the only possible form: the spelling ✳*aswell* is never acceptable. In particular, avoid writing ✳*aswell* as for *as well as*.

Vernacular Canadian English allows *as well* to begin a sentence, as in ??*As well, there were three other problems*. This usage is not regarded as standard English, and it bewilders other English-speakers, even Americans. Canadians are advised to avoid it in writing: write *moreover* or *furthermore* instead.

at any rate This must always be written as three words: the form ✳*at anyrate* is wrong.

atheist See **agnostic**.

at this moment in time This is one of the most frequent and most wearisome examples of **wordiness**. Avoid it, and write *at present*, *today*, *currently* or just plain *now* instead.

attribute This verb means 'ascribe', 'assign'. Its correct use is illustrated by the following example: *Many English spellings are attributed to Samuel Johnson*. But the next version is wrong: ✳*Samuel Johnson is attributed many English spellings*. It is not possible to use *attribute* without *to*.

at your earliest convenience This ridiculous and dishonest expression should never be used. Write instead something plainer and more direct, such as *promptly*, *soon* or *as soon as possible*.

auger, augur An *auger* is a tool for drilling holes. An *augur* is a fortune-teller, and the word is also used as a verb meaning *bode*: *These results do not augur well for our hopes*. The common error is writing *auger* where *augur* is intended.

Austen, Austin The novelist is *Jane Austen*, but almost everybody else with this name spells it *Austin*.

Australian English The variety of English used in Australia. At present, there is no distinctive Australian form of standard English. Australia traditionally adheres to the written norms of British English, but pressure from American English is large and growing. For example, even though the British spelling *labour* is usual in Australia, one of the chief political parties calls itself the *Labor Party*, with the American spelling.

autarchy, autarky You are unlikely to need either of these unusual words. But, just for the record, *autarchy* is absolute power, the sort of power enjoyed by an absolute monarch, while *autarky* is merely self-sufficiency.

authoritarian, authoritative An *authoritarian* person or regime is tyrannical: *There are fears that Russian democracy may succumb to another authoritarian regime*. An *authoritative* person or text is one that commands respect through being knowledgeable and reliable: *I recommend her authoritative essays on Shakespeare*. The first is related to *authority* in the sense of 'being in charge', the second to *authority* in the sense of 'knowing one's business well'.

auxiliary The word is always so spelled: do not write *✳auxillary* or *✳auxilliary*.

avenge, revenge When you *avenge* a wrong, you are delivering retribution to an evildoer, and so you are bringing a modicum of justice into the world: *Mehmet avenged the destruction of his family by killing the evil Aga who had caused it*. The word is rather elevated in tone. However, when you *revenge* something, your motives are less high-minded: you are merely getting even for an earlier setback, and your motivation may even be malicious, though not necessarily: *Chelsea revenged their earlier defeat with a 3–1 win in the second leg*. The derived noun is *vengeance* in both cases.

average This word has a precise mathematical sense. If I announce that the average score on a particular exam is 57.6, then this number results from a simple but precise calculation, and describing 56 or 61 as an 'average' score constitutes a broadening of the sense. Of course, this broad sense is now so well established that no one could possibly object to it, but, before you write *an average household* or something similar, recall that English provides lots of other adjectives: *typical, ordinary, unremarkable, unexceptional, commonplace*, and others. Perhaps one of these would serve your purposes better. As always, good writing requires you to choose your words carefully, and not merely to plonk down the first overused word that pops into your head.

Averroës The name of the Arab philosopher is so written in English.

averse See **adverse**.

avocado, advocate An *avocado* is an oily vegetable resembling a pear, while an *advocate* is a person who speaks for you, often a lawyer. The common error here is writing *advocado for the vegetable.

awfully Colloquial English makes frequent use of *awfully*, *terribly*, *fearfully*, *horribly* and other such words as substitutes for 'very', as in *It was terribly good*. This colloquial usage is out of place in formal writing, where such words should be restricted to their literal senses, as in *He was terribly wounded*.

awhile The adverb *awhile* means 'for a while'. You may write either *stay awhile* or *stay for a while*, but not *stay for awhile*.

Azerbaijani The people from Azerbaijan are *Azerbaijanis*, not *Azeris*.

background This word is used far too freely. Before writing it, consider whether another word might be more explicit: *origin*, *history*, *explanation*, *motive*, or something else.

bacterium, bacteria The singular is *bacterium*; the plural is *bacteria*. Write *a deadly bacterium*, not *a deadly bacteria*.

Bagehot, Walter The writer's name is so spelled.

Baghdad, Bagdad The spelling *Baghdad* is preferred everywhere.

Bahrain, Bahrein Almost all authorities prefer the form *Bahrain*.

bail, bale These are often confused, and some of the confusions have now become accepted in British English. In all varieties of English, the spelling is *bale* when we are talking about a large bundle, as of hay or cotton, but *bail* when we are talking about the sum of money deposited with a court to obtain the temporary release of an accused person, or about one of the carved wooden dowels used in cricket, or about the bar on a typewriter that holds the paper in place. The difficulty arises with removing water and with jumping out of a plane. The traditional spelling in both these cases is *bail*, and this is still the only possibility in American English, where you *bail out* a waterlogged boat and *bail out* of a plane. In British English, however, the originally erroneous spelling *bale out* has now become so widespread that most authorities today recommend it as the preferred spelling in Britain for both these cases.

bait, bate The noun *bait* denotes something used as a lure to attract prey, as in *fishing bait* or *bait for a trap*. The related verb is also *bait*, as in *She baited the trap*. The rare word *bate* is hardly found outside the expression *with bated breath*. Avoid the common error *✳with baited breath*.

baleful This word means 'malignant'. It is now mostly a literary word, applied chiefly to expressions and glances. Long ago it could also mean 'gloomy' or 'miserable', but these senses are obsolete.

balk, baulk The American spelling is *balk* in all senses. The British spelling is usually *baulk* for the noun, but *balk* is perhaps more common than *baulk* for the verb.

Balliol The name of the Oxford college is so spelled, with three Ls.

Bangladesh The official form of the name is *Bangladesh*, not *✳Bangla Desh*.

banns The public declaration of a forthcoming marriage is the *banns*, not the *✳bans*.

barbaric, barbarous It is difficult to draw a clear line between these two. Both can mean 'appalling' or 'cruel'. However, only *barbaric* can have the more neutral meaning 'typical of, or produced by, barbarians (uncivilized peoples)', while *barbarous* is often preferred for 'savagely cruel'. Only *barbarous* can mean 'extremely unsatisfactory', as in *barbarous English*.

barbecue This word is so spelled: the joke spellings *✳barbeque* and *✳bar-b-q* are not acceptable in careful writing.

baritone, barytone The Greek accent is *barytone*; the musical term is *baritone*.

baseball In baseball, batting and fielding averages are normally expressed to three decimal points, with *no* leading zero. So, a batting average is *.326*, not *✳0.326*, and a fielding average is *.992*, not *✳0.992*. A perfect average is *1.000*, but this cannot be achieved except over a very short period. However, an earned-run average, for the rare pitcher who gets it below one, must have a leading zero: hence *0.95*, not *✳.95*.

basically This adverb means 'fundamentally', 'in essence', and it is much overused. Typical misuses are the following: *✳Basically, she was a tyrant*; *✳A wallaby is basically a marsupial*. In both cases, the word *basically* contributes nothing to the sense and should be deleted. If the second is felt to be inexplicit, it can be written *A wallaby is a kind of marsupial*. Every time you find yourself writing *basically*, check to see if it can be removed without damage; if it can, remove it.

basis It is a bad habit to write *??on an equal basis* or *??on a fair basis* when all you mean is *equally* or *fairly*. The pompous and wordy longer forms are typical of bureaucratic prose, but no one in her right mind would take bureaucratic prose as a model for anything, except, I suppose, more bureaucratic prose.

Basque The *Basques* are an ancient people of western Europe, at the western end of the Pyrenees along the Bay of Biscay. Their language, related to no other, is *Basque*. The territory they inhabit is called *the Basque Country*, and this territory is conventionally defined as containing the four Spanish provinces of Vizcaya, Guipúzcoa, Alava and Navarra, plus the western half of the French department of Pyrenées-Atlantique. (In Spain, however, the name *País Vasco* is applied only to the first three provinces named, excluding Navarra.) The Basques call their language *euskara* and themselves *euskaldunak*. The name *Euskadi*, originally invented as a name for a hypothetical Basque political entity, is now officially applied to the territory administered by the Basque Autonomous Government in Spain (the first three provinces listed above), but it is sometimes extended by Basque nationalists to the entire Basque Country. In any case, avoid the silly word *✳Basqueland*, which is not standard English. Note that Andorra is not Basque-speaking at all, but Catalan-speaking.

The letter combination *tx* is common in Basque, where it represents the same sound as English *ch*. This sound is frequent in Basque names, such as the common surname *Etxeberria*. Avoid the error of turning these letters round and writing things like *✳Exteberria*.

bate See **bait**.

batter, batsman A baseball player who is batting is a *batter*. The equivalent in cricket is *batsman* – even in women's cricket – though cricketers are said to prefer *batter* among themselves.

baulk See **balk**.

B.C. B.C.E. See **A.D.**

because There are two points to be noted with *because*. First, it makes a very big difference whether we do or do not set off the *because* phrase with a comma. Consider this example, from a book I've been reading: *Scientists cannot rule out heaven or hell because they are beyond the reach of empirical investigation.* Now, as written, this sentence has the following meaning:

'There may be a number of reasons for scientists to rule out heaven or hell, but their being beyond the reach of empirical investigation is not one of them.' But I suspect that this is not what what the writer meant. Most likely, he meant what should have been written like this: *Scientists cannot rule out heaven or hell, because they are beyond the reach of empirical investigation.* This means 'Scientists cannot rule out heaven or hell *at all*, and the reason for this is that they are beyond the reach of empirical investigation.' This is a big difference. The commaless version allows scientists to rule out heaven and hell, only not for the reason named, while the second does not allow scientists to rule out heaven and hell at all.

Second, there are some peculiarly journalistic uses of *because* which are best avoided in careful writing. Here is one: *Don't think that this will change your life, because it won't.* Use a colon instead, and write *Don't think that this will change your life: it won't.* Another example, less obviously journalistic: *It's raining in the mountains, because the river is flooded.* On the face of things, this sentence appears to say that the flooding of the river is the reason for the rain in the mountains, which is nonsense. What it really means, of course, is this: '[I conclude that] it is raining in the mountains, because the river is flooded. This 'BBC *because*', as a friend of mine has dubbed it, is not appropriate in formal writing. Write something more explicit instead.

See also **reason is because**.

Bedouin Though this a plural form in Arabic, it is used in English as a singular; the plural may be either *Bedouin* or *Bedouins*, according to taste.

beg the question Originally, to *beg the question* was to argue in a circle, to argue by assuming at the outset the truth of what you are trying to prove. For example, the argument *God is all-powerful, because the Bible says so, and the Bible is the reliable word of God* begs the question. Using *beg the question* in this sense will offend no one, though it may baffle many readers, since few people today are aware of this sense.

More recently, *beg the question* has, for many people, acquired a second and quite different sense: it means 'give an evasive answer to a question'. If you ask a political candidate 'Do you support subsidized public transport?' and he replies 'I support a sensible transport policy', then he has begged the question, in this sense. This second sense is now very widespread, and on the verge of becoming accepted as standard English, but nevertheless very many authorities still condemn it as non-standard. On the whole, you are probably best advised to avoid using the words in this sense.

More recently still, *beg the question* has begun to be used in yet another sense: 'raise the question'. Journalists frequently write things like this: *Sinn*

Fein's refusal to condemn the violence begs the question of whether the party is truly independent of the IRA. This use is never acceptable in careful writing, and it must be avoided.

behoove, behove The form *behove* is British, while *behoove* is American. The verb means 'be necessary' or 'be appropriate' (for someone to do something), and it can only be used with the impersonal subject *it*: *It behoves* (or *behooves*) *us to set aside our regulations in this case*. Any other subject is wrong: *The circumstances behove us to take action*. This verb is very formal.

being that Avoid the ghastly ✱*being that*, which has no place in standard written English. Write *Since we have a surplus, . . .*, not ✱*Being that we have a surplus . . .* The same goes for ✱*being as how*: don't use it.

Belarus This is now the preferred form for the name of the country, replacing earlier *Byelorussia* and *Belorussia*. The adjective is *Belarusian*.

belie The unusual and decidedly formal verb *belie* means 'contradict', 'misrepresent', 'disguise': *His educated accent belies his humble working-class background*. The word does not mean 'betray', and it certainly does not mean 'bespeak', 'exhibit', 'show off'.

Belgian See **Dutch**.

Bennet, Bennett Most people with this surname spell it *Bennett*, but the family in *Pride and Prejudice* is called *Bennet*.

benzene, benzine These are not the same. *Benzene* is an important chemical compound, formula C_6H_6, much used as a solvent and in the manufacture of a number of chemicals. It is toxic. But *benzine* is not a single substance: it is a volatile mixture of hydrocarbons extracted from petroleum (crude oil). In Australia and New Zealand, *benzine* is also occasionally applied to petrol (gasoline).

bereft If you are *bereft* of something, then you used to have it but it has been taken away from you. If you never had it, then you cannot be bereft of it. The word is closely related to *bereaved*, but *bereaved* is applied only to someone who has lost a loved one.

beside, besides Both of these words can be prepositions, but their meanings are different. The word *beside* means 'next to', while *besides* means 'also', 'in addition'.

Betelgeuse, Betelgeux The star in Orion is *Betelgeuse* today; the old spelling *Betelgeux* has almost dropped out of use.

bête noire The phrase is so written, with a circumflex and a final E, and in italics.

better, bettor In the sense of 'one who bets', *better* is preferred in Britain, *bettor* in the USA. The American spelling has the great advantage of avoiding any confusion with the comparative form of *good*.

betting odds Odds are commonly quoted *against* a result. If the bookmakers are quoting odds of 5–1 against a particular horse, then, if that horse wins, a bet of £2 will win you £10. This will commonly be expressed as *5–1*. However, if the odds are given as *3–2 on*, this means that a bet of £3 will win you just £2 if your horse comes in. In effect, *3–2 on* means the same as *2–3* (against).

Accordingly, it is dangerous to write *The bookies are offering 5–1 on Slow Motion* if what you mean is *The bookies are offering 5–1 against Slow Motion*. Be careful with this.

between The only possible construction is *between X and Y*. Write *between eight a.m. and six p.m.*, and not *between eight a.m. to six p.m.* The construction *between X to Y* is always wrong. Likewise, write *We must choose between Prague and Budapest*, not *. . . between Prague or Budapest*, which is also wrong.

You should also avoid the faulty usage illustrated by *between 1940–1960*: the dash already carries the meaning of 'between . . . and . . .' or 'from . . . to . . .' If you must use this abbreviated form, write *The war occurred 1940–1960*, though the longer form is much better.

Moreover, you should avoid the construction illustrated here: *The doubles partners were chatting between each point*. Nothing can be between just one thing. The required form is *between each point and the next*, or, more simply, *after each point*.

Further, avoid writing *in between* where *between* will do. Write *The children were playing between the trees*, not *. . . in between the trees*.

Finally, there is a widespread belief that *between* should be used only with two things, and that *among* must be used with three or more. This belief is not supported by examinations of English usage in the past or today. Nevertheless, you might be wise to follow this rule, since doing so will annoy nobody. So, I recommend writing *relations between Britain and France* but *relations among Britain, France and Germany*.

between you and I Common though this form may be in spoken English, it is never acceptable in careful writing. Write *between you and me*. The same problem arises in many other cases. Here is a recent example from a serious newspaper: *Will Self invited Jim and I back to his flat*. No English-speaker would dream of writing ∗*Will Self invited I back to his flat*, but the presence of that *and* seems to throw many writers into a panic, a panic which inevitably leads to the insertion of an impossible *I* where only *me* is possible.

betwixt Except in the hackneyed expression *betwixt and between*, the word *betwixt* is obsolete in standard English and should not be used.

be used to See **used to**.

Bible, bible The word is capitalized when it denotes the text of the Christian holy book: *the books of the Bible*. It is not capitalized when it denotes an individual copy of this book: *The Gideons place bibles in hotel rooms*. And it is not capitalized when it denotes a standard reference book: *The OSW is the Scrabble-players' bible*.

biennial, semi-annual, bi-annual The word *biennial* means 'happening every two years', while *semi-annual* means 'happening twice a year', 'happening every six months'. The common mistake is writing *biennial* where *semi-annual* is intended.

There is also the somewhat unusual word *bi-annual*, which means 'happening twice a year', but you are advised to avoid this.

billion In American usage, a *billion* is always a *thousand million*. In British usage, the word formerly meant a *million million*. However, the American sense has now become predominant in Britain, and you are advised to use the word only to mean *thousand million*.

biological names In biology, a taxonomic name consists of two parts, the genus name followed by the species name. Both must be written in italics. Crucially, the genus name must have an initial capital, while the species name must not. Two examples are *Bombycilla cedrorum* (the cedar waxwing, an American bird) and *Homo sapiens* (our own species). It is always wrong to write about the genus ∗*homo* or about the species ∗*Homo Sapiens*.

If the genus name has already been identified, it can be abbreviated thereafter to a single letter: *The earliest member of the genus* Homo *was* H. habilis.

blanch, blench Historically, there are two unrelated verbs here, but they have become almost inextricably tangled up. The historical position is that *blanch* means both 'turn pale' and 'scald' (vegetables or other food), while *blench* means 'flinch', 'recoil in fear'. I advise sticking to this. But the use of *blench* for 'turn pale' is now so common that it is recognized by most dictionaries, and it can no longer be regarded as wrong.

blatant, flagrant The word *blatant* means 'glaringly obvious', as in *a blatant lie* (a lie which everybody immediately recognizes as such) or *blatant disregard for her feelings*. The word carries a clear note of disapproval of the action so described. But *flagrant* is stronger: it means 'blatant and outrageous'. A *blatant* lie can be a tiny little fib, so long as it is obvious, but a *flagrant* lie must be a breathtaking whopper.

blazon This is not a fancy word for *blaze*, as in *blaze a trail*. It is an unusual word meaning 'proclaim publicly', and it is usually found in the collocation *blazon abroad*. It is also the term in heraldry for 'describe a coat of arms in the conventional manner'.

bloc This word denotes a collection of people, political parties or countries that have grouped together to further their common interests, as in *the former Communist bloc*. But the system in which a delegate casts a number of votes according to the number of people he represents is the *block vote*, not the *bloc vote.

blond, blonde There is something of a tradition in English of describing a man as *blond*, but a woman as *blonde*. But this distinction is not absolute, and it is not rare to find *blond* applied to a woman – though perhaps never *blonde* to a man. In any case, it is very common to see a woman's hair described as *blond*, even when the woman is *blonde*. This distinction could hardly be more pointless, and you should not worry about it unless doing so pleases you. Note also that referring to a woman as *a blonde* is now widely considered to be sexist, since it classifies a woman in terms of her physical attributes. Non-human things like wood and tobacco are always *blond* in British English, but may be either *blond* or *blonde* in American English. See **brunette**.

blueprint Do not use this word if all you mean is *plan*.

Bodleian The name of the library in Oxford is so spelled.

bona fide, bona fides Of these two, *bona fide* is an adjective meaning 'genuine', while *bona fides* is a noun meaning 'good faith', 'honest intentions'. So, we write *a bona fide offer* but *There are doubts about his bona fides*. The noun is singular: write *His bona fides is not in doubt*, not *... are in doubt*. However, like most Latin expressions, these two are hardly necessary: it is preferable to write *a genuine offer* and *There are doubts about his honesty*.

Boötes The name of the constellation is always so written, with the two dots.

bored The established expression is *bored with*, not *＊bored of*, which should be avoided in careful writing.

bosom This is now a rather affected or jocular word for a woman's breasts. The older sense of 'chest', as in *He clutched her to his bosom*, is too old-fashioned to be used in most types of writing. And note that it is an error to refer to *＊a woman's bosoms*: a bosom is not an individual breast, but the pair of them together.

Bosporus The spellings *Bosporus* and *Bosphorus* are both acceptable, but *＊Bosphorous* is wrong.

both It is possible to use *both* alone, as in *Both are acceptable* and *Both of them have been found guilty*. Note that *both* always takes plural agreement. It is also possible to combine *both* with *and*: *Both the Egyptians and the Israelis will attend the talks*. But it is wrong to combine *both* with *as well as*: things like *＊Both the Egyptians as well as the Israelis will attend the talks* are wrong.

A wrong use of *both* is illustrated by the following example: *＊Both these words are synonymous*. Being synonymous is not a property that a single object can have in isolation, and the correct form is *These words are synonymous*.

Another error occurs in the following quiz question, from a film quiz book. *A thief is saved from lynching by marrying a spinster. Who played both parts?* Nobody played both parts. Jack Nicholson played one part and Mary Steenburgen the other. The question should be 'Who played the two parts?'

If *both* is followed by a preposition, that preposition must be repeated after *and*: write *both in Britain and in America*, and not *＊both in Britain and America*. Another possibility is *in both Britain and America*.

bottle English distinguishes between *a bottle of wine* (a bottle full of wine) and *a wine bottle* (an empty bottle of the sort used to hold wine). This difference particularly confuses foreign learners of English, but even native speakers have been known to get it wrong.

bottom line In accounting, the *bottom line* is the last line of a statement of accounts, showing the net profit or loss. Recently, however, this term has been vastly overused to mean 'final outcome', 'most important consideration', and perhaps other things. Don't do this. Write something more explicit.

bouillabaisse The name of the fish soup is so spelled.

bougainvillaea The word is so spelled.

bowdlerize This verb means 'censor', 'expurgate', especially in a prudish and thoughtless way. It derives from the name of Thomas Bowdler, who was so embarrassed by the naughty passages in Shakespeare that he published a 'family' version with the rude bits cut out. The word does not mean 'mutilate' or 'cut' in any other sense.

B.P. See **A.D.**

bra, brassière The older form *brassière* has now been almost totally supplanted by the clipped form *bra*, and *bra* should be preferred even in careful writing: *She was arrested for removing her bra in public.* Writing *brassière* is now comparable to writing *violoncello* for *cello*: doing so identifies you as an old stick-in-the-mud who doesn't approve of anything that's happened since 1912.

brackets There are some trans-Atlantic differences here. The marks ( ) are called *parentheses* in the US, and often also in Britain, but British English often calls them *brackets*. The marks [ ] are *square brackets* everywhere, though sometimes just *brackets* in the US. The marks { } are *braces* in the US but *curly brackets* or *curly braces* in Britain. The marks < > are *angle brackets* everywhere. All four marks collectively are usually called *brackets* everywhere.

brand new The expression is so spelled, or with a hyphen when preposed, as in *a brand-new production.* The spelling *bran-new* is wrong.

brazier, brasier All authorities prefer the spelling *brazier*.

Brazilian names See **Portuguese and Brazilian names**.

breach, breech The spelling is *breach* in all senses involving gaps, breaks or violations: *a breach in the wall, a breach of the peace, to breach the enemy defences.* The word *breech* means 'rear end', and is confined to a handful of expressions: *a breech-loading rifle, a breech* (or *breeches*) *birth, a breeches buoy,* and, of course, *breeches* (trousers).

Breakspear, Nicholas In spite of *Shakespeare*, the man who became Pope Adrian IV is Nicholas *Breakspear*.

breast In contemporary English, this word almost always means 'mammary gland', as in *Julie Andrews bared her breasts in the film* S.O.B. It can also mean 'white meat' of a fowl, as in *breast of chicken*. But its use to mean 'chest', as in *He clutched her to his breast*, is now decidedly old-fashioned, and should be avoided in most writing.

breath, breathe The noun is *breath*, as in *Take a deep breath*. The verb is *breathe*, as in *I can't breathe*.

breech See **breach**.

Breughel See **Brueghel**.

bridge, contract bridge Except in the official names of one or two organizations and tournaments, the famous card game is *bridge*, and the older name *contract bridge* is obsolete. The longer name was once necessary because there used to be another game called *auction bridge*, but auction bridge has probably not been played seriously for over sixty years, and the game is a fossil serving only to decorate the pages of rulebooks.

Britain, Great Britain, England The name *Britain* is a little ambiguous: it may be short for *the United Kingdom of Great Britain and Northern Ireland*, or only for *Great Britain*, though the first is more usual. In contrast, *England* denotes only one of the four principal territories making up the UK. American writers in particular should be careful to avoid using *England* for *Britain*, or *English* for *British*: this error greatly annoys the Scots, the Welsh and the Northern Irish, who are British but not English.

British Uniquely among the countries of the world, Britain does not put its name on its postage stamps. In a similar vein, names of British institutions rarely contain the word *British*: Britain has the *Automobile Association*, the *Chemical Society*, the *Post Office*, the *Open* (a golf tournament), and many others of this sort. When you are writing only for a British audience, there is nothing wrong with using these names. However, when you are writing for a wider audience, you should consider modifying some of them. Americans and Australians may consider you unbearably arrogant if you write loftily about the *Open*, rather than about the *British Open*. And British writers should bear these things in mind before sneering at the Americans for calling their national baseball championship the *World Series*.

British/American differences See **American/British differences**.

British English An unfortunate and awkward name to which there is no good alternative. In principle, *British English* ought to include all of the many varieties of English used in the UK, or at least in Great Britain, but the term is rarely so broadly used. Most commonly, it means instead something like 'the educated English of England', and often especially the educated English of the south of England. Another possible label is *English English*, and this is occasionally used, but many people find it unbearably clumsy. It appears that we are stuck with *British English*. This label is also applied to one of the two recognized versions of **standard English**, the one used in Britain and elsewhere. In any case, Britons should *never* use *English* in the sense of 'the English of England, or of Britain'. English has long since ceased being the sole property of the English, or of the British. Today a London taxi driver or an Oxford professor has no greater claim to English than does a New Zealand sheep farmer, a Canadian lumberjack, an American baseball player or an Irish musician. See also **American English.**

Briton, Brit, Britisher The standard term for a citizen of the United Kingdom is *Briton*, though some Britons strangely object to this term, even though there is no alternative. The form *Brit* is an informal equivalent, and some Britons object to it strongly, while others are entirely happy with it; in any case, it should not be used in formal writing. The word *Britisher* is strictly American, and it should be avoided in careful writing, since almost everyone in Britain objects to it.

broach, brooch The verb is *broach*, as in *broach the subject* or *broach a cask of wine*. The noun *brooch* denotes a piece of jewellery pinned to a garment.

broccoli This is always so spelled: do not write *brocolli.

Brontë All the members of this famous family wrote their surname with the diaeresis (the two dots), and I advise you to follow suit. So far as your word processor permits, you should always respect the preferences of the owner of a name.

Brueghel, Bruegel, Breughel The recommended spelling for the family of Flemish painters is *Brueghel*. The form *Bruegel* is also acceptable. The form *Breughel* is best avoided.

brunette, brunet In British English, the spelling is almost invariably *brunette* in all contexts. In American English, both *brunette* and *brunet* are in use, the first being far more frequent, but there is no systematic distinction between them, and either may be applied indifferently to a man or to a woman. Note also that referring to a woman as *a brunette* is now widely considered to be sexist, since it classifies a woman in terms of her physical attributes. See **blond**.

brutalize This word means 'make (somebody) brutal'. When you *brutalize* somebody, you treat him in such a way that he becomes brutal himself: *Her terrible childhood extinguished her once affectionate nature and brutalized her.*

Merely treating someone brutally is not brutalizing him, and *brutalize* should not be used to mean only 'treat brutally'.

Brynmawr, Bryn Mawr The place in Wales is *Brynmawr*; the US college is *Bryn Mawr*.

bulimia See **anorexia**.

bulky modifiers Among national tabloid journalists, it has become commonplace to fill headlines with enormously bulky preposed modifiers, usually without any hyphens to guide the perplexed reader, as in *✻Railway Station Murder Inquiry Shock*, which presumably designates a shock coming out of an inquiry into a murder which took place in a railway station. Even a national tabloid journalist would probably not go so far as to stick something like this into the body of his text. But very many writers, and not just journalists, fall into the bad habit of writing long and bulky preposed modifiers, often containing Greek and Latin prefixes like *pre-*, *post-*, *pro-* and *anti-*, in front of nouns. This is bad style, and it results from shoving words down onto the page without careful planning or editing.

Why write something cumbersome like *anti-seal-killing campaigners* when you can write instead the far more elegant *campaigners against seal-killing*? And *✻the pre-Roman-conquest Spanish civilizations* is ghastly beside the more normal wording *the Spanish civilizations before the Roman conquest*.

I have just received the new programme for our local theatre, and it informs me breathlessly that I can see *✻multi Olivier Award-winning Simon Russell Beale* as Hamlet. This is a mess, for several reasons. One, the bulky modifier here is almost out of control. Two, the required hyphenation is mostly missing (see **compound modifier**). Three, there is no such word as *✻multi*. Four, the required word *the* is missing (see **preposed appositives**). This can be patched up after a fashion, as follows: *the multi-Olivier-Award-winning Simon Russell Beale*, or, slightly better, *the multi-Olivier-Award-winning actor Simon Russell Beale*. However, if you are not obliged to write such dense and breathless stuff for a living, you would be wise to scrap the bulky modifier entirely, and to replace it with a more measured piece of English: *Simon Russell Beale, who has won several Olivier Awards*. It is not necessary, or advisable, to cram most of your sentence into the overworked slot to the left of the name.

One possible virtue of **style checkers** is that the better ones may succeed in picking up overly bulky modifiers. But you can do a better job yourself if you merely pay attention to what you have written and shun Graeco-Latin prefixes.

bureau The plural is either *bureaux* (preferred in Britain) or *bureaus* (preferred in the US).

bureaucrat This oddly formed word is so spelled, just like *bureau*, and the spelling ✳*beaurocrat* is wrong.

-burg, -burgh, -borough, -boro, -brough, -bury The Old English word *burg* 'fortified place' occurs in very many place names, and it has acquired several spellings and pronunciations. Those in *-bury*, like *Canterbury* and *Waterbury*, rarely cause any problems, since the pronunciation is distinctive here. But the others can cause a good deal of confusion. In England, the spelling *-borough* predominates, as in *Peterborough, Loughborough, Scarborough, Marlborough* and *Wellingborough*. But there are exceptions. The big one is *Middlesbrough*, which constantly catches people out. But others exist, such as *Aldeburgh* in Suffolk. In Scotland, the spelling *-burgh* predominates, as in *Edinburgh, Jedburgh, Musselburgh* and *Helensburgh*. In the US, the spelling *-burg* predominates, as in *Harrisburg* (PA), *Petersburg* (VA), *Ogdensburg* (NY), *Clarksburg* (WV) and *St. Petersburg* (FL). But again there are exceptions. The big one is *Pittsburgh*, which frequently catches out non-Americans, but note also *Plattsburgh* (NY) and *Edinboro* (PA), among others. If in doubt, consult a good reference book.

burgeon This word originally meant 'sprout buds' (of a plant). However, it has acquired a second sense: 'grow rapidly', 'flourish', as in *a burgeoning business empire*. This second sense is now accepted by almost all authorities as standard, though a few conservative writers still dislike it. In any case, don't overuse it: we have many other words to express this second sense, such as *thriving, flourishing, expanding* and *growing*.

burgle, burglarize Both of these are of fairly recent formation, but both are now regarded as standard English. On the whole, British English strongly prefers *burgle*, while American English shows a clear but not overwhelming preference for *burglarize*. But you may use whichever you prefer.

Burma The current Burmese government has changed the official name of the country to *Myanmar*. However, the legitimacy of this government is doubtful, and I advise retaining the traditional name *Burma*.

Burmese names Burmese names are long and complex, and it may not be easy to identify a surname. But note that the item *U* is a courtesy title, not a name, applied to men, even though the statesman *U Thant* is always so called in English.

bus The plural is usually *buses*, which is recommended. The variant *busses* is considered acceptable by most authorities, but is unusual. Likewise, when the word is used as a verb, the inflected forms are usually *bused* and *busing*, which are recommended, though the less frequent variants *bussed* and *bussing* are also acceptable. The rare verb *buss* means 'kiss'.

but Among its other uses, *but* can be a preposition. When it functions as a preposition, it must, like any preposition, take the object form of a pronoun. So, write *Everyone but him was there*, and *Everyone was there but him*. Writing ✳*Everyone was there but he* is just as wrong as writing ✳*Everyone was there with he*.

By the way, contrary to what someone might have told you, there is nothing wrong in starting a sentence with *but*. But try not to overdo this, since overuse will make your writing wearisome.

buxom This word can be applied only to a woman. In the days when plumpness was regarded as attractive in women, it meant 'attractively plump', 'plump and healthy-looking'. Today, however, *buxom* is only a polite or jocular word for 'having large breasts', and the older sense is obsolete.

by-, bye- The prefix meaning 'secondary' or 'incidental' is best spelled *by-*, as in *by-law*, *by-election* and *by-product* (which can also be spelled without hyphens). The alternative spelling with *bye-* is permissible in British English in the word *bye-election* but is not recommended.

Byzantine, byzantine The capitalized form *Byzantine* must be used when you are referring directly to the medieval Greek city of Byzantium, or to that city's empire, art, architecture, politics or history. The lower-case form *byzantine* is strongly recommended in the transferred sense of 'exceedingly complicated, devious and unfathomable', though the capitalized version is by no means rare here.

cabal, cabbala A *cabal* is a group of political plotters. The *cabbala* is an ancient Jewish mystical tradition. The adjectives, if you need them, are *cabalistic* for the first and *cabbalistic* for the second.

caddie, caddy A *caddie* is a person who carries a golfer's clubs. A *caddy* is a small container for tea. The plural is *caddies* in both cases.

Caernarvon, Carnarvon The Welsh town is *Caernarvon* (or Welsh *Caernarfon*), but the co-discoverer of Tutankhamun's tomb is Lord *Carnarvon*.

Caesarean section The first word is so spelled, and ✳*Caesarian* should not be used. Almost all authorities require the capital C here.

calendar, calender, colander A *calendar* is a table of months and days, or a list of events or appointments. A *calender* is a pair of rollers for pressing paper or cloth, and also a kind of dervish. A *colander* is a kitchen utensil. For the utensil, British English permits the alternative spelling *cullender*, which is, however, rare and not recommended.

calends, kalends Both forms are in use. British usage strongly prefers *calends*, while *kalends* is at least equally frequent in the US.

calipers, callipers The American spelling is *calipers*; the British spelling is *callipers*.

caliph Though this word has received a number of spellings in the past, *caliph* is now established everywhere as the standard spelling, except perhaps in scholarly work, where a more accurate transcription might be appropriate.

calligraphy, graphology Often confused. *Calligraphy* is beautiful handwriting, especially when this is consciously practised as an art form. *Graphology* is the forensic study of handwriting, for example by the police when they are looking for forgery. The label *graphology* is also applied to the dubious practice of trying to deduce personality and character from handwriting.

callipers See **calipers**.

callous, callus A *callus* is a hard patch of skin. But *callous* is an adjective meaning 'indifferent to suffering', as in *his callous behaviour*.

camellia In spite of the pronunciation, the name of the flowering shrub is always so spelled, with two Ls, and ✳*camelia* is wrong.

camomile, chamomile The usual spelling today is *camomile*. The old variant *chamomile* is not wrong, but it is now rare, and you are advised to avoid it.

can In addition to its traditional senses of 'be able to' and 'be free to', *can* has acquired, in standard spoken English, the further sense of 'be permitted to', 'may': *My tutor says I can have an extra week to finish my essay*. In spite of the grumbles of a few conservatives, this extension is recognized by all authorities. However, in very formal styles, *may* is still usual, for example in regulations: *In such circumstances, the Board of Examiners may award the higher* *classification*. It is also normal to prefer *may* when politeness is important: *May we draw your attention to a difficult matter?*

Canaan, Canaanite These Old Testament names are so spelled.

Canadian English The variety of English used in Canada. At present, there is no distinctive Canadian version of standard English. For historical reasons, Canada traditionally adheres to the norms of British English – at least in writing – but the pressure from the American colossus next door is enormous, and it is not at all rare to see American forms and spellings in Canada.

candelabrum, candelabra In earlier English, a branched candlestick was a *candelabrum*, plural *candelabra*. In modern English, however, the singular is usually *candelabra*, with a plural *candelabras*, and the older forms are regarded as fusty.

Cantabrigian The formal adjective meaning 'pertaining to Cambridge University' is *Cantabrigian*, not *Cantabridgian*.

Canuck This colloquial term for a Canadian is too informal to appear in most careful writing. In any case, it is widely regarded by Canadians as offensive, at least when used by non-Canadians.

Canute, Cnut, Knut, Knute The spellings *Canute*, *Cnut* and *Knut* are all found for the eleventh-century king of England, but *Canute* is by far the most usual, and is recommended. The same given name is usually spelled *Knut* in Scandinavia today. But the American football coach was *Knute Rockne*.

canvas, canvass The word *canvas* is a noun denoting a kind of coarse cloth, used for example by oil painters. In contrast, *canvass* is usually a verb, and it occurs most often in the expression *canvassing for votes*. The verb gives rise to the uncommon derived noun *canvass*, meaning 'a search for votes'.

Cape Town The city in South Africa is *Cape Town*, not *Capetown*.

capital, capitol The spelling is *capital* in all contexts but one. In the US, the building in which a national or state legislature meets is a *capitol* building, the best known being the *Capitol* building in Washington (always capitalized). A state capitol building is more commonly called a *statehouse*.

capital letters Initial capital letters are required in English in the following circumstances:

- At the beginning of a sentence: *War has broken out in East Africa*;
- In proper names, including titles attached to names: *the Golden Gate Bridge, the Suez Canal, the Rocky Mountains, Edward Albee, Professor Chomsky, the Winter Olympics*;
- In the first word of a title, and (in the most familiar style) in each other significant word: *War and Peace, All About My Mother, The Name of the Rose*;
- In the names of distinctive historical periods: *the Industrial Revolution, the Bronze Age, the Middle Ages*;
- In the names of holidays, festivals and holy days: *Christmas, Purim, Ramadan, Hallowe'en, the Fourth of July*;
- In most significant religious names and terms: *Vishnu, the Old Testament, the Sabbath, Buddhism, the Prophet, the Lord*;
- In the brand names of manufacturers and their products: *a Ford Escort, a Macintosh Power Book, Sellotape, Trivial Pursuit*;
- In the pronoun *I*;
- In roman numerals (except in the front pages of a book): *XXVII, MCMXXXIV*;
- In the names of languages: *English, Greek, French, Swahili*;
- In nouns and adjectives denoting nationalities or ethnic groups, when these have their literal meanings: *a Basque nationalist, the Finnish landscape, a Russian politician, Italian history*;
- In the names of the days of the week and of the months of the year: *Monday, Thursday, November, July*;
- When poking fun at something: *Many people believe that rock music is Serious Art, deserving of Serious Critical Attention*. The unusual capitals here show clearly that the writer believes rock music to be worthless trash. Such sarcastic capitals should be used sparingly, and not at all in very formal writing.

Capitals are not used in the names of seasons: write *in the summer*, not *in the Summer*. Nor are they normally used in the words *north* and *south*. Nor are they obligatory with nationality adjectives when these have non-literal meanings: you may write *a danish pastry* and *french doors*. Nor is the word *god* capitalized when it denotes a pagan deity: *Poseidon was the Greek god of the sea* (not *the Greek God*).

It is not necessary to capitalize a word merely because there is only one thing it can refer to. Write *the equator, the north pole* and *the universe* in preference to *??the Equator, ??the North Pole* and *??the Universe*.

By far the most frequent error with capitals is using too many of them.

Capital letters are *not* properly used to emphasize a word, to draw attention to it, or to suggest that the word is unusually important. If you use a capital letter, make sure you can explain exactly why it is required. If you can't do this, then that capital is probably out of place. Useless capitals can quickly make your writing look idiotic.

Finally, it is out of order to refrain from using necessary capitals in order to draw attention to yourself. The British Film Institute, which used to be known as the *BFI*, now formally styles itself the *bfi*. This is pretentious, irritating and entirely unnecessary.

For more on capitals, see chapter 7 of the *Penguin Guide to Punctuation*.

carat, karat, **caret** The unit of weight for precious stones is the *carat*, as in *a 20-carat diamond*. The unit for expressing the proportion of gold in alloyed gold is also the *carat* in British English, but a *karat* in American English. A *caret* is a proofreader's mark indicating that material is to be inserted.

carbohydrate, hydrocarbon A *carbohydrate* is one of a class of chemical compounds containing carbon, hydrogen and oxygen. The most familiar carbohydrates are the edible starches and sugars. But a *hydrocarbon* is a compound of carbon and hydrogen only, and most hydrocarbons are not edible. Familiar examples of hydrocarbons are petrol (gasoline), paraffin (kerosene), aircraft fuel, and polymerized forms like polythene (polyethylene).

carburetor, carburettor The American spelling is *carburetor*; the British one is *carburettor*.

carcass, carcase All authorities recommend the first spelling.

cardamom, cardamum, **cardamon** All three forms are in use, but *cardamom* is recommended.

careen, career These are not easy to distinguish, and some authorities suggest that trying to distinguish them is not worth the trouble. However, for what it is worth, to *careen* is to lurch from side to side while moving, while to *career* is to move madly, at high speed, as though out of control. Either may be applied, for example, to a car rattling headlong down a bumpy hill, and in practice few people bother to distinguish the words.

caret See **carat**.

Caribbean The name is so spelled, with one R and two Bs. Avoid errors like *⁂Carribean*.

carnivore This word is used by biologists in two different senses: informally, to denote any non-human animal which lives entirely or chiefly on meat, such as a tiger, an eagle, a crocodile or a weasel, and formally to denote any member of the order *Carnivora*, including a few creatures, such as the giant panda, which eat no meat at all. Its use by some vegetarians to denote a human being who eats meat is at best jocular and at worst offensive, on a par with *gerbil* for a vegetarian. Unless you deliberately intend to make a political point, you should not apply the word to a human being: write *meat-eater* instead. Human beings are strictly omnivorous, not carnivorous.

carousal, carousel Often confused. *Carousal* is boisterous and often drunken celebration; the word consists of the verb *carouse* and the same ending -*al* found in *arrival* and *dismissal*. A *carousel* is a device for delivering baggage at an airport. The second is also another name for a merry-go-round; in this sense, the spelling *carrousel* is also possible but neither usual nor recommended.

case A word to watch out for, since it frequently forms part of needless padding. If you find yourself writing *in many cases*, check whether *often* might be an improvement. And be doubly vigilant with *in the case of*, which often represents no more than a bit of time-wasting. Consider the following passage: *The great twentieth-century poets have been very right-wing. In the case of Yeats, he was almost off the political scale.* Here the second sentence would profit greatly from being rewritten as follows: *Yeats was almost off the political scale.*

cashmere, Kashmir The soft fabric is *cashmere*; the disputed territory in the Himalayas is *Kashmir*.

Cassandra For some reason, many people have gained the impression that a *Cassandra* is merely someone who makes gloomy predictions. Not so. The legendary Cassandra made predictions which were always correct but which were unheeded. So, today, a Cassandra is someone whose warnings are ignored.

Cassiopeia The name of the constellation is so spelled.

caster, castor These are complicated. A person or a machine that casts metal or type is a *caster*. A bottle with a perforated top for sprinkling its contents is usually a *caster*, though *castor* is also acceptable. Very fine granulated sugar, in Britain, is usually *caster sugar*, though *castor sugar* is also possible. The small swivelling wheel on an item of furniture is usually a *caster*, though *castor* is also acceptable. The fancy word for 'beaver', often especially for its fur, is always *castor*. The bean and its oil are always the *castor* bean and *castor* oil. Finally, the twin brother of Pollux in Greek mythology is *Castor*.

Castile, Castilian The place in Spain is *Castile*, and the other name for Spanish is *Castilian*. The spellings *Castille and *Castillian are wrong.

casual See **causal**.

casus belli This Latin expression means 'cause of war', and it is traditionally used to denote the formal grievance which permits a country to declare war. The rarely used plural is also *casus belli*: the form *casi bellorum is an ignorant howler.

catarrh The word is so spelled – eccentrically.

catalyst In chemistry, a *catalyst* is a substance which greatly increases the speed of a chemical reaction without itself being affected. It is acceptable to use the word metaphorically to denote a small action which triggers larger consequences. But the word should not be used as a fancy equivalent for *cause* or *agent*.

catchup See **ketchup**.

category The word is so spelled, with an E in the middle, and *catagory is wrong.

category mistakes Informal English permits things like *cold temperatures, *a young age, *cheap prices and *fast speeds. But these should be avoided in careful writing, since they are category mistakes. A day may be cold; the air may be cold; even the weather may be cold. But a temperature, being only a number, cannot be cold. Likewise, people can be young, but an age cannot be young; goods may be cheap, but a price cannot be cheap; and a car may be fast, but a speed cannot be fast. Write *low temperatures*, *an early age*, *low prices* and *high speeds*.

In the same vein, avoid things like this: *The number of mistakes is remarkably few. It is true that the mistakes are few, but the number of mistakes cannot be few: it can only be small.

Some further genuine examples follow. *The probability of small wars has become more likely. No; it is small wars which have become more likely: a probability, being only a number, may increase or diminish, but it cannot become more likely.

*The origin of the emissions seemed to be coming from a dim star in Lyra. No;

it was the emissions that seemed to be coming from Lyra, while their origin, being only a location, was not coming from anywhere.

＊*The composition of the migrants consists of Haitians and Africans.* No; it is the migrants who consist of certain groups, and a composition cannot consist of anything.

＊*The maximum extent of the ice stretched from Bristol to the Vistula.* No; it was the ice which stretched from Bristol to the Vistula, and not its extent. Rewrite as follows: *At its maximum extent, the ice stretched from Bristol to the Vistula.*

cater In British English, you *cater for* something; in American English, you *cater to* it.

catholic, Catholic The word *catholic* means 'wide-ranging', as in *She has catholic tastes in music.* But *Catholic* means 'pertaining to or belonging to the Roman Catholic Church'.

Catiline The name of the treacherous Roman statesman is so spelled, and ＊*Cataline* is wrong.

catsup See **ketchup**.

causal, casual The derived adjective from *cause* is *causal*, not *casual*. Do not write ＊*a casual connection* if what you mean is *a causal connection*.

caviar, caviare Both spellings are acceptable, but *caviar* is overwhelmingly preferred in the USA, and is now preferred also by most dictionaries in Britain.

C.E. See **A.D.**

celebrant A *celebrant* is a person taking part in a religious ceremony – among Christians, particularly a priest officiating at a service. Happy people who are having a good time are not celebrants, but *revellers*.

celibacy Traditionally, *celibacy* is the state of being unmarried, especially as the result of a religious vow which requires its taker to abstain from sex as well as from marriage. Today, however, the word is far more commonly used to mean *chastity*, abstinence from sexual relations: *He remained celibate throughout his marriage.* This second sense is now so dominant that almost all readers will assume that it is the meaning intended. Your choice is to use the word in the second sense and to annoy the minority of conservative readers who object to it or to avoid the word altogether, since using it in its traditional sense will now bewilder most readers.

cello The word is so spelled, with no apostrophe. See **violoncello**.

Celt, Kelt, **Celtic**, **Keltic** In spite of the pronunciation, the spellings *Celt* and *Celtic* are universal today, and the variants with K are now obsolete.

censor, censure, **censer** To *censor* material is to remove from it passages which are regarded as harmful or impermissible, and a person who censors things is a *censor*. To *censure* a person or an act is to criticize him or it severely, to condemn him or it, and such condemnation is also *censure*. A *censer* is a container in which incense is burnt, especially one which is swung back and forth in church in certain Christian denominations.

centenary, centennial Both are correct for 'hundredth anniversary', but British English prefers *centenary*, while American English prefers *centennial*.

cf. This abbreviation stands for Latin *confer* 'compare', and it should only be used to mean 'compare'. For example, you might write *This is the view advanced by Pinker (1993), but cf. Bickerton (1994)*. This means that Bickerton defends a view different from Pinker's, and that you are inviting the reader to compare the two views. It is wrong to use *cf.* to mean only 'consult', 'refer to'. You should not write *✲The Australian language Dyirbal has a remarkable gender system; cf. Dixon (1980)*; the correct form is . . . *see Dixon (1980)*. As usual, you can avoid this common error if you refrain from using Latin abbreviations in your text: the recommended form is *compare Bickerton (1994)*. If you do use this thing, make sure you punctuate it correctly: illiterate forms like ✲*c.f.* and ✲*cf* are never acceptable.

challenge This verb cannot be followed by the connecting word *that*: it is wrong to write ✲*I challenge that this is the case*. Write instead *I challenge the suggestion that . . .* , or something similar.

chamomile See **camomile**.

chaos A much-overused word. *Chaos* denotes a state of extreme and utter disorder, and it is best reserved for this purpose. For the more everyday instances, it is best to use *disorder* or even *confusion*.

chaos theory In everyday English, we apply the label *chaos* to a state of utter disorder. But *chaos theory* is a branch of mathematics dealing with certain types of dynamical systems, known as *chaotic* systems. The point here is not that such systems are truly disorderly – they are not – but rather that their *seeming* disorder in fact derives from rigorously orderly behaviour coupled with extreme sensitivity to starting conditions. Chaos theory has proved useful in modelling certain real-world phenomena, but the prominence of its perhaps unfortunate name has led to a vulgar perception that scientists are telling us that the world is more disorderly than we once believed. This is the very opposite of the truth, and the mathematical sense of *chaos* should not be confused with its everyday sense.

chaperon, chaperone Both spellings are standard, but *chaperon* is much preferred on both sides of the Atlantic, and is recommended.

characterize This verb cannot be followed by the connecting word *that*. Do not write ✳*Linguists characterize that Japanese is a verb-final language*; write instead *Linguists characterize Japanese as a verb-final language*.

charge The following is wrong: ✳*Dionysius Exiguus was charged to calculate the new Easter tables*. The correct version is this: *Dionysius Exiguus was charged with calculating the new Easter tables*. You can only be charged with doing something, not charged to do it.

Furthermore, it is poor style to write *charge* in the sense of 'assert'. ✳*Thousands of teachers are incompetent, charges Woodhead* is not good English.

Chautauqua The name of the lake and of the associated arts centre in western New York State is so spelled.

chauvinism *Chauvinism* is fanatical and unquestioning patriotism. The word derives from the name of Nicolas Chauvin, a fanatical follower of Napoleon. More recently, the expression *male chauvinism* has been coined to denote an attitude of smug and arrogant superiority among men who look down on women. This is fine, but the unqualified word *chauvinism* should not be used in the sense of *male chauvinism*: doing so is rather like writing *cocktail* when *Molotov cocktail* is meant.

cheap This word can mean either 'inexpensive' or 'of poor quality'. If you can see any possible ambiguity, choose another word.

check, cheque British English uses *cheque* for the banking instrument (as in *chequebook*) but *check* in all other senses. American English has *check* in all senses.

checkered, chequered In all senses, the British spelling is *chequered*, the American one *checkered*.

checking facts A recent magazine article describes the linguist Johanna Nichols as working on comparisons among languages 'separated by tens of thousands of miles'. Well, *tens of thousands of miles* can hardly mean anything less than 20,000 miles. But the earth is a globe with a circumference of only 25,000 miles, and so no two languages can possibly be separated by more than 12,500 miles. Check your facts.

cherubim, cherubs The plural of *cherub* is *cherubim* if we are talking about junior angels, but *cherubs* in all other circumstances.

childish, childlike Though *childish* is occasionally used neutrally to mean 'appropriate to a child', as in *my childish efforts at using a fork*, it is much more commonly encountered as a term of contempt applied to an adult, as in the familiar expostulation *Don't be so childish!* In contrast, *childlike* is an approving term meaning 'having the attractive qualities of a child, such as honesty and trust'.

children's The possessive form of *children* is, of course, *children's*, as in *Children's Hour*. There is no such word as *childrens, and so there can be no such word as *childrens'. See **apostrophe**.

chili, chilli, Chile For the name of the fiery vegetable, the US spelling is *chili* (plural *chilis*); the British spelling is *chilli* (plural *chillies*). However, the name of the Mexican dish *chili con carne* should always be so spelled: it is a comical blunder to write *chilli con carne*, rather like writing *champane for *champagne*.

The country in South America is *Chile*.

Chinese names Chinese is not written in the roman alphabet (or in any alphabet). Consequently, we need a system for rendering Chinese words and names into English. Several such systems have been devised. For many years, the most widely used system was the Wade-Giles system, devised by two British academics. However, in 1958 the Chinese government published a new system called Pinyin. Several decades ago, most English-language publications switched to Pinyin, which is preferred by the Chinese, except that the tone marks used in Pinyin are usually omitted. This is why so many Chinese names abruptly changed their English forms: *Peking* to *Beijing*, *Mao Tse-tung* to *Mao Zedong*, *Sinkiang* to *Xinjiang*, and so on. Except in historical contexts in which older spellings seem appropriate, you are advised to stick to the Pinyin versions.

A Chinese name is given with the surname first (one syllable), followed by the given name (usually two syllables, occasionally one). The given name may be written solid (*Deng Xiaoping*), hyphenated (*Deng Xiao-ping*) or written with a space (*Deng Xiao Ping*). On the whole, names of people from China are written solid, while names in Hong Kong are usually hyphenated, and names in Taiwan, Malaysia and Singapore are written with a space. A

Chinese Christian will usually add a western Christian name, which precedes all others: *Sophia Kuo Li-chen*.

But note that Chinese-speakers who have extensive dealings with the west may turn their names around to conform to the western order.

chlorophyll The word is so spelled.

Christchurch, Christ Church The English town and the New Zealand city are *Christchurch*. The Oxford college is *Christ Church*, never **Christ Church College*.

Christian name The name conferred upon you at birth by your parents has several different labels. In Britain, the established term is *Christian name*, but this is very awkward in speaking of non-Christians: *??Nasser's Christian name was Gamel* is positively comical, and may give offence. In most contexts, it is best to avoid the term in favour of *first name* or *forename*. The usual American term is *given name*, which is acceptable in Britain but not widely used there.

chronic See **acute**.

Cincinnati The name of the city in Ohio is so spelled, and *Cincinatti is wrong.

Cinderella The name is so spelled (it is related to *cinders*), and *Cindarella is wrong.

circa This Latin word means 'around', 'approximately', and neither it nor its abbreviation *c.* (US *ca.*) should be used in the body of a text. Do not write things like *There were circa *5000 people present* or **Modern humans reached western Europe* circa *35,000 years ago*. Write *about*, *around* or *approximately* instead.

circumlocutions One of the commonest offences against good style is using six or eight vague words in place of one or two explicit words. Here is an example: *The Serbian army has been accused of numerous human-rights violations*. Much better is this: *The Serbian army has been accused of torture, rape and murder*. Likewise, *an economically viable enterprise* is probably only *a profitable business*. Most of the time, calling a spade a spade is good writing, while calling it a long-handled garden tool is not. See **wordiness**.

circumstances Both *in the circumstances* and *under the circumstances* are standard English, though a few purists still object to *under* here because of the etymology. The *Oxford English Dictionary* suggests that, on the whole, a state of affairs exists *in* the circumstances, while an action is performed *under* the circumstances. Write whatever seems natural to you.

cirrhosis The word is so spelled.

citing words When you cite a word – that is, when you name it so that you can talk about it – you must show that you are doing this by setting it off in some way. You can do this either by italicizing the word or by enclosing it in single quotes. Consider the following examples: *Men are physically stronger than women*; *'Men' is an irregular plural*. Here the first sentence is using the word *men* normally, to denote male human beings, while the second is not mentioning any human beings at all: rather, it is talking about the *word* 'men'.

The other day, I opened a novel written by Susanna Gregory, and read the following sentence: *Susanna Gregory is a pseudonym*. Well, this is a bizarre thing to say about Ms Gregory. It is fine to write *Susanna Gregory is a former police officer*, which is apparently true, but a woman cannot be a pseudonym. What was intended, and what should have been written, is this: *'Susanna Gregory' is a pseudonym*. In other words, the blurb-writer should have made it clear that he was talking about the *name*, not about the *author*.

Be careful about this, since you can easily flummox your reader if you are not. Here is an example of sloppy use: *The word processor came into use about 1910*. This statement is wrong by about seventy years: what the writer intends is *The word 'processor' . . .*

city Informally, we apply the label *city* to any town which is reasonably large and important by some suitable standards. This is the only way of using the word in most historical contexts. For example, the settlement of Jericho around 8000 B.C. had a population of not much more than 1000, but it is counted by archaeologists as the first known city, since it was so much larger than other settlements. Today, though, in both the UK and the USA, the title of *city* is one formally conferred on a town by a suitable authority: by a royal charter in Britain, by the state in the USA. Note also that, for historical reasons, the label *City of London* is applied only to about one square mile of London, roughly the area of the medieval city within its walls, and not to the entire vast metropolis of London. Since this area is the home of most of Britain's principal financial institutions, the term *the City* is used in Britain to denote the financial world, much as *Wall Street* is used in the USA.

claim When you *claim* that something is true, you are insisting that it is true even though there appears to be evidence against you, or at least little or no evidence supporting you. You should not apply this word to another person when you mean no more than 'assert', 'say' or 'report'. Doing so is rather offensive: you are implying strongly that the person you are quoting is making unsubstantiated assertions. Write *Dawkins argues that ...* or *Dawkins concludes that ...*, not *Dawkins claims that ...*

classic, classical As a noun, a *classic* is an outstanding and enduring object of its kind. The *classics* are the literary and artistic works of ancient Greece and Rome, or, more generally, of western civilization. As an adjective, *classic* means either 'outstanding and enduring of its kind', as in *a classic book* on a particular subject, or merely 'outstandingly typical', as in *a classic example*. But *classical* means 'pertaining to the civilization of ancient Greece and Rome', except in music, where *classical music* is the usual label for serious music of any period, as opposed to popular music.

cleanse This is not a fancy word for *clean*. To *cleanse* something is to clean it scrupulously and thoroughly, to scour it, to purify it. The word is most commonly met in religious contexts, as in *cleanse us of our sins*.

clear From a newspaper article on a large-scale computer crash: *The LSE was not clear how serious the problem was*. This informal use of *clear* is not appropriate in formal writing. In our example, it is the degree of seriousness of the problem that was not clear, and not the LSE. Write instead *The LSE was not sure how serious the problem was*.

cliché A *cliché* is an expression which was fresh and vivid the first time it was used but which has been repeated so often that it is now colourless and trite, perhaps even annoying. There are hundreds of these wearisome things, and all I can do here is to provide a sample and to warn you to be on your guard. The sample:

> *acid test*
> *add insult to injury*
> *better late than never*
> *bolt from the blue*
> *calm before the storm*
> *coin a phrase*
> *crack of dawn*
> *draconian measures*
> *dyed in the wool*
> *easier said than done*
> *flat as a pancake*

for love or money
head over heels in love
horns of a dilemma
last but not least
look a gift horse in the mouth
make a long story short
needle in a haystack
none the worse for wear
pretty as a picture
quick as a flash
ripe old age
sad but true
sadder but wiser
sigh of relief
sneaking suspicion
spread like wildfire
straw that broke the camel's back
take the bull by the horns
through thick and thin
tried and true
worth its weight in gold

You may feel free to use one of these phrases if you are satisfied that it expresses your meaning better than any alternative, but you should not trot these things out routinely. Good writing requires careful choice of words, not merely the stitching together of hackneyed expressions.

For more on clichés, see the *Penguin Dictionary of Clichés*. See also **omissible phrases**.

climatic, climactic The adjective *climatic* derives from *climate*, and it means 'pertaining to climate', as in the *climatic zones* of the earth. But *climactic* is related to *climax*, and it means 'involving a climax', as in *the climactic moment*.

clipped forms Clipped forms are words obtained by extracting pieces from longer words of identical meaning: *gym* from *gymnasium*, *bus* from *omnibus*, *flu* from *influenza*, *fridge* from *refrigerator*, *phone* from *telephone*, *gator* from *alligator*, and so on. There are three points here.

First, many people mistakenly believe that clipped forms are abbreviations, but they are not. An item like *phone* or *gym* is a real word, not an abbreviation, and it can be used like any other word: for example, it can take the usual grammatical inflections (*phoned up*, *gyms*), and it can be legally played in a game of Scrabble. If this puzzles you, see **abbreviation**.

Second, when you write a clipped form, you should not add an apostrophe: write *phone*, not *'phone*, and *gator*, not *'gator*.

The third point is the difficult one: when is it appropriate to use a clipped form in formal writing? There is no blanket answer here, since clipped forms vary in acceptability. At one extreme, *bus* is now the only possibility: apart from one or two frozen expressions like *the man on the Clapham omnibus*, the longer form *omnibus* is obsolete, and cannot be used. Close to this extreme are *cello* and *bra*, which are now preferred to *violoncello* and *brassière* in all but the most formal contexts. At the other extreme, clipped forms like *tec* for *detective* and *tache* for *moustache* are surely too colloquial to appear in careful writing.

But this leaves a great many clipped forms of intermediate formality, and with these you must use your own judgement. Your decision will depend partly on the nature of your text. For example, if you are writing a vivid account of wildlife, then clipped forms like *rhino*, *hippo*, *croc* and *gator* might be entirely appropriate, especially if the animal names occur frequently, whereas the clipped forms might seem out of place in a starchily formal text. If in doubt, choose the longer form.

cloth, clothes A *cloth* is a piece of fabric used for a specialized purpose, such as a dishcloth or a tablecloth. The plural is *cloths*. But *clothes* are garments, and this word has no singular form other than *item of clothing*. Do not write *cloths* when you mean *clothes*.

Cnut See **Canute**.

coarse, course To my surprise, I have seen these two confused again and again, most recently in another handbook of English usage. The word *coarse* is an adjective meaning 'rough', 'unrefined', 'not fine', and also 'vulgar, crude'. We may write of *coarse sand* or *coarse language*. But *course* is a noun denoting the layout of a race or a programme of study, among other things.

cockatiel, cockateel For the small parrot, the spelling *cockatiel* is recommended.

cognizant Avoid this silly word, and write *aware* instead.

cohort Originally the name of a division of a Roman legion, this word has various technical senses, but it always denotes a group of people (or sometimes other creatures) having something in common. In Britain, it denotes the group of students who enter a particular university in a particular year; the American equivalent is *class*, as in *the class of 1992*. It is wrong to apply the word to a single person in the sense of 'follower', 'colleague' or 'associate': you should not write *Che Guevara was a cohort of Fidel Castro*. This last usage is now very common in American English, but it is still best avoided by careful writers.

colander See **calendar**.

collaboration, cooperation, collusion In most contexts, *collaboration* means only 'working together', and it has no negative connotation. However, wars provide an exception: in wartime, *collaboration* means working with the enemy and betraying your country. The word *cooperation* (normally so spelled today, with no hyphen and no two dots) is always positive: it implies working together for common benefit. But *collusion* is always negative: it means working together in secret for a dishonest purpose.

collective nouns In American English, a noun or a noun phrase which is singular in form but collective in sense normally requires singular agreement in the verb: *The Administration has decided . . .* ; *Monsanto has announced . . .* ; *The committee has met . . .* ; and so on.

In British English, the verbal agreement may be either singular or plural. It is always plural when the writer has the several members of the group in mind, as in *The committee are not in agreement*. But it is commonly plural even when the group is thought of as a unitary entity, and Britons frequently write *The Government have decided . . .* ; *Monsanto have announced . . .* and *The committee have met . . .*

British writers may choose singular or plural agreement in such cases. However, it is essential to be consistent. The following genuine example, slightly adapted, illustrates an unacceptable absence of consistency: *While they await the results of their research, the company has refused to issue a statement*. Here the collective noun phrase *the company* is given both plural and singular agreement in the same sentence. Either the first part must be changed to *while it awaits* or the second part must be changed to *the company have refused*. Whichever choice is made must be continued into any following sentences mentioning the company.

See also ***range* nouns**.

college There is an awkward trans-Atlantic difference here. In Britain, a *college* can be any of the following: a high school that prepares students for university (roughly equivalent to US *prep school*), a specialist training institute (such as a college of music), or a semi-autonomous unit within a large university (such as King's College and University College within the

University of London). In the US, *college* is a generic term for any institution of higher education, in locutions like *go to college* (equivalent to UK *go to university*), but the word is also applied to a university-level institution which offers only undergraduate degrees, such as *Swarthmore College*. In addition, a few American universities apply the term *college* to an internal division corresponding to what is more commonly called a faculty, such as the *College of Engineering*.

colon The colon is the two dots, one above the other (:). The colon has only one important function: it indicates that what follows it is an explanation or elaboration of what precedes it. Look at the example in the last sentence.

What precedes the colon must normally be a complete sentence. What follows it may be a sentence, a phrase, a list, or even a single word. Here are some examples.

> *We propose the creation of a new post: School Executive Officer.*
> *Africa is facing a terrifying problem: perpetual drought.*
> *The situation is clear: if you have unprotected sex with a stranger, you risk AIDS.*
> *One name dominates modern linguistic theorizing: Chomsky.*
> *Only four contenders remain: Sampras, Agassi, Rafter and Henman.*

The colon is never preceded by a white space, and it is *never* followed by a hyphen or a dash. Especially in Britain, one of the commonest of all punctuation errors is following a colon with a pointless hyphen or dash. This practice is unacceptable in careful writing.

Note also that the semicolon (;) is not a substitute for the colon. All of the examples above would be wrong if the colon were replaced by a semicolon. See **semicolon** for the use of the other mark.

A colon should not interrupt a sentence which flows smoothly without it. For example, you should not put a colon after a form of *be*. Write *The Magi were Caspar, Melchior and Balthazar*, not *✻The Magi were: Caspar, Melchior and Balthazar*. Such a sentence reads perfectly without the colon, and the colon does no work: it merely irritates the reader by interrupting the flow of the sentence.

You should also never put a colon after the preposition *like*. It is wrong to write something like this: *✻This occurs in several languages, like: Hindi, Basque and Georgian*. Use no punctuation at all here, since none is required.

Likewise, no colon should follow the word *including*. Do not write *✻Ireland has produced a number of remarkable writers, including: Yeats, Synge, Joyce, O'Faolain and O'Brien*. Again, the sentence reads perfectly smoothly without that colon, which should be dropped.

Columbus, Colombia, Colombo The English form of the explorer's name is *Christopher Columbus*. All related American and Canadian place names have U: *Columbus, Ohio*; *Columbia, South Carolina*; *District of Columbia*; *the Columbia River*; *British Columbia*; *Columbia, the Gem of the Ocean*. The Italian-American surname is usually *Columbo*, as in the name of the TV detective. The indigenous civilizations of the Americas are *pre-Columbian*. But the country in South America is *Colombia*, and the city in Sri Lanka is *Colombo*.

combining form This is a lexical stem, especially one of Greek or Latin origin, which cannot stand alone as a word, but must be combined with something else within a larger word. The best examples of combining forms in English are the Greek elements used in constructing our technical terms. Examples of initial combining forms are *bio-* 'life', *tele-* 'far', *geo-* 'earth', *micro-* 'small', *thermo-* 'heat, temperature', *eco-* 'household, environment' and *phono-* 'sound'; examples of final combining forms are *-logy* 'study', *-nomy* 'law', *-graphy* 'writing', *-scope* 'seeing', *-metry* 'measurement' and *-phone* 'voice, sound'. We combine these elements with great freedom to produce technical terms like *biology, biography, telephone, microphone, telescope, microscope, geography, geology, geometry, telegraphy, thermometry, ecology, economy* and *phonology*.

These combining forms are not properly called 'prefixes' or 'suffixes'. A true prefix or suffix is added to an existing word to make a new word, while a combining form is not usually added to an existing word, but only to another combining form.

comic, comical Something is *comic* if it is intended to be funny. The word is mainly applied to skits, songs, plays and the like: *Tom Lehrer is famous for his comic songs*. But something is *comical* if it is funny unintentionally: *Her portrayal of Ophelia was comical*.

comma The *comma* is this little mark: (,). It has four distinguishable uses in English.

First, the *listing comma* is used to separate items in a list of the form *X, Y and Z* or *W, X, Y or Z*. Example: *The Three Musketeers were Athos, Porthos and Aramis*. In most British usage, no comma is used before the word *and* or *or*, unless such a comma is required to avoid ambiguity, as in the next example: *My favourite opera composers are Mozart, Puccini, Gilbert and Sullivan, and Rossini*. Here the final comma is required to show that it was Gilbert and Sullivan who worked together, and not Sullivan and Rossini.

However, in American English, it is usual – though not universal – to use the extra comma, and so most Americans prefer *The Three Musketeers were Athos, Porthos, and Aramis*. This style is also preferred in certain quarters in Britain, notably at the Oxford University Press, as a result of which British editors call it the *Oxford comma*.

Second, the *joining comma* is used to join two complete sentences into a single sentence. This is only possible when the comma is followed by a suitable connecting word, the most important such words being *and, or, but, while* and *yet*. Example: *A dropped goal counts three points in rugby union, while in rugby league it counts only one point*. If a suitable connecting word is not present, a comma is impossible, and a **semicolon** must be used instead: *A dropped goal counts three points in rugby union; in rugby league it counts only one point*. Two complete sentences may *never* be joined by a comma alone.

Third, the *gapping comma* is used to show that words have been omitted rather than repeated. Example: *Italy is famous for her composers and musicians; France, for her chefs and philosophers*. Here the gapping comma shows that the words *is famous* have been omitted rather than repeated.

Fourth, and most importantly by far, a *pair* of *bracketing commas* is used to set off a weak interruption to a sentence – that is, an interruption which does not disturb the smooth flow of the sentence. And note that word *pair*: bracketing commas always come in pairs, except when one of them would logically fall at the beginning or the end of a sentence, or when one of them is outranked by a colon, a semicolon or a dash in the same position. The great majority of comma errors involve bracketing commas, and most of these errors involve omitting one of the two required commas.

Correct examples: *Darwin's* Origin of Species, *published in 1859, revolutionized biological thinking*; *The Pakistanis, like the Australians before them, have exposed the shortcomings of the England batting order*; *Rupert Brooke, who was killed in the war at the age of twenty-eight, was one of our finest poets*; *She groped for her cigarettes and, finding them, hastily lit one*; *Stanley was a determined, even ruthless, figure*. In all of these examples, the sequence enclosed by bracketing commas could in principle be removed from the sentence without destroying it. Check this.

The punctuation of these five examples is perfect and cannot be changed. Removing any comma, or moving one to a different place, will in every case give a result which is wrong. Note in particular that the first comma in the fourth example must follow *and*, and not *cigarettes*, and that the comma after *ruthless* in the last example must be present. These are common errors.

Finally, note that any construction of the form *✳between X, and Y* is always wrong: no comma can appear in this position.

For more on commas, see chapter 3 of the *Penguin Guide to Punctuation*.

comma after subject The subject of a sentence can never be separated from the following predicate by a single comma, no matter how long that subject is. All too frequently, we read dismal things like this: *The fairy-tale castle of Neuschwanstein, stands on a mountain overlooking a plain. That comma has no business there and must be eliminated.

commence *Commence* is a very formal word for *start* or *begin*. It is only appropriate in a very starchy context, especially a ceremonial context. It is out of place in most writing: use one of the everyday words instead.

common This adjective can be compared either *common, commoner, commonest* or *common, more common, most common*. You may choose whichever you prefer.

common sense This is traditionally written as two words, as shown here. The spelling *commonsense, while widespread, is not at present regarded as standard, and should be avoided. But, when the phrase is used as a preposed modifier, it is hyphenated as usual: *a common-sense solution*. The derived adjective is written *common-sensical*.

communicate An overused word, and often a pretentious one. Do not write *communicate with* when *talk to* or *write to* will serve your purpose.

communication This five-syllable word is hardly ever necessary, but it has become one of the great vogue words of our day. It has been pressed into service to mean everything from 'letter' or 'e-mail' on the one hand to 'public relations' or 'propaganda' on the other. Unless you are obliged to write vapid dross for a living, avoid this word except when you are certain that no other word can possibly express your meaning.

comparatively, relatively Both these words have long been used as modifiers in the sense of 'fairly', 'moderately', 'rather': *Comparatively few Chinese households have a TV set*; *She obtained relatively good marks*. Some authorities now accept this use as beyond reproach, while others condemn it. The problem here is the standard of comparison: compared to what? If the standard of comparison is overtly expressed, or at least implicitly obvious, there can be no objection. Otherwise, you are advised to avoid this loose use of *comparatively* and *relatively*. Use *rather* or *fairly* or *reasonably* or some other word instead, one that does not appeal to a comparison that does not exist.

compare to, compare with Careful users of English make a useful distinction between these. To *compare X to Y* is to say that X is similar to Y, as in Shakespeare's line *Shall I compare thee to a summer's day?* But to *compare X with Y* is to note the similarities and differences between X and Y: a shop assistant must *compare your signature with* the signature on your credit card.

compatible, comparable Things are *compatible* if they can work together or be used together successfully: *I can't mail her this attachment because her PC is not compatible with my Mac.* But *comparable* means 'of roughly the same kind or size': *House prices in London are now comparable to those in Zurich.* The common error is to write *compatible* where *comparable* is intended: avoid errors like *Prices are now compatible with those in Zurich*. And note the difference in preposition: *compatible with*, but *comparable to*, not *comparable with*.

compendium A compendium is a concise collection of materials, especially materials extracted from a larger work or collection. It is not a vast and comprehensive work.

complacent, complaisant A *complacent* person is well satisfied with himself, even smug. A *complaisant* person is eager to please.

Compleat Angler, The The title of Izaak Walton's book is so spelled.

complement, compliment A *complement* is something which is necessary or suitable for completeness or harmony: *a ship's complement* (the officers and crew required to sail it), *our full complement* (all that we need or are entitled to), *the complement of a verb* (a phrase whose presence is required by the verb). The related verb meaning 'go well with' is also spelled *complement*: *This necklace will complement your outfit.*

A *compliment* is an expression of admiration: *He paid her a number of flowery compliments*. The related verb is spelled identically: *He complimented her on her outfit.*

The common mistake here is to write *compliment* where *complement* is intended. This error is easy to avoid if you recall the similarity in spelling between *complement* and *complete*.

complex, complicated These near-synonyms are not quite interchangeable. The more formal word is *complex*, which in technical use means 'having an elaborate structure', 'not easily treatable'. The more informal *complicated* means 'hard to understand or to resolve'. So, a difficult problem in mathematics is complex, while somebody's messy personal life is complicated.

comply, conform These verbs mean about the same, but they take different prepositions: we *comply with* our instructions, but we *conform to* the required standards.

compound In everyday use, the verb *compound* means 'make worse', as in *to compound the error*. In law, however, to *compound* a felony is to refrain from prosecuting (for that felony) in return for money or another reward. In this special use, the word does not mean 'aggravate', 'make worse', 'complicate' or 'multiply'.

compound modifier A *compound modifier* is a phrase consisting of two or more words which modifies a following noun, and a compound modifier *must* be written with a hyphen (or hyphens). Write *her new-found freedom*, and not *∗her new found freedom*; write *a shoulder-high catch* and not *∗a shoulder high catch*; and write *her Swiss-German ancestry*, and not *∗her Swiss German ancestry*. Failure to write these essential hyphens can bewilder your reader: a *nude-revue producer* (a producer of nude revues) is hardly the same as a *nude revue producer* (a revue producer who is nude). For more on this topic, see section 6.1 of *The Penguin Guide to Punctuation*.

comprehensible, comprehensive Something which is *comprehensible* can be understood. But something which is *comprehensive* is more or less exhaustive. So, a *comprehensible* explanation is one you can understand, while a *comprehensive* explanation is one that explains pretty much everything.

comprise, consist, compose, constitute These four verbs are very frequently confused, producing awful things like *∗The NATO forces are comprised of soldiers from eight countries*, and *∗Thirty-two pieces comprise a chess set*.

A whole *comprises* its parts: *The NATO forces comprise soldiers from eight countries*. This verb can never be passivized or followed by *of*: hence *∗comprises of* and *∗is comprised of* are always wrong. The bad example above should be written as follows: *A chess set comprises thirty-two pieces*.

Note also that *comprise* does not mean 'contain', 'include', unless what follows it is an exhaustive list. So, the following example is wrong: *∗Not a single television news programme comprises a majority of tabloid content*.

A whole *consists of* its parts: *The NATO forces consist of soldiers from eight countries*.

A whole *is composed of* its parts: *The NATO forces are composed of soldiers from eight countries*.

Its parts *constitute* a whole: *Soldiers from eight countries constitute the NATO forces*.

computer, terminal A *computer* is a machine which can do useful things all by itself, without being connected to any other machine, even though a computer may sometimes be connected to other computers in a network. But a *terminal* is a machine which, even though it looks for all the world like a computer, does nothing of interest unless it is connected to a computer. That computer may be in another room, another building or even another town, but all the terminal does is to allow its user to perform tasks on the computer and to see the results. Confusingly, it is possible to use a computer as a terminal. For example, the Mac on my desk is a perfectly good computer, but I often use it as a terminal when I do work on the very powerful computer downstairs.

conciseness, concision The noun derived from the adjective *concise* is traditionally *conciseness*. In spite of *precise*, *precision*, the formation *concision* is not established and is widely disliked. Use *conciseness*.

Concord, Concorde All the American towns are *Concord*, but the aircraft is *Concorde*.

concur If someone else expresses an opinion, then you may *concur* (agree), or you may *concur with* that opinion. But you cannot *✱concur* that opinion: the verb is never transitive. Note also that only a human being can concur with anything. It is wrong to write *✱These results concur with earlier findings*. Write *agree with* or *confirm* instead.

condone When you *condone* something, you let it pass without interference, even though you very likely disapprove of it. The word does not mean 'endorse', 'approve of' or 'permit'.

conducive The word is so spelled, and *✱condusive* is wrong.

conform See **comply**.

connection, connexion The American spelling is *connection*; the traditional British spelling is *connexion*. However, the American form is now predominant in Britain, and is recommended for British writers.

connive To *connive at* a piece of wrongdoing is to tolerate it, to know about it but to keep silent and do nothing. But the word has acquired a second sense of 'conspire', 'plot', 'plan a crime', as in *The local police were conniving with burglars*. Both uses are now standard. The derived noun is *connivance*.

connoisseur The word is so spelled.

consensus Note the spelling, with three Ss. Here is a useful mnemonic: a *consensus* is something to which everybody *consents*. The word has nothing to do with *census*, and the spelling *❋concensus* is wrong. Further, note that a consensus is, by definition, an opinion shared by practically everybody, and hence that expressions like *❋general consensus* and *❋consensus of opinion* are **pleonasms**. Finally, don't write *consensus* when *agreement* will do as well.

conservative, Conservative In the sense of 'traditional in outlook or style', the word takes a small C: *Mike has conservative tastes in music; Mike was wearing a conservative suit.* The spelling *Conservative*, with a capital C, is only appropriate in connection with a political party of that name: *Britain may not see another Conservative prime minister in my lifetime.* The same goes with other words which can be the names of political parties: *democratic* versus *Democratic*; *liberal* versus *Liberal*.

consonant *Consonants* are speech sounds, not letters. Most accents of English have exactly 24 consonants, though a few accents have a different number. The 24 usual consonants occur in the following words, at the beginning unless otherwise specified: *pale, tale, kale, bale, dale, gale, chain, Jane, fail, thin, sale, shale, hale, vale, this, zoo,* (in the middle of) *measure, mail, nail,* (at the end of) *sing, lay, rail, wail, Yale.* Not one of these consonants is spelled in a completely consistent way in English, and some of them are spelled very oddly and inconsistently indeed. Note that our alphabet has no single letters for spelling the consonants in *chain, thin, shale, this, measure* and *sing*. Those letters which are commonly used for spelling consonants may be called *consonant letters*, but calling these letters *consonants* is loose and misleading. See **vowel**.

constellation, asterism A *constellation* is a group of stars recognized by astronomers as occupying a well-defined part of the sky, such as Orion the Hunter or Aries the Ram. There are several prominent and familiar groups of stars which are not recognized as constellations. Among these are the Plough (UK) or the Big Dipper (US), the Great Square and the Summer Triangle (or Right Triangle). These groupings are *asterisms*, not constellations.

consult You *consult* a person for advice. Informal English allows you to *consult with* somebody, but this colloquial use is best avoided in careful writing.

consummate a marriage A couple *consummate their marriage* by having sex for the first time after the wedding. This is chiefly a legal term, since failure to consummate a marriage has at times been grounds for annulment. The term may safely be used in formal writing, but only in its accepted sense: it does not mean 'go through the wedding ceremony', and using it in this way is a hilarious blunder. The TV announcer who advised his audience to 'tune in next week, when a couple will consummate their marriage on stage' had a crimson face after the meaning was explained to him.

contemporary This word is potentially dangerous, since it can mean either 'at the same time as the historical events I am writing about' or 'of the present day'. To repeat the example used by all other handbooks, consider the following: *Shakespeare's* Twelfth Night *is to be staged with contemporary music*. Now: is the music under discussion contemporary with Shakespeare or contemporary with us? Either interpretation is possible, and the thoughtless use of *contemporary* may badly mislead your readers, even if you yourself are certain what you mean.

continuous, continual Strictly, there is a subtle but clear distinction between these words. Something which is *continuous* is unbroken, un-interrupted: *England's canals once provided a continuous waterway from the Thames Estuary to the Irish Sea*. In contrast, the word *continual* means 'repeated', 'recurring', and it is most often applied to nuisances: *Our computing system is suffering continual crashes; Her work was disturbed by continual interruptions*.

If you have trouble remembering this, or if you fear that your readers may be misled, you can always use some other word. Try 'unbroken' instead of *continuous*, and try 'recurring' instead of *continual*.

contract bridge See **bridge**.

contractions A handful of words are always or usually written in their contracted forms, with apostrophes representing the omitted material. Some examples: *Hallowe'en, jack-o'-lantern, will-o'-the-wisp, o'clock, fo'c's'le*.

Certain word sequences, especially those involving auxiliary verb-forms, have contracted forms which are extremely frequent in speech. The more frequent of these may be used sparingly in writing that is no more than moderately formal: *we'll, she's, they'd, can't, won't*, and the like. But the more colloquial contractions, like *she'd've*, are out of place in all but the most informal writing. And very formal writing, such as we find in the minutes of a meeting, tolerates no contractions at all.

contractual The adjective derived from *contract* is *contractual*, as in *contractual obligations*. Avoid the misspelling *contractural, which perhaps arises by contamination from words like *structural* and *procedural*, in which the *r* is part of the stem.

convince, persuade Careful writers make a distinction here which is rare in speech. We *convince* somebody that something is true (we make him believe it), but we *persuade* somebody to do something. So, we write *I convinced her that she would enjoy streaking* (she came to believe this, regardless of whether she did any streaking or not), but *I persuaded her to streak through the pub* (she did it, though not necessarily believing that she would enjoy it). If annoying no readers is one of your goals, it is best not to write *??convince someone to do something* at all, even if you naturally say it – as almost all of us do.

coolabah The name of the Australian gum tree is so spelled. The colloquial variant *✳coolibah* is popularized in the song *Waltzing Matilda*, but should not be used outside that song.

corporal, corporeal Both words are uncommon. The word *corporal* means 'pertaining to the body', and is rare outside the phrase *corporal punishment*, which means 'beating'. Even rarer is *corporeal*, which means 'bodily', 'physical', 'material', as opposed to *spiritual*.

correct There exists a great deal of confusion about the meaning of the word *correct* in connection with language. Many people appear to believe that the rules for correct usage in English are engraved in stone somewhere, that they have not changed for centuries, that they can never change, and that any departures from these rules must always be 'errors' or 'corruptions' or instances of 'slovenly' language. But all of this is false.

A splendid, and astonishing, example of this attitude occurs in an entry in another guide to English usage, published in 2000, under the heading **dice**, **die**:

Although **die** is the correct singular for the plural **dice** (*the die is cast*), nobody in their right minds [*sic*] today would say to his [*sic*] fellow Ludo player, *Hey, Bill, hurry up and throw that die!*

Now, there are several problems here, including the shaky English and the fact that the statement about English usage is false. But the point of interest is this: the writer is asserting with a straight face that nobody in his right mind would use the 'correct' English form. In other words, the writer appears to believe that correctness in English is an issue entirely dissociated from the question of what English-speakers say. Apparently 'correct English' just sits there, independent of usage, and readers are advised to refrain from using the 'correct' form when we find that hardly anyone else uses it. This is rather different from the more widespread view that nobody should ever be allowed to depart from the 'correct' forms at all, and that a 'correct' form remains 'correct' even when nobody is using it at all, in which case every English-speaker on the planet is simply getting it wrong.

Both views are nonsense. A correct form is, by definition, a form that English-speakers use, and there is no higher court of appeal. In the case of our topic, standard written English, a form or usage is correct if it is regularly used by most of those people who write in standard English. Since forms and usages come and go among the writers of standard English, standard English is always changing. The function of this book is to tell you what is or is not currently accepted as part of standard written English, to point out doubtful cases, and to urge caution in these doubtful cases.

See also the **etymological fallacy**.

correspondence This is the only possible spelling in all senses, and the spelling *correspondance* is wrong.

correspond to, correspond with To say *X corresponds to Y* is to say that X and Y match up in some systematic way, that X and Y occupy comparable places in two different systems, or simply that X and Y are in agreement. For example, you can write *These findings correspond to the predictions of the theory*. In contrast, *X corresponds with Y* means only that X and Y are exchanging letters, as in *I'm corresponding with a scholar in Poland*. Do not write *These results correspond with what we expected*. Though now acceptable in some quarters, this last will annoy many readers.

Moreover, do not write *corresponds to* when *matches* will suffice.

corruption *Our word 'skullduggery' is a corruption of the Scots word 'skul-duddery'*. No, it isn't. When a word changes its form, either within a single language or on being taken from one language into another, the result is not a corruption, but only an alteration. You should never apply the term *corruption* to a mere change in the form of a word.

cosy, cozy The British spelling is *cosy*, while the American spelling is *cozy*.

could of There is no circumstance at all in which the sequence *could of* is possible in English. Most usually, this occurs as an error for *could have*, which sounds similar. Write *She could have been a lawyer*, not *She could of been* ... The same goes for other such non-existent sequences, like *should of*, *would of* and *must of*: they require *have* in every case.

councillor, counsellor A *councillor* (US spelling *councilor*) is a member of a council. A *counsellor* (US spelling *counselor*) is an advisor, or, in American usage, a lawyer representing a client in court.

countenance This is not just a fancy word for *face*. Rather, it denotes the face together with its expression, or with the mood or the character which is revealed there.

counterpart See **equivalent**.

course See **coarse**.

courtesy When you are toiling over your word processor, it is easy to allow your passions or your arrogance to run away with you, and to write something very rude about other people or their work. You may very well regret this if the person you have written about happens to read your words. This is particularly true with e-mail, which is often written hastily, and electronic lists are full of rash words followed by red-faced apologies. But it can happen even in carefully edited writing. My advice is this: when offering criticism of someone else's work, always write as though your subject were looking over your shoulder. That way, you are less likely to give offence, unless you have made up your mind that you intend to give offence and to live with the consequences – as I have done in several places in this book.

Court of St James's Ambassadors to Britain are formally accredited to the *Court of St James's*, not to the *∗Court of St James*.

cozy See **cosy**.

credible, credulous Something which is *credible* is easy to believe; this is the opposite of *incredible*. A person who is *credulous* is all too ready to believe things – in other words, he is gullible.

creole, pidgin A *pidgin* is a crude auxiliary language, with a tiny vocabulary and little or no grammar, stitched together for use between people who have no language in common. It is no one's mother tongue. A *creole* is a mother tongue which has developed out of a former pidgin. Unlike a pidgin, a creole is a real language, with a large vocabulary, a rich grammar, and all the expressive powers of any other language. Do not confuse the two.

The word *creole* is capitalized only when it forms part of the name of a particular language, as in *Haitian Creole*, or when it is used as the name of a particular language, as in *My Guyanese friend speaks Creole* (= *Guyanese Creole*).

In some communities, the label *Creole* is applied to a person of some particular ancestry, though the details differ greatly from place to place.

crescendo A *crescendo* is a steady increase in the volume of a sound. The word does not mean 'peak', 'climax', and it is wrong to write ✳*The music reached a crescendo*, since the crescendo is not the finishing point but the growth. It is unwise to apply *crescendo* to anything other than a sound: ✳*Their complaints reached a crescendo* is not standard English.

crimson, scarlet These colour terms are not equivalent: *crimson* denotes a deep shade of red, while *scarlet* denotes a bright shade.

crisis A *crisis* is a very extreme state of affairs, one which will shortly lead to one dramatic outcome or another. The word should not be used loosely to mean no more than 'big problem' or 'period of uncertainty'. It is silly to describe a current shortage of nurses as a ✳*crisis in nursing*. And note that a crisis cannot get worse: it is wrong to write of a ✳*deepening crisis* or a ✳*worsening crisis*.

   The plural is *crises*.

criterion, criteria The singular is *criterion*; the plural is *criteria*. Write *this criterion* and *these criteria*, not ✳*this criteria* or ✳*these criterion*.

criticize, criticism Originally, to *criticize* something was merely to evaluate it, to point out its good and bad points, and this activity was called *criticism*. The noun *criticism* still has this sense in certain fixed phrases, such as *literary criticism*. Otherwise, however, both *criticize* and *criticism* are now almost invariably used, and understood, in a purely negative sense: to criticize something today is merely to say bad things about it, and criticism is likewise always negative. Some people may deplore this shift in meaning, but it is now a fact, and trying to use these words in neutral senses will merely confuse your readers.

critique Very many readers will object to the use of *critique* as a verb. Write *He criticized the report* or *He evaluated the report*, not ✳*He critiqued the report*.

Crome Yellow The title of Aldous Huxley's novel is so spelled, eccentrically, since the English word is always *chrome*.

crotch, crutch The delicate area between your legs is your *crotch*. The vernacular British variant *crutch* is not recommended for careful writing: not everyone in Britain likes it, and it will certainly bewilder non-British readers, for whom a *crutch* is strictly an implement used for walking with a broken leg.

crucial, vital, essential Words of this type cannot be qualified: if something is *crucial*, then that is the end of the matter, and usages like ✳*very* *crucial*, *most vital and *highly essential are unacceptable. Nothing can be only slightly crucial, and nothing can be more vital than something else which is vital.

crucifixion This is the noun derived from the verb *crucify*. There is no such word as *crucification.

crutch See **crotch**.

cui bono? This Latin phrase means 'Who stands to gain?', and its implication is that crimes and other misdeeds are most likely perpetrated by those who stand to profit from the outcome. The phrase does not mean 'What is the point?' or 'What good is it?'

culminate Originally, *culminate* meant 'reach its highest point', and it still often means this. By extension, the word now commonly means 'reach a dramatic climax'. But you should not use the word thoughtlessly to mean no more than 'end', 'conclude', as in **??**Our financial problems have culminated in several dismissals. Doing so is inattentive and perhaps even a little pretentious.

cultivated, cultured Someone who is knowledgeable about the finer things in life may be described with either of these words, but most authorities recommend *cultivated* in preference to *cultured*, which in some contexts may suggest falseness. Of course, both words have other uses: we speak of *cultivated* flowers but of *cultured* pearls.

cum This Latin word means 'with', and it is sometimes used to identify a person or a thing as having two natures at once: *a kitchen-cum-dining-room*, *a composer-cum-critic*. This is a usage you can easily do without: prefer instead *a composer and critic*. But, if you do use it, at least spell it correctly: I was recently dumbfounded to see someone described, in a book written by an academic, as *the philosopher-come-mathematician.

cumin, cummin In spite of the pronunciation, the spelling *cumin* is now usual, and the older *cummin* is not recommended.

cupful, spoonful These are the names of measures, and their plurals are *cupfuls* and *spoonfuls*. Do not write *cupsful or *spoonsful, or, still worse, *cups full or *spoons full if what you have in mind is measures. You can add two teaspoonfuls of paprika to your goulash without problems, but, if you add two teaspoons full of paprika, your guests are going to find a couple of spoons floating around in their dinner.

curb, kerb In American English, the spelling is *curb* in all senses. In British English, the spelling is *kerb* for a raised edge along a road or a path, but *curb* otherwise.

curly brackets See **brackets**.

curtsy The word is so spelled, and *＊curtsey* is wrong. The plural is *curtsies*.

cynic, sceptic, skeptic A *cynic* is a person who has difficulty in finding much that is good in anyone or anything, a person who takes the worst possible view of everything. A **sceptic** (US **skeptic**) is a person who refuses to believe anything until he has seen convincing evidence that it is true.

czar See **tsar**.

Czechoslovakia This country no longer exists. It has split into the *Czech Republic* and *Slovakia*.

Dacca See **Dhaka**.

dachshund The word is so spelled.

daddy-longlegs This is the preferred spelling, not *＊daddy-long-legs*. In Britain, this name denotes a crane fly, an insect resembling a giant mosquito. In North America, it denotes a harvestman, a spider-like creature with a tiny body and enormously long legs.

daemon See **demon**.

Dáil Eireann This, often shortened to the *Dáil*, is the lower house of the Irish parliament. The name should keep its accent.

dais See **lectern**.

Dame See **Sir**.

dangling modifier (also **unattached modifier**) This is one of several conventional labels for a modifying phrase which is in no way grammatically connected to the rest of its sentence, and which therefore just 'hangs' or 'dangles' helplessly on the page, leaving the reader scratching her head about what to do with it. Here is a simple example: *＊Driving down the road, a deer leapt out in front of me*. In this, the modifier *driving down the road* is dangling: it cannot be grammatically attached to anything except *a deer*, which is absurd. You can fix this in two ways. First, you can add something to which the modifier can be attached: *Driving down the road, I saw a deer leap out in front of me*. Second, you can rewrite the modifier so that it no longer requires something to be connected to: *As I was driving down the road, a deer leapt out in front of me.*

Another example: *∗At 53, fans still adore Cher.* This appears to say that fans who reach the age of 53 still adore Cher – probably not what the writer intended.

Misplaced modifiers can easily produce absurdity or offence. Consider the following example, from a major newspaper, commenting on the problems of the football manager Ruud Gullit: *∗Lying in last place in the Premiership after Newcastle's worst start in forty seasons, his girlfriend Michelle Cruyff is begging him to return to the Netherlands.* It is unlikely that Ms Cruyff is amused to read that she is lying in last place.

See also **misplaced modifier** for some examples of a different kind.

dare This unusual verb can be used in two different ways: like *want* or like *must*, though the second usage is decidedly formal. So, you can write either *She does not dare to do it* (like *She does not want to do it*) or (more formally) *She dare not do it* (like *She must not do it*). But do not tangle these constructions up: you cannot write *∗She does not dare do it* or *∗She dares not do it*. After all, you would not write either *∗She does not want do it* or *∗She musts not do it*. In the past tense, only the first construction is now available: *She did not dare to do it.* The past tense of the second is now archaic, and you should avoid it: *∗She durst not do it.*

dare say The chiefly British expression *I dare say* is uncommon in most types of writing. When it does occur, the traditional form is *I dare say*, and this is recommended, but the variant *I daresay* is now so frequent that it is recognized by most British dictionaries, and can no longer be regarded as wrong.

dash The *dash* is the long horizontal bar (–), somewhat longer than a **hyphen**. The dash has only one important use: a *pair* of dashes sets off a strong interruption, an interruption which violently disrupts the flow of a sentence. Examples: *An honest politician – if such a creature exists – would never agree to such a plan*; *The destruction of Guernica – and there is no doubt that the destruction was deliberate – horrified the world.*

The second dash is not written if it would logically come at the end of the sentence: *In those days Martina was the queen of Wimbledon – as she still is.*

The dash is also used, in preference to a hyphen, in separating numbers and dates in ranges, as in *the 1939–45 war.*

A dash never follows a colon; see **colon**.

For more on the dash, see chapter 6 of the *Penguin Guide to Punctuation.*

data Originally, *data* was strictly plural, with a singular form *datum*, and the custom was to write *This datum is interesting* but *These data are interesting*. However, for the great majority of speakers today, *data* has become a singular, and the customary form is *This data is interesting*. In this use, the word has no plural, and a single result can only be referred to as 'a piece of data'. In spite of this widespread use, there remain a number of conservative speakers who are greatly annoyed by the use of *data* as a singular. It is possible that, within a generation or so, there may be no such speakers left. Meanwhile, though, you are advised to use *data* as a plural: writing *These data are interesting* will surprise many readers but annoy no one, while writing ??*This data is interesting* will certainly annoy a number of readers.

Incidentally, the form ✻*a data* is acceptable to no one.

Finally, note that *data* should only be used to denote results obtained from observation or experiment, particularly results which consist of numbers or which can be put into numbers. Mere statements do not constitute data, and it is wrong to write *data* if all you mean is *results*, *findings* or *evidence*.

dates In Britain, as in most of the world, an abbreviated date is written day-month-year, and so, to a Briton, *7/11/93* means '7 November 1993'. In the USA, such dates are traditionally written month-day-year, and so, to an American, *7/11/93* usually means 'July 11 1993'. The international form is now gaining ground in the USA, but is still far from established there. Meanwhile, if you are writing something that might be read on the other side of the Atlantic, it is best to avoid this abbreviated format altogether, and to write the date out in full.

debate We can debate an issue, and we can debate whether something is the case or how to do something. But we cannot debate *about* or *on* anything: ✻*We are debating on the proposed new dam* is not generally regarded as standard English, and it should be replaced by *We are debating the proposal for a new dam*, or, somewhat less formally, *We are debating the new dam* (with *the new dam* seen here as representing an issue).

A quite different issue is illustrated by the next example: *Kennedy debated Nixon on television*. A few conservative writers object to *debate* in the sense of 'debate against (an opponent)'. However, this use is unquestionably standard in American English, and it is difficult to find an authority in Britain who takes exception to it. Still, British writers might prefer to err on the side of caution and avoid this use.

decimals In almost all circumstances, a decimal number less than one must be written with a leading zero, as in *0.768*. The principal common exception occurs with gun calibres, as in *a .22 rifle*. But see **baseball** for some special cases.

decimate Literally, to *decimate* an army is to kill ten per cent of its soldiers. By extension, the word is now acceptable in the more general sense of 'inflict heavy casualties on'. But you should never use the word to mean 'annihilate' or 'destroy': *✳Three battalions were completely decimated* is wrong. Moreover, you should not use the word with a number: avoid things like *✳Over half the troops were decimated*.

décolletage, décolleté *Décolletage* is a low neckline on a woman's garment or a garment having a low neckline: *All eyes were on Cher's startling décolletage*. But *décolleté* is an adjective meaning 'having a low neckline' (of a garment) or 'wearing a low neckline' (of a woman): *Cher's décolleté outfit attracted great attention.*

decorative, decorous The adjective *decorative* means 'ornamental': *She wore a decorative plume on her hat*. But *decorous* means 'conforming to conventional ideas of propriety', especially in clothing or behaviour: *Please behave decorously in church.*

defence, defensive, offence, offensive The British spellings are *defence* and *offence*, while the American ones are *defense* and *offense*. But all varieties of English write *defensive* and *offensive*.

define This verb can never be followed by the connecting word *that*: it is wrong to write *✳Linguists define that a language must possess open-endedness*. A better version is *Linguists define a language as a system possessing open-endedness.*

definite Note the spelling, and avoid the common error *✳definate*. It may help if you recall that *definite* is related to *definition*.

definitive This is not a fancy form of *definite*. The word means either 'conclusive', as in *We have obtained a definitive solution to the problem*, or 'authoritative', as in *She has written the definitive book on the subject.*

Degas, Edgar The painter's name is so written, with no accent.

deism, theism These are not identical. *Deism* is a belief in God based solely on reasoning, without reference to revelation. But *theism* is a belief in one God as the transcendent creator and ruler of the universe, with or without appeal to revelation.

déjà vu This French phrase was originally a technical term in psychology, but it has passed into the language generally. It means 'the illusion that something which is being experienced for the first time has been experienced before', and the phenomenon is common both in healthy people (especially young ones) and in sufferers from certain types of mental illness. However, journalists have frequently given it the quite different sense of 'experiencing something for the second (or third, or fourth) time'. It should not be so used in careful writing, and indeed it should not be used at all except as a technical term for the psychological phenomenon.

delusion, illusion, allusion The first two words both denote a false impression, but they are quite different in sense. An *illusion* is something which appears to us to be true even though we know it is false, or can easily be persuaded that it is false. A familiar example occurs in the expression *optical illusion*. In great contrast, a *delusion* is pathological and can only be held by someone who is mentally ill, or at least by someone who is impervious to rational argument and evidence. Finally, an *allusion* is merely an act of inexplicit mentioning; see under **refer**.

de luxe, deluxe British English prefers *de luxe*; American English prefers *deluxe*.

demon, daemon A *daemon* is an ancient Greek spirit. In all other contexts, the spelling is *demon*.

dependant, dependent The word *dependant* is a noun meaning 'someone who depends upon someone else to live', especially the members of a breadwinner's family who have no incomes of their own. In American English, though not in British English, the noun may optionally be spelled *dependent*. In British English, the word *dependent* is strictly an adjective meaning 'depending (on)', as in *She is dependent upon her pension*. You should not write *dependant* when you mean *dependent*: this is never acceptable. The opposite of *dependent* is, of course, *independent*.

deprecate, depreciate To *deprecate* something is to express disapproval of it, to deplore it: *She deprecated the decision*. To *depreciate* something is to belittle it, to treat it as insignificant: *She depreciated his promotion*. A person who plays down her own achievements is therefore best described as *self-depreciating*, but usage has now made *self-deprecating* so familiar that we can hardly object to it any longer.

The verb *depreciate* has the further sense of 'decrease in value': *Japanese cars don't depreciate as fast as American cars*.

deprive *They deprived gullible people from their money*. This is wrong: you deprive somebody *of* something, not *from* it. Write *They deprived gullible people of their money*.

derisive, derisory These words are not always interchangeable. We commonly use *derisive* to mean 'mocking', 'contemptuous', as in *Her performance was greeted with derisive laughter*. Most authorities recognize *derisory* as an alternative here, as in *derisory laughter*, but this use is less frequent and is not recommended. More commonly, we use *derisory* to mean 'worthy of derision' and most particularly 'absurdly small', as in *a derisory pay rise*. In this sense *derisive* is not possible.

Derry See **Londonderry**.

descent, decent A *descent* is a trip downward, and the word is related to the verb *descend* 'go down'. But *decent* is an adjective meaning 'honest, proper'.

describe It is all too common to encounter things like the following: *The word 'aye-aye' describes an animal resembling a lemur*. This is wrong. The word *aye-aye* does not describe anything at all: rather, it *labels* or *denotes* a particular kind of animal. If you want to *describe* the creature in question, you must write something like this: *a nocturnal tree-dwelling primate of Madagascar, somewhat resembling a lemur*. Otherwise, you should simply write *An aye-aye is an animal resembling a lemur*. Writing about things, rather than about words, will make it easier to cultivate a good style.

description We provide a description *of* something, never *about* something.

desiccate This word, which means 'dry out, dry up', is so spelled: one S, two Cs. Do not write *dessicate*. It may help if you remember that the word derives from Latin *de* 'out' and *siccus* 'dry'. Desiccated coconut is so called because it has been dried, not because it is chopped up.

desirable The word is spelled with no E in the middle. Avoid the common error *desireable*.

despite, in spite of These are equivalent in meaning, but note the difference in usage: *The match went ahead despite the weather; The match went ahead in spite of the weather*. You must not write *despite of the weather*.

destruct, self-destruct The verb *destroy* yields an irregular derived noun *destruction*. From this, a new compound *self-destruction* was coined, and from this in turn a new verb *self-destruct* was coined by a popular TV show. In the rare instance in which you need to explain that an object is programmed to destroy itself, you are probably safe in writing that it will *self-destruct*. However, be wary of extending this form to anything that falls apart: rather than *??Their political movement self-destructed*, you are advised to prefer *collapsed* or *disintegrated* or another better-established word.

The American space programme has introduced yet another new verb, *destruct*. This is most commonly encountered as an intransitive verb meaning 'explode' or 'crash', usually as a result of a malfunction: *The craft destructed before reaching orbit*. Occasionally the word is also found as a transitive verb meaning 'destroy' (a craft which is malfunctioning). In both senses, the word is best left to NASA scientists: prefer a plain English word.

deteriorate This verb means 'become steadily worse', and it is strictly intransitive. Do not write things like *✳The wet weather has deteriorated the roof*. Oh, and note the spelling: avoid errors like *✳deteriate*.

detrimental The plain word *harmful* should usually be preferred.

develop The word is so spelled, and *✳develope* is wrong. The word is not related to *envelope*.

devil's advocate In the Roman Catholic Church, when a person is proposed for canonization, an official is appointed to argue *against* sainthood for the candidate. This official is called the *devil's advocate*, and his function is to ensure that the case for sainthood is strong enough to withstand criticism. By extension, a devil's advocate is anybody who argues against a popular view, not out of conviction, but merely in order to test that view for weaknesses. The term is not properly applied to anyone who defends evil people, evil actions or evil views.

dexterous, ambidextrous In all varieties of English, the spelling *dexterous* is preferred to the variant *dextrous*. However, *ambidextrous* is the only possibility for this word, and *✳ambidexterous* does not exist.

Dhaka, Dacca The spelling *Dhaka* is now preferred everywhere, and the older spelling *Dacca* is obsolete.

diacritics Diacritics, informally called *accents*, are the little dots and squiggles written above or below letters of the alphabet to indicate something about their pronunciation. Unlike most European languages, English makes practically no systematic use of diacritics. There is just one case in which their use is essential: in foreign proper names containing them. So long as you can possibly produce them – and almost all word processors can produce at least the commoner diacritics – then you should use them in foreign names containing them: *José María Olazábal, François Mitterrand, Luis Buñuel, Albrecht Dürer*. (But note that German *ü* and *ö* can always be replaced by *ue* and *oe*, respectively.)

Otherwise, the *diaeresis* (US *dieresis*) is regularly used in writing certain names, to show that the letter bearing it is a separate syllable in pronunciation: *Zoë Wanamaker, Charlotte Brontë*. You should respect the preference of the owner of the name.

Once, the diaeresis was also often used in writing ordinary words, as in *coöperate* and *aërate*, but this style is now decidedly old-fashioned, and you are advised to write merely *cooperate* and *aerate*.

The grave accent may be placed over the *e* in the ending *-ed* to show that this is pronounced as a separate syllable: *a learnèd man, an agèd scholar*. This is now considered old-fashioned.

Finally, ordinary words of foreign origin are often written in English with their original diacritics, but only if the words are regarded as not yet fully anglicized. As soon as the word becomes accepted as an ordinary English word, we usually drop the diacritics. Today, for example, we prefer *cafe* to *café, elite* to *élite, role* to *rôle*, and *facade* to *façade*. But a few words which are very firmly established in English still stubbornly retain their diacritics, such as *sauté* and *fiancée*. However, in other words still regarded as essentially foreign, we always retain the diacritics, as in *déjà vu, bête noire, Gemütlichkeit, mañana*, and *olé*.

If in doubt, consult a good dictionary.

dialect, patois A *dialect* is a regional or social variety of a language which also has other varieties. It is wrong to use *dialect* to mean 'language of low prestige': the 460 or so languages of Nigeria are just that, and you should not write *dialect* if what you mean is a local language of no national importance.

The word *patois* may only be used to denote a local language or dialect of no great importance, especially one used by rural people of little education, and most especially in a historical context. When applied to a present-day variety, the word is offensive, and it should be avoided in this context.

dialectal, dialectical The word meaning 'pertaining to dialects' is *dialectal*: write *The dialectal differences in British English are substantial*, not ＊*dialectical*. The rare word *dialectical* means 'pertaining to the dialectic', where *dialectic* is a narrowly specialized term found in the philosophy of Friedrich Hegel and of his follower Karl Marx.

dialogue This is the only possible spelling in British English, though American English also permits *dialog*. However, the word should not be used when *discussion* will do: this is pretentious and empty. And don't even think of writing the ghastly expression *meaningful dialogue.

dichotomy A *dichotomy* is merely a division into two starkly distinct groups: *There is a dichotomy between his theory and his practice.* The word does not mean 'discrepancy' or 'difference', and it certainly does not mean 'dilemma' or 'conflict'.

dictionary I hope that every reader of this book is already familiar with English dictionaries. If you are not, there are three important things you should know.

First, a dictionary can only record the facts of the language as it is used by educated native speakers. If most educated speakers say things like *Hopefully we'll be there in time for lunch*, then this use of *hopefully* is recorded in the dictionary, and that is the end of it. There is no possibility of recording instead some variety of English which is used by no one or by almost no one, even if that variety was widely used in the past. After all, if you look up the United Kingdom in an encyclopedia, you expect to read about the population, wealth and industry of the UK as it is today, and not about the UK a hundred or two hundred years ago, and you certainly do not expect to see an account of what the editors would *prefer* the UK to be like. Why would you expect a dictionary to be different?

Second, no dictionary is completely up to date. Even the most modern and efficient publisher takes years to convert a database into a dictionary, and, by the time any dictionary appears, it is already slightly out of date. English, like any living language, changes very fast. Moreover, lexicographers (writers of dictionaries) do not rush to include every new word they've encountered: instead, they wait to see if a new word manages to establish itself in the language before they include it. So, a new word you've suddenly started seeing everywhere may not appear in any dictionary until several years have passed.

Third, no dictionary of ordinary size can include all the words of English. There are just too many words for this, and every dictionary publisher must make some prudent choices if he wants to produce a book which people can afford to buy.

So, the familiar notion that a word of English exists only if it is 'in the dictionary' is false. A word exists if people use it. But that word may fail to appear in a *particular* dictionary published at a *particular* time because it is too new, or too specialized, or too localized, or too much confined to a particular social group, to make it into that edition of that dictionary.

die, dice Traditionally, *die* is singular and *dice* is plural: you throw *a die* but you throw *the dice* if you are throwing two or more of them. This usage is still almost universal in American English. In Britain, however, *dice* is now commonly used also as the singular: *throw a dice*. This usage is now recognized by most British dictionaries, even though it has the curious consequence that many Britons do not understand the origin of the phrase *the die is cast*. If you are writing for a British readership only, you can use *dice* as a singular, but, if you have a wider readership in mind, you should use *die* as the singular. In any case, avoid the confused locutions illustrated by *throw two die and *throw two dices.

die, dye The verb *die* 'pass away' has past tense *died* and present participle *dying*. The verb *dye* 'colour' has past tense *dyed* and present participle *dyeing*.

different Formal written English requires *different from*: *His new work is different from all his earlier pieces*. Colloquial English often has *different to* or *different than*; these are familiar in speech, but they should be avoided in careful writing.

The word *different* is often used pointlessly, as in *She consulted five different reference books*. This should read *She consulted five reference books*, since no reader will assume she was mad enough to consult five identical books.

See also **dissimilar**.

digraph A *digraph* is a sequence of two letters used to represent a single speech sound. English examples include the *sh* of *ship* and *fish*, the *ch* of *cheap* and *much*, the *th* of *thin*, the *ng* of *sing*, the *ea* of *head* and the *ou* of *route*. Do not confuse a digraph with a **diphthong**.

dike, dyke The word for an embankment is traditionally spelled *dike*, and still so in American English, but now more commonly *dyke* in British English. The possibly offensive word for a lesbian, especially a butch lesbian, is usually spelled *dyke* on both sides of the Atlantic.

dilate To *dilate* something is to widen it. So, when the pupils of your eyes are *dilated*, they are larger than usual, as happens when you are in dim light. It is wrong to write *His pupils were dilated* if you mean they were very small.

dilemma Strictly, a *dilemma* is a choice between two options, both of which are unappealing. *Moe faced a dilemma: if he confessed, he would go to jail, but,* *if he kept quiet, his friend Homer would go to jail unjustly*. Some authorities, though not all, are willing to countenance the extension of the term to an instance of three or four unattractive choices, providing the number of choices is precisely known. But it is wrong to use *dilemma* as no more than a fancy word for 'problem' or 'difficult decision': deciding who to appoint to a vacant post may be difficult, but it is not therefore a dilemma.

dimension Be very careful with this word outside of its mathematical sense: most often, it means no more than *aspect*, and the plainer word should be preferred.

dinosaur Today there is an almost universal tendency to apply this word to almost any person or thing viewed as outdated in style or views, from pop singers whose popularity has waned, through left-wing members of Britain's Labour Party, to teachers who fail to see the value of mountains of paperwork. This is a **cliché**, and so to be avoided for this reason alone. But it is also ignorant. The implication is that the dinosaurs were too stupid, too lumbering, and too fixed in their habits to survive in a changing world. In fact, the dinosaurs were a magnificently adaptable and successful group of animals which dominated the earth for nearly 200 million years and whose disappearance probably resulted only from a catastrophic asteroid hit which changed the earth's climate and killed the dinosaurs' food. Sneering at the dinosaurs because they died out is like sneering at Abraham Lincoln because he died.

diphthong The word is so spelled, with two Hs. Avoid the common error *✻dipthong*. (And foreign learners of English should avoid the other error *✻diphtong*.) A diphthong is a vowel which changes its quality between beginning and end, such as the vowels in the words *pie*, *now*, *play* and *boy*. Do not confuse a diphthong with a **digraph**.

dis-, dys- The Latin prefix *dis-*, literally 'apart', has a range of functions in English centring on negation, deprivation, removal and reversal: *disinfect*, *disability*, *disassemble*, *discharge*, and many others. The Greek prefix *dys-* means 'bad, defective, abnormal', and is largely confined to names for pathological conditions, like *dyslexia*, *dyspepsia* and *dystrophy*, though it also occurs in the word *dystopia* 'an imaginary place where everything is bad'. If in doubt as to which prefix is required, consult a dictionary.

disabuse See **abuse**.

disastrous The word is so spelled, and *✻disasterous* is wrong.

disc, disk The preferred British spelling is *disc*; the preferred American one is *disk*. However, because of American predominance in computer technology, the spelling *disk* is now usual in Britain in formations like *hard disk* and *compact disk*, though *disc* is always acceptable in these usages in Britain. And *diskette* is now widely preferred to *floppy disk*.

discomfit When you discomfit somebody, you embarrass or bewilder him, or, sometimes, you frustrate his plans. The related noun is the unusual *discomfiture*. The word has nothing to do with *discomfort* (noun and verb), and it should not be used when *discomfort* is intended – nor should *discomfort* be used when *discomfit* is intended. And there is no such word as *＊discomforture*.

discreet, discrete The adjective *discreet* means 'circumspect', 'tactfully avoiding embarrassment' or 'unobtrusive': we may write of *a discreet conversation* or *discreet behaviour*. The derived noun is *discretion*: *Because of her lack of discretion, the story is all over the office*. But *discrete* means 'separate', 'distinct', 'consisting of separate or distinct parts': *An utterance can be decomposed into a sequence of discrete speech sounds*. The derived noun is *discreteness*. The common error is writing *discrete* where *discreet* is intended.

discriminating, discriminatory A *discriminating* person has excellent taste. A *discriminatory* person is bigoted. Laws, rules, policies and attitudes can also be discriminatory, but only a person can be discriminating.

discuss This verb can never be followed by the grammatical connective *that*: it is wrong to write ＊*They discussed that being raised bilingually is an advantage*. You must use a connecting phrase like *the suggestion* or *the proposal*: *They discussed the suggestion that being raised bilingually is an advantage*.

In the same vein, the expression ＊*as discussed* is not regarded as standard English, and should be avoided. Write *as explained above* or *as proposed above*, not ＊*as discussed above*.

It is also wrong to write ＊*discuss about* (something). We *discuss* something, or *have a discussion about* it; we do not ＊*discuss about* it.

disintegrating syntax I have invented this feeble label in order to provide an entry for a problem which is very common but not easy to put into a pigeonhole. The problem is this: the writer starts a (typically long) sentence with one construction, then introduces an ellipsis (an omission of words that would repeat earlier words), then loses track of the construction he started with and lurches into a different construction, leaving the reader bewildered as to which pieces of the sentence are meant to be joined with which other pieces. The result is likely to be unintelligible. Here is an example.

The proposed cuts would mean the loss of all crèches and adult education, school meals and 400 teachers' jobs, the closure of all citizens' advice bureaus, and nearly a third of all homes for the elderly and mentally handicapped.

Let's go through this. The cuts would mean the loss of all crèches. That's clear. Now comes *adult education*. Presumably we are meant to read this as *the loss of all adult education*. So far, so good. Next is *school meals*, but only after a comma. Should we read this as *loss of* [some] *school meals* or as *loss of all school meals*? It's not clear, but the best guess is to retain the *all*. That decision made, we now bump into *400 teachers' jobs*. This is a jolt, because we've decided to retain that *all*, and yet *loss of all 400 teachers' jobs* sounds dubious. Perhaps *loss of 400 teachers' jobs* is better, but now we may begin to suspect we were mistaken in retaining the *all* earlier. Just how much of the sentence is that *all* meant to apply to, anyway? How can we tell? The writer is giving us no help.

Next comes *the closure of all citizens' advice bureaus*. This doesn't fit at all with *loss of all*, or even with *loss of*, so presumably the ellipses have been completed. But now we find *nearly a third of all homes for the elderly and mentally handicapped*. How on earth is this supposed to join up with anything before it? Should we connect it to *the closure of*? If so, why is there a listing comma after *bureaus*? The punctuation suggests that *loss of* applies to everything up to *jobs*, with its following comma, and therefore that *closure of* applies only up to *bureaus*, with its following comma plus *and*. But this is impossible, since the final phrase now cannot be connected to the rest of the sentence at all. The sentence appears to have the form *X, Y, and Z*, but it is unintelligible with this structure.

Just to provide one last little puzzle, that final phrase is ambiguous. Are the homes under discussion inhabited only by individuals who are *both* elderly and mentally handicapped? That's what the sentence seems to say, but this interpretation sounds a bit odd. More likely, the writer has in mind *both* homes for the elderly *and* homes for the mentally handicapped. But, if that's what he means, why didn't he write *homes for the elderly and for the mentally handicapped*, which is unambiguous?

Our writer has clearly not read what he has written. Instead, he has lurched clumsily through his sentence, starting things and then forgetting what he has started. The result is bewildering. Now, assuming that I have managed to divine his intended meaning correctly, here is a corrected version which removes all the problems: *The proposed cuts would mean the loss of all crèches, of all adult education, of all school meals and of 400 teachers' jobs, and the closure of all citizens' advice bureaus and of nearly a third of all homes for the elderly and for the mentally handicapped.* This, I think, is unambiguous – though of course I cannot be quite certain that it expresses the sense our writer had in mind.

disinterested, uninterested Though popular usage often differs here (and has long done so), standard English makes a clear distinction. To be *uninterested* is to be apathetic, to have no trace of enthusiasm, while to be *disinterested* is to have nothing to gain or lose from any outcome. A judge presiding over a case is obliged to be disinterested (otherwise he must disqualify himself), but he is certainly not expected to be uninterested.

disparate This is not merely a fancy word for *different*. It means 'fundamentally different', 'utterly different'. Things which are merely different can often be compared, but things which are disparate can scarcely be compared at all.

dissatisfied, unsatisfied When you are *dissatisfied* you are disappointed, frustrated, unhappy. When you are *unsatisfied*, you feel that you need more of something. Only a person can be dissatisfied, while an abstract thing like hunger or a demand for goods can be unsatisfied.

dissect The word is so spelled, with two Ss. Avoid the error *disect: the word is not spelled (or pronounced) like *bisect*.

dissemble, disassemble To *dissemble* is to conceal your motives or emotions: *She felt obliged to dissemble* means either 'She felt obliged to conceal her feelings' or 'She felt obliged to conceal what she was up to.' But *disassemble* means 'to take apart': *She disassembled her bookcases.* The common error here is to use *dissemble* where *disassemble* is intended.

dissent, dissension These words are not equivalent. *Dissent* is disagreement with an opinion or a decision, especially with a majority view: *The new regulations were adopted without dissent.* But *dissension* is serious and persistent disagreement among a group of people, especially ill-natured disagreement which leads to quarrels: *The Pakistani cricket team has been plagued by dissension.* And note the spelling of the second: *dissention is not acceptable.

dissimilar One thing is *dissimilar to* another thing, never *dissimilar from it. That is, *dissimilar* works like *similar*, not like *different*.

dissociate, disassociate Both are possible, but *dissociate* is more usual, and is recommended.

dissyllable See **disyllable**.

distinguish, differentiate, discriminate Both *distinguish* and *differentiate* can mean all of 'be the difference', 'recognize the difference' and 'point out the difference'. *The bonobo's elaborate social life distinguishes* (or *differentiates*) *it from the common chimpanzee; Bonobos can distinguish* (or *differentiate*) *between clan members and outsiders; Only recently have scientists distinguished* (or *differentiated*) *bonobos from common chimps*. But *discriminate* means only 'recognize the difference': *Bonobos can discriminate between dangerous snakes and harmless ones*. Of course, *discriminate* has another and today more familiar meaning: *That company discriminates against* (or *in favour of*) *handicapped people*.

distrust, mistrust There is a subtle distinction here which should be maintained. To *distrust* somebody is to suspect that he is dishonest, while to *mistrust* him is merely to lack confidence in him. If you consider your deputy to be wholly honest but somewhat incompetent, then you may mistrust him, but you don't distrust him.

disyllable, dissyllable Each of these terms denotes a word of two syllables, but the strangely formed *dissyllable* is now rather old-fashioned, and *disyllable* is recommended.

divergent When things *diverge*, they move steadily farther apart. Therefore, *divergent* things are things which are moving steadily apart. You should not write *their divergent views* if all you mean is *their differing views*.

diverse, divers The word *diverse* means 'of various kinds', and it cannot be applied to a single person or thing: *French cinema is diverse* is wrong. You must write *French cinema is varied* or *French films are diverse*.

The word *divers* is an archaic word for 'several', as in *divers acquaintaices*: it should not be used.

dobermann pinscher The name of the breed of dog is so spelled, with *dobermann* as a less usual alternative.

Domesday Book In spite of the pronunciation, this is the only possible spelling, and *Doomsday Book* is wrong.

domineering A *domineering* person is overbearing and tyrannical, a bully. Only a person can be domineering, and it is wrong to write of *a domineering conviction*. The required word here is *dominant* or *powerful*.

donate This verb means 'give' only in the sense of 'give to a charity, a fund, an institution, or the like'. You can donate money to the Red Cross, or donate works of art to a museum, but that's about it. Use *give* otherwise. Note also that standard English does not accept the use of *donate* illustrated by the following example: *She donated the Liberal Party £500. The only acceptable construction is *She donated £500 to the Liberal Party*.

double letters One of the best-known differences between British and American English is the use, or not, of double letters. Americans write *traveled, traveling* and *traveler*, while Britons write *travelled, travelling* and *traveller*. But everybody writes *referred, referring* and *referral*.

In American English, the rule is simple: never double a final letter unless the stress falls on the final syllable of the stem. This rule automatically produces the correct American forms *traveled* but *referred*. In the case of a final L, American English sidesteps the issue by spelling all verbs with final stress with a double L: *enthrall, extoll, instill, fulfill*, and so on, in contrast to British English *enthral, extol, instil, fulfil*.

In British English, things are more complicated. A final L is always doubled: *travel* but *travelled, extol* but *extolled, pencil* but *pencilled*, and so on. But most other final letters are not doubled: *bracket* produces *bracketed*, not *bracketted, *bother* produces *bothered*, not *botherred, and *ration* produces *rationed*, not *rationned.

Of course, a final consonant in a monosyllabic verb is normally doubled in all varieties, when doing otherwise would suggest the wrong pronunciation: *brag, bragged; pit, pitted; stab, stabbed; hum, hummed; sin, sinned; quiz, quizzed; star, starred*. If the pronunciation is obvious, no doubling takes place: *load, loaded; teem, teemed; stain, stained; fear, feared; boil, boiled*.

Words with final S are more complicated. Most authorities on both sides of the Atlantic prefer *focuses, focused* and *focusing* to *focusses, focussed* and *focussing*, and most prefer *buses* to *busses*, and *bused* and *busing* to *bussed* and *bussing*.

double meaning Carelessness in writing can easily produce a meaning you don't intend, often with hilarious results. Here is an example from a newspaper: *[EURO MP Linda] McAvan tabled proposals to prevent indirect discrimination on grounds of race, religion or belief in the European Parliament*. The only way to avoid gaffes like this one is to read what you have written.

double negatives Unlike the standard English of the past, and unlike the standard forms of some other modern European languages, standard English does not, in most circumstances, permit two negative words in one clause.

Most forms of vernacular English are quite different here, and vernacular speakers may have to learn, rather painfully, to avoid writing things like *The defendant didn't say nothing*, and to prefer the standard versions *The defendant didn't say anything* or *The defendant said nothing*.

But even careful speakers sometimes get lost in syntactically complex constructions. Here is an example: *I wouldn't be surprised if the Government didn't call a snap election*. What the writer means, almost certainly, is this: *I wouldn't be surprised if the Government called a snap election*. The second negative has wrongly crept into the original example, producing a result which appears to assert exactly the opposite of what was intended.

Matters can become still more complex in the presence of words which are negative in sense but not in form, such as *refuse* and *deny*. Here is an example: *Few observers are convinced by the heated denials from the Pentagon that American forces were not present in Cambodia*. What the Pentagon was denying, of course, is that there *were* US forces in Cambodia. Denying that forces were *not* present is tantamount to insisting that forces *were* present.

Note also that certain words which are not negative in form nevertheless are somewhat negative in sense, and cannot be combined with overt negatives. Among these are *hardly* and *scarcely*. You must write *We hardly achieved anything*, not *We didn't hardly achieve anything*, since *hardly* cannot be combined with *not*.

However, standard English *does* permit overt double negatives in two circumstances. The first case occurs when both negatives are logically required, because each is negating something different. Example: *We can't not take this opportunity*. This means 'It is impossible for us not to take this opportunity', though in writing you might well prefer a less intricate wording, such as 'We must take this opportunity' or 'We cannot fail to take this opportunity'.

The second case combines *not* with a negative prefix like *un-* or *dis-*, and it has the effect of producing a weak or polite positive. Examples: *This proposal is not unattractive* (it is somewhat attractive, but not outstandingly attractive); *I am not inclined to disagree* (but my agreement is less than whole-hearted); *Your behaviour has not gone unnoticed* (we have certainly noticed it, but we are telling you so politely).

double passive Sometimes it is fine to follow one passive with another: *Our new server is scheduled to be installed next week*. But this construction can easily get out of hand, producing monstrosities: *His orders were attempted to be carried out*. This is close to unintelligible, and it must be rewritten so as to remove at least one of the passives. If we know who was trying to carry out the orders, then we should say so: *His staff attempted to carry out his orders*. Here both of the passives are removed. If we don't know who was trying to carry out the orders, then we must settle for something like this: *An attempt was made to carry out his orders*. Here just one of the original passives has been removed, but this is enough to produce a decent English sentence.

A similar problem occurs with the following example, which I recently encountered at my university: *Was any action decided to be taken? The minimal improvement here is *Was it decided to take any action?*, though *Did we decide to take any action?* or *Was any action taken?* would be better.

double perfect The following example illustrates a common error: *I would have liked to have met Einstein. The problem here is the repetition of the verb *have*, which grammarians call the 'perfect auxiliary': this example therefore illustrates the *double perfect*.

There are two ways of fixing this. One is *I would have liked to meet Einstein*. This means that I was alive at the same time as Einstein, that I might conceivably have managed to meet him, and that such a meeting would have given me pleasure *at the time*. The other is *I would like to have met Einstein*. This does not imply that Einstein and I were alive at the same time, or that I ever had even a conceivable chance of meeting him. Instead, it means this: I would be happy *now* if – somehow – I had managed to meet Einstein in the past. This distinction is important in careful English: you should respect it, and you should avoid the double perfect.

doubt This simple verb sometimes causes havoc in what follows. Here is a common error: *I began to doubt that we would not get our money back. Presumably what the writer means here is what is properly expressed either as *I began to doubt that we would get our money back* or as *I began to suspect that we would not get our money back*. Choose one construction or the other, and don't tangle them up.

doubtless, no doubt, undoubtedly These are not interchangeable. The items *doubtless* and *no doubt* do not express certainty at all. Each means only 'I have no reason to doubt' or 'I am too polite to express any doubt'. Much stronger is *undoubtedly*, which means 'beyond question'. Equally strong are *without doubt* and *beyond any doubt*.

doughnut This is the only possible spelling in standard English, where the joke spelling *donut is not acceptable.

douse, dowse To *douse* something is to plunge it into water or to throw water over it. To *dowse* is to look for water or another material with a divining rod.

Dow–Jones average This is the only acceptable spelling.

doyen The *doyen* is the senior member of a group or of a profession: *Roger Angell is the doyen of baseball writers*. For a woman, the form is *doyenne*. The word cannot be applied merely to someone who is experienced or respected: there cannot be more than one doyen in a group.

draconian This adjective has nothing to do with Dracula. The ancient Greek lawgiver Draco laid down an extraordinarily harsh code of laws, in which the penalty for everything was death. Accordingly, *draconian* means 'extremely harsh', and the word is commonly applied to laws and punishments. But the word is overused: don't write it thoughtlessly when *harsh* or *severe* will do.

draft, draught British English uses *draft* for a bank's written instruction for payment, for an unfinished version of something that will be polished later (and in the derivative *draftsman*), and for several specialist military and engineering senses. It uses *draught* in all other senses, including those involving moving air, beer and other liquids, animals that pull things, and a ship's displacement. American English has *draft* in all senses. However, the board game called *draughts* in Britain is *checkers* in the USA.

drier, dryer There is great variation here, and neither spelling can be called wrong in any sense. But most authorities prefer *drier* for 'more dry', and *dryer* for any machine that dries, such as a *hair dryer* or a *spin dryer*. For the material added to paint to make it dry faster, British English somewhat prefers *dryer*, while American English somewhat prefers *drier*.

drily, dryly Both spellings are acceptable, though British English favours *drily* while American English favours *dryly*.

dual, duel The word *dual* is an adjective meaning 'consisting of two parts', as in the British *dual carriageway* (= US *divided highway*) or *dual controls*. In grammar, it is also a noun or an adjective labelling a grammatical form denoting exactly two, such as *both*. The word *duel* is a noun denoting a fight or a contest between two opponents.

dubious There is a problem with this word. Suppose a stranger offers to sell you a used car, but you have grave doubts about the origin or the reliability of the car. In this case, you can say *I've been offered a dubious car*, and no one will object to this. But consider another sentence: ??*I'm dubious about that car*. Does this use of *dubious* represent standard English or not?

Opinion is divided. Most authorities now agree that this use of *dubious* is entirely acceptable in formal English. But a conservative minority disagree, and reject this as merely a colloquial use which has no place in careful writing. As usual, I advise you to err on the side of caution, and to refrain from using *dubious* in this way. Reserve *dubious* for 'suspect' or 'untrustworthy', and for the other sense prefer *doubtful*, *sceptical* or *suspicious*.

duel See **dual**.

due to, owing to The expression *owing to* is acceptable in all positions: *Owing to the bad weather, our fête has had to be cancelled*; *My plane was late, owing to the fog.* (However, the alternative *because of* is often more elegant.) But things are more complicated with *due to*. Many careful writers object to the following: ??*Due to the bad weather, our fête has had to be cancelled*; ??*My plane was late, due to the fog*. The problem here is that, in conservative eyes, the word *due* is strictly an adjective, and should be used like one. So, for example, the following are perfectly acceptable to everybody: *The fire was due to careless smoking*; *The displacement of plague-bearing rodents, due to climatic change, brought plague to the African coast.*

Should you worry about this? After all, very many eminent writers have felt free to use *due to* in the questionable ways illustrated above. In all likelihood, the reservations about *due to* will disappear in another generation or so, and all usage handbooks will allow it to be used as freely as *owing to*. But this has not quite happened yet, and the free use of *due to* will still annoy a number of your readers. It seems best to play safe: use *due to* only in adjectival position, or, if you're not sure what counts as an adjectival position, avoid the expression altogether.

But you should not write the wordy and clumsy ✳*due to the fact that* when a simple *because* will do fine.

dungarees The word is so spelled, and ✳*dungerees* is wrong.

Dutch, Flemish, Belgian A citizen of the Netherlands is *Dutch*, and the language spoken there is also Dutch. A citizen of Belgium is *Belgian*. But Belgium is linguistically divided. About half the population speaks French, while the other half speaks Dutch. Not Flemish, but Dutch. Until several decades ago, the Dutch-speakers of Belgium were eager to develop their own standard form of Dutch, distinct from that in the Netherlands, and they gave the name *Flemish* to this proposed standard. However, they have long since abandoned this policy, and accepted standard Dutch. Today, the name

Flemish is applied only to the non-standard local dialects of western Belgium. But *Flemish* is also appropriate in speaking about Flanders during the time when Belgium did not yet exist, as in *the Flemish painters*.

Dutch names In Dutch names, the surname is very often preceded by a particle such as *van*, *de* or *den*, or sometimes two of these. These particles are almost always written separately. In the Netherlands, the particles take no capital letter: *Hans van den Broek*. However, in Belgium (and also in South Africa), it is more usual to capitalize these things, and so a Belgian or a South African with this name would probably write it *Hans Van Den Broek*.

When a Dutch surname is cited alone, the particles, if any, are almost always included. So, for example, *Rudolf de Rijk* is referred to as *de Rijk*. This is in great contrast to what usually happens with comparable particles in German, French and Spanish. Nevertheless, the particles are ignored when placing names in alphabetical order, so that *de Rijk* is listed under R, not under D.

Finally, observe that English surnames of Dutch origin are often written differently from their originals, as in *Dick Van Dyke* and *Cornelius Vanderbilt*. See also **Vandyke**.

dwarfs, dwarves The traditional plural of *dwarf* is *dwarfs*. However, the variant *dwarves* has been popularized by several writers, notably the fantasy writer J. R. R. Tolkien, and it is now perhaps usual in the context of fantasy writing or of fantasy games. In other contexts, *dwarfs* should be preferred.

dye See **die**.

each other, one another There is something of a superstition that *each other* should be used with two people, as in *Hitler and Franco detested each other*, while *one another* should be used with three or more, as in *The four teams in each group must play one another in the first round*. In fact, this notion has no basis in usage, and few if any authorities attach any importance to it. There is no harm in sticking to it, if you like, but ignoring it will rarely attract attention.

More important is avoiding the use of *each other* as a subject: it is wrong to write *They always know where each other is*. Write instead *Each always knows where the other is*. It is well to remember that English has a pronoun *each*. Failure to use *each*, with resulting tangles, is a common feature of semi-literate English.

The possessive forms of *each other* and *one another* are *each other's* and *one another's*; these may be used freely, as in *Susie and Natalie often borrow each other's clothes*. There is no such form as *each others'*: write *at each other's throats*, not *at each others' throats*.

early on, earlier on There is no point in writing *early on* or *earlier on*, if all you mean is *early* or *earlier*. Write *He recognized its importance early*, not *... early on*.

earth This word is not normally capitalized, except when we are thinking of the earth as one of the several planets of the solar system: *Mercury, Venus, Earth* ... The written version *the Earth* is always wrong, though *the planet Earth* is acceptable.

earthy, earthly, earthen These adjectives are all different. Something which is *earthy* is either similar to earth (as in *an earthy texture* or *an earthy smell*) or coarse and vulgar (as in *earthy language*). But *earthly* means 'pertaining to our human existence on earth', as opposed to *heavenly* or *celestial*: *our earthly existence, earthly powers*. It also occurs as a meaningless modifier in fixed expressions like *no earthly use*. Finally, *earthen* means 'made of earth or of clay', as in *an earthen floor* or *earthenware*.

eclectic This word means 'choosing from a variety of sources'. A person with eclectic tastes in music enjoys quite a variety of very different kinds of music – perhaps Gregorian chant, cajun, Indian ragas and bluegrass. The word carries no suggestion of high standards, of good taste, or of fastidiousness. It is not a compliment, but neither is it an insult.

ecology This technical term denotes the study of animals and plants in connection with their environment. It does not mean 'environment'.

economic, economical The adjective *economic* means 'pertaining to economics or to the economy', as in *an economic advisor* or *current economic conditions*. But *economical* means 'using a minimum of money or resources', as in *an economical meal* or *an economical manufacturing process*. Hence an *economic* solution to a problem is a solution which involves economics, while an *economical* solution is one which saves money. The common error here is to write *economic* where *economical* is intended: *an economic meal*.

ecstasy This is so spelled, with *-sy*: the spelling *ecstacy* is wrong, and so are *extasy* and *extacy*.

-ed, -ing Which of the following sentences do you prefer? *My car needs its battery changed; My car needs its battery changing*. The second is normal only in certain parts of England, especially in the north, while the first is normal in almost all the rest of the English-speaking world. Few if any authorities are willing to pass judgement on these competing forms. However, it is a fact that most speakers will be bewildered by the second form, and so you would be wise to use the first in your formal writing, even if you find it unnatural.

edible, eatable The word *edible* is strongly recommended in almost all contexts, and it is the only one possible in the sense of 'not poisonous', as in *edible mushrooms*. The word *eatable*, which is rather informal, should be reserved for the sense of 'good to eat', 'reasonably tempting to the palate'.

-ed participles English permits an unfortunate ambiguity in the use of certain participles derived from the names of parts of fruits and vegetables and other foodstuffs. On the one hand, we normally understand *shelled peas* as peas from which the shells have been removed, and *boned meat* as meat from which the bones have been removed. On the other, we understand *salted peanuts* as peanuts to which salt has been added, and *spiced ham* as ham to which spices have been added. This might seem clear enough so far, but what about *seeded mustard*, which I encountered recently in a recipe? Was I supposed to use mustard with seeds or without seeds? Since mustard naturally contains seeds, we might suppose, by analogy, that mustard with the seeds removed is what was meant. But in fact the writer wanted mustard containing seeds – not my first guess. Be careful with these expressions, and, if you can see any possible ambiguity, write something else which is more explicit.

-ee In recent years, this suffix has been blossoming as a way of deriving nouns from verbs. Alongside such established formations as *employee*, *refugee*, *absentee* and *payee*, we now have *escapee*, *retiree*, *examinee* and *attendee*, and new formations of this kind constantly strike our eyes. I myself have encountered *kissee*, *seducee* and even *murderee*, though admittedly one or two of these were facetious. Apart from those that are very well established, use such formations with caution, and always prefer an established word of the required sense, if one exists. Prefer *captive* to *capturee, *audience* to *lecturees, and *victim* to *torturee.

effectively, in effect The adjective *effective* means 'producing a satisfactory result': an *effective* solution is one that works. Accordingly, the adverb *effectively* means 'with a satisfactory outcome': *The salmonella outbreak has been effectively contained* means that salmonella poisoning is no longer spreading. The phrase *in effect* means 'in practice', and it is usually applied to something which is officially or notionally not done but which gets done anyway. Example: *The government's new measures in effect prevent refugees* *from entering the country legally at all*. Here *in effect* indicates that no such outcome was intended or sought, but that this outcome has arisen in practice regardless. A problem arises because many people make a habit of writing *effectively* in the sense of *in effect*. Consider my example, rewritten: *The government's new measures effectively prevent refugees from entering the country legally at all*. A reader of this version might very well conclude that the government had been seeking all along to ban all refugees, and that it had finally found a way of doing so.

If you mean *in effect*, then write *in effect*, and save *effectively* for its traditional sense.

effete This word originally meant 'exhausted', 'worn out', 'drained of the capacity to produce'. Once it was applied to land which could no longer produce crops or to animals which could no longer produce offspring. Today it is commonly applied to people, and it means 'decadent', 'feeble', 'unable to produce valuable work', especially as a result of over-refinement. An effete civilization is one which has lost its vigour and can no longer advance; an effete poet is one who can no longer write anything but shallow and derivative poetry. The word does not mean 'sophisticated', and it certainly does not mean 'effeminate'.

effrontery See **affront**.

e.g. This Latin abbreviation means 'for example'. If you use it at all, you must punctuate it as shown: monstrosities like *e.g,*, *eg.* and *eg* are never acceptable. But, like all Latin abbreviations, this one should not be used in the body of your writing: write *for example*, not *e.g.* And do not confuse this abbreviation with **i.e.**

egotist, egoist These words are not as clearly differentiated as we might like. But most authorities agree that *egotist* is best reserved for a person who is full of himself, a self-important person, while the rarer *egoist* is best applied to a person who takes the philosophical position that self-interest is the best basis for social organization.

egregious This word means 'conspicuously bad', 'exceptionally terrible'. An *egregious blunder* is a truly awful mistake, and an *egregious reputation* is a reputation for persistent failure, incompetence or misbehaviour. The word does not mean 'distinguished' or 'celebrated', and should not be so used.

ei See **ie**.

Eire See **Ireland**.

eke out Originally, to *eke out* something was to make it go further by supplementing it in some way: *She eked out her student grant by working as a barmaid*. This sense is still normal. Today the expression has another sense, 'support (one's existence) with effort and frugality': *She eked out an existence as a pavement portrait artist*. Otherwise, the word *eke* is archaic and should not be used.

elder, older The form *older* should be used in almost all contexts. It is permissible to use *elder* with kinship terms, as in *my elder brother*, but *my older brother* is more usual and is recommended. Only in the fixed phrase *an elder statesman* can *older* not be used. As a noun, *elder* is used chiefly within certain religions, in which it often has an established significance, as in *Vernon Law was an elder of the Mormon church*. It also occurs in a few fixed expressions, such as *his elders and betters* and *Susannah and the elders*.

electrocution The word *electrocution* means 'death by electric shock'. Do not apply it to a shock which is not fatal.

electronic writing These days most writing is done electronically, but not all electronic writing is equivalent. At one extreme, a book written on a word processor is still a book, and it needs to be written in carefully edited formal standard English. At the other extreme, e-mail messages to close friends are typically dashed off in haste, with no planning and no editing, and, as a result, they are often composed in non-standard English and they often contain typos and errors of every sort. Such unedited writing is perhaps acceptable in private messages when speed is more important than careful crafting. But, in other electronic contexts, planning and editing are essential.

I belong to the panel of an Internet service which offers to answer questions on language, and every week several dozen questions arrive from all over the world. Some of the questioners are careful to plan their questions thoughtfully and to compose them in good English. These questioners usually receive several patient and useful answers from the members of the panel. But many other questioners merely dash off their questions without a moment's thought or editing, and then fire off the result. Consequently, quite a few of the questions we receive are so badly written as to border on the illiterate, and some of them are actually incomprehensible. Naturally, the members of the panel, who are busy people offering their services for free, are less inclined to spend their own time compiling careful answers when they can see that the questioners cannot be bothered to spend a minute or two in framing their questions clearly and accurately. And, of course, an incomprehensible question is very unlikely to receive any responses at all.

So, if you have occasion to send an e-mail to someone you don't know, and especially if you are seeking advice or assistance, it is vital for you to devote the same time and effort to writing your posting as you would to any other piece of serious writing. E-mail is no excuse for sloppiness, and the person you are mailing will not be inclined to put in more effort than you have put in yourself.

Likewise, if you set up your own Website, it is foolish to spend hours making it look pretty if your text is full of mistakes. Only the illiterate will be impressed by dreadful English wrapped in cute graphics.

Naturally, in all your electronic writing, you should make every effort to be as courteous as possible. See **courtesy**.

On another topic, e-mail and the Web have brought into the language a large number of coinages, some moderately formal, others very informal, and there is now a great deal of confusion about how to handle this new terminology in careful writing. The main problem here is that usage has so far not settled down to any kind of recognized standard. For example, on your letterhead stationery or on your business cards, you will want to add a third contact line after those labelled *Tel.* and *Fax*, but should that line be headed *email* or *e-mail* or *E-mail* or perhaps something else? No standard format has yet appeared, and you will just have to make your own choice.

If you want to add your Website, you face the similar problem that there is no agreement as yet as to whether we should write *Website*, *website*, *Web site*, *web site*, or even something else. You can avoid this altogether by simply writing *URL*, the internationally understood label for a Web address (this stands for 'universal resource location'). But how do you write your URL? Suppose it is this:

http://www.zeus.srstc.edu/users/miket/home.html

It is always safe to write this out in full, of course. However, since *all* URLs begin with the sequence *http://*, there is a growing convention now of omitting this part and writing only the rest:

www.zeus.srstc.edu/users/miket/home.html

It is safe to use this abbreviated form as long as you are confident that anybody who might want to consult your site will be sophisticated enough to add the automatic prefix. If you're not so sure, use the full form. In any case, though, don't assume you can leave out the *www.*, since not all URLs contain this element.

As for the flood of new terminology, unless you are doing journalism and require a brash style, you would be wise to steer clear of any coinage you have doubts about, particularly all those starting with *e-*. There may be little objection to *e-commerce* for *electronic commerce*, but writing *e-conomy* for the financial side of the Internet is going too far for anything that purports to be formal writing.

One final point. The business Websites that are so much in the news these days typically have URLs ending in *.com* – pronounced 'dot com'. This last phrase is now very prominent in newspapers, but the often-seen spelling *dot.com* should be avoided, since this is logically 'dot dot com' – not what is intended. If you must write this, prefer *dot-com* instead.

elegy, eulogy An *elegy* is a poem of mourning for someone's death. A *eulogy* is a very formal speech praising someone, who may be either dead or alive.

elemental, elementary The adjective *elemental* means 'pertaining to or involving the brute forces of nature', as in *our elemental needs* (food, water, sex, survival) and *the elemental forces* (storms, tides, earthquakes, and the like). In mythology and occultism, it also means 'pertaining to the primitive and powerful creatures and forces which are supposed to exist just beyond human perception', as in Yeats's line 'About my table, to and fro, the elemental creatures go.' But *elementary* means only 'basic', 'involving first principles', 'simple', as in *elementary mathematics* and *an elementary lesson*.

elicit, illicit The verb *elicit* means 'call forth', as in *My complaint elicited only a pompous reply*. The adjective *illicit* means 'illegal' or 'contrary to prevailing mores', as in *illicit trading*. Do not write *illicit* when you mean *elicit*.

embarrass This is so spelled: two Rs and two Ss.

emend See **amend**.

emigrate See **migrate**.

émigré An *émigré* is a person who is forced to leave his country for political reasons. The word is most commonly applied to those citizens of the former Russian Empire who were obliged to flee after the Bolshevik revolution, but it may also be safely applied to others fleeing a change in the political order back home. But do not think that this word is only a fancy synonym for *emigrant*; see **migrate**.

emotional, emotive These words overlap somewhat in their meanings. But *emotional* is usually preferred in the sense of 'displaying emotion', as in *an emotional outburst*, and also in the sense of 'calling forth emotions', as in *an emotional moment*. In contrast, *emotive* is a rather dry and abstract word, encountered most commonly in the expression *emotive language*, meaning language which is carefully crafted to induce emotions, such as the language of some poems and of some political speeches. If it's spontaneously and artlessly affecting, it's emotional; if it's coldly calculated to produce an emotional response, it's emotive. When in doubt, prefer *emotional*.

empathy, sympathy The word *sympathy* means 'pity', while *empathy* means more specifically identification with the other person. You can sympathize with anybody who is in a bad position, but you can only empathize with her if you can readily see yourself in her shoes.

emporium At various times, this word has meant all of 'marketplace', 'general store' and 'large store'. Today it is largely obsolete except as a facetious term for 'store' or 'store selling a wide variety of unusual goods'. The plural is usually *emporiums*; the alternative *emporia* is almost always facetious.

empowerment A vogue word of somewhat fuzzy meaning, almost entirely confined to the trendier kinds of social commentary. The general idea is that a social group which is seen as oppressed, exploited or otherwise marginalized should enjoy the same opportunity to make choices and decisions as anybody else. This is a fine idea, but, in practice, those who use the word are more inclined to brandish it as a slogan than to come forward with explicit proposals which can be scrutinized.

empty The past tense and the participle are spelled *emptied*, and **emptyed* is wrong.

emulate This word does *not* mean 'imitate' or 'copy'. Instead, it means 'try to equal or surpass, especially by copying'. So, for example, *Every young cricketer emulates Ian Botham* means 'Every young cricketer tries to do as well as Botham, or even better'. Accordingly, the wording **try to emulate* should not be used, since *emulate* already includes the notion of trying.

Encyclopedia Britannica This is now the official spelling, with *e* and not *ae*. Note also: one T, two Ns in the second word.

endemic, epidemic, pandemic An *endemic* disease is one that persists for a long time in a particular area: *Malaria is endemic in tropical Africa*. An endemic disease does not necessarily affect large numbers of people at one time. An *epidemic* disease is one that affects very many people at one time in one place: *There is an epidemic of flu in California*. A *pandemic* disease is an epidemic that affects a vast area, such as the Black Death in the fourteenth century or the flu outbreak of 1919.

ending a sentence with a preposition See **preposition stranding**.

energy This word has a precise meaning in physics, and it may safely be extended to everyday use in the sense of 'vigour'. But the role of the word stops there. You should not use it as a meaningless piece of padding for 'something or other pretty amazing which I can't explain'.

Energy cannot be counted, and the plural of the word is not in common use. If you find yourself writing *an energy* or *energies*, then you clearly have not the faintest idea what you are talking about, and you should give up.

enervate, invigorate, **energize** The first two words have almost opposite meanings. When you are *invigorated*, you become filled with energy and enthusiasm. But, when you are *enervated*, you are drained of energy, for example by a gruelling ordeal or by a serious illness. Do not write *enervate* when you mean *invigorate*. The word *energize* means the same as 'invigorate', but many people dislike it. Prefer *invigorate*.

England See **Britain**.

English The language whose standard written form is the subject of this book. English belongs to the huge Indo-European family, which includes most of the modern languages of Europe and many of those of western and southern Asia. It belongs to the Germanic branch of that family, and its closest living relatives are therefore Frisian, Dutch, Afrikaans, German, Yiddish and the Germanic languages of Scandinavia. Today English has more native speakers than any other language but Mandarin Chinese. However, if we count non-native speakers, English has perhaps more speakers than any other language.

English derives from a group of Germanic dialects spoken along the North Sea coast of continental Europe. After the collapse of Roman power in Britain, speakers of these dialects moved into Britain, where their speech rapidly displaced the existing Celtic language, the ancestor of modern Welsh, and developed into a distinctive group of dialects which we call **Old English**. After the Norman Conquest of England, English was temporarily submerged as the prestige language, but it soon reappeared, though much changed, with thousands of new words taken over from Norman French, words which displaced more than half of the native lexicon.

The elaborate Germanic system of grammatical endings found in Old English has mostly disappeared, leaving English today the European language with the fewest grammatical endings. Attempts at fixing the spelling of English were soon overwhelmed by enormous changes in pronunciation, changes which have left us with an archaic and mysteriously complex system of spelling. Far more foreign words have been taken into the language, from Latin, from modern French, and from a hundred other languages, and we have resorted to elements extracted from ancient Greek to coin most of our constantly growing technical vocabulary. From Britain, the language spread to every inhabited continent. The result is a language which is very peculiar indeed, but which is nevertheless wonderfully flexible and expressive, and which, for political, economic and cultural reasons, has today become the most influential language on the planet, and the first truly global language the world has ever seen. See also **American-British differences**, **American English**, **British English** and **standard English**.

enjoin A troublesome word. To begin with, it is not a fancy equivalent of *join*. Most commonly, it means 'urge' or 'order', and it is used as in the following example: *The mayor enjoined the crowd to go home.* In legal language, however, it means 'prevent', and it is used as follows: *He is seeking to enjoin our newspaper from publishing an article on his business dealings.* In this last sense, the word is related to *injunction*.

enormity An *enormity* is a terrible crime. We may write of *Stalin's enormities* or of *the enormities perpetrated by the Serbian army in Kosovo*. In spite of its resemblance to *enormous*, the word does not mean 'large size', and should not be used to mean this. Write *the vastness of the universe* or *the immensity of the universe*, not **the enormity of the universe*.

enquire, inquire, enquiry, inquiry The forms in *en-* and in *in-* are both correct, and you may use whichever you prefer. However, American English overwhelmingly prefers the forms in *in-*. British English also prefers the forms in *in-*, except that many people prefer *enquire* in cases like *enquire after her health*.

enrol, enroll British English prefers *enrol* and *enrolment*; American English uses *enroll* and *enrollment*. But the inflected forms are *enrolled*, *enrolling* everywhere. There is no such word as *enrole.

enter (into) You *enter* a building or a profession, but you *enter into* something abstract: *The robbers entered the bank*; *He entered the priesthood*; but *They entered into an agreement.*

enthuse This colloquial verb is out of place in formal writing: write *They were enthusiastic about his music*, not *✻They enthused about his music*.

envelop, envelope The noun is *envelope* (the thing you put a letter into), while the verb is *envelop*, with no E on the end, just as in the verb *develop*.

envisage, envision There are several points here. First, *envisage* is more usual in British English, *envision* in American English, though neither is confined to one side of the Atlantic. Second, many careful writers prefer to restrict *envisage* to the sense of 'form a mental picture of' and *envision* to the sense of 'conceive as a possibility'. With this distinction, then, you can *envisage* your dream house (you can see it clearly in your mind), but you can only *envision* early retirement (you can regard it as a possibility). Third, both words are best used with a following object, as in the examples just cited. The use of these verbs with a following *that* clause, while now commonplace, is still regarded as distasteful by many conservatives, as in *??We envisage/envision that we will be in profit by next year*. Finally, neither word should ever be used to mean no more than 'think', 'believe', 'expect' or 'imagine': this is pompous. Write *We expect a profit next year*, not *✻We envisage/envision a profit next year*.

epicentre The *epicentre* of an earthquake is the point on the earth's surface directly above the focus of the earthquake. The word should not be used as a fancy synonym for *centre*. Do not write drivel like *✻Galliano is at the epicentre of women's fashion*: all this means is 'Galliano is important in women's fashion, and I am a pretentious twit.'

epidemic See **endemic**.

epigram, epigraph, epitaph, epithet An *epigram* is a pithy statement, especially a witty one. An *epigraph* is an inscription on a building or a monument, or a quotation at the beginning of a book or a chapter suggesting its theme. An *epitaph* is an inscription on a tombstone, or any remark commemorating a dead person. An *epithet* is a descriptive word or phrase added to somebody's name, or used in place of his name, as when King Richard I of England is called *the Lionheart*. A term of abuse hurled at somebody, such as *You bastard!*, is strictly an *abusive epithet*. Today, though, most people use *epithet* to mean merely 'term of abuse'. This extended sense can no longer be regarded as wrong, but most careful writers still avoid it.

eponymous When you are writing about the book *Tristram Shandy*, there is little point in explaining that the character Tristram Shandy is the *eponymous hero* of the book. If Tristram is not the hero of the book, then why is the book named after him? Prefer *hero*.

equal Either things are equal or they are not. So, we can describe two things as *not equal* or *almost equal* or *exactly equal*, but we cannot write that one thing is ✳*more equal* than something else. If you need to express the meaning of *more nearly equal*, then write this. Of course, George Orwell famously violated this rule when he wrote *All animals are equal, but some are more equal than others*, but he was being overtly ironic, and you should not follow his lead unless you too are being ironic.

equally The expression ✳*equally as* is always wrong. Do not write ✳*His new book is equally as good as his last one*. Write instead *His new book is just as good as his last one*, or *His last two books are equally good*.

equate You can *equate* one thing *with* another, or (less commonly) you can equate one thing *and* another. But you cannot equate one thing *to* another.

equation A somewhat overused word. Do not write *equation* if all you mean is *circumstances*, *position* or *matter*. Avoid ✳*This greatly complicated the equation*, and prefer *This greatly complicated things*.

equity, equality Quite apart from its several legal and financial senses, *equity* means 'impartiality', 'fairness', 'lack of favouritism'. It is an error to use this word when you mean *equality* – the state of being equal.

equivalent, counterpart Strictly speaking, two things are *equivalent* when one can be readily substituted for the other: *Eight ounces of dried rice is equivalent to 24 ounces of cooked rice*. Note that we write *is equivalent to* but *is the equivalent of*.

However, when two people or things occupy comparable positions in different systems, they are best referred to as *counterparts*, not as *equivalents*: *The British Foreign Secretary is meeting his Israeli counterpart* (not ✳*his Israeli equivalent*).

But you should not use *counterpart* to mean only 'colleague'. The phrase *her male counterparts* is wrongly used when it means no more than 'the men on the committee with her', or something similar.

-er See **-re**.

ere This ancient word for 'before' is now obsolete and should not be used: write *before long* and not *ere long. If you take this advice, you will not have to worry about confusing the word with *e'er*, the archaic contraction of *ever*.

ergo This Latin word means 'therefore', and, in English, the English word is always to be preferred. It is pretentious to write *ergo* in place of *therefore*.

erratum, errata The singular is *erratum*; the plural is *errata*. Do not write **I found only a single errata*; write *I found only a single erratum*, or, better still, *I found only a single error*.

Erse See **Gaelic**.

erupt, irrupt To *erupt* is to burst out violently; to *irrupt* is to enter violently. So, the Huns erupted out of Asia and irrupted into Europe. The derived nouns are *eruption* and *irruption*.

Eskimo The plural is *Eskimos* or *Eskimo*, but not *Eskimoes. The old spelling *Esquimau is obsolete and should not be used. However, since the name is somewhat offensive in origin, it is disliked by the people themselves, who prefer their own names for themselves. There are two groups: the *Inuit*, who occupy Greenland and Canada, and the *Yupik*, who occupy most of Alaska and a small part of Siberia. The *Aleut* people of the Aleutian Islands are not Eskimos at all, though they have a similar culture and though their Aleut language is related to the Eskimo languages.

esoteric, exotic Something which is *esoteric* is known only to the privileged few. The word was formerly applied to mystical or religious doctrines knowledge of which is confined to a select handful of initiates. In this sense it has a little-used opposite, *exoteric*, labelling those morsels of information which can be freely handed out to those not fully initiated. But *esoteric* is commonly applied today to any knowledge possessed by few people, such as the ability to read Egyptian hieroglyphs or to do quantum mechanics, especially when such knowledge is perceived as wonderfully strange and well outside ordinary human concerns.

The word *exotic* means literally 'foreign', 'coming from outside the country', as in *exotic vegetables*. However, it has acquired the much broader sense of 'strange', often 'excitingly or alluringly strange', as in *exotic costumes*. But note the special sense in *exotic dancer*, which denotes a woman who prances about while taking her clothes off or without wearing any clothes.

especially, specially These are not yet quite interchangeable. The adverb *especially* means 'most notably', 'even more so': *She is a brilliant student, especially of languages*; *As volleyball players go, she is not especially tall*; *Turkish cuisine is memorable, especially the lamb dishes*. In contrast, *specially* means 'for a particular occasion or for a particular purpose': *I bought this specially for your birthday*; *We had this machine specially made*. The adjective is almost always *special* in all senses; the form *especial* is extremely formal and now close to obsolete.

-ess The female suffix *-ess* has never established itself more than marginally in English, and now it is close to disappearing. Such formations as *✳poetess* and *✳authoress* are generally regarded as patronizing, and should be avoided. The more familiar word *actress* is seemingly declining in frequency, and performers like Meryl Streep and Gwyneth Paltrow describe themselves as *actors*, not as *actresses*. Even the everyday word *waitress* is giving way to *waiter*. Perhaps only *hostess* is still in regular use alongside *host*, though the now-frequent use of *hostess* to denote a kind of sex worker may well drive the neutral sense of the word out of the language. And, of course, the designations *air hostess* and *stewardess* have already been officially replaced by *flight attendant*.

Only with a few animal names is the suffix still normal: there is no objection to *lioness* and *tigress* (not *✳tigeress*).

essential See **crucial**.

et al. This Latin abbreviation means 'and other people'. It has only one function: when you are citing in your text a work with three or more authors or editors, you can cite the first name alone followed by *et al.* Example: *This is explored in Hualde* et al. *(1998)*. Note that *et al.* is usually italicized, and note the punctuation.

etc. This is an abbreviation for the Latin phrase *et cetera* 'and other things', and it should be written as shown. Do not write ghastly things like *✳etc*, *✳ect.* or *✳e.t.c.* Furthermore, you should never use this expression to refer to people: doing so is inappropriate and rather offensive. Finally, as with all Latin abbreviations, you should not use this in the body of your text. Doing so is lazy and sloppy on your part: in effect, you are saying 'I cannot be bothered to say exactly what I mean, so I'll leave the reader to work it out.'

Using *etc.* repeatedly in your writing is simply terrible style, and very wearying for your readers. Worst of all is the construction *✳such as X, Y, Z, etc.* The presence of *such as* already shows that you are providing only some representative examples, and not an exhaustive list, and so that hideous *etc.*

does no work at all here. Finally, do not write *etc. etc. in any circumstance at all: this is simply abominable.

etymological fallacy This name is given to the wrongheaded belief that the 'true' meaning of a word is what it meant at some time in the past, and not what it means now. Everything changes in languages, and the meanings of words change rather faster than most things. At various times in its past, the word *nice* has meant all of 'ignorant', 'foolish', 'wanton', 'fussy', 'fastidious', 'discriminating', 'subtle', 'precise', 'skilful', 'delicate', 'satisfactory' and 'agreeable'. At the moment, it usually means 'agreeable', as in *a nice person* or *a nice day*. I'm sure you will realize at once that any attempt at declaring that *nice* 'really' means 'ignorant' or 'wanton' or 'fussy' is a foolish waste of time. But the same is true of other words. If *gay* now means 'homosexual', then that's what it now means, and insisting that it must mean 'cheerful' is likewise a waste of time.

euchre The name of the card game is so spelled.

eulogy See **elegy**.

euphemism, euphuism A *euphemism* is an inoffensive expression used in place of one which may be considered painful or vulgar, such as *pass away* for *die* or *wee* for *urinate*. But *euphuism* (the word is not countable) is an absurdly overblown and affected style of writing.

ever, -ever Pairs like *what ever* and *whatever* are often confused. The single word *whatever* means 'anything at all' or 'no matter what': *You can take whatever you like; Whatever you do, remember to be home by 6.00.* The two words *what ever* mean 'what, eventually?', and they most often occur in questions like this one: *What ever happened to Helen Shapiro?* It is wrong to write *Whatever happened to . . .* The film title is *What Ever Happened to Baby Jane?*, even though most reference books give it wrongly as *Whatever Happened . . .*

everybody, everyone, every one The words *everybody* and *everyone* mean the same thing, though *everyone* is sometimes considered slightly more formal than *everybody*. These words can only be applied to people. But *every one* is different. This means 'each one', 'every single one of them', and it can be applied to things as well as to people: *He left several dozen notebooks, but his widow burned every one.*

every day, everyday The adverbial phrase is *every day*: write *This happens every day*, not *This happens everyday*. But the adjective is *everyday*, as in *an everyday occurrence*.

evidence See **prove**.

evidently See **apparently**.

evoke, invoke To *invoke* something is to call upon it, or to appeal to it, for help or inspiration. For example, we can invoke a clause in our contract, or we can invoke a legal precedent, or we can invoke the assistance of a powerful patron. Invoking is done deliberately, and only a human being can invoke anything.

In contrast, to *evoke* something is to call it up in somebody's mind. For example, a song, a play or a story may evoke memories of your childhood, or an unpleasant act may evoke an angry response. Evoking is not usually deliberate, and it is not usually done by human beings.

evolution In biology, *evolution* is the process by which species change over time and develop into new species. Observe carefully that the word carries no suggestion of 'improvement' or 'perfection': later species are never seen as being in any way superior to earlier ones, but only as different from them. Consequently, when you apply this word to something other than living creatures, you should be careful to avoid any implication of improvement. It is fine to write *the evolution of the Internet* if all you mean is the development of the Internet over time, but the phrase should carry no crucial implication that the Internet has been getting better.

ex- Except in the colloquial phrase *my ex*, meaning 'my former spouse', which is rarely appropriate in formal writing, *ex-* is strictly a prefix and should be written as one. It is wrong to write *＊ex minister* or *＊ex ambassador*. Write instead *ex-minister* and *ex-ambassador*, if you must use this prefix. However, in most cases it is better style to write *former*: *former minister* and *former ambassador* should be preferred.

except See **accept**.

exception that proves the rule, the The sense of this expression is often lost. What it means is this: since we have an exception to the rule, that proves that there *is* a rule in the first place. It is foolish to apply this phrase to every exceptional case you come across, and it is positively asinine to invoke the phrase in the hope of defending a rule which has been shown not to work.

excess of, in See **in excess of**.

exciting Advertising has reduced this word to a cipher. In an advertisement, the phrase *an exciting magazine* means no more than 'a magazine which we are selling'. Unless you are obliged to write such dross for a living, you are advised to confine this word to its literal sense of 'thrilling'.

execute Though it earlier meant only 'carry out' (a sentence), this has become our usual word for 'put to death' (after due process of law). Recently, however, journalists have made a habit of writing things like this: *Two of the hostages were executed by the hijackers*. It is an insult to the families of the victims of terrorists to assert that those victims were 'executed'. They were not: they were merely murdered.

exhaustive This word has nothing to do with *exhaust* in the senses of 'use up' or 'wear out'. It means 'comprehensive', 'omitting nothing'. An *exhaustive* list of the guests at a party is a list that includes every guest without exception.

exorbitant The word is so spelled, and *exhorbitant* is wrong.

exotic See **esoteric**.

expatriate An *expatriate* is a person who lives outside his own country, usually by choice. This is the only possible spelling: the word has nothing much to do with *patriot*, and there is no such word as *expatriot*.

expeditious, expedient The adjective *expeditious* means 'quick and efficient'. It is not applied to people, but only to actions and procedures, as in *an expeditious solution*. But *expedient* means 'convenient in the circumstances', and it carries a strong whiff of disapproval: the word suggests something a trifle unfair or dishonest.

expertise A vastly overused word. Before you write it, think whether *experience*, *knowledge* or *skill* might serve your purposes just as well. In any case, *expertise* should be reserved for outstandingly unusual skill.

exponential This word has a precise meaning in mathematics, and it is not just a fancy word for 'fast'. Do not write *It has been growing exponentially* unless you know what exponential growth is and you are sure that you are looking at an instance of it.

exterminate To *exterminate* something is to wipe it out, to destroy it utterly, leaving not a single individual behind. You can only exterminate an entire population or species: *Human settlers in New Zealand exterminated the moa; British settlers in Tasmania exterminated the native Tasmanians*. You cannot exterminate a single individual or a limited number of individuals: you cannot write *The new Sultan exterminated his rivals* or *We have* *exterminated several thousand rabbits*. Use another word instead, such as *murder* or *destroy*.

It is acceptable to extend the use of the verb to cases in which the sense of 'annihilation' is retained: *The World Health Organization hopes to exterminate smallpox* (eradicate it from the face of the earth).

extraordinary The word is so spelled, with no hyphen, and the form *✻extra-ordinary* is wrong.

extravert, extrovert The traditional, and well-formed, version is *extravert*. But, by contamination from *introvert*, this has now been almost universally replaced by *extrovert*. The newer form is reluctantly recommended, but, if your tastes are very conservative, you might prefer the older form, which is still in limited use.

exuberant The word is so spelled, and *✻exhuberant* is wrong.

-ey See **-y**.

eyewitness Since there are few witnesses other than eyewitnesses, *witness* alone is usually sufficient.

eyrie, aerie Of the several spellings of the name of an eagle's nest, these are the most widespread, and the only ones recommended. You may use either, though *eyrie* is perhaps a little more frequent than *aerie*.

façade, facade You may retain the cedilla in this word if you can produce it – and most word processors can. But *facade* is now more usual, and recommended though will still annoy a few people.

facile This is not a synonym of 'easy'. Something which is *facile* is superficially simple and easy but ill-thought-through and unlikely to work. The word is not complimentary.

facility, faculty These two are very often confused. If you have a *facility* for doing something, then you can do it easily, as in *Susie has a facility for making people feel at home*. In the plural, *facilities* are amenities or services, such as *recreational facilities* (like playgrounds and swimming pools). But a *faculty* is an inherent ability or power, such as the *faculty of hearing* or the *faculty of memory*; these are collectively called one's *faculties*, as in *She has lost her faculties*. The common error is to write *facility* where *faculty* is required.

In many universities, *faculty* has two further meanings: a large division, as in *Faculty of Arts*, and the entire teaching staff.

fact The problem here is the use of *the fact that*. Naturally, you should only use these words to introduce something which you are presenting as a fact, and not merely as a suggestion, a hypothesis or a tentative conclusion. It is wrong to write *This suggests the fact that women's brains are structured differently from men's*; write instead *This suggests that* . . . And it is a comical blunder to write *I do not accept the fact that genetically modified food is dangerous*: you cannot reasonably reject a fact. Write instead *I do not accept the suggestion that* . . . English is rich in appropriate alternatives to *the fact that*: *the proposal that, the observation that, the inference that,* and others.

Moreover, do not write clumsy and wordy things like *due to the fact that* for *because*, or *in spite of the fact that* for *although*.

Faerie Queene, The The title of Spenser's poem is so written.

Faeroes, Faroes Both spellings are standard.

faint, feint The spelling is *feint* for the mock attack and for the related verb, and also for the closely ruled paper. It is *faint* in all other senses.

fake French English has curiously invented and adopted some 'French' expressions which do not exist in French. Two examples are *nom de plume* 'pen name' and *bon viveur* 'person who enjoys luxuries', the genuine French equivalents of which are *nom de guerre* and *bon vivant*. There seems little point in embracing these creations: either use the genuine French expressions, or, better, use English equivalents.

fancy words See under **pomposity**.

Faneuil Hall The name of the historic building in Boston, Mass., is so spelled.

fantasy The preferred spelling is *fantasy*, and *phantasy* is now archaic. But *phantasm* is still spelled with PH.

Faroes See **Faeroes**.

Farsi, Persian The chief language of Iran is today usually called *Farsi*, rather than *Persian*.

farther, farthest, further, furthest Any of these words may be used in the literal sense of distance. You may write *Mars is farther from the sun than is the earth* or *Mars is further* . . . Some writers prefer to use only *farther* and *farthest* in this literal sense, and you may follow suit, if you like. But, in all metaphorical senses, only *further* and *furthest* are possible: *She read further; This office is closed until further notice; Are there any further questions?*

fascist, Fascist The capitalized version is correct only when you are mentioning a political party with this name. In all other contexts, prefer *fascist*. But do not fall into the trap of using this word as a meaningless term of abuse.

fatal, lethal Though both pertain to death, these words are not equivalent. We apply *fatal* to something which has caused someone's death: *a fatal accident* is an accident which has killed someone involved in it, and *a fatal disease* is a disease which has killed the person contracting it. In contrast, we apply *lethal* to something which is capable of killing someone: a *lethal weapon* is a weapon which can kill, regardless of whether it has yet killed anybody, and a *lethal disease* is a disease which is capable of killing those who suffer from it.

There is, however, a complication with diseases. A disease which invariably kills its victims may be described as *fatal*.

fatwa A *fatwa* is a formal legal opinion handed down by a Muslim religious leader. A fatwa need have nothing to do with death, or with punishment of any kind, and the word should not be used loosely to mean 'sentence of death' or anything similar.

fauna, flora The *fauna* of a region consists of all the animals living there in the wild, and the *flora* consists of all the wild plants found there. Both words are singular: *The fauna of Madagascar is exotic.* The plurals can be either *faunas* and *floras* (recommended) or *faunae* and *florae*, though you will hardly ever need these plural forms.

February For many speakers, especially in Britain, the pronunciation of this word has strayed so far from the spelling that the spelling must now simply be memorized.

fed up Though the expression is rarely appropriate in formal writing, the accepted form is *fed up with*, and not *＊fed up of*.

feedback A much-overused word. This is a technical term in several scientific disciplines, generally involving the response of some system to its own behaviour. Today it has become something of a vogue word for anything along the lines of 'comment', 'criticism', 'evaluation', or just plain 'response', and it is enormously overused. Before rashly committing this word to paper, think whether one of the plainer words might serve your purpose perfectly well. This is one of two words banned a few years ago by the Provost of the University of Cincinnati. The other was **input**.

feel When constructing an argument, you must not write *I feel that . . .* in order to introduce a conclusion. For example, you should not write *I feel that this hypothesis is not supported by the evidence*. Feelings are emotional, not rational, and you should write instead *I suggest that . . .* or *I conclude that . . .*, depending on how strong you judge the evidence to be. The frequent use of *I feel that . . .* will make your writing appear childish.

feint See **faint**.

feminism In western society, as elsewhere, women have long been the victims of discrimination, subjugation, exploitation, contempt and violence. This is wrong and should be put right. Feminism, insofar as it addresses these issues, is admirable and deserves the support of every right-thinking person. Sadly, however, the name has been appropriated by an array of irresponsible and self-serving people who promote every kind of ignorant and vicious but apparently career-advancing drivel in the name of feminism. So much sludge now appears in print, littered with invocations of 'herstory', 'the Goddess', 'feminist science', 'the elemental power of the female', 'women's ways of knowing', and like claptrap, that real feminism is in some danger of being submerged, and the word is now difficult to use in its proper sense.

The expression 'feminist science', for example, is, at best, contemptuous of women, since it implies that women are not good enough to do real science, and must content themselves with a fifth-rate substitute. At worst, it is an abomination on a par with lunacy like 'Marxist science', 'Aryan science' and 'creation science'.

few, a few These two have quite different senses: *few* means 'hardly any', while *a few* means 'some, but not many'. The first implies that the total is not far from zero, while the second implies that the total is greater than zero. So, *Few of my students speak French* means 'Hardly any of my students speak French', while *A few of my students speak French* means 'I have some students who speak French'.

fewer, less Though colloquial English is often different, standard written English uses *fewer* with things that can be counted and *less* with things that cannot be counted: *fewer people* but *less money*. Do not write *less students* or *less players*.

However, do not write *fewer than six weeks*. Here the expression *six weeks* denotes only a single period of time, and not a collection of six individual objects, and so the required wording is *less than six weeks*.

fictitious, fictional Both of these words mean 'made up', 'invented'. But they are not quite interchangeable. The word *fictional* means 'pertaining to fiction', 'found in fiction', as in *Shangri-La is a fictional country* and *Macbeth was a historical King of Scotland, not a fictional one*. In contrast, *fictitious* means 'false', 'fraudulent', 'non-existent', as in *Cyril Burt's supposed collaborator was found to be fictitious*.

fiery The word is so spelled, and *firey* is wrong.

figures See **numbers**.

filigree, filagree The usual and recommended spelling is *filigree*. The variant *filagree*, though recognized by most dictionaries, is rare, and it looks wrong to many readers.

finalize Though it is recorded from 1901, and has been widely used since the 1920s, this word still attracts great hostility in some quarters. There are perhaps a few authorities who still condemn it, but most now accept it as established. For many people, the word neatly expresses the sense of 'put the finishing touches to', and alternatives like *finish* and *conclude* are not quite adequate. There no longer seems any reason to object to it, but you might be wise to use it advisedly, and not too freely.

find favour with *Do you find favour with that approach?* This is wrong. The correct form is *Does that approach find favour with you?*, though this is merely a coy and wordy way of asking *Do you like that approach?*

fine-toothed comb The traditional and recommended form is *fine-toothed comb* or its variant *fine-tooth comb*, both denoting a comb with fine teeth set close together and hence, metaphorically, close scrutiny. The British variant *fine toothcomb* is eccentric and should be avoided: what is a *toothcomb*, anyway?

Finnegans Wake The title of James Joyce's novel is so written, eccentrically, with no apostrophe.

fiord See **fjord**.

first, firstly There is absolutely no agreement here among the authorities. Whatever you write, it will be approved by some but condemned by others. I recommend writing *first, second, third, . . .* But others prefer *firstly, secondly, thirdly, . . .* , while still others like *first, secondly, thirdly, . . .*

first floor A trans-Atlantic difference. In the USA, the *first floor* is the ground floor. In Britain, the first floor is the floor above the ground floor.

This difference continues all the way up, of course, and it can lead to serious misunderstandings between Americans and Britons.

fjord, fiord Both spellings are acceptable, but *fjord* is preferred by most authorities, and clearly predominates in American English.

flagrant See **blatant**.

flaunt See **flout**.

flautist, flutist Each of these may be applied to a flute-player. American English prefers the more traditional *flutist*; British English prefers the newer form *flautist*.

Flemish See **Dutch**.

flora See **fauna**.

flout, flaunt These unrelated but similar-looking words are often confused. To *flout* something is to disobey it or ignore it, and you can only flout a law, a rule, a convention or another such established standard. You cannot flout a person: the newspaper headline *❋Meacher flouts Blair* is wrong, and should have read *Meacher defies Blair*.

To *flaunt* something is to show it off ostentatiously: *She was flaunting her engagement ring* means that she was making sure that everyone nearby got a good look at the ring, which was presumably expensive and spectacular. Only a person can flaunt anything, and so the following newspaper headline is wrong: *❋Carole Vorderman's flaunting ambition*. Ambition cannot flaunt anything.

fluorescent The word is so spelled: avoid common errors like *❋flourescant*.

foetus, fetus The traditional British spelling is the somewhat eccentric *foetus* (eccentric, because the word derives from Latin *fetus*, from the same root as *female*); the American spelling is *fetus*. The adjective is likewise *foetal*, *fetal*. However, the American spelling is gaining ground in Britain, and is now preferred by some authorities.

for-, fore- As a general rule, we write *fore* or *fore-* or *-fore* when the meaning is 'in front (of)' or 'earlier in time'. Thus we write *in the fore, before, foreleg, forehead, foretell, forebear* ('ancestor'), *forewarn, foresee, foregoing* ('preceding'), *foregone* (as in *a foregone conclusion*) and *foreground*. But we write *for* or *for-* or *-for* when these meanings are absent, as in *for the time being, forget, forbid, forbear* ('refrain'), and *forgo* ('do without'). However, there are some irregular exceptions, which you must learn: we write *forward* and *forwards*, even though the E should logically be there, and we write *therefore*, even though the E should logically be absent. Note in particular the difference between *forgo* and *foregoing*: these are very often confused. And note also the spelling of *foreword*: a foreword is an introduction to a book, and neither *foreward nor *forward is a possible spelling here.

forbid, prohibit These words have the same meaning but behave differently. We *forbid someone to do something*, but we *prohibit someone from doing something*. It is wrong to confuse the two: do not write *The students were forbidden from visiting the bars in town or *The students were prohibited to visit the bars in town.

With a simple object, however, either verb may be used: *The police forbade demonstrations* and *The police prohibited demonstrations* are both fine.

foreign names There are countless proper names in the world's 6000 or so languages: names for countries, cities, buildings, rivers, peoples, languages, and so forth. Only a small minority of these names are familiar enough to have accepted English versions. When an English version does exist, you should normally use this, and not the foreign original, which will seem pretentious to your reader and may even be incomprehensible. So, for example, write *Munich*, not *München*, *Spain*, not *España*, *Montreal*, not *Montréal*, *Saxony*, not *Sachsen*, *the Eiffel Tower*, not *le Tour Eiffel*, and *Basque*, not *Euskara*.

In a few cases, the accepted English name is of an unexpected form. For example, the German football club *Bayern München* has a name which is literally 'Bavaria Munich', but it is always known in English as *Bayern Munich*, and you should respect this convention.

Particularly awkward are the names of musical compositions, especially operas. For example, *The Magic Flute* and *The Marriage of Figaro* are always called in English by these English names, while *Der Rosenkavalier*, *La Traviata* and *La Cenerentola* are always known by their foreign names. If in doubt, consult a good reference book.

forensic This word means 'pertaining to courts of law', and it has nothing to do with medicine or with scientific testing. *Forensic medicine* is the application of medical knowledge and techniques to providing evidence in lawcourts, and the *forensic department* of a police force is a unit dedicated to finding evidence that will stand up in court, usually by means of rigorous testing.

forever, for ever In the USA, *forever* is the only possible spelling. In Britain, *for ever* is traditional in the sense of 'for always', and many publishers still insist upon it, but *forever* is gaining ground rapidly and is now recognized by most dictionaries. However, *forever* is everywhere the only possibility in the sense of 'continually', as in *She's forever having accidents*.

formulae, formulas In a mathematical context, the plural of *formula* is usually *formulae*; elsewhere, it is *formulas*.

fortuitous This word means 'accidental', not 'fortunate'. It is wrong to write *a fortuitous event* if what you mean is *a fortunate event*. This example well illustrates the dangers of trying to use fancy words when you're not too sure what they mean.

In fact, this word is now often applied to something which is *both* accidental and lucky. In this sense, *a fortuitous meeting* is a meeting which happens by chance but which turns out well for the people who meet. It may be that the word will eventually settle down into this sense, but this has not happened yet, and avoiding the word is still the best policy.

forty In spite of *four* and *fourteen*, this word is spelled *forty*, not *fourty*. No reason: it just is.

forum When this word means 'place for discussion', its established plural is *forums*. The Latin plural *fora* is now increasingly used, especially by academics, but it is rather pretentious, and it is frowned upon by many (not all) usage manuals. However, when *forum* is used in its ancient sense of a Roman marketplace and site of public business, the plural is always *fora*.

Frankenstein In the novel by Mary Shelley, *Frankenstein* is the name of the scientist who creates the monster, and not of the monster, who has no name. You can describe a horrible creation as *a Frankenstein monster*, but you can't describe it as *a Frankenstein*.

fraught The adjective *fraught* means 'charged (with)', especially 'emotionally charged (with)', and it is normally followed by *with*: *The atmosphere in the room was fraught with barely concealed anger*. The word is very formal, and best reserved for the most formal styles. Using it without a following phrase is common in informal styles, but best avoided in careful writing: *The atmosphere in the room was fraught*. In no circumstances should the word be used as a preposed modifier: *There was a fraught atmosphere in the room*.

French names There is just one complication with French names: the surname is sometimes preceded by a particle *de*, *d'* or *du*. When a French-speaker with such a name is cited in English by surname alone, the particle is usually dropped. For example, the great Swiss linguist *Ferdinand de Saussure* is always called *Saussure*, and never *de Saussure. There are, however, a few established exceptions. The general and politician *Charles de Gaulle* is normally *de Gaulle*, and the writer *Simone de Beauvoir* is *de Beauvoir*. An unusual case is *Madame du Barry*, mistress of Louis XV, always so known in English; this name, exceptionally, is alphabetized under D, not under B.

Note that these particles, especially *du*, are sometimes fused onto the surname, as in the cases of the composer *Henri Duparc* and the painter *Marcel Duchamp*. These names cause no difficulty, apart from making sure you don't inadvertently insert a space that shouldn't be there.

French surnames carried to English-speaking countries are treated variously. Note, for example, the English cellist *Jacqueline du Pré*, the English writer *Daphne du Maurier*, the American historian *W. E. B. Du Bois*, the American businessman *Pierre Du Pont*, and the American general *Samuel Dupont*. If in doubt, check a good reference book.

fruition Historically, this word means 'enjoyment', especially 'pleasure in something one owns', and it has nothing at all to do with *fruit*. However, by a mistaken association, the word has come to be used almost exclusively in the phrase *come to fruition*, meaning 'come to completion', 'become accomplished'. Whatever the dictionaries may tell you, this is now the only possible sense, and the older sense is extinct. If you are still trying to use it in its older sense, it is time for a reality check.

frustum The geometrical term is *frustum*, and *frustrum is wrong.

fuchsia The name of the flower is so spelled.

Fuji The Japanese mountain is *Fuji*, *Mount Fuji* or *Fujiyama*, but never *Mount Fujiyama, since *yama* means 'mount(ain)'.

-ful The suffix is always *-ful*, and never **-full*: *spoonful*, *roomful*, *cupful*, and so on. But note the big difference between *-ful*, which always expresses a quantity, and *full*, which doesn't. If you drop a *spoonful of mayonnaise* onto your salad, then you have mayonnaise on your salad, but, if you drop a *spoon full of mayonnaise* onto your salad, then you have a piece of cutlery in your salad.

fulfil, fulfill British English requires *fulfil*, while American English requires *fulfill*, and the derived noun shows the same difference: UK *fulfilment*, US *fulfillment*. But the verb-forms are *fulfilled* and *fulfilling* in all varieties of English.

fulsome The adjective *fulsome* derives from *foul* and it means 'so excessive as to cause embarrassment or disgust'. Hence, *fulsome praise* of a person is praise which is laid on absurdly thick, and there may even be a suggestion that the praise is hypocritical. For example, the obligatory ritualized praise that was lavished publicly on the leaders of the formerly Communist countries was certainly fulsome, and the term is not a compliment. Recently, however, there has been a tendency to use the word in a positive sense, and *fulsome praise* is now often written to mean 'great but sincere praise'. Using *fulsome* in this second sense will annoy many readers, but, unfortunately, using it in its traditional sense will now mislead many others, who are unaware of the established meaning. Unless you are sure of your readership, it is probably best to avoid the word altogether: write *lavish praise* or *warm praise* if you mean to be complimentary, and *excessive praise* or *hypocritical praise* if you do not.

furor, furore The British spelling is *furore*; the American one is *furor*.

gabardine, gaberdine There is considerable variation here, but most authorities recommend *gabardine* for the fabric and *gaberdine* for the short coat worn in medieval Europe.

Gaelic, Gallic, Erse, Irish Strictly, the name *Gaelic*, when pronounced GAY-lik, denotes a branch of the Celtic language family including Irish, Scots Gaelic and the recently extinct Manx. Gaelic in this sense was formerly also called *Erse*, but this other name is now more or less obsolete, except in crossword puzzles, and you are advised to avoid it. When pronounced GAL-ik (rhymes with *italic*), *Gaelic* denotes instead the Celtic language of northwestern Scotland. The second national language of Ireland is properly called *Irish*, not *Gaelic*. And note that the other Celtic languages, such as Welsh, Breton and the extinct Cornish, are not Gaelic languages at all: these belong to another branch of Celtic, called *Brythonic* or *Brittonic*, and writing ✳*Welsh Gaelic* is absurd.

In contrast, *Gallic*, which also rhymes with *italic*, means 'pertaining to France' or 'typically French'.

gainsay This is a somewhat archaic word for 'deny' or 'contradict', found most usually in the negative, as in *This cannot be gainsaid*. The word is too archaic for ordinary writing: avoid it.

Gambia See *the* **in names of countries**.

gambit, gamut In chess, a *gambit* is the deliberate sacrifice of material for the sake of gaining a superior position. The term may be extended to any kind of calculated manoeuvre made by someone who hopes to gain an advantage, as in *a conversational gambit*, but it should not be used more broadly to label any kind of manoeuvre at all.

And do not confuse this word with *gamut*. This word means 'the whole range', as in the example *She ran the gamut of emotions*, meaning that she exhibited every possible emotion.

game names The name of a proprietary game, like the name of any commercial product, must be capitalized: *Monopoly*, *Cluedo* (US *Clue*), *Diplomacy*, *Trivial Pursuit*. But the name of a traditional game owned by no one does not need a capital: *bridge*, *chess*, *draughts* (US *checkers*), *ludo* (US *parcheesi*), *backgammon*.

Gandhi Note the spelling of this famous name, and avoid the common error ✳*Ghandi*.

gaol See **jail**.

garda, gardai The Irish police are the *gardai*; one Irish policeman is a *garda*. The official name of the force is the *Garda Síochána*.

gelatin, gelatine The American spelling is *gelatin*, while the British one is *gelatine*. But, in scientific writing, the spelling is always *gelatin*.

gender, sex Strictly speaking, *gender* is a grammatical phenomenon found in certain languages in which nouns are classified into two or more classes requiring different agreement. In contrast, *sex* is a matter of biology: you are born into one sex or the other. You should not use *gender* when you mean *sex*: write *She was discriminated against because of her sex*, not ✳ *. . . because of her gender*. Using *gender* for *sex* sounds prissy: it suggests that you are too embarrassed to use the word *sex* in any sense at all.

gendarmes In France, the *gendarmes* are soldiers used to police rural districts. The ordinary French police are just that: *police*. Do not write *gendarmes* if all you mean is (French) *police*.

genealogy The word is so spelled: avoid the common error ✳*geneology*.

geographical names There are a few problems with geographical names consisting of a proper name combined with an ordinary word like *street*, *lane*, *island*, *lake* or *desert*. The usual English pattern is to put the ordinary word last: *Wall Street*, *London Road*, *Park Lane*, *the Pacific Ocean*, *Long Island*, *the Caspian Sea*, *the Barossa Valley*. But there are complications, especially with the names of mountains, deserts, lakes and rivers.

A mountain name containing the word *mount* reverses the usual pattern, putting the proper name last: *Mount Everest, Mount McKinley, Mount Snowdon, Mount Aconcagua*. But most other mountain names follow the usual pattern: *Pike's Peak, Sca Fell, Table Mountain*. The name of a particularly famous mountain may be used without *mount*: *Everest, Snowdon*. A Scottish or Irish mountain name containing the word *ben* 'mountain' never takes either *mount* or *mountain*: *Ben Nevis*, never *＊Mount Ben Nevis* or *＊Ben Nevis Mountain*. The famous Japanese mountain may be any of *Fuji, Fujiyama* or *Mount Fuji*, but never *＊Mount Fujiyama*, since *yama* is the Japanese word for 'mountain'. Untranslated foreign names should be left in their original forms: *Mont Blanc, the Matterhorn*.

A very famous mountain range is usually named by its proper name alone, usually in the plural: *the Alps, the Himalayas, the Pyrenees, the Andes, the Urals*. We never write *＊the Himalaya Mountains* or *＊the Pyrenee Mountains*. Other names are variable: you can write either *the Appalachian Mountains* or *the Appalachians, the Great Smoky Mountains* or *the Great Smokies*. The shorter form is recommended. A few names are unusual: *the Cascade Range* or *the Cascades*, but never *＊the Cascade Mountains*.

Desert names follow the usual pattern: *the Sahara Desert, the Gobi Desert, the Mojave Desert*. However, a desert name may be abbreviated, and commonly is among those who use the name frequently: *the Sahara, the Gobi, the Mojave*. (Note: some writers object to *the Sahara Desert*, since *sahara* means 'desert' in Arabic, but the form is established and beyond objection, like *the Mississippi River*, literally 'the bigriver river', and *the La Brea Tar Pits*, literally 'the the tar tar pits'.)

Lake names are more complex. Names of large lakes almost always reverse the usual pattern: *Lake Victoria, Lake Ontario, Lake Maracaibo*. But names containing *great* follow the usual pattern: *Great Slave Lake, Great Salt Lake*. Names of small lakes are variable: *Lake Amadeus* (in Australia) but *Cuba Lake* (in New York State). The Welsh lake is usually *Bala Lake*, but *Lake Bala* is also used. The English lake is sometimes *Lake Windermere*, but more often *Windermere*, since *mere* means 'lake'. Names not containing the word *lake* follow the usual pattern: *Coniston Water, Wast Water*. Scottish and Irish lakes with *loch* or *lough* ('lake') always follow the reversed pattern: *Loch Ness, Lough Neagh*.

River names always follow the reversed pattern in Britain and Ireland: *the river Thames, the river Avon, the river Shannon*. In the US, they always follow the usual pattern: *the Ohio River, the Thames River* (in Connecticut), *the Colorado River*. You are advised to follow the style of the country in which the river is located, since *＊the Ouse River* and *＊the river Ohio* both sound strange or worse to those on the side of the Atlantic where the river is.

If in doubt, consult a good reference book.

geriatric This adjective means 'pertaining to the illnesses or other difficulties of elderly people'. It does not mean 'elderly' or 'senile', and you should not use it so.

German names There is only one complication with German names. A German surname is sometimes preceded by the particle *von* (or rarely *van*, in a family of Dutch origin). As a rule, when the surname is cited alone in English, the particle is dropped. So, for example, the general and politician *Paul von Hindenburg* is usually *Hindenburg* in English, not *von Hindenburg*, and the composer *Ludwig van Beethoven* is always *Beethoven*, never *van Beethoven*. But usage is not always consistent. The Nazi diplomat *Joachim von Ribbentrop* is often called *von Ribbentrop*, though *Ribbentrop* is more usual, and is recommended. Of course, these particles are always ignored in alphabetical listings.

But there is a complication with German-speakers who have migrated to English-speaking countries. These people often retain their *von* in all circumstances. For example, the Hungarian-born (but German-speaking) mathematician *John von Neumann* and the rocket scientist *Wernher von Braun*, both of whom migrated to the US, are always called *von Neumann* and *von Braun*, though their particles continue to be ignored in alphabetical lists.

A different case is represented by the American film director *Joseph von Sternberg* and the American actor and director *Erich von Stroheim*, both born in Austria. Not only do these two keep their particles, but their names are even alphabetized under V. This is partly because their names have been adapted to the usual English practice, and partly because both names are stage names: neither man was born with the name he is known by. If in doubt, consult a good reference book.

German *ü*, *ö* and *ä* should be reproduced if possible. If this is not possible, then the sequences *ue*, *oe*, *ae* make an adequate substitute. But note that the name of the writer *Goethe* is always so written, and never as *Göthe*.

gerrymander The word is so spelled, with G, and *jerrymander* is wrong.

gerund, verbal noun English has several different grammatical forms ending in *-ing*, all of which differ in function and behaviour. Two of these are the *gerund* and one kind of *verbal noun*. We will begin by distinguishing these, since many contemporary handbooks fail to distinguish them, even though the difference is important.

A *gerund* is derived from a verb by adding the suffix *-ing*. The result is still a verb, and it exhibits ordinary verbal properties, such as taking objects and adverbs. Example: *In football, deliberately tripping an opponent is a foul*. Here the verb *trip* occurs in its gerund form *tripping*, but this *tripping* is still a verb: it takes the adverb *deliberately* and the object *an opponent*. However, the entire phrase *deliberately tripping an opponent*, because of the gerund within it, now functions as a noun phrase, in this case as the subject of the sentence. So, a gerund is still a verb, but the phrase built around it is nominal, not verbal.

Very different is a *verbal noun* constructed with *-ing*. Though derived from a verb, a verbal noun is strictly a noun, and it exhibits nominal properties: it takes determiners like *the* and *this*, it permits adjectives (but not adverbs), it permits following prepositional phrases (but not objects), and it can even be pluralized if the sense permits. Example: *In football, the deliberate tripping of an opponent is a foul*. Here the verbal noun *tripping* takes the determiner *the*, the adjective *deliberate* and the prepositional phrase *of an opponent*, but it exhibits no verbal properties at all. In other words, *tripping* in this case is a perfectly ordinary noun, behaving just like any other noun, with no verbal properties in sight. Compare the last example with one involving the unremarkable noun *attack*: *In football, a deliberate attack on an opponent is a foul*.

Every verb in the language forms a gerund in *-ing*, apart from the modal verbs like *can*, *must*, *will* and *should*, which are defective verbs (they lack some of the forms exhibited by other verbs). But not every verb forms a verbal noun in *-ing*. Some do, like *trip* above and *kill*, which forms the verbal noun *killing*: *We must put a stop to these killings*. Some don't, and can only form verbal nouns with other suffixes. For example, *arrive* does not form a verbal noun *✳arriving*: *✳Her constant late arrivings annoy me*. The verbal noun of this verb is *arrival*: *Her constant late arrivals annoy me*. And still other verbs form no verbal noun at all. For example, the verb *despise* forms no verbal noun: *✳Her despising/despisal/despision of David was obvious*.

Now, suppose we need to identify the person responsible for the action. With a verbal noun, as with any other noun, we must use a possessive form like *John's*, *the boss's*, *my*, *your* or *his*. Example: *I was not happy with John's handling of the contract*. This is probably natural for everyone, and I don't suppose there is an English-speaker alive who is tempted to say, or write, *✳I was not happy with John handling of the contract*.

But, with the gerund, there is a possible surprise: the gerund *also* requires a possessive form. Example: *I was not happy with John's handling the contract for us*. In standard written English, this is the only possibility, and it is wrong to write *I was not happy with John handling the contract for us*. In my experience, the standard possessive form comes far more naturally to Americans than to Britons, but all authorities – British as well as American – agree that the possessive is the only possibility here. Another example: standard *I don't like his coming here* against non-standard *I don't like him coming here*.

If you find this possessive form unnatural – as you very likely do – then I am afraid you will just have to grit your teeth and learn it. Though the other form is now overwhelmingly predominant in spoken British English, and gaining ground in American English, it is not yet regarded as part of standard written English. Maybe in another generation, but not yet.

For another common problem with gerunds, see **to plus gerund**.

get passive The *get* passive is firmly established in informal English: *My dog got hit by a car*. However, this construction is too informal for careful writing, where the *be* passive should be preferred. Write *Constantinople was sacked by the Crusaders*, not *. . . got sacked*.

gift The noun *gift* should not be used as a verb in careful writing. Write *Pollok House was given to Glasgow*, not *Pollok House was gifted to Glasgow* – which is what it says on the sign in Pollok House.

gild, gilt, guild To *gild* something is to cover it in gold. The gold covering so applied is *gilt*. An association of craftsmen is a *guild*.

ginkgo The tree name is so spelled. The rare variant *gingko* is best avoided.

gipsy See **gypsy**.

Giuseppe The Italian given name is so spelled. Avoid the common error *Guiseppe*. The same goes for other names with the same first syllable, like *Giulio* and *Giulietta*.

given In spite of its seeming illogicality, a phrase starting with *given that*, in the sense of 'since', may occur at the beginning of a sentence with any continuation. Example: *Given that we are faced with a large deficit, we must reach into our reserves*.

glean To *glean* something is to gather it in a painstaking and laborious manner. So, for example, to *glean* information from a coded message is to extract that information by hours of hard work, and there is a clear implication that the information gained is partial. The word does not mean 'realize', 'notice' or 'discover', and it should not be so used. It may help to recall that *glean* originally meant 'collect the edible residue from a cornfield whose crop has already been harvested'.

Note also that *glean* cannot be followed by the connecting word *that*: you can *glean information about his wealth*, but you cannot *glean that he is wealthy*.

Glen The name of a Scottish glen is written as two words: *Glen Garry*, *Glen Coe*, *Glen Carron*. If there is a town taking its name from the glen, the town name is written as one word, like *Glencarron*.

goodbye The hyphenated spelling *good-bye* is now widely considered old-fashioned, and *goodbye* is recommended.

Gorbachev, Gorbachov Even though *Gorbachov* represents the pronunciation better, *Gorbachev* matches the Russian spelling better, and is preferred by most authorities.

gourmet, gourmand A *gourmet* is a person who is knowledgeable about food and who can readily judge its quality. A *gourmand* is merely someone who eats too much. The first is a compliment; the second is not.

government, administration In Britain, a *government* is the tenure of a particular prime minister, or the people who hold office during that tenure, as in *the Thatcher government*. The American equivalent is *administration*, as in *the Carter administration*. In the US, *the government* is the entire body of federal, state and local officials and laws, the whole structure with which a citizen must deal in official matters. There is no real British equivalent.

graffito, graffiti The little-used singular is *graffito*: *There was an obscene graffito on the wall*. The familiar form *graffiti* is always plural: *These graffiti are disgusting*. Do not write *This graffiti is disgusting*. In either case, note the spelling: two Fs, one T. Avoid the common error *grafitti*.

-gram, -gramme There are complications here. Certain words always take *-gram* in all varieties of English; examples are *diagram*, *telegram* and *epigram*. Other words take *gram* in American English but either *-gram* or *-gramme* in British English. This group includes all the metric units of mass: *gram(me)*, *kilogram(me)*, and the like. Most British authorities prefer the shorter forms, which in any case are normal in scientific writing. And see **program** for an unusual case.

grammar The word is spelled as shown: do not write *grammer*. It may help you to recall that the derived adjective is *grammatical*.

The word has several quite distinct senses. First, it is the collective label for all of the rules present in a language which pertain to the proper construction of words, phrases, clauses and sentences. In this sense, grammar is divided into two parts: *morphology* (the structure of words) and *syntax* (the structure of phrases, clauses and sentences – in other words, the assembling of words into larger units). The frequent collocation *grammar and syntax* must therefore be avoided, since syntax is merely a part of grammar.

Note that every variety of English has its own rules of grammar: there is no variety of English which lacks grammar. For example, the sentence *He don't have no car* is fully grammatical in the local variety of English spoken where I grew up, and in many other local varieties, but it is not grammatical in standard English. In contrast, *He doesn't have a car* is grammatical in standard English, but it is not grammatical in my local variety.

Some linguists extend the term *grammar* to the entire assembly of rules governing the structure and use of a language, including rules of pronunciation and of conversation, but this extended sense is neither usual nor recommended.

Second, *grammar* is applied to any particular approach to the study of grammar. This is the sense found in labels like *traditional grammar* and *transformational grammar*.

Third, a *grammar* may be a book containing a description of the grammar of a particular language, as in *a grammar of Latin* or *an English grammar*.

See also **grammatical**.

grammar checkers Today many word processors come equipped with grammar checkers, programs which are supposed to check your writing for errors in grammar. These things are, at best, in their infancy. They may succeed in catching a few slips of the keyboard which you have overlooked, but they are often helpless in the face of more subtle errors. For example, the following attempt at a sentence is quite ungrammatical, and would be spotted at once by a competent human copy-editor: *The Austrian advance had given no thought to secure their flank*. Try typing this into your word processor, and then ask your grammar checker to check it. Does your checker pick up the error, and correct the faulty *secure* to the required *securing*? If it does, your checker is better than most. But, if it doesn't – and it probably won't – you have a vivid demonstration of the feebleness of these programs. See also **spellcheckers**, **style checkers**.

grammatical A particular linguistic form is *grammatical* if it conforms to all the requirements of the grammar of the language variety it belongs to. So, as explained in the entry for **grammar**, the sentence *He don't have no car* is grammatical in the non-standard variety of English spoken where I grew up, but not in standard English, while *He doesn't have a car* is the other way round.

But a form may be fully grammatical in standard English and yet still fail to be normal, acceptable or intelligible. Here are some examples of grammatical sentences which are more or less nonsensical, marked with the hash mark (#): #*Booth killed Lincoln, but Lincoln didn't die*; #*The square root of seven is green and squishy*; #*Colourless green ideas sleep furiously* (this last is the famous coinage of the linguist Noam Chomsky).

You might think that such things are of no relevance to this book, but not so. The writer Keith Waterhouse has uncovered a splendid example produced by a British prime minister: #*Trial by television is the day that freedom dies*. This is fully grammatical, but it is senseless, since a trial cannot be a day. Writing this is rather like writing #*Trial by television is six feet tall* or #*Trial by television is Guy Fawkes Day*.

As always, read what you've written.

grasslands English uses a number of labels for broad grassy plains, depending on where the plains are located. North America has the *prairie*. South America has the *pampas*. Eurasia has the *steppe*. Most of Africa has the *savannah* (the preferred British spelling) or the *savanna* (the preferred American one). South Africa has the *veld* (the preferred spelling today) or the *veldt* (an older spelling, still acceptable but now little used). No one of these has become accepted for labelling grasslands all over the planet, though *savanna(h)* is perhaps most often used for this purpose.

gray See **grey**.

Great Britain See **Britain**.

Greek names Greek is not written in the roman alphabet, and Greek names must be converted for use in English. For ancient Greek names, there is a precise and detailed scholarly system involving numerous diacritics, but this system is rarely used in everyday English.

Otherwise, there are two systems for writing ancient Greek names in English. The first uses a fairly consistent rendering of the Greek spelling, producing names like *Sokrates*, *Oidipous*, *Akhilleus*, *Herodotos* and *Herakles*. This system is occasionally used in popular accounts written by scholars, and in translations of literature, but it is not common.

The second system involves spelling the name according to the conventions of Latin. In this system, the first four names just cited become *Socrates*, *Oedipus*, *Achilles* and *Herodotus*, and these are the usual English forms. Sometimes the Latin form is significantly different from the Greek original: for example, the last of the five names becomes *Hercules*, also the usual English form.

Occasionally, however, the accepted English form of the name has an unpredictable form. A good example is the philosopher *Aristoteles*, who is always known in English as *Aristotle*.

Non-native speakers should note that the English form of a Greek name is sometimes different from the form common in Europe. For example, we write *Plato* for the philosopher, and never *✳Platon*.

Today we always refer to the ancient Greek divinities by their Greek names. The former custom of using the names of their Roman counterparts is now dead. So, for example, the Greek divinities are *Ares*, *Aphrodite* and *Artemis*, never *Mars*, *Venus* and *Diana*; these last names are reserved for the Roman deities.

Modern Greek names are usually rendered into English by converting the Greek spelling letter by letter, regardless of the pronunciation. For example, the Greek forms of *Anthony* and *George* are usually *Antonios* and *Georgios*, reflecting the Greek spelling, rather than *✳Andonios* and *✳Yoryos*, which represent the pronunciations more accurately. And again there are a few odd cases, an example being the poet *Kavafis*, always known in English as *Cavafy*.

If in doubt, consult a good reference book.

grey, gray For the colour term, the British spelling is *grey*, while the American form is *gray*. However, even in Britain, the surname is usually spelled *Gray*.

grievous The word is *grievous*, not *✳grievious*.

grisly, grizzly The adjective *grisly* means 'gruesome', as in *a grisly crime*. But *grizzly* means 'streaked with grey', and is little used outside the name *grizzly bear*.

ground rules In cricket and baseball, the *ground rules* are the special rules introduced to deal with the features of individual playing grounds, such as the tree growing within the Canterbury cricket ground and the ivy on the wall at Chicago's Wrigley Field. Ground rules are thus quite different from the fundamental rules, and you should not write *ground rules* if what you mean is the fundamental rules.

guerrilla This word is so spelled: note in particular the two Rs. The misspelling *✳guerilla* is now so frequent that it is recognized by many dictionaries, but you should avoid it in careful writing. The word derives from Spanish *guerra* 'war', related to French *guerre*.

Guiana, Guyana *Guiana* is a region of the north coast of South America, divided into three countries: *Guyana* (the former *British Guiana*), *Surinam* (the former *Dutch Guiana*) and *French Guiana*.

guild See **gild**.

Guildhall The famous building in the City of London is *Guildhall*, and not *∗the Guildhall*. Don't ask me why.

Guinness The names of the Irish beer, of the book of records and of the actor Alec are all so spelled, with two Ns. Do not write *∗Guiness*.

Gujarat, Gujarati These spellings are recommended; *Gujerat* and *Gujerati* are less good.

Gulf of Lions The gulf next to southern France is so called, and both *∗Gulf of Lyons* and *∗Gulf of Lyon* are wrong. The name of the gulf has nothing to do with the name of the city of Lyons.

Gurkha The word is so spelled; avoid the error *∗Ghurka*.

guttural The word is so spelled, with two Us, and *∗gutteral* is wrong. The word is not spelled like *gutter*.

Furthermore, avoid the common blunder of applying the meaningless label *guttural* to every language or speech variety that doesn't sound like Italian. If you can't explain precisely which speech sounds are guttural and which not, then you don't know what the word means, and shouldn't use it.

Guyana See **Guiana**.

gypsy, gipsy Almost all authorities prefer *gypsy* for the common noun and *Gypsy* for the proper noun, the spelling preferred by the Gypsies themselves.

Haarlem, Harlem *Haarlem* is a city in the Netherlands; *Harlem* is a district of Manhattan.

had have In standard English, there is no circumstance whatever in which the sequence of auxiliaries *∗had have* is grammatical, and the same goes for the contracted forms *∗'d have* and *∗'d've*, when the first element represents *had*, and not *would*. Accordingly, all of the following are wrong: *∗If we had have received the data earlier, we could have solved the problem*; *∗If she'd've appealed, she might have won*; *∗Had he have made that pot, he might have cleared the table*. As you can see, this error usually arises after *if*. In every case, the error is the presence of that following *have*. If this word is eliminated, the result is fine in each case: *If we had received the data earlier . . .* ; *If she'd appealed . . .* ; *Had he made that pot . . .*

Hague, The Unusually, the name of the Dutch city is *The Hague*, with two capital letters.

hajj, haji A *hajj* is a pilgrimage to Mecca; a *haji* is a person who has made it. Other spellings exist, and are not wrong, but these appear to be the most widely used.

halve There is a pitfall in using this word. If you write *The population has more than halved*, this is not wrong, but it is certainly less than instantly clear. Prefer a less troublesome form of words, such as *The population has fallen to less than half of its earlier value*.

Hamitic, Hamito-Semitic These names are no longer in use in linguistics. The whole family of languages is now called *Afro-Asiatic*, not *Hamito-Semitic*, and the languages formerly classed as *Hamitic* are no longer recognized as a single group.

handgun, pistol A firearm held and fired with one hand is traditionally a *pistol*. In American English, the alternative term *handgun* is now well established, and may be used freely by Americans. This new word is gaining ground in Britain, but many people still object to it, and British writers are advised to avoid it.

hang, hanged, hung Standard English makes a curious distinction here. In most circumstances, the verb *hang* is irregular and has the parts *hang*, *hung*, *hung*: *Icicles hung from the eaves*; *The picture was hung in the living room*. However, when *hang* means 'put to death with a rope', it is regular, and has the parts *hang*, *hanged*, *hanged*: *They hanged him*; *He was hanged*. It is not recommended to write *⁎They hung him* or *⁎He was hung*.

hangar, hanger You put your coat on a *hanger*, but you keep a plane in a *hangar*.

hara-kiri The word is so spelled, and *⁎hari-kari* is wrong.

harass Note the spelling: one R, two Ss.

hare-brained The word is so spelled, and *⁎hair-brained* is wrong. The calumny here is directed against hares.

Harlem See **Haarlem**.

having said that If you introduce a sentence with these words, the very next word or phrase must name the person who has said that. Example: *Having said that, Susie burst into giggles* (it was Susie who said that). The common error is illustrated by the next example: *⁎Having said that, there is no feasible alternative*. Here *there* certainly does not name the person who has said something, and *having said that* is now a **dangling modifier** with no connection to its sentence. A legitimate version is this: *That said, there is no feasible alternative*.

Hawaii The established English spelling is *Hawaii*, with two Is. A more accurate rendering is *Hawai'i*, with an apostrophe representing the glottal stop heard in the native Hawaiian pronunciation. This second version is often preferred in scholarly work. In ordinary writing, the second version may be regarded as fussy or pretentious, but that may change, since the State of Hawaii is considering changing the official spelling to *Hawai'i*. The derived adjective is always *Hawaiian*, with two Is and no apostrophe. The form *＊Hawai* is always wrong.

headline adjective I have coined this label here for a feature of journalistic English which seems to have no accepted name. The following example, a newspaper headline, illustrates the phenomenon: *Fury Over Saudi Nurses*. The point is that the two nurses under discussion were not Saudi at all, but British. However, they had entered the news as a result of a death in Saudi Arabia. The headline is therefore to be understood as talking about 'the nurses connected somehow with Saudi Arabia'. This space-saving device is much favoured by headline writers, but it is entirely out of place in careful writing. Compare **transferred epithet**.

healthy, healthful, wholesome You are *healthy* if you are free of illness and injuries, and animals and plants, as well as people, may also be described as *healthy* in the same way. However, in standard English, foods and practices which promote good health are *wholesome* (or, sometimes in American English, *healthful*). You are therefore advised to write *wholesome food* and *wholesome exercise*. The usage illustrated by *??healthy food* and *??healthy exercise* is now very widespread, and perhaps on the brink of being accepted as standard English, but some readers will still object to it, and you would be wise to avoid it.

In any case, avoid writing things like *a healthy profit*. Prefer *a substantial profit* or some other more explicit wording.

Hebrew, Yiddish *Hebrew* is the traditional language of the Jews. The ancient Hebrew language, in which most of the Old Testament (the Jewish holy book) is written, died out as a mother tongue long ago, but the language was remarkably revived as a mother tongue in what is now the State of Israel. Where necessary, we distinguish between *Biblical Hebrew* (the ancient form) and *Israeli Hebrew* or *modern Hebrew* (the modern form).

In contrast, *Yiddish* is a Germanic language, closely related to German, which was widely spoken by European Jews before the Holocaust. It is still spoken to some extent in Europe, in the USA and in Israel, but it is now often regarded by Israelis as inferior to Hebrew, and it is dying, even though it has greatly enriched English.

The *Hebrews* were the famous people of the ancient Near East. It is proper to use the word in this historical context, but it is improper and offensive to apply the word to Jews in general.

hegemonic The problem with this unusual adjective is that it is found almost exclusively in writing which is pompous and pretentious. It means 'involving the (unjust) domination of one group or class over others', and it occurs most commonly – indeed, almost entirely – in the most awful sort of post-modernist drivel. If you find yourself using this word, you might be wise to ask a colleague in a different discipline whether your writing has any detectable content.

The word is not intrinsically bad. But it hardly ever seems to occur in good writing, whereas it is inescapable in certain types of terrible writing.

hermeneutic Except in philosophy, in which it has technical senses, this word means 'interpretive', and most especially 'pertaining to the interpretation of the Scriptures'. It is not a word that you are likely to need. However, it has become a favourite of post-modernist writers, who cannot resist slipping it into every second page. Like most post-modernist habits, this is not one you should imitate. If you mean 'interpretive', then write *interpretive*, and forget about this silly word.

hers This is the correct spelling, and both *her's* and *hers'* are wrong.

hiccup This is the preferred spelling: the strange and somewhat confused variant *hiccough* is not usually considered wrong, but it is pointless, and I advise you to stay away from it.

hierarchy Note the spelling: it is wrong to write *heirarchy*. The derived adjective is *hierarchical*.

hieroglyphs The famous written characters of ancient Egypt are *hieroglyphs*, not *hieroglyphics*. The word *hieroglyphic* is strictly an adjective, as in *hieroglyphic inscriptions*, and there is no such word as *hieroglyphics*.

hijack The word is so spelled, and the hyphenated version *hi-jack* is both pointless and recognized by no major dictionary. The variant spelling *highjack* is recognized by some (but not all) dictionaries, but is not recommended.

hire, rent, charter In all varieties of English, we *hire* a person or a taxi, we *rent* a house or a flat and we *charter* a boat or a plane. But tools and equipment are more complicated: in British English, you *hire* a cement mixer or a chainsaw, while in American English you *rent* it.

historic, historical A *historical* event is one which really happened, which is not fictitious or mythical. In contrast, a *historic* event is one which is so memorable that it will live in people's memories for a long time.

hitherto This word means 'until now' or 'before now', and you should usually prefer these plainer words. It absolutely cannot mean 'until then', and things like this are wrong: ＊*Napoleon had hitherto enjoyed only unbroken success*. There is a word meaning 'until then', *thitherto*, but this is archaic and clumsy, and you should avoid it. Use a plainer word, such as *previously* or *earlier*.

hoard, horde A *hoard* is a stockpile, often a secret one. A *horde* is strictly a large band of marauding barbarians, but we often apply the word more generally to any large group of people who annoy us, as in *a horde of day-trippers*. The common error is writing *hoard* where *horde* is intended: ＊*hoards of football fans*. Note that *horde* can only be applied to people: you should not write ＊*hordes of junk mail*.

Hobson's choice This expression does not mean 'the lesser of two evils'. It means 'no choice at all'.

hockey In Britain and in much of the Commonwealth, *hockey* is a game played on grass. In Canada and the USA, it is a game played on ice. North Americans call the grass game *field hockey*, while everyone else calls the ice game *ice hockey*. There really is no solution to this: we are just stuck with conflicting usages.

hoi polloi This Greek expression means 'the many', 'the masses of ordinary people'. It is commonly used as *the hoi polloi*, but many people object to this, since *hoi* already means 'the'. The simplest way out is to avoid the expression altogether.

holdout In American English, a *holdout* is a person who refuses to agree to something to which most others have already agreed: *All the owners have sold their ancestral homes to summer visitors, apart from one or two holdouts*. The word is virtually unknown in British English, and should perhaps be avoided by Americans writing for a wider audience.

holistic The word is so spelled, and ＊*wholistic* is wrong.

Holland The country in western Europe is properly *the Netherlands*, and, within the Netherlands, the name *Holland* is applied only to the two provinces along the southwest coast. In informal English, *Holland* is commonly applied to the whole country, but this usage is best avoided in careful writing: the Dutch don't like it.

homey, homely The adjective *homey*, which in British English can also be spelled *homy*, means 'reminiscent of home', 'comfortable', 'cosy'. In British English, *homely* means about the same, though it emphasizes plainness and lack of sophistication more than comfort. In North America, however, *homely* is applied to people and it means 'unattractive', 'somewhat ugly'.

hominid, hominoid A *hominid* is any member of the biological family *Hominidae*. At present, this family includes four known genera: *Ardipithecus*, *Australopithecus*, *Paranthropus* and *Homo*, though a minority would split off *Zinjanthropus* as a fifth hominid genus. Within these genera, a number of species are recognized. The known member species of *Homo* are *H. habilis*, *H. rudolfensis*, *H. erectus*, *H. ergaster*, *H. heidelbergensis*, *H. neanderthalensis* and our own species, *H. sapiens*, the only surviving hominid. All of this is likely to change as new discoveries are made.

A *hominoid* is any member of the superfamily *Hominoidea*, which includes the hominids, all the living apes, and a number of extinct species.

Just to complicate things, some biologists are proposing to rearrange our family tree (or, better, family bush) in such a way as to include chimpanzees and gorillas, and possibly even orangutans, within the hominids. Whether or not this is a good decision, it does not represent the ordinary use of *hominid*.

homogeneous, homogenous The adjective *homogeneous* (five syllables) means 'having a uniform composition': *Stir the mixture until it appears homogeneous*. But the adjective *homogenous* (four syllables) is only a technical term in comparative anatomy: homogenous structures are structures in different creatures having a common evolutionary origin, like the forelegs of dogs and the wings of bats. The second should not be used when the first is intended.

homosexual This adjective means 'sexually attracted to members of the same sex', and it applies equally to women and to men, even though we have the word *lesbian* for a female homosexual. The word contains Greek *homos* 'same', and it has nothing to do with Latin *homo*, which in any case means 'human being', not 'man'.

hopefully No one objects to this word in the sense of 'in a hopeful manner': *The students are waiting hopefully for their degree results*. But there are people who object fiercely to its use as a sentence adverb meaning 'it is to be hoped that': *Hopefully, the agreement will be signed by Friday*. Almost all authorities agree that the objections are ill-founded. First, this use of *hopefully* is entirely parallel to our familiar use of other sentence adverbs, such as *frankly, mercifully, honestly, probably, surely* and *fortunately*. Second, contrary to what the critics claim, there is almost never any ambiguity in the use of *hopefully*. Note the clear difference between *Hopefully the students are waiting* (sentence adverb: 'we hope') and *The students are waiting hopefully* (simple adverb: 'in a hopeful way'). Third, like other sentence adverbs, *hopefully* is briefer and more elegant than the alternatives. Probably no one would prefer *it is fortunate that* to *fortunately*, so why should anyone prefer *it is to be hoped that* to *hopefully*?

horde See **hoard**.

hot line A *hot line* is a direct link between heads of government, used for urgent talks in emergencies. Recently the term has come to be used very widely and loosely, an example being the British prime minister John Major's notorious cones hot line for reporting difficulties with traffic cones on highways. As one wag has remarked, it appears that *hot line* is now applied freely to almost any official phone number at the other end of which you might faintly hope to find a human being, rather than the usual maddening recorded instructions to 'press two'. This development is not to be encouraged.

however When this word occurs inside a single clause, it must always be set off by a *pair* of commas. When it comes at the beginning of the second of two clauses within a single sentence, it must be preceded by a semicolon and followed by a comma. The following examples illustrate correct punctuation. *These new findings, however, cast doubt upon his hypothesis. The German forces had taken up their positions; however, their left flank was unprotected.* Any other punctuation here is wrong.

human Once this word was strictly an adjective, and people were *human beings*. Today, however, though a few commentators still object, it is entirely acceptable to use *human* as a noun, and to write *Humans first reached the Americas 13,000 years ago*. This use has the advantage of brevity.

humorous, humerus The word meaning 'amusing, comical' is *humorous*; avoid the common misspelling *humerous*, which I have even seen in a famous art gallery belonging to a distinguished university. The bone in your upper arm is a *humerus*.

hydrocarbon See **carbohydrate**.

hyperbola, hyperbole A *hyperbola* is a certain mathematical curve. But *hyperbole* is overstatement, exaggeration, as in *She is infinitely more talented than her boss*. Hyperbole should be kept under control in careful writing; for this example, see **infinite**.

hyphen The hyphen is the short horizontal bar (-). The hyphen has several uses, all of which involve separating a piece of a word from a larger unit. First, the hyphen is used when a word is broken at the end of a line. Second, it is used in citing a piece of a word in isolation: *The prefix* anti- *is strictly a prefix and should be written as one*; *This shop is family-owned and -operated*. Third, it is used in writing compound words, and words containing prefixes and suffixes, when the absence of a hyphen would make the result hard on the eye: *The judge delivered his summing-up*; *Her hobby is star-gazing*; *I refuse to wade through this semi-illiterate essay*. But we do not write a hyphen between an adjective and the following noun it modifies: for example, we write *semantic structure*, and not **semantic-structure*. Finally, and most importantly, the hyphen must be used in writing a **compound modifier**: see this entry. See also **hyphens in verbs**. A hyphen must never follow a colon; see **colon**. For more on hyphens, see chapter 6 of the *Penguin Guide to Punctuation*. Compare the **dash**.

hyphens in verbs English possesses a number of compound verbs, and these are of several kinds. Writers are frequently confused about whether these compound verbs should be hyphenated or not. But there is a simple rule. If a compound verb consists of a simple verb *followed* by another word, then no hyphen is written. But if the compound verb consists of a simple verb *preceded* by another word, a hyphen must be written (or the two may be written together, if the result is legible). For example, we write *The car speeded up*, not **The car speeded-up*, and *She made up her face*, not **She made-up her face*. But we write *We need to carbon-date these samples*, not **We need to carbon date these samples*, and *She is baby-sitting tonight* (or *She is babysitting tonight*), not **She is baby sitting tonight*. Likewise, we write *Acme wants to take over Imperial*, and not **Acme wants to take-over Imperial*, even though we write of *a takeover bid* and of *a takeover*.

I, me In a title containing no verb, should we write *I* or *me*? In fact, both are perfectly acceptable. The Rodgers and Hammerstein musical is *The King and*

I, and the film is *Withnail and I*, while Michael Moore's autobiographical book is *Roger and Me*, and a recent newspaper article was called 'Christmas and me'. On the whole, you might prefer *I* if you want to sound dignified, *me* if you want to sound informal, but neither is wrong.

After *is*, things are more complicated. Colloquial English requires *It's me*, and the alternative *It's I* sounds ridiculous to most of us. Can you imagine looking at a bad photo of yourself and exclaiming 'Good heavens! Is that really I?' No; I thought not. However, a number of people have somehow got it into their heads that there is something immoral about our native English form, and they maintain that the absurd *It's I* is 'more grammatical' or 'more logical', whatever that means. In order to avoid annoying these people, you might choose to avoid the issue altogether by recasting your sentence. For example, instead of *The last one left was me/I*, try *I was the last one left*.

See also **between you and I**.

-ic, -ical, -ically English has very many adjectives ending in *-ic* and just about as many ending in *-ical*: for example, *phonetic, semantic, despotic, pedantic* but *phonological, tyrannical, musical, typical*. It is rarely possible to predict which form is in use in an individual case, and, if you have trouble with these words, you will have to spend a good deal of time consulting dictionaries until you have learned them. And learn them you must, since your readers will be irritated by non-standard forms like *⁎syntactical* and *⁎despotical*.

Only in a very few cases are both forms equally possible, as with *rhythmic* and *rhythmical*. In a few other cases, both forms exist, but with a difference in meaning, as with **economic** and **economical**, or **historic** and **historical**.

Observe that adjectives in both *-ic* and *-ical* normally form their derived adverbs in *-ically*: *phonetic, phonetically; pedantic, pedantically; musical, musically*. Perhaps the sole exception is *public*, whose adverb is *publicly*, not *⁎publically*. Don't ask me why.

-ics Many disciplines have names ending in *-ics*: *physics, mathematics, economics, statistics, acoustics* and my own field of *linguistics*. As a rule, these words are grammatically singular: we write *Physics is a demanding field*, just as we write *Chemistry is a demanding field*. However, a few of these are treated as plurals when they denote something other than the discipline. For example, though we write *Statistics is essential knowledge for psychologists*, we write *These statistics are surprising*, since the second case does not denote the discipline, but rather some particular numbers. Likewise, we write *Acoustics is a branch of physics*, but *The acoustics in this hall are poor*.

ideogram, logogram An *ideogram* is a pictorial representation of what it stands for, such as a picture of a telephone to represent the location of telephones in an airport, or a picture of a leaping deer on a highway to warn drivers of the presence of deer. A *logogram* is an arbitrary symbol for a whole word, such as 5 for 'five' or % for 'per cent'. No language on earth is, ever has been, or can be written in ideograms. The characters used in writing Chinese and ancient Egyptian are not ideograms but logograms, and it is wrong to refer to Chinese or Egyptian characters as 'ideograms'.

idiosyncrasy Note the spelling, with that final *-sy*. The spelling *✳idiosyncracy* is wrong.

idiot savant See **savant**.

i.e. This Latin abbreviation means 'in other words'. If you use it, be sure to punctuate it correctly: awful things like *✳ie* and *✳ie.* must be avoided. But, like all Latin abbreviations, this one should not be used in the body of your text: write *in other words* or *that is*, not *i.e.* And do not confuse this with **e.g.**

ie, ei For historical reasons, we write *ie* in *believe* and *relief* but *ei* in *deceive* and *ceiling*. Keeping track of the distinction is a chore if you are a poor speller, but you must learn when to use each.

When the two vowel letters represent different syllables, there is generally no problem, since the pronunciation is a reliable guide: we write *diet* and *fiery*, but *deity* and *reify*. The problems arise when, as in most cases, the two vowel letters represent a single vowel.

The general rules are as follows.

First, after the letter C, the spelling is almost always *ei*: *receive, deceive, deceit, conceit, ceiling, perceive, conceive*, and so on.

Second, when the letters spell the sound of 'ay' (as in *day*), then the spelling is also *ei* (usually followed by *gh*): *weigh, weight, sleigh, inveigh*, and so on.

Otherwise, the spelling is usually *ie*: *believe, belief, relieve, relief, chief, bier, siege, niece*, and so on.

But there remain some exceptional spellings, and these must simply be learned. Chief among these are *either, neither, weird, foreign, seize, leisure, height, feisty* and *inveigle*. And note also the spelling of the unusual word *gneiss*, which denotes a kind of rock.

if For a counterfactual (unreal) condition in the past, standard English requires the construction illustrated by *if I had known* and *if I had had the* *chance*. These may be informally contracted to *if I'd known* and *if I'd had the chance*, but such contractions are rarely appropriate in formal writing. However, the common vernacular form illustrated by *if I'd've known* and *if I'd've had the chance* is completely unacceptable in any variety of standard English, and must be avoided. The same is true of their expanded forms, *if I would have known* and *if I would have had the chance*.

Likewise, the inverted alternative illustrated by *had I known* is always acceptable, but *had I have known* is not.

if and when This expression is beyond reproach, and occasionally necessary, but it is often used when either *if* alone or *when* alone would suffice. If you find yourself using the expression, check to see whether it is strictly necessary.

if ... was/were When the subordinator *if* introduces a counterfactual clause – that is, a clause representing something which is not true – then, in formal writing, the verb-form *were* is required, not *was*. Examples: *If I were dictator, I would ban men from wearing shorts; If Susie were not so plain-spoken, she might be a cabinet minister by now*. Spoken English commonly uses *was* here, but writers should learn this formal and possibly unnatural use of *were*.

ignore This verb cannot be followed by the connecting word *that*. It is wrong to write *He ignores that new evidence has been discovered*. Write instead *He ignores the new evidence that has been discovered*, or something similar.

ilk A small word that arouses passions out of all proportion to its size or importance. As any reference book will tell you, the traditional Scottish use is illustrated by *McTavish of that ilk*, which means either 'McTavish of (the family) McTavish' or 'McTavish of (the place) McTavish'. No one will object to this, if you ever have occasion to use it.

The problems arise because *ilk* has passed into vernacular English as a synonym for 'kind', 'sort', though often with a somewhat dismissive air about it, as in *politicians and others of that ilk* or *mass murderers of Saddam Hussein's ilk*. Some people find this normal and unremarkable. Other people hate it. Some authorities say it's OK. Other authorities warn us against it. That's enough for me: don't use the word this way unless you enjoy annoying your readers. You can always find another phrase, such as *of that stripe*, to serve your purpose, and many of your readers will remember that skunks have stripes.

ill See **sick**.

illegal, illicit The word *illegal* means 'prohibited by law'. The word *illicit* can also have this meaning, but more commonly it means 'contrary to prevailing social mores', as in an *illicit love affair*.

illegible, unreadable An *illegible* text is one in which the letters and the words cannot be made out, and hence one which cannot be interpreted. An *unreadable* text is one which is so poorly written that a reader cannot be expected to struggle through it.

illicit See **elicit, illegal**.

illusion See **delusion**.

imaginary The word is so spelled, and *⁕imaginery* is wrong.

imbue, inculcate You *imbue* a person *with* ideas: *My teachers imbued me with a strong sense of professionalism*. But you *inculcate* ideas *in* a person: *My teachers inculcated a strong sense of professionalism in me*. The mixed construction illustrated by *⁕My teachers inculcated me with a strong sense of professionalism* is widely encountered, but it has been condemned by generations of commentators, and you are advised to avoid it.

immanent See **imminent**.

immediately All varieties of English use *immediately* as an adverb: *Seeing him collapse, we immediately ran to help*. In addition, British English, though not American English, permits this word to be used as a subordinator meaning 'as soon as': *I dashed off immediately I had finished dinner*. This construction perplexes Americans and is disliked by some Britons; you would be wise to avoid it in formal writing.

immigrate See **migrate**.

imminent, immanent The common word *imminent* means 'about to happen', as in *A storm is imminent*. The rare word *immanent* means 'inherent', 'permanently present throughout the universe', and is chiefly confined to religion and metaphysics.

immolate To *immolate* something is to sacrifice it to the gods. The word does not mean 'burn'.

immoral See **amoral**.

immune Should you write *immune to* or *immune from*? Not all authorities agree here, but you are advised to write *immune to* a disease or persuasion, but *immune from* most other things, such as taxation or punishment.

impeach As the Clinton case has reminded us, to *impeach* someone is to bring charges against him or to make an accusation against him. The word is now little used in Britain, while in the US it has acquired the more specific meaning of 'bring charges against (a public official, for crimes committed in office)'. The mere bringing of the charges is the impeachment, and impeachment need not lead to conviction or to removal from office. Recall that an *unimpeachable* reputation is one against which no charges can be brought.

impersonal passive The *impersonal passive* is any construction which begins with *it is* or *it was* followed by a passive participle and *that*. Examples: *It is believed that* . . . ; *It was thought that* . . . ; *It is suspected that* . . . There is also a second form, without the *it*. For example, *It is believed that cuts are on the way* can be expressed equally impersonally as *Cuts are believed to be on the way*. Impersonal passives are extremely formal, and they should only be used in the most frostily formal writing. Elsewhere, they are out of place. In all other writing, you are advised to explain just who it is doing the believing, the thinking, the suspecting, or whatever. So, with my last example, prefer *The directors believe that cuts are on the way*, or whatever is appropriate.

imply See **infer**.

imposter, impostor The spellings *impostor* and *imposter* are both widespread and acceptable, but many authorities prefer *impostor*. The action of an impostor is *imposture*.

impractical, impracticable If something is *impractical*, it can be done, but doing it would require more time, money or effort than it's worth. If something is *impracticable*, it can't be done at all.

imprimatur This is strictly formal permission for a book to be printed or published. There is no need to trot this word out every time you need to mention approval: just write *approval*.

in-, un- The negative prefixes *in-* and *un-* have been competing in English for centuries. Of these, *in-* is spelled *im-* before *p, b* or *m, il-* before *l*, and *ir-* before *r*, while the spelling of *un-* is invariable. The general rule is that *in-* is used with words of Latin origin, as in *impossible* and *indescribable*, while *un-* is used with native English words, as in *unhappy* and *unwelcome*. However, there are very many exceptions in which *un-* is found with Latinate words, as in *uncommunicative, undistinguished* and *unintentional*. There are also curious pairs like *unequal* but *inequality* and *unstable* but *instability*. Only in a very few cases are both forms in current use, an example being *undecipherable* and *indecipherable*, though here the form with *in-* predominates.

If you are in doubt about a particular case, you must consult a good dictionary.

in case This expression properly means 'in the event that'. Examples: *Let's take an umbrella, in case it rains; She took an umbrella in case of rain.* Oddly, both British and American English have extended these words to vernacular uses which can puzzle other speakers, and which are best avoided in careful writing.

In Britain, *in case* is familiarly used to mean 'lest': ??*In ice hockey, there is a plastic screen around the rink, in case spectators are hit by the puck.* This is virtually incomprehensible to other users of English, who require . . . *lest spectators be hit by the puck* (formal) or . . . *to keep spectators from being hit by the puck* (less formal). A normal form for all speakers is *There is a nurse standing by, in case spectators are hit by the puck.*

In the USA, *in case* is often used for 'if': ??*In case it rains, we'll have to cancel the picnic.* This too sounds very strange to other users of English.

Both of these idiosyncratic usages are best avoided in careful writing.

Another distinctively American habit, largely confined to academics, is the use of *just in case* to mean 'if and only if': ??*A Basque noun phrase takes the ergative case-suffix just in case it is the subject of a transitive verb.* While now perhaps standard in American academic use, this form is best avoided in favour of the more traditional *if and only if*, which will be understood by everyone.

inchoate This word means 'just beginning to form', 'only partly developed'. It has nothing to do with chaos, and it does not mean 'chaotic' or 'incoherent'.

incompatible words The other day I came across this: *This conclusion is arguably indisputable.* By definition, there is no arguing about something which is indisputable, and it is absurd to assert that an indisputable conclusion can be argued for. As always, read what you have written, and you should not fall into gibberish like this.

incredible This word means 'beyond belief', 'not capable of being believed', and it should be used accordingly. It should not be used to mean merely 'surprising' or 'unusual', and it certainly should not be used to mean no more than 'excellent' or 'large'. Misuse of this word will quickly make your writing appear childish and make you appear semi-literate, as in this howler from a student essay: *It was incredible to the point of being beyond* *belief*. Likewise, do not write *This test is incredibly useful*: use *enormously* or something similar instead if that is what you mean, and *very* instead if that is all you mean. If you find yourself writing *incredible* or *incredibly*, check to see if the word is truly appropriate; if it is not, replace it with a more suitable word.

Finally, do not confuse *incredible* with *incredulous*, which means 'sceptical', 'reluctant to believe something', and is applied only to people.

inculcate See **imbue**.

independent This word, and its derived noun *independence*, are so spelled, with E: avoid the common errors *independant* and *independance*.

in-depth These days, it appears, no analysis, no survey, no investigation deserves mention or respect unless it is an *in-depth* analysis, or whatever. Before you write this word for the eight hundredth wearisome time, recall that English has other modifiers, such as *careful, thorough, detailed, exhaustive* and *scrupulous*. Might one of these serve your purpose?

index, indexes, indices When an *index* is an alphabetical listing at the back of a book, its plural is *indexes*. In all other uses, and particularly in mathematical senses, the plural is *indices*.

India, Indian Formerly the name *India* was applied to the entire huge territory lying between Afghanistan, the Himalayas and Burma. Today, however, *India* is applied only to the Republic of India, and the whole territory is called *the Indian subcontinent*, or occasionally just *the Subcontinent*.

With *Indian*, things are more complicated. It is no longer appropriate to apply this label to anyone other than someone who lives in, or originates from, the country of India. Indians, Pakistanis, Bangladeshis, Nepalis and Sri Lankans collectively can only be called *Asians* – hardly an ideal term, since Thais, Chinese, Koreans, Japanese and others are also Asians in the ordinary sense of the word.

As for the Americas, it is now often seen as politically incorrect to apply the name *Indians* to the indigenous inhabitants, and the term *native Americans* is widely preferred.

Indian English The variety of English used in India and in the Indian subcontinent generally. Indian English is distinguished not only by an unusually large proportion of localized vocabulary, such as *crore* '10,000' and *dacoit* 'bandit', but also by a number of grammatical features not found in standard British and American English, such as the use of the progressive with stative verbs, as in *He is not knowing that*. Opinion in the Subcontinent is divided on the status of these numerous local forms, but it may be that India is closer than any other English-speaking country to developing its own distinct version of standard English, contrasting with the existing British and American versions.

indicate This verb means 'suggest rather strongly', and it should not be used as a coy synonym of *say*. It is fine to write *The Chancellor indicated that he would raise petrol taxes* if what you mean is that he gave clear hints that he would do this. But you should not write this if the Chancellor merely asserted, in so many words, that petrol taxes would be going up. Doing so is coy and pompous.

Furthermore, do not write *indicated* in order to express 'advisable' or 'necessary'.

Indo-European The great language family to which English belongs is called the *Indo-European* family, or *IE* for short. It was formerly also called the *Indo-Germanic* family and the *Aryan* family, but both these other names are dead. The remote and unrecorded language which is the ancestor of the family is called *Proto-Indo-European*, or *PIE* for short. Do not write *Indo-European* when you mean *Proto-Indo-European*. See also **Aryan**.

in effect See **effectively**.

in excess of Don't use this. Write *more than £50 million*, not *✳in excess of £50 million*, which is wordy and pretentious.

in fact This is always written as two words: the spelling *✳infact* is never acceptable.

infamous This word means 'disgraceful', 'worthy of hatred'. It is not directly related to *famous*, and something which is infamous is not necessarily well known. The Serbian atrocities in Kosovo were infamous even before anyone outside had heard of them. The word does not mean 'famous' or 'celebrated', and it certainly does not mean 'quaint'. Compare **notorious**.

infer, imply When you *imply* something, you suggest indirectly that it is true. When you *infer* something, you conclude that it is true. Thus, implying is usually done by a speaker or a writer, while inferring is always done by a listener or a reader, though note that a state of affairs can also imply something. Here are examples of correct use: *The Prime Minister implied that a decision was imminent* (the PM hinted at such a conclusion); *Their silence* *implies that they will not object; The authors infer from their findings that teenage girls take up smoking in order to declare sexual maturity and sexual availability* (the authors draw this conclusion). The common error here is to write *infer* when *imply* is intended: it is wrong to write ✱*The Prime Minister inferred that a decision was imminent* if you mean that the PM was suggesting this. Compare **insinuate**.

infinite This word means 'uncountably or immeasurably vast', and it should be used with caution, especially in its adverbial form *infinitely*. It is usually better to write *vastly more dangerous* rather than *??infinitely more dangerous*, since the latter phrasing is unlikely to be strictly accurate. Note also that *infinitesimal* is usually preferable to *??infinitely small*.

inflammable, flammable The word *inflammable* means 'capable of burning', and it derives from *inflame* 'set on fire'. However, so many people interpreted the word, because of its initial *in-*, as meaning 'not capable of burning' that insurance companies and consumer groups pleaded with manufacturers to do something, and the result was the new word *flammable*, which also means 'capable of burning'. In this literal sense, then, you may use either form, though a few conservative speakers will still insist on *inflammable*. Something which does not burn is *non-inflammable* (or sometimes *non-flammable*).

in front of This compound preposition is always written as three words, and ✱*infront of* is wrong.

ingenious, ingenuous, disingenuous The word *ingenious* means 'extremely clever', and it may be applied either to a person or to a plan or a device constructed by such a person. But *ingenuous* means 'naive', 'easily deceived' when applied to a person and 'naive, foolish' when applied to a plan or an action. The opposite of the second, *disingenuous*, means 'calculating', 'deceptive', 'slightly dishonest'.

ingratiate The only way of using this word is as follows: *She ingratiated herself with her boss*. Constructions like ✱*She ingratiated her boss* are not acceptable.

inimitable, inimical The word *inimitable* means 'unique', 'not capable of being imitated'. It has been so vastly overused in show business that it is now best avoided. The word *inimical* means 'hostile'. The second should not be used when the first is intended.

initialisms See **acronyms**.

inning, innings In baseball, the principal unit of play is an *inning*; in cricket, it is an *innings*. The plural is *innings* in both cases. In baseball, though not in cricket, an inning is divided into two parts called *half-innings*: the *top half* and the *bottom half*.

inoculate Note the spelling, with no double letters.

input The noun *input* is a technical term in several disciplines, especially computing. But now it is very widely used, especially in bureaucratic writing, to represent anything from 'contribution' to 'comment', as in *I would like your input on this*. Though probably all authorities now accept this use as standard, it will still greatly annoy many conservative readers, and in this sense the word is unquestionably vastly overused and lacking in explicitness. Note also that this is one of two words banned a few years ago by the Provost of the University of Cincinnati, who was sick of reading it every twelve seconds. Try to avoid it in favour of a more explicit word. See also **feedback**.

inquire See **enquire**.

insinuate To *insinuate* something is to suggest it indirectly, by means of hints or innuendo. Only a human being can insinuate anything: it is wrong to write *These results insinuate that our current model needs revision*. Use *imply* instead.

in situ This Latin phrase is a technical term in archaeology and palaeontology, where an artefact or a fossil is *in situ* if it is still lying just where it was discovered, and has not been moved. The phrase has a few other technical uses, but it has no place in everyday English, and it should certainly not be used merely to express 'in place' or 'in position'.

intellectual As an adjective, this word causes few problems. It means 'pertaining to, or requiring the use of, the intellect, as opposed to the emotions'. For example, *an intellectual pursuit* is a pastime demanding sobriety, intelligence, alertness and analytical skill. It is the use of *intellectual* as a noun that causes the problems. There is almost no agreement about how an intellectual might be distinguished from anybody else. Some of us use the word as a compliment: an intellectual is a profound thinker. But others of us use the term as an insult: an intellectual is somebody who is hopelessly out of touch with everyday life. It is best not to use the noun at all, since you will very likely be misunderstood.

intercourse Traditionally this word means no more than 'dealings between people'. Jane Austen could therefore write of the very genteel Miss Anne Elliot and her former suitor Captain Wentworth that *they had no intercourse but what the commonest civility required*. More recently, however, the expression *sexual intercourse* has been created as a delicate way of saying *copulation*. This in turn is now commonly shortened to *intercourse*, and as a result it is difficult to use the term in any sense other than the sexual one without producing sniggers: consider the effect of Jane Austen's sentence upon a modern reader, and consider what is likely to happen if you write *The Serbs and the Croats have resumed normal intercourse*. It is best to use another word.

interface This is a technical term in chemistry and some other disciplines. Since the 1960s, it has been a vogue word, invoked ceaselessly to mean 'connection', 'relation', 'discussion', 'debate', 'conflict', and almost anything else a sloppy writer might have in mind where two things, two groups or two positions are involved. It is perhaps less fashionable now than formerly, but it has not vanished. Don't use it.

intermittent This adjective means 'on and off', 'happening now and again, but not continuously'. For example, an intermittent fault in your TV set is one that comes and goes. The word does not mean 'intermediate', 'in-between', and it should not be so used.

internalize The verb *internalize* is a technical term in the social sciences, but it should be avoided in ordinary prose, where it is usually inexplicit and pretentious. Children *learn* their first language; they don't *internalize* it.

in the range of See **on the order of**.

into Spoken English often uses *in* for *into*: ✱*She fell in the water*; ✱*She ran in the house*. This is out of place in careful writing. Write *She fell into the water* and *She ran into the house*.

The word *into* can never be written as ✱*in to*. However, *in to* must be written when the *in* and the *to* are unrelated, as in *She dropped in to see me*, which means 'She dropped in for the purpose of seeing me.'

Colloquial English uses *into* to mean 'involved in' or 'interested in', as in *She's into feng shui*. But this popular use has no place in formal writing.

invidious When you are in an *invidious* position, you are in a position in which, regardless of what you do, you are bound to upset somebody, and an invidious job is therefore a job which few people would want to take. In spite of its etymology, the word does not mean 'envious', but rather 'unenviable'. A job or a position can be described as invidious, but a person cannot be. However, an invidious remark is a remark which is somewhat offensive.

invigorate See **enervate**.

invoke See **evoke**.

Ireland, Eire The island is *Ireland*. The country occupying most of it is *the Republic of Ireland*, which for short is called *Ireland*, or, when the context makes the meaning clear, *the Republic*. The name *Eire*, once used officially, is now obsolete, and should not be used except in a suitable historical context. The smaller part in the northeast is *Northern Ireland*; see **Ulster** for some discussion.

Irish See **Gaelic**.

Irish names See **Scottish and Irish names**.

ironically This word is very frequently misused. Narrowly, an *ironic* remark is one characterized by good-natured sarcasm, one which means the opposite of what it says; by extension, an *ironic* event is an incongruous event, one at odds with what we might have expected. But *ironically* should not be used to mean no more than 'curiously' or 'engagingly' or 'by an odd coincidence': it is bad style to write *Ironically, Botham scored his final run on the same ground on which he had scored his first run. There is nothing ironic about this.

By the way, the related adjective is *ironic*, not *ironical.

irregardless There is no such word: write *regardless*, not *irregardless.

-ise See **-ize**.

is, is Curiously frequent these days is the blunder illustrated by the following example: **The only thing we need to do is, is to minute our response*. There is no justification for repeating the word *is*: write *The only thing we need to do is to minute our response*.

Islamic See **Muslim**.

island constraints I have borrowed this technical term from linguistics to introduce a certain problem for which no other label is readily available. The following sentence is normal: *John has been sent to prison, and his mother wants to visit him there*. Here *there* refers to *prison*, which is fine. But the next version is not fine: **John has been imprisoned, and his mother wants to visit* *him there*. This is no good, because *prison* is now wrapped up inside the word *imprisoned*, and so it is not available to be picked out by a word like *there*.

is when, is where You should never use either of these phrasings when you are giving a definition. Awful things like *A suffix is when you add something to the end of a word* and *Statutory rape is where a man has sex with an underage girl* are simply illiterate; they must never be used in careful writing. Write instead *A suffix is an affix added to the end of a word* and *Statutory rape is sex with an underage girl*. Failure to master this will stamp you for ever as semi-literate.

If the awfulness of this construction is not obvious to you, consider another example: *In the Basque Country, a* txapeldun *is when they award a trophy to the winner of a competition*. Now: what do you suppose a *txapeldun* is? Is it the trophy? Is it the person who receives the trophy? Is it the ceremony of handing over the trophy? Is it the competition? Can you tell? No? Do you see why this construction is so hopeless as a way of defining or explaining anything?

(OK; the answer: it's the person who receives the trophy. Now try rewriting my awful sentence in good English.)

its, it's Illogically enough, given the regular use of the apostrophe in writing possessives, the possessive form of *it* is *its*, as in *The bull lowered its head*. There are few quicker ways of persuading your reader that you are illiterate than writing things like *The bull lowered it's head*. The form *it's* is properly used only as a contraction for *it is* or *it has*, as in *It's raining* and *It's been a long time*. Note also that no such form as *its'* exists in English.

Italian names Italian personal names rarely cause problems for English-speakers. But it is worth noting that medieval and Renaissance Italians often had no surname. For example, *Leonardo* had no other name, and our custom of calling him *Leonardo da Vinci* comes about only because he was born in the town of Vinci. He can never be referred to as *da Vinci*.

-ize, -ise There are two groups of words here, and these should not be confused.

The first group consists of words which are always spelled with *-ise* in all varieties of English. The most frequent verbs in this group are *advertise, advise, apprise, chastise, circumcise, comprise, compromise, despise, devise, disguise, excise, exercise, improvise, supervise, surmise, surprise* and *televise*, to which we may add the nouns *demise, enterprise, franchise* and *merchandise*, some of which are occasionally used as verbs. These words do not contain the Greek suffix *-ize* and may never be spelled with *-ize*. British writers attempting to use American spelling sometimes slip up here and write, for example, **advertize*, which is never acceptable.

The second, and much larger, group consists of verbs containing the Greek suffix *-ize*. Among these are *realize, civilize, ostracize, jeopardize, organize* and *trivialize*; there are far too many to list here, and new ones are coined almost at will, like *hospitalize, finalize* and *prioritize*. These words *must* be spelled with *-ize* in American English. In British English, the spelling with *-ize* is traditional, and is still preferred in many conservative quarters, for example at the Oxford University Press. But the newer spelling in *-ise* is now widespread in Britain and is preferred in other quarters. British writers may use whichever spelling they prefer, unless they are writing for a publishing house which insists upon one or the other.

Whichever spelling you prefer, you must, of course, be consistent, and use it exclusively, not only with the verbs but with their derived nouns like *realization* and *civilization*.

There is a complication with the verb *exorcize, exorcise*. Historically, this word contains the suffix *-ize*, and so it should be spelled *exorcize* in the style that uses *-ize*. However, many people no longer perceive this as containing the suffix, and so it is sometimes spelled *exorcise* even in the style with *-ize*.

Note also the unusual word *capsize*, which is spelled *-ize* in all varieties.

See also **-yze, -yse**.

jail, gaol The old form *gaol* is now little used in Britain, and it is completely dead in the USA. Write *jail*, and also *jailer*, as opposed to *gaoler*.

Japanese names Japanese is not written in the roman alphabet (or in any alphabet). Consequently, we need to have a system for rendering Japanese words and names into English. Several such systems have been devised. The two most important are the Romaji and the Yale system. The Romaji, which is preferred in Japan, has the advantage of making the pronunciation of consonants more obvious to English-speakers. Consequently, the Romaji is commonly used for ordinary purposes, except that the double vowels of Romaji are frequently omitted. Thus, for example, we write *Tokyo* where strict Romaji has *Tookyoo*, and *sumo* for Romaji *suumo*. The Yale system was devised by linguists and is superior for linguistic purposes, since it exhibits the structure of the language more clearly: for example, a number of regular verbs remain regular in the Yale system but appear to be irregular in Romaji. Yale departs noticeably from Romaji in the spelling of consonants: for example, it writes *tunami* for familiar *tsunami* and *Huzi* for *Fuji*.

jargon This word has been used in a large number of rather different senses. Here we focus on just two.

First, *jargon* is the technical terminology of particular disciplines. Every professional group, from lorry drivers to lawyers, from electrical engineers to etymologists, has its own special technical terminology. It is normal to use the specialist jargon of your field when you are writing only for your specialist colleagues, but you should refrain from doing the same when writing for a wider audience. For example, in writing for my own colleagues in historical linguistics, I might write the following: *Basque* arrain *'fish', the modern reflex of Pre-Basque* ✻arrani, *results not from metathesis but from intervocalic nasal loss with concomitant nasalization of adjacent vowels, followed by unpacking of the nasality into a following segment.* This makes perfect sense to a historical linguist, but probably not to many other people. Whatever your job, and however much time you commonly spend in writing jargon-ridden prose for your professional colleagues, you must refrain from specialist jargon when you are writing for other people. If you do not, you are wasting your time in writing at all, for your readers will not understand you.

Second, the word *jargon* is now often applied to a style of writing which is pompous and pretentious, which deliberately rejects plain words in favour of fancy ones, whether in the hope of dazzling or intimidating the reader, whether with the clear intention of deceiving the hapless reader, whether with the hardly less dishonest intention of impressing that reader with the writer's importance, or whether merely in the hope of disguising the fact that the writer has nothing of interest or value to say. Other names for the same thing are *gobbledygook* and (with apologies to those sociologists who can write in English) *sociologist-speak*.

All of us are familiar with jargon of this kind. Here is a sample, taken from a standard customer contract used by a company which sells goods by mail order:

10.4. Notwithstanding that the property in all Products to be delivered to the Customer by the Company shall remain vested in the Company until the Company has received payment in full, the risk of damage to or loss of all or any such goods shall pass to the Customer forthwith upon delivery or deemed delivery thereof to the Customer and as from such date of delivery or deemed delivery the Customer shall be liable to pay to the Company the contract price for such Products whether or not the same are damaged or lost prior to the dates that the property therein shall pass to the Customer.

What do you suppose this largely unpunctuated paragraph means? After much study, I *think* it probably means this:

If you buy something from us, you don't own it until we get your money. However, if it's broken when you get it, or if you never get it at all, you have to pay us anyway.

You may draw your own conclusions about the company's reasons for preferring the jargon-ridden version of its contract. But companies and their lawyers are hardly the only users of jargon. The US Air Force, for example, will sometimes admit to *inflicting collateral damage*, but it never admits to *killing innocent civilians*.

You might reasonably expect that academic scholars, who are supposed to be dedicated to finding out the truth about things, would refrain from indulging in such pompous and dishonest wordiness. But you would be disappointed. In our day, large sections of the academic community have been taken over by pretentious wannabees who are all too eager to disguise their lack of interesting ideas with reams of unintelligible verbiage. Here is a modest sample, the name of whose author I will kindly conceal:

These new approaches have also traced the inscription of sexual meanings in widely scattered fields of cultural production, while detecting the inscription of diverse cultural meanings in the practices and discourses of sex . . . The project ultimately has an oppositional design: its purpose is to map more precisely the available avenues of cultural resistance to contemporary institutional and discursive practices of sex.

Did you follow that? No? Any idea what *cultural production* might be? Any thoughts on how cultural production, whatever it is, could bring about the *inscription of sexual meanings*? How do you suppose a project with *an oppositional design* differs from other projects? And what's all this about *institutional practices of sex*? Kinky sex in jails or universities? And how can the practices of sex (whatever they are) be *discursive*? This word normally means 'jumping from one topic to another', 'failing to stick to the point'.

People who write like this – and, sadly, there are now thousands of them in universities – should be encouraged to give up writing altogether, and save a few trees.

jejune This word means 'thin', 'insipid', 'unsatisfying', and it is so spelled: the spelling *jejeune* is wrong. In any case, this is not a word which you are likely to need very often, since more familiar synonyms exist. About a century ago, by some kind of misunderstanding, the word acquired a new meaning of 'childish', 'puerile'. Most authorities are still uncomfortable with this new sense, and you are advised to avoid it.

Jew, Jewish, Judaism, Judaic The religion espoused by Abraham and Moses is *Judaism*. A follower of this religion is a *Jew*, and the derived adjective is *Jewish*. Because of long-standing prejudice, many non-Jews, and even a few Jews, are nervous about using the word *Jew*, but the word is in fact respectful and inoffensive.

The adjective *Judaic* means 'pertaining to Jewish religion, culture or traditions'. The derived noun is *Judaica*.

However, it is *extremely* offensive to use *✳Jew* or *✳jew* to mean 'tightfisted or unscrupulous person', or to use *✳jew down* to mean 'bargain unfairly', 'cheat'. It is also considered offensive to write *✳Jewess* for a Jewish woman.

Opinion varies with *jew's-harp*, the name of a rustic musical instrument held between the lips. Though it is not obvious why this name should be offensive, some authorities recommend *mouth harp*.

See also **Hebrew**, **Yiddish**.

jewellery, jewelry Only the first is acceptable in British English, while the second is preferred in American English.

jibe, jive The prepositional verb *jibe with* is an informal expression meaning 'correspond to', 'agree with', 'match': *These data don't jibe with our earlier results*. The expression is a little too colloquial for the most formal kinds of writing. But *jive* is not a verb at all: it is a noun denoting a kind of jazz, or the argot associated with this. It is wrong to write *✳jive with* when you mean *jibe with*.

journal It is now unusual to apply this word to a newspaper, daily or otherwise, and you are advised not to use the word in such a way. Only two senses are now current in non-specialist use: a book in which a person regularly records events or thoughts (not necessarily every day), and a periodical publication devoted to reporting scholarly or scientific work.

judgement, judgment Both spellings are acceptable in all varieties of English, though British English prefers *judgement* and American English prefers *judgment*.

judicial, judicious The word *judicial* means 'pertaining to judges or to the courts', as in *a judicial review* or *a judicial separation*. In contrast, *judicious* has nothing to do with the law: it means 'prudent', 'carefully considered', 'showing good judgement', as in *a judicious choice* and *judicious advice*.

jurist, juror A *jurist* is a person who is knowledgeable about the law, especially one who writes about legal matters. The word is not a fancy equivalent for *judge*. A *juror* (note the spelling) is a member of a jury.

just deserts The phrase is so spelled, with only a single S in the second word. It may help to remember that your *deserts* are what you *deserve*. The phrase has nothing to do with *dessert*, the sweet course served at the end of a meal.

just in case See **in case**.

kalends See **calends**.

Kansas, Kansas City The name of the American state is *Kansas*; the name of the city in Missouri is *Kansas City*. British writers should avoid the error of writing *Kansas* when they mean *Kansas City*: the city is never called *Kansas*.

karat See **carat**.

karma In certain religious and mystical systems, this word has a more or less specific meaning, though the meaning differs substantially from one system to another. As an ordinary English word, it is almost entirely devoid of identifiable meaning, and it represents no more than another piece of California psychobabble. Avoid it in favour of some more explicit word, such as *destiny* or *atmosphere*.

Kashmir See **cashmere**.

Kelt, Keltic See **Celt**.

kerb See **curb**.

ketchup, catchup, catsup In British English, *ketchup* is now the only form in use. American English still recognizes all three forms, though *ketchup* is most frequent and is recommended for American writers, while *catsup* is losing ground and *catchup* is almost obsolete.

key Especially in journalistic prose, the noun *key* is often used as a modifier meaning 'most important', 'central' or 'crucial': *a key appointment*, *the key play of the match*, *a key figure*. This use is not to everyone's taste, and might well be avoided in careful writing. In any case, the word is not an adjective, and should not be treated like one: locutions like *a very key appointment* and *That decision was key* are not at present regarded as standard English.

Khrushchev The name of the former Soviet leader is so spelled in English. Such versions as *Krushchev* and *Khruschev* are wrong, and *Khruschchov*, while not wrong, should be avoided.

Kilimanjaro The African mountain is always so called: do not write
*Mount Kilimanjaro.

kind, sort Though very common in speech, locutions like *these kind of
and *these sort of are never acceptable in formal writing. The words *kind*
and *sort* are grammatically singular, and should be treated accordingly: write
either *this kind of* or *these kinds of.*

kinda, sorta These colloquial forms, though common in speech and sometimes seen in representations of speech, are strictly out of order in even
moderately formal writing. Write out *kind of* and *sort of* in full if you use
these at all, but note that both of these are inappropriate in careful writing
in the sense of 'somewhat', 'rather'. Write *It was rather good*, not *It was
kind of good*, or, still worse, *It was kinda good.*

kinky Not so long ago, this word meant 'quirky', 'idiosyncratic', 'eccentric'.
However, it is now so strongly established as a label for deviant sexual
practices that it can hardly be used in any other sense, except perhaps in
kinky hair, which seems to raise no sniggers. Use *quirky* or *eccentric* instead.

kith and kin Your *kin*, of course, are your relatives. Your *kith* were originally your friends. The now-fossilized expression *kith and kin* therefore once
meant 'friends and relatives', but, because of the disappearance of *kith* in all
other contexts, it has come to be understood as merely 'relatives'. Rather
than engage in tiresome discussions of proper use, I advise you to forget this
archaic cliché altogether. Write *relatives* if that is what you mean, and write
friends and relatives if that is what you mean.

knickers A word capable of causing unintended giggles. In Britain, *knickers*
are women's underpants, called *panties* in the USA. In the USA, however,
knickers (also *knickerbockers*) are baggy trousers gathered just below the knee,
of the type once commonly worn by golfers.

knock up Another phrase which can produce giggles and confusion. In
Britain, if you *knock up* a woman, you awaken her in the morning by banging
on her bedroom door. In the USA, if you knock up a woman, you make her
pregnant. The American use is now beginning to be heard in Britain.

knot In nautical usage, a *knot* is 'a nautical mile per hour', a unit of speed,
and not 'a nautical mile', a unit of distance. It is accordingly wrong to write
thirty knots per hour: write *thirty knots.*

Knut, Knute See **Canute**.

Koran, Qur'an For everyday purposes, the preferred spelling of the name of the Muslim holy book is *Koran*. In scholarly work, however, the more accurate rendering *Qur'an* is often appropriate. The compromise version *Quran* is also found, but is not recommended in any context, while ✽*Qu'ran* is simply a blunder.

Korean names Koreans give their names with the surname first, followed by the given name, which usually comes in two parts. So, for example, *Kim Jong Il* becomes *Mr Kim* or *Kim* at a later mention. But Koreans who live in the west or deal with the west often turn their names round to conform to the western custom, so watch for this. Many of these, however, thoughtfully join their given names with a hyphen, or even write them solid, so that *Lee Soo Man* may present himself as *Soo-Man Lee* or as *Sooman Lee*. A Korean who is a Christian will additionally take a western Christian name, and so our Mr Lee may present himself as *Noah Lee*.

Only a handful of surnames are used in Korea, with the ubiquitous *Kim* by far the most frequent.

krona, krone Four Scandinavian countries have the crown as their unit of currency, but the local names differ. In Sweden, the unit is the *krona*, plural *kronor*. In Iceland, it is also the *krona*, but with the plural *kronur*. In both Norway and Denmark, it is the *krone*, plural *kroner*. Unless you are stuck without a reference book, it is best to use the correct local form, rather than falling back on *crown(s)*.

kudos This word means 'praise', and it is grammatically singular, with no plural. Write *this kudos*, not ✽*these kudos*. There is no such word as ✽*kudo*.

laissez faire, laisser faire Both spellings are acceptable, but most authorities prefer the form with z: *laissez faire*. As a preposed modifier, this must, of course, be hyphenated: *a* laissez-faire *economy*.

lama, llama A *lama* is a Buddhist monk in certain Buddhist countries. A *llama* is a South American animal related to the camel.

lambast(e) The American form is *lambaste*. Some British sources give *lambaste* as the preferred British form, too, but, in practice, *lambast* is much more frequent.

language, writing system You should not write *language* when you mean *writing system*. It is wrong to write ✽*The Chinese language uses thousands of characters*. Chinese is a spoken language, and it uses no characters at all: it is the Chinese writing system which uses thousands of characters.

language names In English, the name of a language is always written with an initial capital. We write *English*, *French*, *Greek* and *Chinese*, not *english, *french, *greek and *chinese. Only in rare circumstances is it necessary to identify a language name as such: write *English has no grammatical gender*, not *??The English language has no grammatical gender*. While not wrong, this last version is needlessly wordy, and tiresome when repeated: *??The English language has taken many words from the French language*. See also **nationality words**.

languor The word is so spelled in all varieties of English, and neither *langor nor *languour is acceptable anywhere.

largess, largesse Both forms are acceptable everywhere, but *largesse*, with a final E, is by far the more usual form, and is recommended.

larva The singular is *larva*; the plural is *larvae*.

last, latest, **previous** These words are sometimes interchangeable, but not always. First, of course, *last* alone can mean 'final': *Wilhelm II was the last emperor of Germany*. Both *last* and *latest* can mean 'most recent': Spielberg's newest film may be called either his *last* film or his *latest* film. This means, of course, that *Spielberg's last film* is potentially very ambiguous: it can mean either 'the final film that Spielberg ever made' or merely 'Spielberg's most recent film'. Moreover, with reference to his most recent film, *Spielberg's last film* can also mean 'the film before his most recent one'. Often the context is enough to distinguish these, but you should be very careful about using *last* in writing: if you can detect any possibility of misunderstanding, choose a different word.

If the point of reference is not the present, then normally *previous* is required, and *last* is unacceptable. If you have just mentioned *Raiders of the Lost Ark*, then *Spielberg's previous film* means the one he did just before *Raiders*, and *Spielberg's last film* is improper in this sense.

Latin abbreviations English recognizes a number of Latin abbreviations for familiar English words and phrases. Among the commonest are **e.g.** 'for example', **i.e.** 'in other words', **cf.** 'compare', **viz.** 'namely', **etc.** 'and other things' and **et al.** 'and other people', though many others exist, such as *sc.* 'which means'.

The principal rule for using Latin abbreviations is simple: *don't use them*. It is very poor style to splatter your text with these things: they all have simple English equivalents which should usually be preferred. It is far more important to make your writing easy to read than to save a few seconds in writing it. The only Latin abbreviations which are always acceptable in a text are **A.D.** and **a.m.** and **p.m.**

If you *do* find yourself using these abbreviations, there are several important things to bear in mind.

First, make sure you choose the right one. Far too often, a writer slips up by writing *✻i.e.* when he means 'for example', *✻e.g.* when he means 'in other words', *✻cp.* when he means 'compare', and, most frequently of all, *✻cf.* when he means 'consult', 'refer to', 'see', for which the Latin abbreviation is *v.*

Second, make sure you punctuate the abbreviation correctly. No punctuation other than what is shown above is acceptable for the common abbreviations, and ghastly but frequent errors like *✻e.t.c.*, *✻ect.*, *✻eg.* and *✻et. al.* will make your prose look illiterate. Today a few publishers make a practice of omitting all full stops from these abbreviations, and hence of requiring *✻eg* and *✻ie*, but this practice will infuriate many of your readers, and you should not imitate it.

Third, don't forget to punctuate the rest of your sentence correctly: using a Latin abbreviation does not relieve you of the responsibility of punctuating your sentence. Here is an example of good style: *Several British universities were founded in the Victorian era; for example, the University of Manchester was founded in 1851.* The following version is worse: *??Several British universities were founded in the Victorian era; e.g., the University of Manchester was founded in 1851.* But it is disastrously wrong to write this: *✻Several British universities were founded in the Victorian era e.g. the University of Manchester was founded in 1851.* Here the necessary punctuation has been lost.

If you avoid Latin abbreviations, you will automatically avoid all of these pitfalls.

Latin America See **South America**.

Latin names A Roman citizen normally had three names, but the full form is used in English only in reference books or, sometimes, when introducing a character for the first time in a history. Otherwise, usually only one name is used. For example, the general *Publius Cornelius Scipio* is usually known as *Scipio*, and *Marcus Tullius Cicero* as *Cicero*. But there are exceptions: for example, *Gaius Julius Caesar* is known to us as *Julius Caesar*, though often merely as *Caesar*.

In some cases, the Latin ending *-us* or *-ius* is customarily omitted in English. For example, the historian *Titus Livius* is *Livy*, the historian *Gaius Sallustius Crispus* is *Sallust*, and the emperor *Publius Aelius Hadrianus* is *Hadrian*.

The emperors often took additional names, often entirely new names, but usually we use only one in English. For example, the original *Lucius Domitius Ahenobarbus* took the throne name *Nero Claudius Caesar Drusus Germanicus*, but we call him *Nero*. On the other hand, the emperor *Marcus Aurelius Antoninus* is known to us as *Marcus Aurelius*.

If in doubt, consult a good reference book.

latter The words *the latter* mean 'the second of two' and nothing else. If you have just listed three or more items, you cannot refer to any of them as *the latter*: this is rather like trying to refer to three or more things as *both*. And, if you have mentioned only one thing, this cannot be *the latter* either.

In any case, be careful with the phrases *the former* and *the latter*. Even when you are using these correctly, you can easily weary your reader by sending him back to what he has already read, in order to find out just what you're talking about.

launch In standard English, this verb is strictly transitive. So, the following example is wrong: *✻Channel 4 News launched in 1982*. The required form is *Channel 4 News was launched in 1982*.

lawn tennis See **tennis**.

lay See **lie**.

lead, led The verb *lead* has the past tense *led*. The common error here is to write *✻lead* for the past tense: *✻The soldier lead us into a hut*, instead of *The soldier led us into a hut*. The verb *lead* works just like *read* in pronunciation, but not in spelling. Don't ask me why.

leadership This word variously means 'the quality of being a good leader', 'the office of leader' and 'the period during which someone serves as leader'. It does not mean 'leaders': write *the Chinese leaders*, not *✻the Chinese leadership*.

leading question A *leading question* is not a hostile or intimidating question. Rather, it is a question asked in such a way as to try to obtain a particular answer wanted by the questioner. A lawyer who asks a witness in court *You had a good view of the incident, didn't you?* or *You didn't have a good view of the incident, did you?* is asking a leading question, hoping to extract the answer *yes* in the first case, *no* in the second. American and British courts prohibit leading questions. In this case, the neutral question is *Did you have a good view of the incident?*

leastways, leastwise Both forms are now archaic in standard English, and neither should be written. Use *at least* instead.

least worst This informal expression is best confined to journalistic and jocular prose: in formal English, write *least bad*.

leave, let These verbs overlap in function to some extent. However, though colloquial English is often different, standard written English strongly prefers *let* in the senses of 'allow', as in *Let him go!*, and 'stop holding', as in *Let go of the handle!* Here *leave* is widely regarded as non-standard, and should be avoided. However, both *Let me alone!* and *Leave me alone!* are generally regarded as standard in the sense of 'Stop bothering me', though only *leave* is possible in cases like *They went on holiday and left their children at home alone.*

Lebanon See *the* in names of countries.

lecher, lechery These words are so spelled, with no T, and *letcher* and *letchery* are wrong. However, the colloquial verb meaning 'lust (after)' may be spelled either *lech* or *letch*, but this word is rarely appropriate in formal writing.

lectern, podium, dais A *lectern* is a tall, narrow desk on which you place your notes when you are speaking in public. A *podium*, or *dais*, is a platform raised somewhat above the floor level upon which the lectern is placed and upon which you stand while speaking.

lectureship This is the ordinary word for the post held by a university lecturer. The variant *lecturership*, which might seem more logical, is almost never used, except at Oxford University, where it appears to be preferred.

legend, legendary A *legend* is a largely fanciful story, or series of stories, about the past which may have some basis in fact. King Arthur is a good example of a legendary figure: there may well have been a historical Arthur who did something or other fairly important, but the tales of King Arthur and the Knights of the Round Table are entirely medieval fabrications.

The adjective *legendary* may safely be extended to a real person who has achieved such outstanding success in some field as to appear almost larger than life. Good examples are the cricketer Don Bradman, the baseball player Babe Ruth, and Napoleon Bonaparte. But it is out of order to apply the label *legendary* to a real person who is merely well known, or who is known only to a small group of specialists. The Egyptian Pharaoh Peribsen is a well-documented historical figure. Nobody apart from Egyptologists has ever heard of him, but this fact does not make him legendary.

lend, loan In formal British English, the verb is *lend* while the noun is *loan*: *She lent me some money* but *She gave me a loan*. In American English, however, *loan* is freely used as a verb in all but the most frostily formal styles: *She loaned me some money*. In fact, the American use continues an earlier pattern which has largely disappeared in Britain. But the verb *loan* is becoming increasingly frequent in Britain, above all in descriptions of museum displays: *This picture has been loaned by the Cincinnati Museum.*

lengthy There are people who object to this word, regarding it as no more than a clumsy way of writing *long*. But the word deserves its place in the sense of 'tediously long', 'excessively long': *a long book* may be a splendid book, but *a lengthy book* is overly long and rather wearisome to read.

lèse majesté, lese majesty Both forms are in regular use. But note that the phrase, which is literally 'wounded majesty', means only 'an affront to the dignity of an important person'. It does not properly mean 'treason' or 'rebellion'.

less See **fewer**.

let See **leave**.

let alone, much less These two expressions are sometimes used backward. When you write *not X, let alone Y* or *not X, much less Y*, then Y must be something more ambitious, more difficult or more spectacular than X. It is fine to write *He can't order a cup of coffee in French, let alone converse in the language*, but it is wrong to write *He can't converse in French, let alone order a cup of coffee in the language*. The phrases *let alone* and *much less* do not mean 'not even'.

levy, levee A *levy* is a tax or a fine, or (in historical writing) a requirement that a community should provide soldiers. A *levee* is a formal reception, and, in American English, an embankment along a river.

liaise The bureaucratic verb *liaise*, as in *You should liaise with the standards committee*, is best avoided in most types of writing. Use *consult* or *confer with* instead.

libel, slander The distinction is easy in principle: *libel* is written, while *slander* is spoken. In this electronic age the distinction has become a little blurred, but, if you send an offensive e-mail, you are more likely to be sued for libel than for slander.

libertine, libertarian A *libertine* is a person who does whatever he feels like doing, especially in sexual matters, without regard for moral or social conventions. The word is now somewhat old-fashioned. A *libertarian* is, in principle, a believer in freedom of thought and expression, and hence an opponent of tyranny and censorship. These days, however, *libertarian* is most commonly applied to a holder of the extreme view that governments should not be allowed to interfere with such behaviours as using drugs, engaging in prostitution or owning deadly weapons.

licence, license In British English, the noun is *licence* but the verb is *license*. So, write *You must get a TV licence* but *James Bond is licensed to kill*. In American English, however, the spelling is *license* in all cases.

licorice, liquorice The British spelling is *liquorice*; the American spelling is *licorice*. The curious British spelling is by contamination from *liquor*, which is unrelated.

lie, lay Very few vernacular forms of English retain a distinction between these two verbs, most having only *lay* in all circumstances. But standard English absolutely requires a distinction between intransitive *lie* and transitive *lay*. The first verb has the parts *lie, lay, lain*: *I'm going to lie down*; *She lay on the bed*; *This must have lain here for a long time*. The second has the parts *lay, laid, laid*: *Please lay the towels on the table*; *They laid down their weapons*; *I have laid out your suit*. Native speakers of vernacular English will often find this distinction unnatural and difficult, but mastery of it is essential if you want to be regarded as literate.

lifelong A controversial word. Its familiar use is illustrated by the following example: *She has a lifelong interest in Japanese art*. Many people object to this on the ground that her interest could hardly have arisen at birth, and therefore is not strictly 'lifelong', but only 'through all her adult life', or something similar. Three points. First, the word is completely established in standard English in this use. Second, no one meeting this sentence would be so stupid as to conclude that she came out of the womb fascinated by Japanese art. Third, there is perhaps no circumstance in which we urgently need to distinguish a passion conceived in infancy from a passion conceived only in adolescence or adulthood. Just go ahead and use *lifelong* in the familiar and natural way, and don't worry about the pettifoggers.

life-threatening This polysyllabic coinage has its place, but it should not be used thoughtlessly where *dangerous* or *lethal* would be adequate.

lighted, lit The past tense and the past participle of the verb *light* may be either *lighted* or *lit*: *She lighted a cigarette* or *She lit a cigarette*; *They had lighted torches* or *They had lit torches*. However, in these functions, *lit* is strongly preferred in British English and moderately preferred in American English.

As an adjective, the preferred form is *lighted* everywhere: *She waved her lighted cigarette*; *They were carrying lighted torches*. But an exception occurs when the adjective is modified: *a well-lit room; an ill-lit street*.

lightning The word that goes with *thunder* is so spelled, and ✻*lightening* is wrong. There exists a form *lightening*, but this is only the *-ing* form of the verb *lighten*, as in *lightening the load*.

light year A *light year* is a unit of distance, not of time. It is the distance light travels in a year, around six trillion miles. You should not write things like ✻*light years ago*.

like Only things of the same category can be compared, and the following example illustrates a common error: ✻*Like all sharks, the skeleton of the hammerhead is made of cartilage*. The error here is to compare a skeleton with sharks. Write *Like all sharks, the hammerhead has a skeleton of cartilage*, or *As with all sharks, the skeleton of the hammerhead is made of cartilage*. The same is true of *unlike*: write *Unlike other textbooks, this one has illustrations in full colour*, not ✻*Unlike other textbooks, the illustrations in this one are in full colour*.

like, as In formal English, *like* cannot be used as a conjunction. Though common in speech, the usage illustrated by ✻*We should proceed like we did last time* must be avoided: write *We should proceed as we did last time*. Similarly, write *He batted as though he were possessed*, not ✻*He batted like he was possessed*. But do write *He batted like a man possessed*, not ✻*He batted as a man possessed*.

However, it is not true that *as* cannot be a preposition. It can be, but its meaning is different from that of *like*. If I write *Like your teacher, I advise you to learn algebra*, then I am not your teacher, and I am merely comparing myself to your teacher. However, if I write *As your teacher, I advise you to learn algebra*, then I am indeed your teacher, and I am speaking in my capacity as your teacher.

likeable, likable Both spellings are acceptable on both sides of the Atlantic, but British English strongly prefers *likeable*, while American English slightly prefers *likable*.

likewise This word means 'the same thing', 'in the same way', as in *Our competitors are cutting prices; we must do likewise*. But it is nor properly used to mean 'and': write *They were dismayed by his fierce appearance and his surly manner*, not ∗ *. . . by his fierce appearance, likewise his surly manner*.

limbo In Christian mythology, *limbo* is a resting place for the souls of those who have committed no sins, and so cannot go to hell, but have not been baptized, and so cannot go to heaven. The word now has two extended senses, both standard. First, *limbo* is an imaginary place for lost or forgotten people or things: *The dreadful word 'albeit' is best consigned to the limbo of unnecessary baggage*. Second, *limbo* is the position of a person who is stuck helplessly waiting for a decision about his future, and meanwhile unable to function: *Paul is in limbo until his misconduct case is resolved*. But the word does not mean merely 'gap' or 'interval', even a tedious one. It is wrong to write ∗*We needed to fill the limbo between our return and the beginning of the academic year*. A limbo cannot be 'between' anything.

The plural is *limbos*.

linear, non-linear These are technical terms in mathematics and physics. If you are not using them in their strict technical senses, then you should not be using them at all. Unfortunately, in much post-modernist writing, *linear* has become an all-purpose term of abuse and *non-linear* an all-purpose term of approval. If you find yourself using the terms in this way, then you need help. Ask yourself this question: can you explain the difference between a *linear equation* and a *non-linear equation*? If you can't, then don't use these words, unless you are interested in making a fool of yourself. It is ignorant drivel to suggest that mathematics, or science, or the world generally, has somehow changed from being 'linear' to being 'non-linear'. It has not.

linguist A *linguist* may be either a practitioner of linguistics (the scientific study of language) or a polyglot (a person who speaks several languages). Both uses are fine, but you should take care to avoid any ambiguity: out of context, the word may be misunderstood. For the practitioner of linguistics, the label *linguistician* is occasionally met, but this cumbersome word is disliked by linguists and little used by anyone. Avoid it.

liquefy The word is so spelled, and ∗*liquify* is not acceptable. And no such word as ∗*liquidify* exists. The derived noun is *liquefaction*.

liquor, liqueur In American English, *liquor* is the equivalent of British English *spirits*: both words denote distilled alcoholic beverages like whisky and gin. The word *liquor* is little used in Britain. A *liqueur* is a sweetened and flavoured alcoholic beverage, usually based on a distilled spirit, such as Cointreau or Tía María.

liquorice See **licorice**.

lira, lire The Italian currency is the *lira*, and the plural form is *lire*. Write *two million lire*, not ✳*two million lira*.

lit See **lighted**.

litany, liturgy A *litany* is a form of Christian prayer consisting of a series of invocations, each followed by an unvarying response. The *liturgy* of a particular Christian church is the entirety of the forms of public worship laid down by that church.

literally Something which is *literally* true is true in fact: you can only write *She was literally foaming at the mouth* if there was indeed foam coming out of her mouth. Do not write things like ✳*They were literally glued to their seats* unless you really mean that someone had placed glue on their seats.

However, even when the word is correctly used, it is often unnecessary: what is conveyed by writing ⁇*He was literally furious* that is not equally conveyed by *He was furious*?

livid Originally, this word denoted a greyish-blue colour, the skin colour exhibited by someone with a black eye. By extension, the word has come to mean 'furious', 'so angry as to be almost out of control', and this sense is acceptable in formal writing. But the word does not mean 'red' or 'intensely coloured', and should not be so used. For 'intensely coloured', the word is *vivid*.

llama See **lama**.

loan See **lend**.

loath, loathe The word *loath* (formerly also spelled *loth*) is an adjective meaning 'reluctant' or 'unwilling': *She is loath to return to her home town.* But *loathe* is a verb meaning 'detest': *She loathes rhubarb.* The first rhymes with *both*; the second doesn't. If these words trouble you, why not just avoid them in favour of 'unwilling' and 'detest'?

locate, location Overused and rarely necessary. Prefer *find* to *locate* and *place* to *location*.

loc. cit. See *op. cit.*

-log, -logue British English accepts only *-logue* in these words; American English accepts either spelling but often prefers *-log*: hence British *analogue*, *catalogue*, *dialogue*, *epilogue*, but often American *analog*, *catalog*, *dialog*, *epilog*.

logogram See **ideogram**.

Londonderry, Derry A political problem. The historical name of the Irish city is *Derry*. Under British rule, the name has been officially changed to *Londonderry* – though *Derry* is acceptable to the post office. Irish nationalists call it *Derry*, while Unionists call it *Londonderry*, and there is no politically neutral name.

lorry, truck Traditionally, a large road vehicle is a *lorry* in Britain but a *truck* in the US and in much of the rest of the world. However, *truck* is now rapidly displacing *lorry* in Britain. Indeed, one recent guide to British usage states bluntly that '*lorry* has now given way to *truck*.' This judgement is perhaps a little premature, but it shows the way things are going, and *truck* is now acceptable in British English.

lose, loose The verb *lose* means 'cease to have', as in *When did you lose your keys/virginity/leg?* The word *loose* is most often an adjective meaning 'not tight', 'not fastened', 'not tied up', as in *Those trousers are too loose* or *The dog is loose*. But *loose* can also be a verb meaning 'release', as in *She loosed her hold on his neck*. The common mistake here is to write *loose* where *lose* is intended, as in *✻He always looses at tennis*.

lots of, a lot of Normal in spoken English, these expressions still look rather strange in formal writing. Quite a few people are now happy to use these things in formal writing, and write *Lots of research has been done*, but many readers will still find this objectionable. You are advised to write *A great deal of research has been done*, or, in very formal writing, *Much research has been done*.

lusty, lustful The adjective *lusty* means 'robust', 'vigorous' or sometimes 'invigorating': *a lusty cheer*, *a lusty young man*, *a lusty glass of ale* (this last is old-fashioned). But *lustful* means, unsurprisingly, 'full of (sexual) lust'. *A lusty young man* is a healthy and vigorous one, while *a lustful young man* is one who is consumed by sexual desire. Confusing these can lead to embarrassment.

Luxembourg The country and city in Europe, the province in Belgium and the palace in Paris are all properly spelled *Luxembourg* in

English, not *Luxemburg*. But the German political activist was *Rosa Luxemburg*.

luxuriant, luxurious The word *luxuriant* means 'lush, rich', as in *luxuriant vegetation*. But *luxurious* means 'sumptuous', as in *a luxurious apartment*. Misuse is common in both directions, but is as yet tolerated by no commentator. In any case, *luxurious* is increasingly replaced as a preposed modifier by *luxury*, as in *a luxury apartment*. This new form has a small advantage in brevity, but no other advantage I can think of. Stick to *luxurious* in careful writing.

-ly Adverbs of manner commonly end in *-ly*: *slow, slowly*; *happy, happily*. However, quite a few adjectives happen to end in *-ly* as well, such as *lonely*, *silly*, *unearthly* and *lovely*. Adding the adverbial *-ly* to one of these produces something which is unacceptably clumsy and hard to pronounce: *lonelily*, *sillily*, *lovelily*. You should avoid these by writing instead *in a lonely manner*, and so on. But note the special case of *gingerly*, which in this form can be either an adjective or an adverb: *a gingerly examination*; *He examined it gingerly*.

Lyons The French spelling is *Lyon*, and this should be used when giving names in French. However, the established English form is *Lyons*, and this spelling should be used. See also **Gulf of Lions**.

lyric, lyrics Formerly, the words to a popular song were its *lyric*, but this singular form has now been almost completely replaced by the plural *lyrics*. There is no point in trying to revive the older usage.

madam, ma'am, **madame** In all forms of English, the polite way of addressing a man you do not know is *Sir*, both in speech and in writing. In American English, the female equivalent in speech is *Ma'am*, as in *Excuse me, Ma'am*. But this is impossible in Britain, where *Ma'am* is reserved for addressing the Queen and other female members of the royal family. In fact, spoken British English has *no* polite way of addressing an unfamiliar woman – a fact which is astonishing. In Britain, as elsewhere, the long form *madam* is used in writing letters, as in *Dear Madam*, and it has special uses in phrases like *Madam Chairman* and *Madam Mayor*, but *madam* simply cannot be used otherwise – except, of course, as a label for a woman who runs a brothel.

There is no such English word as *madame*, and this French spelling should never be used except in front of the name of a foreign (especially French) woman, as in *Madame Mitterrand*.

Magdalen, Magdalene The Oxford college is *Magdalen*; the Cambridge college is *Magdalene*. In both cases, the pronunciation is 'maudlin'.

magistrates' court The term is so spelled, with an apostrophe as shown.

Magna Carta, Magna Charta The spelling *Magna Carta* is recommended by authorities on both sides of the Atlantic, even though *Magna Charta* is widely used in the USA. This name is used without the article: *King John signed Magna Carta*, not ✳. . . *signed the Magna Carta*.

major A much overused word. It is well-established in certain locutions like *major surgery* and *a major highway*, in which it implicitly contrasts with *minor*. But it should not be used on every occasion. Before writing it, think whether another word might be better, such as **principal** or *important*. The word cannot be compared or modified: avoid writing ✳*very major*.

Majorca, Minorca Though the Spanish forms are *Mallorca* and *Menorca*, the spellings *Majorca* and *Minorca* are established in English and should usually be used.

majority, plurality In British English, a political candidate who wins an election is always said to have a *majority*, even if he has not gained fifty per cent of the votes. If he gets more than half of the votes, he has an *absolute majority*; if not, he has a *relative majority*. However, in the USA and Canada, he has a *majority* only in the first case, and a *plurality* in the second.

In other contexts, *majority* always means 'more than half', but note that the word can be used only with things that can be counted: it is acceptable to write *the majority of my students* or *the majority of the committee*, but you cannot write ✳*the majority of the book* or ✳*the majority of Siberia* or ✳*the majority of the money*.

Use this word carefully: in most cases, it is better style to write *most of my students*, rather than *the majority of my students*.

Malaysian names As is the case in other predominantly Muslim countries, Malaysian personal names offer formidable difficulties. In particular, it is often difficult to locate a surname among the several names borne by an individual. For example, the statesman *Tunku Abdul Rahman Putra Al-Haj* is usually known in English as *Abdul Rahman*. There is no simple rule for picking out the surname. But note that *Tunku* is a title, not a name.

male, masculine, female, feminine The words *male* and *female* denote the biological sexes: *a male lion, a female engineer*. The words *masculine* and *feminine* are applied to characteristics perceived as typical of each sex, or to individual people seen as exhibiting these characteristics: *a masculine man* is a man perceived as having manly characteristics, and *a feminine style* is a style perceived as appropriate to women. You should not use *masculine* and *feminine* to mean merely *male* and *female*: it is wrong to write *a masculine name* for *a male name* (like *Henry*) or *the feminine gender* for *the female sex*. See **gender**.

The adjective *effeminate* is a contemptuous label applied to a man perceived as exhibiting stereotypical female characteristics. The nearest counterpart for a woman perceived as exhibiting the characteristics of a man is *mannish*.

mannequin, manikin, mannikin A *mannequin* is a plastic human figure displayed in the window of a clothing store. Occasionally the word is also applied to a human model on the catwalk. A *manikin* is a tiny man, either a boy or a dwarf, and it is also a model of the human body used in teaching medicine or art. For the second, a variant spelling *mannikin* is recognized by some dictionaries, but this is widely disliked and should be avoided.

manoeuvre, maneuver The British spelling is *manoeuvre*; the American spelling is *maneuver*. But the spelling *maneuvre* is never acceptable.

manqué This postposed adjective means 'who might have been but failed to become': thus, *a poet manqué* is somebody who had hoped or tried to become a poet but failed. Logically, the form should be *manquée* when the word is applied to a woman, but almost all English dictionaries recognize only the form *manqué*. Nevertheless, careful copy-editors often prefer *manquée* for a woman.

marinade, marinate The noun is *marinade*; the verb is *marinate*. You marinate your food in the marinade.

Marseilles The French spelling is *Marseille*, and this should be used when names are being given in French. Otherwise, the spelling *Marseilles* is established in English, and should be used.

marten, martin A *marten* is a tree-dwelling mammal somewhat resembling its relative the weasel. A *martin* is a bird of the swallow family.

masonry The word is so spelled, and *masonery* is wrong.

masterful, masterly The adjective *masterful* means 'dominating', 'exercising authority very effectively'. We may write, for example, of *King Alfred's masterful leadership*. But *masterly* means 'very skilful': we may write of *a masterly analysis of the problem*.

maudlin, mawkish The word *maudlin* means 'foolishly tearful or sentimental', and is best applied to the moans of somebody who is drunk and
feeling sorry for himself. But *mawkish* means 'falsely sentimental', and is
best applied to the kind of exaggeratedly sentimental writing that makes a
discerning reader want to throw up.

Mauretania, Mauritania The country in West Africa is *Mauritania*,
while *Mauretania* is the name of an ancient region along the Mediterranean
coast of Africa, in modern Morocco and Algeria.

mawkish See **maudlin**.

may, might In the present tense, either of these is acceptable, though the
first perhaps suggests a somewhat greater degree of confidence than the
second: *We may have a peace treaty this month* and *We might have a peace
treaty this month* are both permissible.

The difficulties begin in the past tense. A past-tense verb-form can normally only be followed by *might*, and not by *may*. So, the required form is
Susie said that she might be here, and not *✳Susie said that she may be here*.
Likewise, write *We believed that we might have a chance*, and not *✳We believed
that we may have a chance*. The use of *may* in such sentences is decidedly
non-standard, and it will cause many readers to grind their teeth.

An even greater problem arises with the pair *may have* and *might have*. In
standard English, these two are very sharply distinguished, as follows. If I
write *We may have won*, this means 'Maybe we won, and maybe we didn't:
I don't know what the facts are.' But, if I write *We might have won*, this
carries the very different meaning 'We didn't win, but, in slightly different
circumstances, our winning was possible.'

In other words, *might have* is counterfactual: it is always followed by
something which is not true. But *may have* is not counterfactual: it is
followed by something which is not known to be false. This contrast is of
central importance in standard English, and mastery of it is essential. So,
ignore all those football coaches who routinely intone *✳If it hadn't been for
that dodgy call, we may have won*. Standard English absolutely requires *might
have won* here, and, if you find this unnatural, you will simply have to grit
your teeth and learn it. You can't imagine how awful that non-standard
may have sounds to careful writers.

maybe, may be These two are often confused. But there is a simple way
to tell them apart: the single word *maybe* can always be replaced by *perhaps*
without changing the meaning, while the two words *may be* cannot. So,
write *Two decisions may be more important than others* but *Two decisions, maybe*

more, will be more important than others. Note that *perhaps* can replace *maybe* in the second example, but not *may be* in the first.

mayhem A word which is frequently met but not always understood. In law, *mayhem* is the deliberate infliction of violence on somebody, resulting in injury. By extension, the word has come to be used in the everyday language to mean 'violent disorder'. But it does not mean 'murder', nor does it mean merely 'confusion' or 'peaceful disorder'.

me See **I**.

mean A gravely overused verb. In careful writing, this verb is best confined to its central sense of 'denote', 'signify'. Colloquial English has extended its uses greatly, but these extended senses are best avoided. Here are some examples of poor use. **The inspection means we have to have our paperwork in order.* Choose a more precise verb: *The inspection requires us to have our paperwork in order.* **Our low rating probably means a budget cut.* Improved version: *Our low rating probably indicates a budget cut.*

meaningful A vastly overused word, and one often used inexplicitly. Before writing it, consider whether some more explicit word might serve your purposes better. Possibilities include *important, fruitful, significant, serious, far-reaching* and *knowing*.

measles This word is normally grammatically singular: *Measles is deadly among people with no resistance to it.*

Mecca, mecca The city in Saudi Arabia is *Mecca*. But a revered centre of activity is a *mecca*: *Cooperstown is a mecca for baseball fans.*

mediator See **arbiter**.

medieval, mediaeval The preferred spelling in all varieties of English is *medieval*.

Mediterranean Note the spelling, with two Rs and an EAN, and avoid common errors like *Mediteranean and *Mediterranian.

medium, media Traditionally, *medium* is singular while *media* is plural, at least in speaking of ways of transmitting information, though, for a person who claims to be able to speak to spirits, the plural is *mediums*. So, you should write *The mass media are vastly important today*, not **The mass media is . . .* Journalistic prose almost invariably uses **The media is . . .* , but you should avoid this use in careful writing, since it will set many readers' teeth on edge.

meet with The expression *meet with* is very common in journalistic prose, but it should be avoided in formal writing. Write *Mr Clinton met Mr Putin*, not **Mr Clinton met with Mr Putin*.

mega- This is a prefix and should be written as one, as it is in scientific use: *megabyte*, *megaparsec*. If such informal words as *megastar* and *mega-hit* are used at all, they should likewise be written as single words: forms like *mega hit are never acceptable. But the vernacular use of *mega* as an adjective meaning something like 'highly successful' is entirely out of place in good writing.

memento This word for 'souvenir' is so spelled, and *momento does not exist.

memorabilia This word is grammatically plural: *These memorabilia are not very valuable.*

memorandum The singular is *memorandum*; the plural is usually *memoranda*. A plural *memorandums* is also found but is not recommended. The common error here is treating *memoranda* as a singular and writing things like *these memorandas, which is always wrong.

men's wear, menswear The only form you will ever see in a clothing store is *menswear*, which is now recognized by most dictionaries. However, the more conservative *men's wear* is recommended, since the one-word style annoys many readers.

meteor, meteorite A *meteor* is a bright streak of light in the sky produced by a small body from space travelling through the atmosphere at enormous speed, what is informally called a *shooting star*. The word is also applied to the small body producing the light. A *meteorite* is a lump of stone or metal on the earth's surface, the remains of a meteor which was big enough to survive passage through the atmosphere without being burned up.

methodology A *method* is a single procedure for achieving some end. In contrast, a *methodology* is a set of conventional procedures, always principled and usually scientific or at least scholarly, for working in a particular discipline. The longer word is only appropriate in scientific and scholarly contexts, and it should not be used thoughtlessly as a fancy synonym for the shorter word.

meticulous A controversial word. It earlier meant 'fussy', 'finicky', 'pernickety', 'over-attentive to insignificant details', and it was not a compliment. Today, however, almost everyone uses it in a positive sense to mean only 'very careful', 'thorough', and somebody who calls your work *meticulous* is almost certainly complimenting you. Authorities are divided on this shift of meaning, but most now embrace it. For the negative sense, we must now use *fastidious*, *over-meticulous* or one of the other synonyms just cited.

metre, meter British English uses *metre* for the unit of length, and for its several derivatives like *kilometre* and *centimetre*. But it uses *meter* for any measuring instrument, as in *gas meter* and *thermometer*, and also for a poetic measure, as in *iambic pentameter*. American English uses *meter* in all circumstances.

mews Though it was originally a plural, this British word for a small residential street containing houses converted from former stables is today usually singular: *I'm buying a place in a pretty little mews*. The word is little known outside Britain.

migrate, emigrate, immigrate To *migrate* is to move from one place to another. This movement may be more or less permanent, as when persistent drought forces people to leave their homes and migrate to a new area, or it may be temporary or cyclical, as when nomadic hunter-gatherers migrate from place to place according to the seasons. To *emigrate* is to leave one's homeland: *The potato blight forced many Irish people to emigrate*. To *immigrate* is to travel to a new home: *During the nineteenth century, millions of Europeans immigrated here to the USA*. Of course, a migrant always travels *from* one place *to* another place, and your choice of word depends on whether you want to emphasize the leaving or the arrival. So, we speak of *emigrants* from the Ireland of the famine, but of *immigrants* from elsewhere to the USA.

See also **émigré**.

militant My dictionary defines this adjective as 'aggressive or vigorous, especially in support of a cause'. But the word is used all too freely in the feebler sense of 'holding or expressing views which are unpopular or which I don't like'. In Britain, for example, Christians have demanded and won compulsory religious education in state schools and compulsory religious programmes on television. Some Christians ring the doorbells of strangers at 9.00 on Sunday morning demanding to talk about the Bible, while others display large and often lurid posters in public places with messages like 'The wages of sin is death'. Somehow none of this activity ever seems to draw forth the label 'militant'. But, when the biologist Richard Dawkins is asked about his religious beliefs and replies 'I'm an atheist, and I have no time for religion', he is at once accused by tabloid newspapers and other commentators of being 'a militant atheist'.

So, if you find yourself writing this word, stop and think whether it has any clear meaning, or whether you are just using it as a swearword.

militate, mitigate These similar-looking but unrelated verbs are often confused. The verb *militate* normally only occurs in the expression *militate against*, which means 'disfavour', 'work against': *Her punk hairstyle and pierced face militate against her chances of getting a teaching job*. It is not possible for a person to militate against anything, or for anything to militate against a person.

The verb *mitigate* means 'soften', 'reduce the severity of': *The seriousness of her crime was mitigated by the appalling treatment she had endured*. It is not possible to follow *mitigate* with *against*. You are probably familiar with the phrase *mitigating circumstances*, which means 'circumstances that reduce the seriousness of an offence'.

millennium Note the spelling: two Ls and, more critically, two Ns. The spellings *millenium and *milennium are wrong. The plural is either *millennia* or *millenniums*, though the first is often preferred in scholarly writing. The derived adjective is *millennial*. But the word *millenarian* 'consisting of one thousand' is not directly related and has only one N.

millipede, millepede Traditionally, the British spelling is *millepede* and the American one *millipede*. However, the spelling with I is now predominant in Britain and preferred by most dictionaries.

mini-, mini Before about 1960, English had neither a prefix *mini-* nor a word *mini*. Today both are everywhere, and both are overused. These things are most usual in informal writing, and they should be used carefully, if at all, in formal writing. It is usually better to write *miniature sausages* rather than ??*mini-sausages* or *mini sausages*, and it is always better to write *a brief affair* rather than *a mini-affair*. If you do find yourself obliged to use *mini-*, note that it is strictly a prefix in formal writing: write *miniskirt*, not *mini skirt*.

Minorca See **Majorca**.

minuscule This word is so spelled, and *miniscule is wrong. The word is related to *minus*, not to **mini-**.

misuse See **abuse**.

mischievous The word is so spelled: avoid the common error *mischievious*.

misplaced modifier Consider the following sentence from a newspaper: *BBC Radio One has decided to revive its rock programme after three years off the air*. The problem here is that the sentence appears to imply that it is Radio One which has been off the air for three years, rather than its rock programme.

If this is not clear to you, consider another example with the same structure: *BBC Radio One has decided to revive its rock programme after three years of indecision*. This time it should be obvious that the phrase *after three years of indecision* applies to *BBC Radio One*, not to *its rock programme*, and so the same is true of the phrase in my first example.

Here is a further example: *No longer requiring tremendous time and energy, the new Bessemer process made steel cheap enough for common use*. This appears to say that the new Bessemer process no longer requires tremendous time and energy, which makes no sense. What the writer intended to say is that, thanks to the new Bessemer process, the manufacture of steel no longer requires tremendous time and energy. He should have said so.

My final example concerns a group of native Americans, one of whose number discovered that the Spaniards were planning to murder all of them while they were attending Mass on Sunday, and warned the others. The writer's conclusion was this: *Forewarned, no Indians appeared in church on Sunday*. This is nonsense, since it appears to say that no Indians were forewarned, whereas in fact all of them were.

As always, the cure for these blunders is to read what you have written. See **dangling modifier**.

misquotations More than a few famous quotations have become garbled in common use. Before thoughtlessly writing down what you *think* might be the quotation, you would be wise to check the wording in a dictionary of quotations. Here are a few of the commonest misquotations:

* *All power corrupts*. Lord Acton wrote 'Power tends to corrupt, and absolute power corrupts absolutely.'
* *Blood, sweat and tears*. Winston Churchill's phrase was 'blood, toil, tears and sweat'.
* *The Devil can quote Scripture*. Antonio's line in *The Merchant of Venice* is 'The Devil can cite Scripture for his purpose.'
* *Gild the lily*. In *King John*, Salisbury's line is 'to gild refined gold, to paint the lily'.
* *In the sweat of thy brow shalt thou eat bread*. Genesis 3:19 has 'In the sweat of thy face shalt thou eat bread.'

* *A little knowledge is a dangerous thing.* Pope's line is 'A little learning is a dangerous thing.'
* *Money is the root of all evil.* In I Timothy 6:10, St Paul says 'The love of money is the root of all evil.'
* *Play it again, Sam!* In the film *Casablanca*, Humphrey Bogart's character says 'If she can stand it, I can. Play it!'
* *A poor thing, but mine own.* In *As You Like It*, Touchstone says of his beloved 'An ill-favoured thing, sir, but mine own.'
* *Pride goeth before a fall.* In Proverbs 16:18, we read 'Pride goeth before destruction, and an haughty spirit before a fall.'
* *The best laid plans of mice and men.* Robert Burns's line is 'the best laid schemes o' mice an' men'.
* *There's method in my madness.* In *Hamlet*, Polonius observes 'Though this be madness, yet there is method in't.'
* *Water, water, everywhere, and not a drop to drink.* Coleridge's line in *The Ancient Mariner* reads 'Water, water, everywhere, nor any drop to drink.'

missing *and* The following example illustrates a very common error: *I had a secure contract, a salary of £21,000 and was surrounded by trained journalists*. The problem here is that a necessary *and* is missing. If you work through this faulty example, you will see that the writer is effectively writing *I had a secure contract, I had a salary of £21,000, and I had was surrounded by trained journalists*, which is gibberish. This must be rewritten as *I had a secure contract and a salary of £21,000, and (I) was surrounded by trained journalists*, in which the second *I* is not essential but is recommended.

Similarly, the following sentence, adapted from a newspaper article, is wrong: *John Williams, his wife and sister are missing after a plane crash*. The reader sees *John Williams, his wife and sister* and expects a continuation with *and* . . . which is not there. Write instead either *John Williams and his wife and sister* . . . , or, much better, *John Williams, his wife and his sister* . . .

missing preposition In a construction with *and* or *or*, it is easy to miss out a required preposition. Here is a genuine example: *Peter Mandelson has no special knowledge or interest in Northern Ireland*. You cannot have knowledge *in* something, but only knowledge *of* something. Rewrite as follows: *Peter Mandelson has no special knowledge of, or interest in, Northern Ireland*. This example represents one type of failure to maintain a **parallel construction**, and it further illustrates the dangers of **right-node raising**.

For another case of a missing preposition, see **ambiguous comparative**.

missing subject The following example, written about a new computer operating system, illustrates an error that is easy to commit: *It's too big to be able to remove the bugs completely*. The problem is that *be able* has no subject here, other than the initial *it* (the operating system), which makes no sense. Write instead *It's too big for anyone to remove the bugs* or *It's too big for the bugs to be removed*.

mistrust See **distrust**.

mitigate See **militate**.

Mitterrand The former French president's name is so spelled, with two Ts and two Rs.

mixed language In linguistics, a *mixed language* is an unusual language which did not descend from a single ancestor in the ordinary way, but which was deliberately constructed by bilingual speakers, for reasons of their own, from the two (or possibly more) languages which they knew and then passed on to children as a mother tongue. A good example is Michif, spoken along the US–Canadian border, which is a highly orderly combination of elements from the Algonquian language Cree and from Canadian French. Mixed languages are rare. Often the term *mixed language* is used very loosely, to label any language which has been heavily influenced by one or more others, such as English, which has made great use of French, Latin and Greek. This loose sense is best avoided, since, in this sense, there are hardly any unmixed languages.

mixed metaphor Here is a line that recently turned up on the radio: *It was clear that the germs of a compromise policy would have to be sown*. This is a fine example of a mixed metaphor: germs cannot be sown. Such mixed metaphors can easily slip out in unplanned English, but, in careful writing, you must be on guard against them. In my example, replacing *germs* by *seeds* would repair the metaphor.

mogul, Mogul, Mughal The Muslim rulers of India were formerly called *Moguls* in English, but today the spelling *Mughals* is increasingly preferred and is recommended here. But our informal word for a powerful person, often especially in the entertainment industry, is always written *mogul*, as is the unrelated word *mogul* for a mound of hard snow on a ski slope or a snowboard course.

mold See **mould**.

Moldova, Moldavia The official form of the name is *Moldova*, which should be used, except in historical contexts in which the older form *Moldavia* is appropriate.

momentarily In standard English, *momentarily* means 'for a moment', and not 'in a moment', 'very soon'. It is therefore wrong to write *We'll find out momentarily*. The correct use is illustrated by *She was momentarily flummoxed*.

money You should not write a sum of money with two units of currency. For example, 'five pounds and fifty pence' is written £5.50, and not *£5.50p*.

moneys, monies Though the plural of *money* is hardly ever required in ordinary contexts, that plural is the regular *moneys*. But an exception occurs in legal language, in which the irregular plural *monies* is usual in the sense of 'sum(s) of money'.

mongoose The plural is *mongooses*, not *mongeese*.

monotonous, monotonic Both these words originally meant 'having an unvarying pitch or tone'. Today, however, *monotonous* is almost always used in the sense of 'wearisomely unchanging', and the original sense can only be usefully expressed by *monotonic*. Bear in mind, however, that *monotonic* also has a quite distinct technical sense in mathematics and logic, roughly 'increasing (or decreasing) steadily, with no interruptions'.

more than From a newspaper: *Our DNA and that of chimpanzees is more than 98.3% identical*. It is pointless to combine a qualifier like *more than* with a precise number like *98.3%*. Write either *98.3%* or *more than 98%*. (And, by the way, that *is* should be *are*.)

moribund This word means 'almost dead'. A moribund language is one which is no longer being learned by children, and a moribund industry is one which now barely exists and which will not exist much longer. The word does not mean 'troubled', 'beleaguered', 'in difficulties'.

morphic A meaningless word with no existence outside pseudo-scientific drivel. I include it here only as a touchstone: any text containing this word may be safely left unread.

mortar The spelling is *mortar*, with an A, in all of the several senses of the word, and there is no such word as *morter*.

Moslem See **Muslim**.

most well-known This form is clumsy or worse: write *best-known*, not
*most well-known. The same goes for other such items: *best-informed*, not
**most well-informed*; *best-looking*, not **most good-looking*.

mould, mold In all senses, the only British spelling is *mould*, while the
only American one is *mold*.

mouse, mice Everyone knows that the plural of *mouse* is *mice* when we are
talking about rodents, but what is the plural when we are talking about the
gadgets connected to our computers? After some vacillation, the plural *mice*
seems to have won out here too, and is recommended.

much less See **let alone**.

Mughal See **mogul**.

Muhammad, Mohammed, Mahomet The accurate spelling *Muhammad* is now usual for the name of the Prophet. The older spelling *Mohammed*
is not wrong but is not recommended. But the spelling *Mahomet* is now
archaic and should be avoided. Of course, with a person who has this as a
given name, you should use the English spelling preferred by the owner of
the name.

Muslim, Moslem, Mohammedan, Islamic A follower of the religion
promulgated by the Prophet Muhammad is a *Muslim*. The older spelling
Moslem is not exactly wrong, but it is not recommended, and some Muslims
dislike it. However, the old-fashioned term *Mohammedan is gravely offensive to Muslims, and must be avoided. Finally, the archaic variant *Mussulman*
is no longer in use. The name of the religion is *Islam*: the word **Mohammed-
anism* is likewise offensive, and should not be used. We speak of *Islamic art*,
Islamic architecture, *Islamic literature*, and so forth.

mutual The entry for this word is one of the most difficult to write in any
handbook of usage. The reason for this is that there exists a long-standing
and powerful view among careful writers that *mutual* means A but not B,
while at the same time we can see that the word has been used to mean B
by eminent writers from Shakespeare to the present. So, should I endorse
the opinion or the usage?

Here is the opinion. The word *mutual* means only 'reciprocal', and a
mutual connection between you and me is one such that you are connected
to me and I am connected to you in the same way. For example, if Alice
dislikes Susie, and Susie dislikes Alice, then we can speak of Alice and Susie's
mutual dislike. However, if Alice dislikes Zelda, and Susie dislikes Zelda,

then there is no reciprocal relation, and we cannot speak of Alice and Susie's mutual dislike of Zelda, but only of their *common* dislike of Zelda. Thus *mutual* does not mean 'common'.

So far, so good. But now we turn to the facts. And here we find that *mutual* has been used in the sense of 'common' for centuries. The *Oxford English Dictionary* reveals examples of this from the sixteenth century without interruption. One of the best-known is Dickens's title *Our Mutual Friend*, and the phrase *our mutual friend* is recorded from 1658.

What to do? All authorities on usage are uneasy about making recommendations here, and most exhibit a measure of caution. There is, of course, no problem with *mutual* for 'reciprocal', as in *our mutual admiration* ('we admire each other'). Probably everyone is willing to allow *mutual* also in the slightly different sense of 'equally involved', as in *This agreement will be to our mutual benefit*, meaning that we will both benefit from the agreement, but not necessarily that we will be directly benefiting each other. Beyond this point, the ice becomes thin. Most commentators find themselves obliged to accept the particular phrase *our mutual friend*, because it has been in use for centuries, because Dickens made it famous, and because the alternative *our common friend* may suggest the unfortunate sense of a friend who is vulgar and not refined.

My advice? If *common* expresses your intended meaning, and if this word can be used without sounding unnatural or badly chosen, then use it: write *their common ancestry* and *our common interests*. But, if *common* sounds clumsy or misleading, then probably not many readers will complain if you choose *mutual* – though one or two doubtless will.

my one Colloquial British English permits locutions like *my one* and *your one*, but these are not standard English. Write instead *mine* and *yours*.

myself In formal writing, this word should never be used as a fancy variant of *me*: write *Please keep Roberta or me informed*, not ✳*Please keep Roberta or myself informed*. After all, nobody would write ✳*Please keep myself informed*, and the presence of *or* does not change the structure of the sentence.

mystery Something which is not known is not necessarily a *mystery*. For example, we don't know exactly who built Stonehenge, or why, but calling the origin of Stonehenge 'a mystery' may be wrongly interpreted as implying that there is something inexplicable about the monument.

myth Originally, a *myth* was a fanciful story invented to explain some phenomenon or tradition, usually one involving gods or heroes. Today the word is commonly used to denote a widespread but false belief, such as *the* *myth that French is more logical than other languages.* Almost all authorities now regard this sense as acceptable in formal writing, though there are still a few people who object to it. The derivative *mythical* means 'false', 'fictitious', while *mythological* means 'pertaining to myths and mythology' (in the older sense).

naive In French, *naïve* is a feminine form, but, in English, *naive* is invariable as an adjective and applied to both sexes. Write *He was naive*, not **He was naif*. The spelling with the diaeresis, *naïve*, is now less common and is not recommended. The rather rare word *naïf* is a noun only, as in *He was a naïf*; this is almost always written with the diaeresis. The abstract noun derived from *naive* is variously written *naivety*, *naïvety* or *naïveté*; all are acceptable, and none seems to be winning out over the others.

names Many dozens of individual names which often give trouble are entered separately in this book. For discussions of some general issues, see the following entries: **apostrophe in names**, **Arabic names**, **Burmese names**, **Chinese names**, **Christian name**, **Dutch names**, **foreign names**, **French names**, **geographical names**, **German names**, **Greek names**, **Italian names**, **Japanese names**, **language names**, **Latin names**, **Malaysian names**, **personal names**, **place-name derivatives**, **place names**, **Portuguese and Brazilian names**, **Russian names**, **Scottish and Irish names**, **Spanish names**, **team names**, ***the* in names of countries**, **Turkish names**, **Ukrainian names**, **Vietnamese names**, **Welsh names**.

napkin, serviette The thing you wipe your mouth with at table is everywhere a *napkin*. Curiously, the British equivalent *serviette* is widely regarded as vulgar, and should probably be avoided in careful writing.

nationality words A word denoting a nationality must be capitalized when it has its literal meaning of 'from or associated with a place'. So, for example, we must write *American history*, *Albanian refugees*, *the Canadian flag*, and *Thai cuisine*. However, when such a word does not have a literal meaning, the capital is optional: we may choose to write *russian dressing*, *french windows* and *danish pastry*, since these things have no literal connection with Russia, France or Denmark. Here you may use capitals or not, as you prefer, but be consistent.

natural As any good dictionary will tell you, this word has a large number of senses, most of them centring on 'occurring without human intervention', 'normal', 'typical of people generally or of a particular person', 'spontaneous'. But the word is often used foolishly or even dishonestly, especially in advertising, and above all in connection with foods, medicines and hygiene. The usual suggestion is that there exists a class of 'natural' substances and practices which are invariably wholesome, as opposed to those produced or engineered by human beings, which are invariably harmful. This is nonsense.

The organisms which cause and transmit malaria, cholera, tuberculosis, bubonic plague, influenza, leprosy, syphilis, AIDS, and other horrifying diseases are wholly the products of nature. So are earthquakes, floods, blizzards, tornadoes, hurricanes, volcanoes, and other terrifying varieties of destruction and death. So are the insects and other vermin which destroy the crops on which subsistence farmers depend to feed their families, and so are the droughts which devastate their farms. In all these cases, it is the thoughtful efforts of informed human beings to fight off these horrors which deserve applause, and not the ghastliness visited upon us by nature.

Don't fall into the foolish trap of using *natural* as an all-purpose term of approval, and its opposite *artificial* as an all-purpose term of abuse. Honey is not superior to refined white sugar merely because it is 'natural'. In any case, there is virtually no foodstuff consumed in the western world that is obtained without substantial human intervention. Even our cereals, fruits, vegetables and livestock have been developed by many generations of purposeful breeding, and bear little resemblance to their wild ancestors, which most of us would find deeply unpalatable.

Anyone who tells you that natural things are good by definition should be invited to spend a year in a remote third-world village with no running water, no sewers, no electricity and no medical treatment, but plenty of vermin and diseases.

naught, nought The word meaning 'the digit zero' is spelled *nought* in British English and usually also in American English, where it is much less common. British examples include *noughts and crosses* (the game Americans call *tic-tac-toe*) and *nought point five* (the decimal o.5, usually read *oh point five* in American English). In all forms of English, *naught* means 'nothing', but this word is now somewhat archaic and confined to one or two fixed expressions like *come to naught* 'come to nothing'.

nauseated, nauseous If you stumble across a dead rat, and the sight makes you somewhat ill, then the rat corpse is *nauseous*, while you are *nauseated* – not *nauseous*.

Navaho, Navajo Both forms are in use, but *Navaho* is recommended.

Neandertal, Neanderthal The traditional form is *Neanderthal*, and this may be retained in informal writing. However, for scientific purposes, the spelling *Neandertal* is now preferred, and this form is recommended for scientific work.

near to Do not write ✳*near to*, in which the *to* does no work. Write *Villages with these names were located near Roman roads*, not ✳ *. . . near to Roman roads*.

necessary This is so spelled, with one C and two Ss; the spelling ✳*neccessary* is wrong.

neither In most circumstances, the word *neither* is grammatically singular and requires a singular verb. Write *Neither Hitler nor Stalin was a competent military commander*, not ✳*Neither Hitler nor Stalin were . . .* The only time *neither* can take plural agreement occurs when the item after *nor* is plural: *Neither Hitler nor his advisors were militarily competent*.

nemesis A *nemesis* is an agent of vengeance and retribution, and sometimes of doom. The word should not be used to mean no more than 'persistent opponent'. Write *Professor Lacey is the scourge of the food industry*, not ✳*Professor Lacey is the nemesis of the food industry*.

net, nett In phrases like *net weight* and *net profit*, the spelling is everywhere *net*, with one T. In Britain, and only in Britain, there exists a variant spelling *nett*, but this variant is pointless, widely disliked and condemned by some authorities. Don't use it.

New Age Bookshops today are obliged to devote a depressingly large amount of shelf-space to books churned out by crackpots and charlatans on everything from dubious self-improvement practices and dream interpretation to astrology, witchcraft, fork-bending and alien abductions. This sad waste of trees is commonly labelled 'mind, body and spirit', but the label *New Age* is also widely used. This coy label is overly respectful, in that it suggests that the books have some detectable content. You may use it, if you prefer to refrain from blunter descriptions, but it is a prime candidate for **scare quotes**.

New York The name *New York* is given both to the large American city and to the state containing it. If there is any possibility of misunderstanding, the American practice is to write *New York City* for the city and *New York State* for the state. Writers elsewhere are advised to follow suit, though *New York* may be written alone if there is no possibility of misunderstanding.

New Zealand English The variety of English used in New Zealand. At present, there is no distinctive New Zealand variety of standard English, though of course there exist a number of local words, such as *pa* 'village' and *kit* 'Maori basket'. New Zealand traditionally adheres to the written norms of British English, but pressure from American English is large and growing, and recently there was a proposal to shift wholesale to the American standard.

nexus This unusual word means 'connection', 'bond'. Its plural may be either the Latin *nexus* or the English *nexuses*. Avoid the non-existent *nexi, which is an ignorant howler.

Nietzsche The philosopher's name is so spelled.

night-time The word is so spelled, with two Ts, and *nightime is wrong.

no doubt See **doubtless**.

noisome This adjective has nothing at all to do with noise. Rather, it means 'disgusting' or 'offensive to the senses', and it is most usually applied to foul smells.

no-man's-land This is the spelling preferred by most dictionaries.

nomenclature This is not a fancy word for 'name'. Rather, a *nomenclature* is a system for naming things. For example, chemists have a nomenclature for chemical compounds, biologists for living creatures, and astronomers for stars.

non- The prefix *non-* is just that: a prefix. It must never be written as though it were a separate word. Write *non-smokers*, not *non smokers, and write *non-partisan*, not *non partisan. The hyphen can be omitted whenever the result is easy on the eye: *nonaligned, nonstop.*

none There is a prescriptive rule which requires *none* to be grammatically singular, but this rule may be safely disregarded when the sense appears to call for plural agreement. So, although *None of my children is old enough to vote* may be preferred by those of a prescriptive outlook, you may safely write *None of my children are old enough to vote* if that sounds more natural to you – as it probably does.

none the less, nonetheless In British English, the conventional form is *none the less*. In American English, *nonetheless* is preferred, and this form is now gaining ground in Britain. Still, *none the less* is recommended for British writers. Note, though, that everybody writes *nevertheless*.

non-linear See **linear**.

non-standard English As a rule, non-standard English forms have no place in careful writing. But there are exceptions. A good example is the following expression: *If it ain't broke, don't fix it*. Rendering this conventional expression into standard English, as *If it isn't broken, don't fix it*, would largely destroy its effectiveness. Another example is the word *whodunnit*, which can hardly be replaced by *✳whodidit*.

no one The established form is *no one*; the variant *no-one* is acceptable in British English but may be regarded as old-fashioned. However, *✳noone* is never acceptable.

normality, normalcy The established word is *normality*; the form *normalcy* is widely disliked and should be avoided.

notify This is a very formal word for 'tell', 'inform', and one of the simpler words should usually be preferred. In British English, this word has a second sense of 'announce', as in *The exam results have been notified to the students*. This is not possible in American English, and British writers writing for an international readership might be wise to avoid it.

not (only) . . . but (also) Sequences connected by these words must be **parallel constructions**. But it is all too easy to lose track of the parallelism. Here is a genuine example: *✳a kind of miniaturist who not only is unable to see the woods for the trees but the trees for the leaves*. If we follow the structure assigned here by *not only . . . but*, the result is *✳a kind of miniaturist who the trees for the leaves*, which is gibberish. There are several ways of fixing this, the simplest being as follows: *. . . who is unable to see not only the woods for the trees but the trees for the leaves*.

Such errors usually arise because we are careless about putting *not (only)* into the position in which it logically belongs, and drop it thoughtlessly into the sentence too early. Here is another example, from a history book: *✳The plague not only affected Gaul but most other Mediterranean territories as well*. The correction is easy: *The plague affected not only Gaul but . . .*

My last example, from a science book, is harder to fix: *✳It seems as though the galaxy started not as pure hydrogen, but was already a mix of hydrogen and helium*. This sentence has gone badly wrong, and it requires substantial rewriting. One solution is this: *It seems as though the galaxy started not as pure hydrogen, but as a mixture of hydrogen and helium*. Another solution is simply to move that *not*, which is causing most of the trouble with its bad placement: *It seems as though the galaxy did not start as pure hydrogen, but was already a mix of hydrogen and helium.*

notorious Something which is *notorious* is not only bad but well known. So, *a notorious torturer* is someone who is widely known as a torturer. Compare **infamous**.

not so much This wording must be followed by *as*, and not by *but*. Write *She is not so much a singer as an entertainer*, and not *✻She is not so much a singer but an entertainer*.

notwithstanding This is a very formal word for 'in spite of', 'despite', and it is best confined to very formal writing. Oddly, it can either precede or follow its object: *notwithstanding this result* or *this result notwithstanding*. The second version is a little more formal than the first.

nought See **naught**.

nouniness Nouniness is the excessive use of nouns, especially abstract nouns, and it is a common fault, especially in bureaucratic prose. Here is an example: *✻Because of the delay in the introduction of new assessment procedures for teaching staff, a postponement of the evaluation programme now appears inevitable.* The presence of all those nouns makes the text stiff, hard to follow, and wearisome to read. Here is a somewhat better version: *Since the new assessment procedures for teaching staff have been delayed, it seems we will have to postpone the evaluation programme.* It would be too much to advise you to prefer verbs to nouns in every case, but, if you suffer from this fault, you would do well to remind yourself that English has verbs.

nouns as verbs For centuries, English has been turning nouns into verbs without any modification. A good example is Shakespeare's use of the noun *beggar* as a verb in his line 'It beggared all description', from *Antony and Cleopatra*, a usage which is now familiar to us. It is easy to think of many similar examples, old and new, ranging from *She combed her hair* and *She smoked a cigarette* to *Her new film premieres tomorrow* and *You can access that utility from the main menu*. Even so, the overzealous 'verbing' of nouns can easily produce results which sound hideous to many people and which are hardly briefer or more elegant than conventional verbs. Writing things like *✻She is parenting three children*, *✻She has authored two books*, and *✻She has critiqued his new book* will impress nobody favourably but will convince many readers that your command of good English style is feeble.

Recently I encountered an article titled *Who Shall Mother?* I found this incomprehensible at first, but reading it eventually revealed that the intended sense was 'Who shall be a mother?' This title was a bad decision.

nubile This word, which is only ever applied to women, originally meant 'of a suitable age for marriage'. But no one uses it that way any more: instead, it has acquired the rather different sense of 'young and sexually attractive', and this is the only way it can now be used.

nuclear This is the only possible spelling, and *nucular* is wrong.

number A phrase beginning *a number of* is grammatically plural: *A number of students have fallen ill*. But a phrase beginning *the number of* is grammatically singular: *The number of students is up this year*.

numbers The numbers from twenty-one to ninety-nine are hyphenated when written out: *Mozart was thirty-seven years old when he died*. But larger numbers do not take any additional hyphens: *A leap year consists of three hundred and sixty-six days*.

The number names up to ten are normally written out: *Three prisoners have escaped; She had ten children*. It is bad style to write *She had 10 children*. With number names from eleven to twenty, there is fluctuation: some authorities prefer to see these too written out, while others are happy with the digits. I advise writing them out: *The US flag has thirteen stripes*. But numbers above twenty are written with digits in most circumstances: *A golf tournament consists of 72 holes; Writing was invented less than 6000 years ago*.

It is *very* bad style to begin a sentence with a number written in digits: *3 prisoners have escaped; *37 people were killed by the bomb*. Either write out the number or rewrite the sentence so that it no longer begins with a number.

oblige, obligate Legal senses aside, these verbs have the same meaning. On the whole, the shorter form *oblige* is more usual and is recommended. Indeed, in British English *obligate* is now all but obsolete, though in American English it continues to find some use.

oblivious In American English, you are usually *oblivious to* something. In Britain, most authorities declare firmly that *oblivious of* is the only possibility, but a substantial number of literate people defy this ruling and insist on *oblivious to*. You may use either, but, if you choose *to*, be prepared for objections.

Traditionally, *oblivious* means 'forgetful', not 'unaware': that is, you can only be oblivious of something which you once knew. However, most people today are happy to use the word to mean 'unaware', as in *She was so engrossed in her work that she was oblivious of the approaching storm*.

But most careful users of English object to the use of *oblivious* to mean 'deliberately paying no attention'. You should avoid writing things like *As we huddled in a circle, our captors, oblivious of/to us, argued among themselves.* Prefer *ignoring us*.

obscene This word means 'outrageously and repellently indecent', and it is best applied to things that are morally shocking or perverted. It should not be used loosely: a dress may be *shockingly expensive*, but it cannot be *obscenely expensive*.

obsess It is quite acceptable to write *She was obsessed with him*. But you should avoid the journalistic form illustrated by *She was obsessing over him*.

obsolescent, obsolete Something which is *obsolescent* is dropping out of use but is not yet entirely gone, while something which is *obsolete* has completely disappeared from use. In the western world, mechanical type-writers are obsolescent, while slide rules are obsolete.

occasional The word is so spelled, with one S, and *occassional* is wrong.

Occitan, Provençal In the Middle Ages, through the French Revolution, and well into the twentieth century, the language spoken in most of the southern half of France was not French at all, but a quite different language. Since outsiders noticed that speakers of this language said *oc* for 'yes', it came to be known first as the *langue d'oc*, and then as *Occitan*. Occitan is still spoken today, though it is now largely confined to rural areas. It has never had an accepted standard form, and it has always been spoken in a variety of regional dialects. One group of dialects, spoken in the Mediter-ranean territory of Provence, became the vehicle of a brilliant literature in the Middle Ages; this dialect was dubbed *Provençal*, and, in English, this name has often been extended to the whole language.

However, you are strongly advised to call the language *Occitan* – the name preferred by its speakers – and not *Provençal*, since using the second name for the language is rather like referring to English as 'East Anglian' or 'Californian'.

occurrence This is so spelled, with two Cs and two Rs. The common mistake is writing *occurence*. The verb *occur* also has the forms *occurred* and *occurring*.

octopus The plural is *octopuses*. Avoid the form *octopi*, which is either a joke or a blunder: the word is not of Latin origin, and it has no business taking a Latin plural.

oculist See **ophthalmologist**.

oe See **ae**.

of age Write *nine years old*, and not the pompous *nine years of age*.

off of Though it is common in vernacular speech, especially in the USA, the preposition *off of* is not acceptable in standard English. Write *He fell off the ladder*, not ∗*He fell off of the ladder*.

Oklahoma, Oklahoma City The American state is *Oklahoma*; its capital city is *Oklahoma City*. British writers must be careful not to write *Oklahoma* when they mean *Oklahoma City*.

Old English The history of English is conventionally divided by scholars into four periods: *Old English* (from the first settlement of Germanic-speakers in Britain to 1100, just after the Norman Conquest, sometimes also called *Anglo-Saxon*), *Middle English* (1100–1500), *Early Modern English* (1500–1700), and *Modern English* (1700 to the present). *Old English* is thus the language of *Beowulf* and of King Alfred the Great. It is wrong to refer to Chaucer's English or Shakespeare's English as 'Old English'. If you need to refer generally to English which is significantly earlier than modern English, write *earlier English*.

older See **elder**.

old language A meaningless term. Except for creoles and sign languages, which are special cases, every natural language (mother tongue) is equally old, in that each is descended, without interruption, from the remote origins of human speech. True, some languages have been established in their present positions longer than others, some were first written down earlier than others, and some have changed less than others in the last few centuries, but none of these circumstances makes a language older than another language. So, you should never describe a language as 'old', or write that one language is 'older' than another, or ask 'how old' a language is. Write something more specific: *Basque has been established in its present position longer than any other living European language*, or *Icelandic is much more conservative than its Scandinavian relatives*.

Olympic, Olympics, Olympian, Olympiad The *Olympic games*, held every four years, can equally be called the *Olympics*. The adjective *Olympic* means 'pertaining to the Olympic games', as in *an Olympic athlete*. The adjective *Olympian* means 'pertaining to Mount Olympus', and, by extension, both 'pertaining to the gods of ancient Greece' and 'celestial, heavenly'. The noun *Olympian* means 'a participant in the Olympic games'. The noun *Olympiad* means both 'a particular staging of the Olympic games' and 'the period of time between one Olympic games and the next', though the first is by far the more frequent.

omissible phrases Quite a few commonly used phrases contribute nothing whatever to your writing and should, in almost all cases, be omitted. Here are some of the most frequent of these:

all things considered
as a matter of fact
for all intents and purposes
for the most part
in a manner of speaking
in a very real sense
in my (honest) opinion
in the final analysis
the point I am trying to make is that
to all intents and purposes
what I mean to say is that

If you find yourself writing one of these, check to see if it makes an essential contribution to your meaning. If it does not, remove it. The frequent use of these things will make your writing appear wordy, padded and empty. See also **cliché**.

omit This is so spelled, with one M, even though *commit* has two Ms. Avoid the common error *＊ommit*. And note that the derived noun is *omission*, not *＊omittance*.

one These days, almost every keyboard has a key with the numeral 1 for 'one'. If you are still using a keyboard that lacks this, you should replace it with a small L (*l*), not with a capital i (*I*). Capital I doesn't look much like a one, and it also happens to be the roman numeral for 'one'. So, if you can't write *1994*, write *l994*, not *＊I994*.

one of the The following example illustrates a very frequent error: *＊Dr Wilson is one of the scientists who opposes research into cloning*. The mistake here is to make the verb (here *opposes*) agree with the word *one*, which is not its subject. The subject here is *the scientists*, and the correct version is *Dr Wilson is one of the scientists who oppose research into cloning*. If you think about this a moment, you will realize that the wording *＊the scientists who opposes* is clearly wrong.

ongoing This word, though by no means a recent one, is widely disliked, and is hardly ever necessary. You are advised to avoid it: write *a continuing process*, not *an ongoing process*; write *a persistent problem*, not *an ongoing problem*; and write *a current controversy*, not *an ongoing controversy*. And, if you value your reputation, avoid the ghastly phrase *an ongoing situation* at all costs. This phrase uses eight syllables to say nothing at all, and using it marks you at once as someone with nothing to say.

on line, online The adverb is *on line*, while the adjective is *online* or *on-line*. Write *This dictionary is available on line*, not *online* or *on-line*. But write *an online dictionary* or *an on-line dictionary*, not *an on line dictionary*.

only In colloquial speech, the word *only* may turn up in surprising places. But, in formal writing, it should be placed directly before the word or phrase which it applies to. For example, you should write *The judge sentenced only one of the defendants to jail*, and not *The judge only sentenced one of the defendants to jail*, since this defective version implies that the judge sent that one defendant to jail but did nothing else to him. See what happens with a continuation: *The judge only sentenced one of the defendants to jail, while he both jailed and heavily fined the remaining defendants*.

Consider a further example. The sentence *An ice-hockey team may only consist of six players* means 'No ice-hockey team is legal unless it consists of exactly six players', while the sentence *An ice-hockey team may consist of only six players* means 'It is legal for an ice-hockey team to consist of six players, even though it usually consists of more players'.

Careless placement of *only* may bewilder your reader. Pay careful attention when you use this word.

onomatopoeia This word is so spelled. The derived adjective is preferably *onomatopoeic*; the variant *onomatopoetic* is now accepted by some (not all) authorities, but is best avoided, since some people dislike it.

on the order of, in the range of We write *temperatures on the order of $30,000^0$* and *temperatures in the range of $20–30,000^0$*. But do not tangle these up: *temperatures in the order of $30,000^0$* is wrong.

onto, on to The choice between *onto* and *on to* is often an awkward one, and not all authorities agree about where to draw the line. But here are some useful rules of thumb.

First, if you could, in principle, stop writing after *on*, and still get a sensible sentence with a related meaning, then you must write *on to*. For example, *We pushed on to the next town* is right, because it is clearly only an extended form of *We pushed on*, and *Let's move on to the next agenda item* is right, because it is an extended form of *Let's move on*.

Second, you should write *onto* only when the thing that is moving literally winds up on top of whatever is denoted by the words following *onto*. For example, *She tossed her books onto the table* is right, because the books really do end up on the table.

Observe the difference between the following two examples: *We drove on to the beach* means 'We continued driving until we had reached the beach' (though we didn't necessarily take the car right onto the sand), but *We drove onto the beach* means 'We moved the car so that its wheels were sitting on the beach.'

If these rules don't seem to be enough, consider whether you would write *into* in a related sentence. Should you write *A streaker ran onto the pitch* or *A streaker ran on to the pitch*? Well, I prefer *onto*, since I would not hesitate to write *A streaker ran into the changing room*.

op. cit., loc. cit. These two Latin phrases mean 'in the work cited' and 'in the place cited'. In scholarly work, they represent an extremely bad way of citing references to published work, and they should not be used. Each one says, in effect, 'This is another reference to something I mentioned some time ago, and, if you want to know what it is, you can leaf back through twenty-five or fifty pages to find it.' For the proper way of citing published work, see chapter 10 of the *Penguin Guide to Punctuation*.

ophthalmologist, oculist, optometrist, optician An *ophthalmologist* is a medical practitioner specializing in diseases of the eye. Another word with the same meaning is *oculist*, which is now rarely used. An *optometrist* is a person who is qualified to examine the eyes and to prescribe spectacle lenses. An *optician* is not qualified to prescribe lenses, but merely sells spectacle frames. In practice, a high-street shop usually contains both optometrists and opticians. In Britain, an optometrist is often called an *ophthalmic optician*, while an optician is called a *dispensing optician*.

optimal, optimum Both of these are technical terms in certain mathematical disciplines. Neither should ever be used where *best* is intended: write *the best result*, not **the optimal result*, or, still worse, **the optimum result*.

optometrist See **ophthalmologist**.

opus, opera The more-or-less technical term *opus* denotes a literary or musical composition, and the rarely used plural is *opera*. However, it is preferable to write *Beethoven's works*, rather than ??*Beethoven's opera*.

But we use the singular word *opera* to denote a dramatic musical composition: *Fidelio was Beethoven's only opera*. The plural is *operas*.

-or See **-our**.

oral, verbal Something which is *oral* is spoken: for example, an oral agreement is one which is made by speaking, with nothing written down. In contrast, anything which is *verbal* is expressed in words, whether spoken or written. Hence a verbal agreement may be either spoken or written down. It is an error to write *verbal* if what you mean is *oral*. It may help to remember that *non-verbal communication* is communication by means of postures, gestures and expressions, without the use of words.

orchestrate To *orchestrate* a piece of music is to take the musical ideas and convert them into notes assigned to the various instruments, so that the whole yields a satisfying result. Orchestrating something therefore involves a great deal more than merely organizing or directing it. Accordingly, *orchestrate* should be used with care: don't write this word thoughtlessly when all you mean is 'organize', 'lead' or 'direct'.

ordinance, ordnance An *ordinance* is a bylaw or a decree. In contrast, *ordnance* is munitions – that is, ammunition, shells or artillery. Curiously, the official map-making body of the British or Irish government is the *Ordnance Survey*.

orient, orientate The traditional form of the verb is *orient*, as in *I couldn't orient myself* and *She was disoriented*. This is still the only possibility in American English. In British English, however, the word is commonly extended to *orientate*, producing *I couldn't orientate myself* and *She was disorientated*. This extended form cannot now be regarded as wrong in British use, but what is the point of introducing a useless extra syllable? The shorter form is recommended.

-os, -oes Writing the plurals of nouns ending in *-o* is one of the most infuriating problems in English spelling. There is absolutely no general rule here for choosing between *-os* and *-oes*, and you will simply have to learn how to write the plural of every one of these words. In fact, though, the great majority of such words take *-os*: *curios, zeros, radios, scenarios, commandos, frescos, piccolos, solos, kimonos, fiascos, weirdos, credos, ratios*, and so on. So the problem reduces to learning the words which don't behave in this way. Fortunately, there are only a few words which absolutely require *-oes*, the most frequent ones being the following: *buffaloes* (but note that the more usual plural is *buffalo*), *dominoes, echoes, embargoes, goes, heroes*,

Negroes, noes, potatoes, tomatoes, torpedoes, vetoes. A number of others can form their plurals in either way: *calicos* or *calicoes*; *cargos* or *cargoes*; *halos* or *haloes*; *mosquitos* or *mosquitoes*; *mottos* or *mottoes*; *volcanos* or *volcanoes*. When in doubt, of course, consult a dictionary.

Note also that a few words of Italian origin may or must form their plurals with *-i*: *graffito, graffiti*; *castrato, castrati*; *basso, bassi*; and a few others.

ostensible, ostensive, ostentatious The word *ostensible* means 'apparent', 'seeming', 'professed': so, for example, *an ostensibly independent assessment* is an assessment which is apparently independent, which is publicly presented as independent. As this example may indicate, today the word almost always carries a suggestion of deception: the writer of this phrase is delicately implying that, even though somebody has *called* the assessment 'independent', it is not really independent. In other words, the assessment has been rigged. Therefore, you should not use *ostensible* if you do not mean to imply any such thing: use 'apparent' or 'seeming' instead.

The rare word *ostensive* is primarily a technical term in philosophy. You should avoid it unless you are sure of its technical sense.

An *ostentatious* action is one which is pretentiously flamboyant, which is intended to impress gullible people: *Her ostentatious clothes struck me as vulgar.*

Do not use *ostensive* or *ostentatious* when you mean *ostensible*, and do not use *ostensible* if you mean only 'seeming'.

-our, -or There exist a number of words which are spelled *-our* in Britain but *-or* in the USA. Among these are *colour/color, labour/labor, splendour/splendor, armour/armor, honour/honor* and *favour/favor*; there are too many to give an exhaustive list here, and you should consult a dictionary if in doubt. But certain words have *-or* in all varieties of English: *terror, horror, squalor, tremor, pallor* and others.

Note, though, that in British English certain derivatives of *-our* words are spelled with *-or*. So, for example, British English has *humour* but *humorous* and *humorist*, *vapour* but *vaporize* and *evaporate*, *colour* and *colourize* but *colorant* and *coloration*. For British writers, mastery of these details may require considerable use of a dictionary. The American standard has a great advantage here, in using the same spelling throughout.

ours This is the correct spelling, and both *our's* and *ours'* are wrong.

overboard This word is an adverb, not a preposition. Hence this is wrong: *He fell overboard the ship*. Write *He fell overboard* or *He fell overboard from the ship*.

overlong sentences It is quite possible to find yourself writing a sentence which is perfectly grammatical, perfectly sensible and perfectly punctuated, but which nevertheless drags on for so long that it may drive your readers to despair. Here is an example. Take a deep breath. *After the Spanish Civil War ended in 1939, many Basque soldiers fled into exile in France, where they soon found themselves caught up in the Nazi occupation of the French coast, including the French Basque Country, with the result that they switched their attention to fighting the occupying Germans as best they could, acquiring in the process new military skills which they were able to put to good use after the German defeat by hiding out in the Pyrenees and conducting armed raids against the troops of the Spanish dictator General Franco, raids which only petered out after the United States welcomed Spain, the last surviving Fascist nation in Europe, into the fold of its Cold War alliance against the Soviet threat.*

Whew. If you find that you have written a monstrosity of this length, go back and break it up into two or three shorter sentences. Your word processor will probably be able to tell you the length in words of the longest sentence in your text; if you discover that it is something like 118 words, do some rewriting.

overview This word, denoting a broad general survey, the 'big picture', is perfectly acceptable in American English. In British English, it is still regarded with some suspicion and distaste. It is now not at all rare in Britain, but British writers might choose to steer clear of it anyway.

owing to See **due to**.

ox We all learn in school that the plural of *ox* is *oxen*. In fact, in colloquial English, *oxes* is more usual when the word is used at all, but formal written English still requires *oxen* for the animals. However, the colloquial word *ox* 'large, clumsy man' always takes the plural form *oxes*.

ozone This is not a fancy word for 'bracing fresh air'. It is the name of a chemical substance with the formula O_3. And ozone is not bracing at all: it is lethal when inhaled. Be grateful there isn't much of it in your seaside air.

paean, peon A *paean* is a piece of extravagant praise. A *peon* is a Latin American peasant. The common error here is *∗paeon* for *paean*.

Pagliacci The name of Leoncavallo's opera is *Pagliacci*, and not, as is often written, *∗I Pagliacci*.

pampas See **grasslands**.

panacea A *panacea* is a universal remedy, a cure-all. The word should not be applied to any old remedy. And *∗universal panacea* is a **pleonasm**.

pandemic See **endemic**.

Panjab, Punjab The spelling *Panjab* is recommended for the region of India, and *Panjabi* for the language. The alternative spellings *Punjab* and *Punjabi* are not recommended, since these induce people to mispronounce the names. And do not write *∗the Panjab*.

pantomime The word is so spelled, with two Ms, and the spelling *∗pantomine* is wrong. If this troubles you, think of *mime*, which nobody ever gets wrong.

paparazzo The singular is *paparazzo*; the plural is *paparazzi*. Paparazzi, of course, are photographers who try to snatch candid or embarrassing photos of famous people.

paradigm In grammar, a paradigm is an orderly list of the forms taken by an inflected word, presented as a model of the behaviour of words of that class. An example is the paradigm of the Latin verb *amo* 'love', often presented in textbooks as a model for the inflection of the class of verbs to which it belongs. By extension, a paradigm is a highly typical or stereotypical example of something, or even an outstandingly good example of something, as when we write *The cold-fusion debacle was a paradigm case of how not to do science*.

But *paradigm* has become a vogue word, and today it is used far too freely, and often pretentiously, when a simpler word would be preferable. Don't use the word when *model*, *pattern* or (*good*) *example* would serve your purpose.

Moreover, be very wary of the expression *paradigm shift*. This term was introduced by Thomas Kuhn into the philosophy of science, but it has been picked up and applied with wearisome frequency to almost any change in policy or fashion. Avoid it in favour of something more explicit.

paraffin The word is so spelled, and *∗parrafin* is wrong. This is an old technical term in chemistry, now generally displaced there by *alkane*. In Britain, it is also the name of a certain fuel; the American equivalent is *kerosene*.

parallel constructions Constructions involving connecting words like *and* and *but* require careful attention, since it is all too easy to lose your way in the middle of one of these and to produce something which fails to be a parallel construction – that is, only some of your words connect properly with the rest of the sentence. Here are a few examples, all of them genuine.

From an advertisement for an English course: *Have you ever wanted to learn English but didn't know how to go about it?* The part after *but* must be taken as *have you ever didn't know . . .* , which is gibberish. The continuation should be *. . . but not known . . .*

From a political statement: *We have never and will never accept this.* The sequence *we have never accept* is not English. Correct if cumbersome is *We have never accepted, and will never accept, this*, though it would be better style to write *We have never accepted this, and we will never accept it.* This is another instance of a **right-node raising** gone wrong.

From an advertisement: *Are you short of time but need a tasty meal in minutes?* Again, *are you need a tasty meal?* is nonsense.

From a speech: *This could not and ought not rule out a settlement.* Here the problem is the sequence *ought not rule out*, which is missing its obligatory *to*.

From an official document: ??*Any person who has submitted an application and who has requested an acknowledgement but has not received one . . .* This is not strictly wrong, but clarity would be improved by adding a third instance of *who* before *has not received one*.

A special problem arises with verbs which can take either objects or complements. It is fine to write *The Vikings discovered America*, and it is equally fine to write *They discovered that it was already inhabited*, but it is an error to combine these: *The Vikings discovered America and that it was already inhabited*. The problem here is that *America* is a noun phrase, while *that it was already inhabited* is a complement clause. The resulting construction is therefore not parallel.

Not all such errors involve *and* or *but*. Here is a different example, illustrating a very frequent error: *Elliot earns as much if not more than Gates*. The problem now is the sequence *as much . . . than Gates*, which is gibberish. The correct form is this: *as much as, if not more than, Gates*. The first version is another example of a **right-node raising** gone wrong.

Yet another example arises with modified nouns. There is no problem with *serious newspapers*, nor is there any with *tabloid newspapers*. However, these two examples are not parallel, since *serious* is an adjective, while *tabloid* is a noun. Consequently, *serious and tabloid newspapers* sounds awful. An acceptable version would be *serious and popular newspapers*, with two adjectives, or *broadsheet and tabloid newspapers*, with two nouns.

Problems of this kind are so frequent with *not . . . but* that I have provided a separate entry under **not (only) . . . but (also)**. See also **missing preposition**.

parameter In mathematical subjects, a *parameter* is a numerical quantity whose value can be varied from case to case but can be held constant, at a desired value, in a given case. It is acceptable to use the word more generally when this sense is held in mind. However, it is out of order to use the word freely to mean no more than 'constraint' or 'limit', or, still worse, 'characteristic'. It is frothy and shallow to write *within the parameters of our budget* when all you mean is *within the constraints of our budget*, and it is diabolical to write *the parameters of her work* when you merely mean *the characteristics of her work*. And avoid the spelling errors *paramater* and *perameter*.

paranoid *Paranoia* is a recognized medical condition, and usually a very grave one. Like all medical terms, *paranoid* should not be tossed around loosely. It is highly inappropriate to write *paranoid* when all you mean is something like 'anxious' or 'nervous'.

partner Today it is commonplace for two people to live together as an established and committed couple, often with children, without going through a marriage ceremony, and *partner* has become the normal word for denoting one of the two. This is so with both heterosexual and homosexual couples. It is always acceptable to write of someone's *partner* in this context, and doing so is recommended, since some people in this position dislike the words *boyfriend* and *girlfriend*.

past experience This is a **pleonasm**. All experience is necessarily in the past. Write *her experience*, not *her past experience*, or, still worse, *her prior experience*.

PC See **political correctness**.

pedagogue This troublesome word behaves differently in British English and in American English. Originally, it meant only 'teacher', and it still does in the US, where it is a formal or respectful word for a teacher, with no negative connotations. The variant spelling *pedagog* is permissible in the US, but not recommended, and it is never acceptable in Britain.

In Britain, however, the word has acquired strong negative overtones, and it is now applied only to a teacher who is pretentious, fussy, dogmatic or pedantic. This pejorative sense is now so prominent that the word cannot be used in Britain in its neutral sense. Indeed, for many Britons, the word has become a virtual synonym for *pedant*, or a label for anyone who shows off knowledge at every opportunity.

penny, pence In several English-speaking countries, the smallest unit of currency, or the coin of smallest denomination, is the *penny*. In all of these countries except Britain, the plural is always *pennies*. In Britain, though, things are more complicated: the plural is *pennies* if you are writing of coins, as in *a pocketful of pennies*, but *pence* if you are writing of a sum of money, as in *A cup of tea costs 75 pence*.

British usage exhibits a further peculiarity. When the old LSD currency was in use, it was usual to write of *a sixpenny piece*. Today, however, very many Britons say, and write, *??a twenty-pence piece* and even *??a one-pence piece* for the coins, and, surprisingly, even *??one pence* for the sum of money. It appears that *pence* is well on the way to displacing *penny* in all circumstances in Britain. Even so, if you write *??a twenty-pence piece*, you may expect some grumbling from your older readers.

penultimate This is merely a fancy word for 'next-to-last', as in *November is the penultimate month of the year*. For some reason, many people have gained the impression that it means something like 'absolutely last', 'latest' or 'most fashionable'. It does not.

per cent, percent The preferred British form is *per cent*, while the preferred American form is *percent*. However, the American form is gaining ground in Britain and is now acceptable in some quarters, though not in all.

Note also the following. If interest rates rise from 10% to 11%, then they have not risen by one per cent, but by ten per cent. (If you were paying £100 a month before, you are paying £110 a month now – an increase of ten per cent.) But you can write that rates have gone up by one percentage point.

perception Originally, you could only *perceive* something that was really there, and a *perception* was thus merely a recognition of existence. More recently, however, *perception* has come to be used to denote the manner in which something is evaluated. For example, when manufacturers worry about the perception of their product by the general public, they are not bothered about whether the public knows their product exists, but rather about whether people regard their product as fashionable and desirable or not. This new use is now so well established that only a handful of conservative commentators still object to it.

peremptory A word which is often misunderstood. A *peremptory* order or a *peremptory* dismissal is not one which is sudden, or brief, or irregular. It is one which is decisive and final, one which permits no argument, no debate, no questioning and no appeal.

perfect progressive passive The perfect progressive passive is illustrated by the following example: *My house has been being painted for two weeks now.* There is nothing here which violates any rule of standard English grammar, and most speakers find such sentences entirely normal. Oddly, though, quite a few people find these unacceptable. These people have no difficulty with any of *has been painting*, *has been painted* or *is being painted*, but the combination of three auxiliaries renders the result unacceptable. I have no idea why this should be so, but, in any case, there is no objection to using such constructions when they are appropriate.

permissiveness A curious word. Nobody *ever* uses it as a term of approval, or even neutrally. It is always used as a complaint: *permissiveness* is, without exception, a label for something that somebody is doing that the writer doesn't approve of. If you find yourself using it, you're obviously fulminating about something. Maybe you should calm down. The neutral equivalent is *tolerance*.

perquisite, prerequisite A *perquisite* is a privilege attached to a certain job, such as a company car or free use of a gym. The word is informally shortened to *perk*. But a *prerequisite* is a condition you must satisfy in order to qualify for something: *A good degree in French is a prerequisite for this job.*

per se This Latin phrase means 'in itself', 'of itself', 'intrinsically': *I don't like pop music* per se, *but I enjoy country and western.* The phrase is usually pretentious and unnecessary: just leave it out.

persecute, prosecute To *persecute* somebody is to deliberately make him suffer, usually because of his race, religion, social group or political beliefs: *Queen Mary persecuted the Protestants.* To *prosecute* somebody is to bring legal charges against him: *Shoplifters will be prosecuted.* There is also a much rarer sense of *prosecute*, 'continue with', now largely confined to war, as in *Beyazit prosecuted his war against the Europeans until Tamerlane's invasion forced him to desist.*

persevere This verb means 'continue', often especially in the face of obstacles. It may be followed either by *with* or by *in*: *She persevered with her studies* or *She persevered in her studies.* Avoid the misspelling *✽perservere*.

Persian See **Farsi**.

personally This word is often used to no purpose. It is pointless to write
*Nixon personally visited all fifty states or *I personally find his latest film
disappointing. Nixon's visits could only be in person, and my opinion can
only be personal. Write instead Nixon visited . . . and I find . . .

personal names When you cite a person's name, you must not only spell
the name correctly but be careful to use the form preferred by the owner of
the name. For example, the palaeontologist Stephen Jay Gould always signs
himself in this way, and you should use the same form if you mention him:
don't call him *Stephen J. Gould or *S. J. Gould. Of course, once you have
introduced him, you can refer to him thereafter as Gould.

Likewise, the linguist Noam Chomsky always signs himself in this manner,
and it is out of order to refer to him as *Avram Noam Chomsky or as *A. N.
Chomsky or as *N. Chomsky. This last style, consisting of first initial plus
surname, is usual in some other European languages, but it is neither usual
nor appropriate in English, except in the rare case in which you happen to
be discussing two people with the same surname and you need to distinguish
them.

With names – most often foreign names – containing diacritics (accent
marks), you should reproduce those diacritics faithfully. Today almost any
word processor can produce the commoner diacritics. So, the Spanish
Basque golfer is José-María Olazábal; the Turkish patriot is Mustafa Kemal
Atatürk; the French politician is François Mitterrand; and the English novelist
is Charlotte Brontë.

Many foreign names contain particles which are not capitalized, such as
von, van, de, du and da. These forms should be respected. Write General von
Moltke, Ludwig van Beethoven, Simone de Beauvoir and Leonardo da Vinci, and
do not capitalize the particle. However, some families with such names have
emigrated to English-speaking countries, and their descendants may choose to
capitalize the particle. This is why we have names like Dick Van Dyke and Yvonne
De Carlo. But not all do so: note the name of the English cellist Jacqueline du Pré.
Moreover, some such immigrants choose to write their surnames solid, with
a single initial capital, as in Cornelius Vanderbilt and Margaret Dumont. As
always, you should respect the preferences of the owner of the name.

In any context in which you are mentioning people by surnames alone,
you must treat women and men in the same way. If you are writing about
tennis, and you mention Sampras and Agassi, then you must also write
Hingis and Davenport, and not *Miss Hingis or *Ms Davenport, which is
unbearably sexist.

personnel This word, which means 'the staff employed by an organization', is so spelled, with two Ns and one L.

perspicacious, perspicuous A *perspicacious* person is one who is shrewd, perceptive or discerning. Only a person can be perspicacious. A *perspicuous* thing is a thing which is clear, lucid and easy to understand, such as a perspicuous explanation. A person cannot be perspicuous. The derived nouns are *perspicacity* and *perspicuity*, respectively. As so often, you can avoid tangling these words up by simply avoiding them in favour of simpler synonyms like *perceptive* and *lucid*.

peruse Traditionally, to *peruse* written material is to read it very carefully, to examine it, study it, scrutinize it. This usage is still normal. Recently, however, by a misunderstanding, the word has come to be used frequently to mean 'glance through', 'read in a casual or idle manner'. This new sense is now so frequent that it is recognized by many dictionaries and by a few usage guides. However, it will annoy many readers, and you are advised to avoid it. As usual, choosing plain everyday words like *glance through* is preferable to sticking in fancy-looking Latinate words whose meanings you're not quite sure of.

In any case, don't write *peruse* when *read* will do just fine.

petite This word means 'small', but it can be applied only to a woman of small stature or to a clothing size suitable for such a woman. When applied to a woman, the word is complimentary: it suggests that her small size is attractive (but note that feminists may find this word sexist and offensive). The word cannot be applied to a man (except as a joke) or to anything else.

petrifaction When organic material is slowly converted into stone, it becomes *petrified*, and the process is *petrifaction*. There is no such word as *petrification*.

petroleum, petrol, petrel The word *petroleum* is a somewhat technical name for '(crude) oil'. In contrast, *petrol* is a petroleum derivative used in car engines; the American equivalent is *gasoline*, often shortened to *gas*. But a *petrel* is a kind of seabird.

phantasy See **fantasy**.

pharaoh The word is so spelled, and *pharoah* and *pharoh* are wrong.

phenomenon, phenomena The singular is *phenomenon*, the plural is *phenomena*. Write *this phenomenon* and *these phenomena*, not *this phenomena* or *these phenomenon*.

phial, vial Both forms of the word for 'small container' are correct. British English somewhat prefers *phial*, while American English strongly prefers *vial*.

Philippines, Filipino Note the spelling of the name of the country: one L, two Ps. Do not write *Phillipines* or *Phillippines*. A person from the Philippines is a *Filipino*. Oddly, many writers make a sex distinction here, using *Filipino* for a male but *Filipina* for a female. This distinction is now so well-established that it cannot be called wrong, but it is certainly unusual: we do not distinguish sex among Cubans, Russians, Koreans or Thais, so why among Filipinos?

phonetic alphabet In everyday English, we apply the somewhat unfortunate term *phonetic alphabet* to any conventional system for spelling out words over a radio link. A familiar example is the US Army's *alpha, bravo, charlie* system. In linguistics and phonetics, however, a *phonetic alphabet* is a system of conventional characters for representing speech sounds. The most widely used phonetic alphabet is the International Phonetic Alphabet.

phonetic spelling This term has become widespread as a label for any system of spelling which matches the pronunciation in a systematic and regular way, so that the pronunciation of a word can almost always be correctly predicted from its spelling. However, the term is strictly inaccurate: in linguistic work, this kind of spelling is properly called *phonemic spelling*, while *phonetic spelling* denotes something quite different, a massively detailed spelling system with a blizzard of diacritics representing tiny details of pronunciation, something which no sane person would propose as a practical orthography. See also **spelling**.

phoney, phony Both spellings are correct. British English prefers *phoney*, while American English prefers *phony*.

phosphorus The name of the chemical element is *phosphorus*, and *phosphorous* is strictly an adjective used by chemists. And there is no such word as *phospherus* or *phospherous*.

-phth- A number of technical terms of Greek origin contain the unusual letter sequence *-phth-*. Here are the most frequent such words:

aphtha
diphtheria
diphthong
monophthong

naphtha, naphthalene
ophthalmic (and related words)
phthalic acid (and its derivatives)
triphthong

pidgin See **creole**.

pied piping See under **preposition stranding**.

pigeon The bird is a *pigeon*, and the spelling *pidgeon* is wrong.

pigmy See **pygmy**.

Pinocchio The name is so spelled, with one N and two Cs. Avoid the error *Pinnochio*.

pistol See **handgun**.

Pittsburgh The name of the city in Pennsylvania is always so spelled, with two Ts and, critically, an H on the end. Do not write *Pittsburg* or *Pitsburg*. Not long ago, I had to fly to Pittsburgh, and my British travel agent's inability to type the name correctly into her computer wasted a good deal of her and my time, since the machine could not understand her misspelled versions. Who says spelling is not important in today's electronic world?

place-name derivatives Unlike some other languages, English has no systematic or orderly way of deriving from place names adjectives meaning 'pertaining to' or nouns meaning 'person from'. Often the suffixes *-er*, *-(i)an* and *-ite* are used in a more or less haphazard way to derive such words: *Londoner, New Yorker, Queenslander, Quebecker, Chicagoan, Floridian, Bristolian, British Columbian, New Jerseyite, Wyomingite*. Some place names appear to have no such derivatives in use: for example, I know of none for Seattle, Edinburgh, Sussex, Christchurch, Natal or St. Louis. But some place names have established derivatives which are highly unpredictable and often little known in the wider world. Below are a few of these which have come to my attention. There are doubtless others.

Birmingham	Brummie
Connecticut	Nutmegger
Glasgow	Glaswegian
Indiana	Hoosier
Liverpool	Liverpudlian
Los Angeles	Angelino
Maine	Down Easter

Manchester	Mancunian
Massachusetts	Bay Stater
Michigan	Michigander
Newcastle	Novocastrian
North Carolina	Tarheel
Sydney	Sydneysider
Utah	Utahn

place names Peculiarly American is the odd habit of following the name of a famous city with the name of its country. There is no point in writing *Paris, France or *Moscow, Russia since every reader will assume that *Paris* and *Moscow* denote the famous cities. It is only appropriate to add a qualifier when you are referring to a less well-known city with the same name: *Paris, Texas* and *Moscow, Idaho* are fine.

plaid, tartan In Scotland, a *tartan* is a woollen cloth with a pattern of stripes of different colours crossing at right angles. Each Scottish clan has its own distinctive tartan. But a *plaid* is a length of tartan fabric worn over one shoulder as part of the traditional Highland costume: look at any Scottish piper. In everyday English, *plaid* has come to be applied to a tartan fabric. This new use cannot now be regarded as wrong, but it should be avoided in a Scottish connection.

plain words See under **pomposity**.

plausible The word is so spelled, and the common error *plausable is never acceptable.

pleasantry A *pleasantry* is a good-natured little joke or a piece of friendly banter. So, *They were exchanging pleasantries* means they were teasing each other and joking in a good-natured manner. The abstract noun derived from *pleasant* is *pleasantness*, not *pleasantry*.

pleonasm A *pleonasm* is the use of a word which merely repeats a bit of meaning which is already present in another word. Here is an example: *The two armies combined together*. Things which combine are necessarily together as a result, and so that *together* is pleonastic. Write instead *The two armies combined*. And here is another example: *There might be potential commercial developments*. Here *might* carries the same meaning as *potential*: write either *There might be commercial developments* or *There are potential commercial developments*.

Below is a list of some of the most frequent pleonasms, with corrected forms.

Pleonastic	Improved
adequate enough	*adequate*
an added bonus	*a bonus*
3 a.m. in the morning	*3 a.m.*
a total of 200 people	*200 people*
basic essentials	*essentials*
close proximity	*proximity*
close scrutiny	*scrutiny*
completely exhausted	*exhausted*
consensus of opinion	*consensus*
each and every	*each*
effective demonstration	*demonstration*
end result	*result*
exactly the same	*the same*
final completion	*completion*
free gift	*gift*
future plans	*plans*
in the field of linguistics	*in linguistics*
minute detail	*detail*
a new innovation	*an innovation*
one and the same	*the same*
particular interest	*interest*
period of two weeks	*two weeks*
personal opinion	*opinion*
prior experience	*experience*
razed to the ground	*razed*
rectangular in shape	*rectangular*
red in colour	*red*
refer back	*refer*
repeat again	*repeat*
revert back	*revert*
shorter in length	*shorter*
small in size	*small*
summarize briefly	*summarize*
surrounded on all sides	*surrounded*
temporary respite	*respite*
track record	*record*
true facts	*facts*
usual custom	*custom*
very widespread	*widespread*

plummet The verb *plummet* means 'fall straight down rapidly', and the key element here is 'down'. Nothing can plummet in any direction but downward, and writing *The balloon plummeted upward* is a hilarious but embarrassing blunder. It may help to remember that the word was once a noun meaning 'ball of lead'.

Since *plummet* already includes the sense of 'down', it is a **pleonasm** to write *The plane plummeted downward*. Settle for *The plane plummeted*.

plurals See **-os**, **plurals in compounds**, **plurals of compounds**, **unusual plurals**.

plurals in compounds Like its Germanic relatives, English forms compounds with great freedom. When the first element of a compound is a noun, then normally that noun must stand in its singular form. (Strictly, it stands in its *stem* form, but the stem is usually identical to the singular.) This happens even when the sense is logically plural. So, for example, a person who watches birds is a *birdwatcher*, not a *birdswatcher*, and a person who tunes pianos is a *piano tuner*, not a *pianos tuner*. It happens even when the noun has no singular. Although *trousers*, *oats* and *scissors* are strictly plural, and have no singular, we say *trouser leg* and not *trousers leg*, *oatmeal* and not *oatsmeal*, *scissor blade* and not *scissors blade*.

As the psycholinguist Steven Pinker has pointed out in his book *Words and Rules*, the only interesting exception occurs with nouns that have irregular plurals, at least when the whole compound is plural. It is quite possible to say *women doctors* rather than *woman doctors*, or *teethmarks* rather than *toothmarks* – even though nobody would say *clawsmarks*.

However, irregular exceptions do occur, and these are perhaps gaining ground in Britain. In American English, almost the only prominent exception is *sports*, which regularly forms compounds like *sportsman*, *sports pages* and *sportscaster*. British English has gone much further than this, though. Britons very commonly say, and write, *students union* instead of *student union*, *greetings card* instead of *greeting card*, *kitchenwares department* instead of *kitchenware department*, *drugs pushers* instead of *drug pushers*, and *trades union* instead of *trade union*. These peculiar departures from the established norms of the language are not to be encouraged. If you find yourself writing one of them, you might consider whether the form without the extra S would serve as well.

See also **penny**.

plurals of compounds Certain compound nouns in English have an unusual structure, with a head noun followed by other material. When one of these is pluralized, it is traditional to attach the plural ending to the head noun, and not to the whole thing. Here is a list of some of the most familiar examples of these, in the plural:

aides-de-camp
attorneys general (and all the other terms in *general*)
commanders-in-chief
courts martial
culs-de-sac
fleurs-de-lis
grants-in-aid
heirs presumptive
listeners-in
men-of-war
mothers-in-law (and all the other terms for in-laws)
notaries public
passers-by
poets laureate
rights of way

These unusual plurals are always acceptable in formal writing, and you are advised to use them. However, for a few of these words, the regular plurals, with *-s* at the end of the whole thing, are now widely used: *mother-in-laws*, *attorney generals*. Unfortunately, the authorities do not always agree as to just which of these compounds can now safely take the regular plurals, and using the regular plurals for any of them will inevitably annoy some conservative readers.

plus This word should not be used in writing to mean 'and': it is wrong to write *✻Martina won the singles title, plus she and her partner won the doubles*. Write *and* instead.

podium See **lectern**.

policy Politicians have a habit of saying *policy* when all they mean is 'ambition' or 'goal'. *✻This party has a policy of low inflation* is absurd, since low inflation is not something that anybody can put in place by fiat, but only an aspiration which may perhaps be pursued by means of real policies.

political correctness There is probably no more vexed topic than this one, and here I can do no more than to suggest a few guidelines. Beyond doubt, the most vexed issues of all are those involving **sexism**, and for these I have provided a separate entry. Otherwise, the PC movement focuses on perceived linguistic ill-treatment of people because of their ethnic background (or 'race'), their sexuality, their disabilities, their religion, and often also their size, shape or physical appearance, or even their tastes in food, clothes or hobbies.

The PC movement is well-meaning in origin, and some of its complaints must be acknowledged as just by any fair-minded person. However, some people in the movement have taken matters to an extreme, often an absurd extreme. This is unfortunate, since the excellent advice to refrain from calling anyone a *dago or a *poof or a *spastic loses its force when it comes together with an insistence on *differently abled in place of disabled, or *hearing-impaired in place of deaf, or *vertically challenged in place of short.

Some general guidelines. First, do not assign anybody to a class when that class is irrelevant. It is fine to describe somebody as a Rasta poet if that poet's work expressly celebrates Rastafarianism. But it is extremely offensive to describe somebody as *a Jewish scientist if that scientist's religious or ethnic background is of no relevance to his work. This is rather like describing a nominee to the US Supreme Court as *a slim and attractive brunette. You should never mention anyone's religion, ethnic background, skin colour or physical appearance unless it is directly relevant.

Second, do not use a label that you would not want someone else to apply to you if you belonged to the group in question. Homosexuals are happy to call themselves queers among themselves, but the term is offensive when used by an outsider. If black Americans have made it clear they want to be called African-Americans, then call them that.

Third, be alert to changes in usage. The names Lapp and Eskimo, for example, were formerly usual in English, but they are now generally considered offensive by the people they denote, and courtesy today demands other words, such as Saami and Inuit. And *mongolism has been entirely ousted by Down's syndrome.

Fourth, if a proposed term seems preposterous to you, then don't use it. If, like me, you find my earlier examples *differently abled, *hearing-impaired and *vertically challenged to be ludicrous, then write something plainer and more direct.

pomposity There is a certain style of writing which never uses a plain word if a fancier word can be found. In such writing, every teacher is an educator, every doctor is a physician, every weatherman is a meteorologist, people don't write books but author them, people don't buy things but purchase them, people don't use things but utilize them, people don't eat things but consume them, people don't *talk* but *communicate*, things are never *different* but always *disparate*, people are never *poor* but only *underprivileged* or *disadvantaged*, and nobody ever has a mere life or career, but only an *odyssey*. This kind of writing is pompous, and it is wearisome to read. If you suffer from this problem, try to teach yourself to use plain words, and to avoid the sickly lure of fancy words, which as often as not will lead you astray, as in some of my examples here.

poo, pooh Often confused, with embarrassing results. The word *pooh* is an interjection expressing disappointment or disdain. But *poo* is a childish word for 'excrement'. The famous bear, of course, is *Winnie-the-Pooh*.

populace This is not another word for *population* or *inhabitants*. It means 'common people', 'ordinary people'.

populous This word means 'heavily populated', 'having lots of people', and only a place can be populous. You can't write *The Chinese language is populous*: write instead *Chinese has a large number of speakers* or *Chinese is widely spoken*.

pore, pour This morning's paper contained this: *I poured over the document*. No. We *pour* a drink, but we *pore* over a document.

Portuguese The word is so spelled, with two Us, and *Portugese* is wrong.

Portuguese and Brazilian names A Portuguese or Brazilian person usually has two surnames, normally the mother's first surname followed by the father's first surname – just the reverse of Spanish practice. Either of these surnames may be preceded by the particle *de* 'of '. Most people use their second surname as the short form. So, for example, the former Portuguese dictator *Antonio de Oliveira Salazar* was commonly known as *Salazar*, not as *de Oliveira*. . However, quite a few people prefer their first surname. Moreover, a few people take both surnames from one parent and wind up with three surnames.

Some names end with a (capitalized) relationship term, such as *Filho* 'son', *Neto* 'grandson' and *Sobrinho* 'nephew'. These indicate merely that the name-bearer has the same name as another member of the family, and no one with such a name can ever be referred to as *Mr Neto* or the like.

Many Portuguese and Brazilian sportsmen prefer to be known by a single name; this may be a given name, a surname or a nickname. Examples include the Portuguese footballer *Eusebio* and the Brazilian footballer *Pelé*.

possess The word has four Ss, and the same is true of its derivatives, like *possession* and *possessive*.

post- This item is strictly a prefix, and not an independent word: *post-Victorian*, *post-traumatic stress disorder*. The hyphen is omitted when the result is easy on the eye: *postscript*. Do not use *post* or *post-* as a cute way of saying *since* or *after*. Write *since Newton* or *after Newton* (as required), not *✳post-Newton*, and write *since Chernobyl*, not *✳post-Chernobyl* or, still worse, *✳post Chernobyl*. See also **pre-**.

posthumous Even though the Latin spelling is *postumus*, the curious spelling *posthumous* is the only possibility in English.

pour See **pore**.

practical, practicable, **pragmatic** A *practical* person or thing is effective and down-to-earth, not concerned with or involving empty flamboyance. The label is a compliment. But something which is *practicable* is merely something which can be done, regardless of whether doing it would be valuable. This word cannot be applied to a person. Except in linguistics and philosophy, in which it has special technical senses, *pragmatic* means 'concerned only with results in the real world, and not with theoretical or moral stances', and the word can be applied to both people and policies.

So, if you have a task to perform, a *practicable* approach is one which can be done, a *practical* approach is a sensible one, and a *pragmatic* approach is one which is meant to be effective.

practice, practise In British English, the noun is *practice* while the verb is *practise*. Hence Britons write *It was time for her violin practice* but *She was practising the violin*. American English, however, uses *practice* in both cases, and Americans write *She was practicing the violin*.

prairie See **grasslands**.

pre- This is a prefix and must be written as one: *pre-soaked*, *pre-examination*. The hyphen is omitted whenever the result is easy on the eye: *prepack*, *prescientific*.

This prefix is often used pointlessly: *✳pre-recorded music* is no different from *recorded music*, and *✳preplanning* is no different from *planning*. Similarly, *✳talks without preconditions* should be replaced by *talks without conditions*, and *✳They were prewarned* should be replaced by *They were warned*.

And, for heaven's sake, do not use *pre* or *pre-* as a cute way of saying *before* or *from before*. Write *before Newton*, not *✻pre-Newton*, and write *from before Newton to the present*, not *✻pre-Newton to the present*. These starred forms are dreadful style. See also **post-**.

precede, proceed The verb *precede* means 'come before': *The Gilded Age preceded the First World War*. The common misspelling *✻preceed* must be avoided. But the verb *proceed* means 'go ahead': *She proceeded with her speech*. A common error is using *proceed* where *precede* is intended: *✻An English adjective usually proceeds its head noun*.

precipitate, precipitous The word *precipitous* means 'very steep', while *precipitate* means 'rash' or 'hasty'.

predication The word *predication* is a technical term in logic, philosophy and linguistics, with several technical senses centring around assertions and the assignment of properties. The word has nothing to do with the everyday word *prediction*, and should not be confused with it.

prefix A *prefix* is an element which cannot stand alone as a word but which can be added to the beginning of an existing word to make a different word. English prefixes include *re-* (as in *rewrite*), *non-* (as in *non-smoker*), *un-* (as in *unhappy*), *trans-* (as in *trans-Atlantic*), *de-* (as in *defrost*), *mini-* (as in *miniskirt*) and *post-* (as in *post-war*), among many others. Note that a prefix must never be written as though it were a separate word: instead, it must be connected to the word of which it forms a part. Compare **suffix**, and note that a **combining form**, like *bio-*, is not really a prefix.

premier, premiere The word *premier* is an adjective meaning 'first' or 'most important': *The Barossa Valley is Australia's premier wine-producing district*. It is also a noun meaning 'prime minister': *The President will meet the Russian premier*. But the word *premiere* is a noun meaning 'first performance': Aida *received its premiere in 1871*. It is permissible, though not necessary, to write this last as *première*.

premiss, premise, premises In logic, a statement upon which a following statement is based is usually a *premiss* (plural *premisses*) in British English, but the spelling *premise* (plural *premises*) is also acceptable in Britain, and is universal in American English. In all varieties of English, the plural form spelled *premises* is a formal or legal term for a property.

preposed appositives Here is an example of a preposed appositive: *the Harvard University palaeontologist Stephen Jay Gould*. In this example, the name *Stephen Jay Gould* is accompanied by an appositive placed in front of it: *the Harvard University palaeontologist.* Such appositives commonly pose two sorts of difficulties.

First, it is essential to include the article *the.* Far too often, we encounter preposed appositives with no article: **Harvard University palaeontologist Stephen Jay Gould is the co-proposer of the theory of punctuated equilibrium.* This irritating journalistic usage has no place in formal writing: if you must use a preposed appositive at all, make sure you include the word *the.*

Second, preposed appositives should be used sparingly, if at all, and they should be short. Some writers, and above all science writers, constantly clog their pages with monstrosities like the following, apparently under the impression that they are writing in English: **University of Southern North Dakota at Hoople physical anthropologist Alice Haney argues that human populations, or 'races', are only about 40,000 years old, but Southern Illinois University at Carbondale evolutionary biologist Jaap van der Velde and Free University of Barcelona palaeontologist Arantxa Villaverde do not agree.*

The constant use of these awful things can quickly reduce your reader to tears. If you believe you must provide so much information about people's professions and affiliations, then spread it out by using more sentences. The dreadful example above might be rewritten as follows: *Alice Haney is a physical anthropologist at the University of Southern North Dakota at Hoople. She argues that human populations, or 'races', are only about 40,000 years old. But others disagree. Among them are Jaap van der Velde, an evolutionary biologist at Southern Illinois University at Carbondale, and Arantxa Villaverde, a palaeontologist at the Free University of Barcelona.*

This is still far from wonderful, but at least it looks like English.

preposition stranding This is the name given by linguists to a construction in which a preposition stands at the end of its sentence or its clause. Examples: *Who were you talking to?* (*to* is stranded); *The true story that* Moby Dick *is partly based on is told in a recent book* (*on* is stranded). Though for generations ignorant prescriptivists have railed against this construction, it is in fact perfectly normal in everybody's English, and there are no sensible grounds for objecting to it. Preposition stranding exists alongside a much more formal construction, amusingly called **pied piping** by linguists, in which the preposition is moved. With pied piping, my examples come out as follows: *To whom were you talking?*; *The true story on which* Moby Dick *is partly based is told in a recent book.*

Most careful writing uses a mixture of the two constructions, and making good choices is a hallmark of sensitivity to the language. Using the stranded construction all the time produces a highly informal style hardly fit for anything but popular journalism, while using the pied-piped construction all the time results in a stiff and stilted tone which will not endear you to your readers.

prerequisite See **perquisite**.

prescribe, proscribe To *prescribe* something is to lay it down as a rule or a procedure to be followed (or, in the case of a medicine, of course, to give instructions to the patient for its use). In contrast, to *proscribe* something is to prohibit it or condemn it. So, a *prescribed* book is a set book, a book which students following a particular syllabus must read or study, while a *proscribed* book is a banned book.

presently In standard usage, this adverb means 'soon', 'shortly', as in *I'll see her presently*. It does not standardly mean 'at present', and you should avoid writing things like *I am presently working in London*. Use *at present*, *currently* or *now* instead.

prestigious This word once meant 'illusory', 'in the manner of a conjuring trick', but this sense is now dead, and there is no point in trying to revive it. Today the word means only 'possessing great prestige'. Some people still dislike this use, but it is too well established and too convenient to moan about any more.

presumptuous The word is *presumptuous*, not *presumptious*. The second form was formerly in use, but it died out in the nineteenth century.

prevalent This is a troublesome word. Consider the following sentence: *The form 'I dove into the water' is prevalent in the northeastern USA*. Now, what does this mean? The choices: (a) Almost everybody in the region says it; (b) Most people in the region say it; (c) Quite a few people in the region say it. For older and more conservative speakers like me, the answer is (b): *prevalent* means 'predominant', 'most frequent'. But recent dictionaries of English, at least in Britain, prefer answer (c): they take the word as meaning no more than 'widespread', and indeed one dictionary describes the sense of 'predominant' as 'archaic' – a conclusion which astounds me.

In spite of the facts of contemporary usage, I advise you to avoid the use of *prevalent* in the sense of 'widespread', which will surely annoy many readers. If all you mean is 'widespread', then the word *widespread* will do the job perfectly well, and nobody will object to this.

I mention this because I recently encountered, in an essay on linguistics, the following sentence: *Both usages are prevalent.* For a reader who uses *prevalent* in its traditional sense, this is simply nonsensical.

prevaricate The word *prevaricate* means 'speak or act evasively or deceptively'. That is, when you prevaricate, you are trying hard to conceal the truth, though usually without telling outright lies. As the British civil servant Sir Robert Armstrong famously put it, after his testimony in an Australian court of law had been shown to be less than the whole truth, 'I did not lie. I was merely economical with the truth.' The word does not mean *procrastinate* ('postpone a task indefinitely'), nor does it mean *hesitate* or 'fail to reach a decision'.

prevent This verb can be used with only an object: *The police prevented a riot.* However, when it is used with an additional complement, it requires the word *from*: *The court order has prevented him from speaking to journalists.* The phrasing *∗ . . . has prevented him speaking to journalists* is now exceedingly common in British English, but it should be avoided in formal writing.

preventive, preventative Both forms are acceptable, but the briefer *preventive* is much commoner and is recommended, especially since some people dislike *preventative*.

primary colours A term of variable and often confused use. In physics and in physiology, the primary colours are red, green and blue, sometimes called the *additive primaries*. These three colours can be added together in varying proportions to produce any other hue we like, and combining all three equally produces white. The retinas of our eyes contain colour receptors for just these three colours, and a colour TV screen likewise produces a picture by combining these three colours. In contrast, the *subtractive primaries* or *primary pigments* are cyan (peacock blue), magenta (purplish-pink) and yellow. Removing these colours from white in varying proportions yields any other hue we like, and removing all of them equally produces black. This is the basis of colour printing, since a pigment removes a certain colour of light by absorbing it: look at the edge of a sheet of postage stamps, and you will see test bars of cyan, magenta and yellow, plus black, since in practice it is difficult to produce a good black with the three primary pigments. Note that red, blue and yellow do not constitute a set of primary colours for any purpose at all.

In fashion and design, the label *primary colours* is sometimes used loosely to mean bold, bright colours like red, green, blue and yellow, as opposed to more subtle colours like chartreuse, burgundy and lilac.

primitive language A meaningless term. There is no mother tongue anywhere on earth which is 'primitive' in any sense. Every human language ever discovered has a large vocabulary and a rich and complex grammar, without exception. There is no mother tongue consisting of 200 words supplemented by grunts and gestures: this is a fantasy born of ignorance and bigotry. The language of a Stone Age tribesman in New Guinea is no less rich than that of a Chicago stockbroker, and the language of a Siberian reindeer herder is no less complex than that of an Oxford professor – but also no more complex.

principal, principle The word *principle* is strictly a noun meaning 'rule', 'law', 'general truth': *She refuses to abandon her principles*. The word *principal* is chiefly an adjective meaning 'chief', 'most important': *Chile's principal export is copper*. But this last can also be a noun meaning 'chief executive officer of a university' (in Scotland) or 'head teacher of a school' (in the USA), and also 'most important character or player', as in *Joseph Fiennes and Gwyneth Paltrow portray the principals*. Be careful not to confuse the two words. I have just seen a document from the Committee of Vice-Chancellors and Principals in Britain in which the phrase *principle applicant* occurs more than forty times. This is deeply embarrassing.

prior Often used pointlessly. There is no point in writing *prior knowledge* or *prior experience*. You can't apply knowledge you don't have before you apply it, and any experience you have is in the past by definition.

prioritize This verb means 'rank (a list of tasks) in order of urgency'. It is a bureaucratic word, best avoided in most types of writing.

prior to This ghastly thing has recently become almost a disease: we constantly see written forms like *prior to 1990*, *prior to the war* and *prior to her arrival*. You should make every effort to avoid this Latinate monstrosity in favour of plain old English *before*. Write *before 1990*, *before the war* and *before she arrived*.

pristine Over the last century or so, the meaning of this word has been shifting. Originally it meant 'ancient, primeval': *the earth's pristine atmosphere* is the atmosphere it had long ago, when it first acquired an atmosphere. This use is still current.

But then the word began to be used in the weaker sense of 'unsullied, uncorrupted, in its original condition', as in *pristine innocence* and *a pristine copy of Gutenberg's Bible*. This is now the most frequent sense of the word, and it is widely accepted as standard, but you should be aware that many people still dislike it.

More recently still, the word has come to be used to mean no more than 'clean, fresh, untouched', with no trace of 'original' or 'ancient' at all, as in *a pristine building* for 'a brand-new building'. This use is best avoided.

privileged This word is fine in certain traditional expressions, such as *in a privileged position* or *a privileged background*. But recently it has come to be badly overused as a meaningless term of abuse: post-modernist writers constantly accuse scientists, scholars and others of unfairly possessing or claiming 'a privileged voice', or something similar, when these targets are doing nothing more than talking about what they know about. The implication here is that, in a post-modern world, the opinions of knowledgeable specialists are of no greater value than the opinions of the ignorant but strident. The frequent use of *privileged* as a term of abuse is one of the surest signs that the post-modernist disease has infected your writing.

The same goes for the use of *privilege* as a verb, something which is almost unknown outside post-modernist writing. Post-modernists constantly use *privilege* to mean 'assign greater importance to' or 'regard as more fundamental', as when certain post-modernists complain that linguists 'privilege' speech over writing. The use of *privilege* as a verb is not found in good writing, and you are urged to avoid it.

By the way, note the spelling: *priviledge(d) is wrong.

proceed See **precede**.

prodigal This word means 'wasteful', 'extravagant': a *prodigal* person is one who throws his money away foolishly. In spite of the New Testament parable, the word has nothing to do with running away or being absent, and you cannot write *the return of the prodigal* if all you mean is 'the return of someone who has been away a long time'.

proffer This is a fancy word for *offer*, and the everyday word should be preferred in most circumstances. If you do use it, be sure to spell it correctly: avoid the common error *profer.

program, programme In American usage, the spelling is *program* in all circumstances. In British usage, the spelling *programme* is preferred for most purposes: *a theatre programme*, *a radio programme*. But even in Britain *a computer program* is always so spelled. In all senses, and in all varieties, the derived adjective is *programmatic*.

pro-life The opponents of abortion commonly apply the label *pro-life* to their stance. But this label is tendentious and highly inaccurate, and you should not use it if you are trying to be at all objective: write *anti-abortion* or *opposed to abortion* instead. After all, no sane person is opposed to life, and the proponents of legalized abortion are certainly not opposed to life.

prolific This adjective means 'fruitful', 'producing quite a lot', and it is applied to that which produces, not to that which is produced. A *prolific* writer produces lots of books, but the books he writes cannot be described as *prolific*. Also wrong is the comment, in another usage handbook, that a certain word *✳has been used prolifically*. The writer should have said that the word has been *frequently* used, or *excessively* used, as required.

prone, prostrate, supine When you are *prone*, you are lying on your face. When you are *prostrate*, you are doing the same, but this time because you are expressing adoration or begging for protection, or, metaphorically, because you are exhausted. When you are *supine*, you are lying on your back. The common mistake here is to write *prone* when *supine* is intended.

By the way, do not write *prostate* when you mean *prostrate*: the prostate is a gland found in male mammals.

pronouns and antecedents A pronoun, such as *it* or *they*, must always be used with an antecedent, another noun phrase with which the pronoun co-refers. There are three common problems here.

The first arises when a pronoun is used without an antecedent. Here is an example. *✳When you converse, you must be cooperative. It must follow the accepted rules of conversation.* The problem here is that the pronoun *it* has nothing to refer to. Clearly, this pronoun is intended to mean something like *what you say*, but no such phrase is present. Change the second sentence to *What you say must follow the accepted rules of conversation*.

The second arises when a pronoun is used with more than one possible antecedent. Here is an example, taken from an account of a battle in the American Civil War. *✳The northerners were faced by an army of unruly but highly motivated rebel soldiers. They were armed with .577 calibre Enfield muskets.* Now, who do you suppose had the muskets? Most readers will naturally assume that the northerners possessed these weapons, since *the northerners* is the subject of the first sentence and *they* is the subject of the second. In this case, though, further reading reveals that the writer intended to say that it is the rebel soldiers who had the muskets. Consequently, the second sentence must be rewritten. The simplest way of fixing the problem is to write *These were armed . . .* Here *these* will be taken, correctly, as referring to the people or things most recently mentioned – in this case, the rebel soldiers. If this solution still appears inadequate, then write something more explicit, such as *The rebels were armed . . .*

The third occurs with the possessive -*'s*. Note the following example, which is wrong: *The Guardian*'s typos are legendary. It has now published a collection of them.* Here the pronoun *it* is clearly meant to refer to the *Guardian*, but in fact *the* Guardian has not been referred to: instead, it is only *the* Guardian*'s typos* which have been mentioned, and hence *the* Guardian is not available to serve as an antecedent. Write instead something more explicit: *The newspaper has now published a collection of them.*

Whenever you use a pronoun, check to see that its intended antecedent is present and unambiguous. The sloppy use of pronouns is maddening for your reader, who must struggle to decipher your intended meaning.

pronunciation Note the spelling, which is similar to what we find with *annunciation, denunciation, renunciation* and *enunciation*. The erroneous spelling *pronounciation must be avoided.

proof See **prove**.

prophecy, prophesy The noun is *prophecy*; the verb is *prophesy*. If you prophesy a fall in share prices, then this outcome constitutes your prophecy. And there is no such word as *prophesize.

proscribe See **prescribe**.

prosecute See **persecute**.

prostitute If you *prostitute* yourself, then you abandon your principles or your dignity in return for money or other material gain. As a noun, *prostitute* is now the usual polite word for *whore*, since *whore* itself is widely regarded as too vulgar for everyday use. Strangely enough, though, it is no longer usual to write *She prostituted herself* to mean 'She worked as a whore'. Don't ask me why.

protagonist, antagonist The word *protagonist* means 'first actor', and it originally denoted the single most important character in a Greek drama. Some people therefore object to recognizing more than one protagonist in a single matter, but all authorities on English usage now agree that this extended sense is perfectly acceptable: you may safely write *He is one of the protagonists in this affair*, meaning 'He is one of the principal actors'.

But it is a serious error to write *protagonist* to mean 'supporter'. Even though an *antagonist* is an opponent or adversary, the word *protagonist* has nothing much to do with *antagonist*, and it does not contain the element *pro-*, meaning 'in favour of'. Write *He is a supporter* (or *proponent*) *of legalized abortion*, not *He is a protagonist of . . .

prove, proof, **evidence** Be very careful with the words *prove* and *proof*. Mathematicians and logicians can prove things, but, in the real world, it is usually very difficult to prove anything at all. Normally the best we can hope for is to show that the evidence for some conclusion is so overwhelming that it would be unreasonable not to accept that conclusion – just as our legal systems require 'proof beyond reasonable doubt' in order to convict.

Consider the following example, taken from an account of several competing theories of intelligence: *All are plausible, but none is proven*. Though non-scientists often fail to realize this, a scientific theory can *never* be proven: this is a logical impossibility. All that scientists can do is to examine the evidence for and against a theory, and to place their confidence in it to the degree that seems appropriate.

Of course, some theories, like the theory of evolution and the theory of special relativity, are supported by such an abundance and variety of evidence that no rational investigator could possibly reject them at present – though there always remains the remote possibility that, one day, new and conflicting evidence might force scientists to modify their understanding to some extent.

So, my example above might better have been written as *All are plausible, but none is yet established beyond reasonable doubt* or . . . *established to general satisfaction*, or something similar.

In the same vein, be careful to distinguish between *proof* and *evidence*. A particular observation or experiment may provide *evidence* in support of a particular conclusion, but in almost no case does this evidence amount to *proof*.

proved, proven The participle of *prove* is usually *proved* in standard English. Examples: *We have proved it*; *This hypothesis has never been proved*. In such cases, the variant *proven* is much less acceptable, especially in British English, though it cannot quite be called wrong there, and it is in fact rather common in American English, where both forms are accepted as standard. However, the adjective is almost always *proven*: *her proven competence*; *a proven remedy*. Note also the special case of *not proven* in Scottish law.

Provençal See **Occitan**.

Punjab See **Panjab**.

pure Some time ago an educated friend of mine assured me solemnly 'Honey is the purest form of sugar.' No, it isn't: since it is in fact only about 70% sugar, honey is one of the impurest forms of sugar we commonly run into. The purest form of sugar we usually encounter is the refined white crystalline material found in a supermarket bag of sugar. The word *pure* emphatically does *not* mean 'natural' or 'unprocessed': instead, it means 'uncontaminated by other materials'. Unprocessed natural substances are hardly ever pure. As a rule, they are grossly impure, and much of the point of processing is removal of the impurities. Do not let the cosy warm feel of the word *pure* seduce you into using it as an inappropriate label for something you happen to approve of.

purge To *purge* something is to rid it of impure or undesirable elements. You can take medicine to purge your bowels. Neil Kinnock attempted to purge the Labour Party of hostile militants. But note that, when supposedly undesirable people are removed from an organization, it is the organization which is purged, and not the people who lose their jobs. It is wrong to write *The militants were purged. The militants may have been sacked, dismissed, expelled, ejected or driven out, but they were not purged.

purport This verb means 'be presented as', 'be superficially', and it is normally applied to things, not to people: *This book purports to be a critique of Gross and Levitt's work.* The word carries at least a hint that the thing under discussion is not what it seems to be: in my example, the writer is suggesting that the book mentioned, while presented as a critique, is at least disappointing and possibly even dishonest. The word does not mean 'claim': write *She claims to hold a PhD*, not *She purports to hold a PhD.* And the phrasing *purport about is always wrong.

pursue The word is so spelled: avoid the common error *persue. The word is not spelled like *persuade*.

putrefy The word is so spelled, with an E in the middle, and *putrify is wrong. The derived noun is *putrefaction*, and there is no such word as *putrefication*, or, still worse, *putrification*.

pygmy, pigmy All authorities prefer the spelling *pygmy*.

Pyrrhic victory A Pyrrhic victory is a victory which costs the victor far more than he can afford. The term derives from the victory of Pyrrhus, King of Epirus, over the Romans in 279 BC, in which Pyrrhus's troops, though victorious, were so badly mauled that he could scarcely continue the war. The term is often misunderstood: it does not mean a hollow victory, or a meaningless victory, or a victory which goes wrong.

q(u) Every schoolchild learns that the letter Q must always be followed by U. This is true for words that have been in the language for some time, but it is not always true for words of recent origin in English or for names of foreign origin – especially of Arabic origin. Exceptional words include *qadi* (an Islamic judge), *qat* (a stimulant leaf) and *suq* (a market), all beloved of Scrabble-players, and all from Arabic. Non-Arabic names include *Qantas*, the airline, *Compaq*, the computer manufacturer, and *NASDAQ*, the stock exchange.

Arabic has a letter qof, which spells a sound absent from English and which need not be followed by anything in particular. This qof is usually rendered in English by Q, and it occurs in names of Arabic origin not only in Arab countries but in most Muslim countries. Examples include *Iraq* and *Qatar* (the countries) and *Abdul Qadir* (the Pakistani cricketer). It is a common error to insert a U into such a name in error, producing mistakes like *Siddiqui* for *Siddiqi* and *Iraqui* for *Iraqi*.

quality The use of this word as a preposed modifier meaning 'of high quality', as in *a quality watch*, is an informal usage typical of journalistic prose, especially advertising. It is out of place in formal writing: write *a watch of good quality* or *a high-quality watch*.

quantum *Quantum mechanics* is a branch of physics dealing with the behaviour of subatomic particles. It is formulated with great mathematical exactness, and it is one of the most successful physical theories of all time. It allows physicists to calculate physical quantities, and to predict the results of experiments, with astounding accuracy. But quantum mechanics is not easy to picture in our minds, since subatomic particles do not behave like familiar everyday objects.

As a consequence, every third charlatan finds that he can sell books by wrapping his content-free dross in a warm, fuzzy, pseudo-mystical cloud of blather featuring the word *quantum* very prominently. This merchandising technique has been dubbed 'quantum mysticism', and it seems to sell piles of books which would have served us better by remaining as trees.

quantum jump, quantum leap In physics, when a particle makes a *quantum jump*, it moves from position A to position B without ever being anywhere in between – that is, the jump is discontinuous (and also very small by everyday standards). Journalistic prose commonly uses *quantum jump* or *quantum leap* to mean 'a sudden and dramatic change, especially an increase', as in *a quantum leap in house prices*. Not only is this expression now a **cliché**, it results from a bad misunderstanding of the physical sense of the term. You should avoid the expression in formal writing, unless you are using it in its physical sense.

Quebec The English form *Quebec* should be written, not the French form *Québec*. The people of Quebec are usually *Québecois*, but this French label is only strictly appropriate for the French-speaking majority. To label the English-speaking minority, or the entire population, the slightly clumsy word *Quebeckers* is acceptable. The capital city of the province is *Quebec City* if there is any possibility of confusion with the province, but *Quebec* when no such possibility exists.

query The verb *query* does not mean 'ask', and cannot be so used. Things like ✳*'Where can I find the director?' he queried* are not standard English. The verb means 'cast doubt upon', and to query something is to suggest that it is wrong: *The shareholders have queried the annual report*. But the noun *query* just means 'question'.

question I saw this in the newspaper the other day: ✳*The French are begin-ning to question how Germany defeated them so easily*. This is wrong. The verb required is *ask* or *wonder*, not *question*. To *question* something is to doubt its truth or validity, not to ask questions about it or to wonder about it.

question mark The *question mark* (?) has only one common use: it stands at the end of a direct question. Examples: *How many languages will die out in the next century?*; *'Can you help me?' she asked*. A common error is writing a question mark at the end of a sentence which has the form of a statement. Here is an example: ✳*I wonder what our grandchildren will think of this?* Like other such sentences, this one requires a final full stop, not a question mark.

For more on the question mark, see chapter 2 of the *Penguin Guide to Punctuation*.

quixotic This adjective means 'hopelessly idealistic and chivalrous'. It does not mean 'foolish' or 'pointless'.

quotation, quote Careful writing requires the long form *quotation*. The short form *quote* is only appropriate, if at all, in informal writing.

quotation marks Quotation marks, also called *inverted commas* in Britain, come in two types: *single quotes* ('like these') and *double quotes* ("like these"). Quotation marks have three uses.

First, they are used to enclose a direct quotation – that is, an exact repetition of somebody else's words. For this purpose, either single or double quotes may be used, and the choice is merely a matter of taste and house style. For example, you may write either of the following: *Napoleon described the British as 'a nation of shopkeepers'*; *Napoleon described the British as "a nation of shopkeepers"*. On the whole, British publishers prefer single quotes, while American publishers prefer double quotes, and, if you are writing for publication, you will probably have to conform to your publisher's house style.

Second, quotation marks are used when you, the writer, want to distance yourself from a word or a phrase. In effect, you are saying 'Hey, look – these are somebody else's words, not mine, and I'm not responsible for them.' Quotation marks used in this way are often called *scare quotes*. For example, you can write this: *Physicists are searching for a 'theory of everything'*. Here the quote marks indicate that the phrase *theory of everything* is one used by somebody else – in this case, physicists – and that you, the writer, are not responsible for these words. Your quote marks here carry the message 'This is what they call it; OK? Don't blame me if you don't like the name.'

Very often scare quotes are used to indicate not just distance, but outright contempt. For example, you can write this: *In the USA, the religious right is trying to enforce the teaching of 'creation science'*. Here the scare quotes will very often mean more than merely 'I'm not responsible for this term.' Instead, they may mean 'Look – I realize that this is a stupid label for a contemptible position, and I want you, the reader, to understand that too.'

Be careful with scare quotes. You should not write things like this: **I have just been 'ripped off' by my insurance company*. Here you are simultaneously using the term *ripped off* and showing that you don't really approve of it, by wrapping it in scare quotes. If you think a term is appropriate, then use it, without any quotes. If you don't think it's appropriate, then don't use it, unless you deliberately intend to be ironic.

In short, then, when you put quotation marks around some words, you are denying all responsibility for those words. So, all those pubs with signs declaring *We sell 'traditional pub food'* are in fact implying that they are serving up microwaved sludge. Quotation marks cannot be used for emphasis.

But be aware that scare quotes express your opinion, and nothing more. Do not try to copy the behaviour of certain post-modernist writers who appear to believe that wrapping a blizzard of terms inside scare quotes constitutes a closely reasoned critical analysis. It does nothing of the sort.

Finally, quotation marks may be used to set off a word or a phrase which is merely being talked about, rather than used. Consider the following examples: *Men are physically stronger than women*; *'Men' is an irregular plural*.

The first sentence is using *men*, as usual, to denote male adults. But the second is doing nothing of the kind: it is not mentioning any people at all, but only the *word* 'men'. For this purpose, single quotes are strongly recommended over double quotes.

For more on quotation marks, see chapter 8 of the *Penguin Guide to Punctuation*.

Qur'an See **Koran**.

raccoon, racoon The North American spelling is *raccoon*. In Britain, where there are no raccoons, the variant spelling *racoon* is acceptable, and is strangely even preferred in some quarters, though not in all.

race In biology, a *race* is a subspecies separated geographically from other populations of the same species, from which it differs in a few minor respects. The extension of this word to human populations is *extremely* contentious, and is best avoided: writing of 'human races' will quickly attract a (possibly well-deserved) charge of racism. Worse still is using *race* to mean no more than 'nationality': the people of England, for example, do not constitute a race in any sense at all, and writing *the English race* is absurd.

racialism, racism Though some people still argue for the older forms *racialism* and *racialist*, these are almost obsolete today, and the preferred forms everywhere are *racism* and *racist*.

rack, wrack Several historically unrelated words have become almost inextricably tangled together here, and different authorities give conflicting advice. The seaweed is always *wrack*. The place where you put your luggage is always a *rack*. The instrument of torture is always a *rack*. The lamb dish is always *rack* of lamb. But now things become complicated.

I recommend the spelling *rack your brains* but the spellings *nerve-wracking* and *wrack and ruin*. But the other spellings are found for all three, and these are widely accepted as standard.

racket, racquet The bat used in playing tennis and related games is either a *racket* or a *racquet*. Both forms are standard, and you may use whichever you prefer, though *racket* is now more usual in all forms of English. However, the game resembling squash is always *rackets* in British English but *racquets* in American English.

racoon See **raccoon**.

random This word has a precise mathematical meaning in statistics, and it should be used with care in non-mathematical writing, especially when there is an implicit appeal to statistics. For example, you should not write *a random sample* if all you mean is a sample selected according to no particular criteria. Such a sample is unlikely to be truly random, and you are advised to write instead *an arbitrary sample* or *an unsystematic sample*.

range **nouns** I have coined this admittedly awkward name to provide a headword for this entry, since I could find no established name. What I have in mind is a set of English nouns of similar meaning, including *range*, *selection* and *choice*. There is really nothing unusual about these nouns at all, but they all cause the same problem very frequently. The problem is this: each one of these nouns is singular (unless overtly pluralized as *ranges, selections, choices*), but each is very often wrongly given plural agreement. Some examples: *A large range of courses are available*; *A selection of wines are available in our cellars*; *A choice of desserts are provided*. In every case, the verb-form required is *is*, not *are*. This should be obvious, since the preceding *a* is singular, not plural, and since perhaps no one would consider writing *Our range are the best in London*.

See also **number**, where the rule is quite different.

rarefy This is the only possible spelling, and *rarify* is not acceptable.

ravage, ravish To *ravage* a territory is to wreak destruction on it. As for *ravish*, this has had several senses, but most commonly it is a quaint or delicate word for *rape*. The common error is writing *ravish* where *ravage* is required, as in this example: *The fighting has ravished Lebanon*.

raze, rase The spelling is *raze* in all varieties of English; the older *rase* is now obsolete. Note that to *raze* a building is to demolish it, to level it, so that nothing remains of it except perhaps the foundation. It is therefore a **pleonasm** to write *The buildings were razed to the ground*. Prefer instead *The buildings were razed*. There is no partial razing.

re This pretentious Latin word should *never* be used as a replacement for 'about', 'concerning' or 'in connection with', except perhaps in headings to business memos.

re- The prefix *re-*, which means 'again', does not usually require a hyphen: *rewrite, repaint, reconsider, rebirth*. But a hyphen is required in two circumstances. First, it is required if the result would otherwise be hard on the eye, especially before an E, as in *re-examine* and and *re-entry*. Second, it is required if the result would otherwise look just like a different word. A good example is *re-cover* 'cover again', as in *She re-covered the sofa*, in order to avoid confusion with *recover* 'get back', as in *She recovered the sofa*. Another such pair is *re-form* 'form again' and *reform* 'improve by correcting abuses'.

Note also that many words beginning with *re-* do not contain the prefix *re-* 'again', and must never take a hyphen. Examples, apart from *recover* and *reform*, include *replace*, *revise*, *recite* and *remember*.

-re, -er There exist a number of words which are spelled *-re* in Britain but *-er* in the USA. Among these are *theatre/theater*, *centre/center*, *calibre/caliber*, *litre/ liter* and *fibre/fiber*. You should use the spelling which is appropriate on your side of the Atlantic. But note that *acre*, *ogre*, *massacre*, *nacre* and *lucre* are so spelled in all varieties of English. Note also the case of *metre/meter*: in Britain, the unit of length is a *metre* (and likewise for derived forms like *kilometre*), while in the USA it is a *meter*, but all varieties use *meter* for a measuring instrument, and for derived forms like *thermometer*, and also for a rhythmic pattern in poetry, and for derived forms like *pentameter*.

reaction A *reaction* is a sudden and spontaneous response to a stimulus, such as jumping, shrieking, laughing or fainting. The word is not properly used as a fancy word for 'opinion' or 'judgement', or for any kind of considered response. If you circulate a policy document, you can ask others for their opinions, or their responses, or their criticisms, or any of a dozen other things, but you cannot ask them for their reactions, unless you really hope to hear responses like 'I burst into uncontrollable laughter'.

realistic Apart from specialist uses in philosophy and literature, this word means 'showing awareness of reality', 'practical in the real world'. It does not mean the same as *real*, and you should not write *∗We are making realistic progress* for *We are making real progress*. In any case, the word is much overused. Instead of trotting out *realistic prices* for the zillionth time, try *sensible prices* or *competitive prices* or some other more explicit expression.

reason is because In formal writing, it is inappropriate to write *∗The reason is because* ... Prefer instead *The reason is that* ...

rebut, refute These words are frequently confused and frequently used wrongly. To *rebut* a statement is to offer clear evidence or a reasoned argument against it. To *refute* a statement is to prove it wrong. Neither word means *deny* or *contradict*, and this is where most of the trouble arises.

Suppose I say to you 'All swans are white.' If you simply reply 'No, they're not', then you have *denied* my statement (and *contradicted* me), but you have neither rebutted nor refuted anything. If you produce an encyclopedia article on black swans or an ornithologist who can report on his experience with black swans, then you have *rebutted* my assertion – that is, you have assembled good evidence against it. If you show me a black swan, then you have *refuted* my assertion – that is, you have proved it wrong.

Do not make the common error of writing *refute*, or even *rebut*, when all you mean is *deny*. It is usually very difficult to prove that a statement is wrong, and *refute* should accordingly be used with great care.

Received Pronunciation (RP) *Received Pronunciation*, or *RP*, is an accent of English – that is, it is one way of pronouncing English. RP is almost entirely confined to Britain, and most especially to England, though a few RP-speakers can be found in the Commonwealth countries. RP appears to have originated in the public schools – that is, the expensive and prestigious private boarding schools in England to which the British elite have traditionally sent their children. Until recently, RP was regularly used by members of the royal family, by members of the aristocracy, by military officers, by senior churchmen, by Oxbridge professors – in short, by almost anyone who could claim to be part of the upper crust in England. It was formerly also required for almost all people appearing on the BBC, but this is no longer the case, and indeed RP is losing ground almost everywhere, in favour of other accents which are more firmly grounded in popular speech. This development disturbs many conservative commentators in Britain, but pronunciation is not the subject of this book, and so I will not pursue the matter here.

But I do want to point out a misunderstanding. Not infrequently, people in Britain confuse RP with *standard English*. This is a grievous error. Standard English is characterized by its particular choices of grammar and word use, and in large measure by its vocabulary (and, in its written version only, by its spelling and punctuation). But pronunciation has nothing to do with it. Standard English can be spoken in virtually any accent of English. There are speakers of standard English who speak it with a Glasgow accent, with a Welsh accent, with a Mississippi accent, with a New Zealand accent, and so on. It is also possible in principle to speak non-standard English with an RP accent, though in practice this combination is rare to non-existent.

recipe, receipt A *recipe* is a set of instructions for preparing a dish. A *receipt* is a piece of paper acknowledging a payment. Since about 1900, this distinction has been standard in written English, and you should stick to it. But before 1900 the words behaved rather differently, and *receipt* was often written where the sense of *recipe* was intended.

recommend This verb behaves differently in British and American English. American usage, both formal and informal, permits only *We recommend that this be done* and *We recommend that this not be done*. Informal and moderately formal British usage prefers *We recommend that this is done* and *We recommend that this is not done*, both of which are ungrammatical for Americans. But very formal British English – for example, in the minutes of formal meetings – uses *We recommend that this be done* and *We recommend that this be not done*, the second of which is also ungrammatical for Americans.

reductionism *Reductionism* is the policy of decomposing a complex problem into a set of smaller and simpler problems, in the hope that these smaller problems can be dealt with successfully, thus allowing progress in addressing the original large problem. Almost all successful scientific work is reductionist, and reductionism has proved to be a hugely successful policy. However, in recent years *reductionism* has come in some quarters to be a sneer word – very unfortunately. It is perfectly in order to condemn an approach which manifestly fails to recognize the complexities of a difficult issue, but, for this purpose, labels like *simplistic* and *facile* are more appropriate than *reductionist*. But the mere condemnation of reductionism in itself is idiotic. *Holistic* approaches have their place, but they rarely achieve anything until reductionist work has first built up a sizeable body of understanding.

refer The inflected forms and derivatives of this word cause difficulties. The spellings are *refer*, *reference*, *referent* and *referee* (with one R), but *referring*, *referred* and *referral*. The key is the pronunciation: for all forms except *refer*, we write one R when the stress is on the first or third syllable, but two Rs when it is on the second. The same is true for other such words and their derivatives, such as *prefer*, *defer*, *infer*, *confer* and *transfer*. And note that the spelling *reffer is wrong.

refer, allude When you *refer* to something, you do so explicitly, citing it by name. However, when you *allude* to something, you do so inexplicitly, without naming it. I can refer to my wife by writing *Jan* or *my wife*, but, if I write *somebody I know*, with Jan in mind, I am only alluding to her.

refer back This expression is condemned by some writers of usage handbooks but used freely by others in their texts. I go along with the first group: except in rare circumstances, *refer back is tautologous and should be avoided. Write *He referred to our earlier discussion*, not *He referred back . . .

refer to All too often, we come across things like the following: *The word 'puma' refers to a large American wild cat*. This is poor usage. A person or a written text can *refer to* something, but an individual word generally cannot: it can only *denote* something – that is, name it or label it. A more proper version of my example would be this: *The word 'puma' denotes a large American wild cat*. But, though correct, this is both wordy and stuffy. It is much better style to write this: *A puma is a large American wild cat*. Cultivating a plain, direct style will help you to avoid verbose tangles like my original example. Unless you are expressly doing linguistic work, talk about things, and not about words: talking about words when your subject matter is not words at all will only get you into trouble.

reflexive pronouns Reflexive pronouns are forms ending in *-self* or *-selves*, such as *myself* and *themselves*. There is just one common error in the use of these items.

A reflexive is often used where a simple pronoun is required. Example: *Please reply to Jenny or myself*. This is wrong. Nobody would write *Please reply to myself*, and the presence of *or* does not change the structure of the sentence. The required form is *Please reply to Jenny or me*, or, a little more carefully, *Please reply to Jenny or to me*.

A somewhat more subtle example of the same thing is illustrated by the following example: *Mr Simpson complained that the CEO had forced himself and his partner out of the company*. The problem here is that *The CEO had forced himself out of the company* can only mean that the CEO had forced the CEO out of the company – an implausible event. Again, the required form is *him*, not *himself*.

Be careful with this. The reflexive pronouns have narrowly circumscribed uses in standard English, and they are not fancy equivalents for the simple pronouns.

refute See **rebut**.

regard, regards The noun *regards* is only appropriate in the construction illustrated by *Give your wife my regards* and in the phrase *as regards*. In all other circumstances, the required word is *regard*. In particular, write *with regard to this issue*, not *with regards to this issue*.

register office The municipal office in Britain where civil marriages are performed and records are kept is a *register office*. The variant *registry office*, though common in speech, is not official and should be avoided in careful writing.

regretful, regrettable The word *regretful* means 'full of remorse', and only a person can be regretful. But *regrettable* means 'unfortunate', and it is applied to circumstances or to behaviour. Write *Her behaviour at the party was regrettable, and she is now suitably regretful*.

Reims See **Rheims**.

relate to Colloquial English uses *relate to* to mean something like 'feel comfortable with', 'feel an affinity with', as illustrated by the following example: *I can't relate to opera*. While now regarded as standard by some dictionaries, this use is decidedly inexplicit, and it is disliked by many people. You are advised to avoid it in careful writing.

relative clause A relative clause is a clause that modifies a preceding head noun, and there are two main kinds.

A *restrictive relative clause* is required to identify the person or thing being referred to. According to circumstances, it may be introduced by any of *who* (or *whom* or *whose*), or *which*, possibly preceded by a preposition, or *that*, or zero, and it must not be set off by commas. Examples: *The volcano that destroyed the Minoan civilization was colossal*; *The firm of builders to which the contract was awarded has gone bankrupt*. Here the relative clauses, *that destroyed the Minoan civilization* and *to which the contract was awarded*, are clearly required to identify the volcano and the building firm under discussion.

A *non-restrictive relative clause* is not required for identification, but serves only to provide additional information. Such a clause must nearly always be introduced by one of *who* (or *whom* or *whose*) or *which*, possibly preceded by a preposition. Example: *His first novel, which became a bestseller, took two years to write*. Here the sequence set off by commas is the non-restrictive clause, and it is clearly not required to identify which novel. A non-restrictive clause is *always* set off by a pair of commas. It will change the meaning to write **His first novel which became* ... Moreover, a non-restrictive clause can never be introduced by *that*: it is equally wrong to write **His first novel, that became* ... The connecting word *that* can never be preceded by a comma, unless that comma is the second of two commas setting off a preceding weak interruption: *She announced, with a shy smile, that she was getting married*.

There are potential difficulties when *and* appears in or near a relative clause of either type. Here is a typical error, involving non-restrictive clauses: **The iMac, which Apple released in 1998 and has become Apple's greatest success, has rescued the company*. This is ungrammatical, and there must be a second *which* before *has become*: *The iMac, which Apple released in 1998 and which has become Apple's greatest success, has rescued the company*. The problem with the first version is that *which* is being required to serve simultaneously as the object of *Apple released* and as the subject of *has rescued* – something which English grammar does not permit. Compare the following good example, in which *which* serves as the subject in both cases: *The iMac, which appeared in 1998 and has become Apple's greatest success, has rescued the company*.

relatively See **comparatively**.

relativity In the early years of the twentieth century, Albert Einstein put forward two related but distinct physical theories, commonly known as the *special theory of relativity* and the *general theory of relativity*. The special theory has been overwhelmingly confirmed and is now a pillar of physical orthodoxy. The general theory has been more controversial, but it has proved to be so successful that it too is now widely accepted.

The name *relativity* is perhaps a little unfortunate, since people who know no physics frequently jump to the conclusion that Einsten is telling us that 'Everything is relative', or something similar. But this is nonsense. The fundamental point about relativity is in fact not relativity at all, but *invariance*. The heart of special relativity is the conclusion that certain things, such as the laws of physics and the speed of light, are constant for all observers: in other words, these things are invariant, and they are not relative to anything. We might almost wish that Einstein had chosen to call his ideas the *theory of invariance*. This choice might have prevented some nonsensical misunderstandings.

relevant This word means 'having a bearing on the topic under discussion'. It should not be used to mean 'modern' or 'socially significant': this use is vapid and pretentious.

relieve The expression is *relieve of*, not *relieve from*. Write *He was relieved of his duties*, not *He was relieved from his duties*.

religiosity This word does not mean merely 'religious belief'. Instead, it means 'ostentatious and somewhat offensive display of religious beliefs and practices', 'sanctimoniousness'. It is not a compliment.

renowned The word is so spelled, and *reknowned* is wrong. The word has nothing to do with *known*. The related noun is *renown*.

repeat To *repeat* something is to say or write it again. Note that the *first* occurrence of something is not a repetition, while its *second* occurrence is its *first* repetition. Accordingly, if something occurs exactly twice in a passage, you cannot write *This is repeated twice*. It is repeated only once, so write *This is repeated*.

repel, repulse Often confused. To *repulse* is to drive back, usually in war: *The Chechens repulsed the Russian attack*. To *repel* is to excite disgust in: *Susie is repelled by the smell of raw fish*.

repellent, repugnant, repulsive All three of these adjectives mean 'loathesome', 'disgusting', 'offensive to the senses or to sensibilities'. But *repulsive* is the strongest word of the three: while you merely keep away from something which is repellent or repugnant, you recoil from something repulsive.

The word *repellent* also means 'resistant' (for example, to water), as in *water-repellent fabric*. And note the spelling, with *-ent*, not *-ant*.

repertoire, repertory The word *repertory* occurs nowhere but in the expression *repertory company*, denoting a theatrical troupe which performs a number of plays one after another. In all other circumstances, the required word is *repertoire*.

repetition The chance repetition of words is inevitable, and this does not cause many problems in most cases. Examples: *We had had our fill; She told me that that would not be necessary*. As always, though, you should read what you have written, and, if you can see a possible problem, you might be wise to rewrite the passage.

More serious is the repeated use of a favourite word which is not required. Example: *She was fairly nervous about starting university, but her first week went fairly well, and before long she was feeling fairly happy about things*. All of us have our favourite words, and all of us fall into this trap on occasion. The only cure is to read what we have written, and to rewrite where necessary.

Many people seem to believe there is something wrong in repeating a name or a label. Such people go to extreme lengths to avoid such repetition, producing as a result some surprising prose. Example: *Darrow faced Bryan in the Scopes trial. When the Illinoian orator foolishly allowed himself to take the stand, the veteran lawyer humiliated the former Secretary of State by demonstrating that the defender of religious orthodoxy held absurdly conflicting views*. This sort of thing is dizzying, and the reader can easily become hopelessly lost. It is much better simply to repeat the names as required: *Darrow faced*

Bryan in the Scopes trial. When Bryan foolishly allowed himself to take the stand, Darrow humiliated him by demonstrating that Bryan held absurdly conflicting views.

replace See **substitute**.

require This is a very formal word for *need*, and the simpler word should usually be preferred. It is pompous to write *require* for *need* in all but very formal contexts.

resilient **Wallace was resilient to tropical diseases.* Presumably what the writer meant was *resistant*. A resilient person is one who recovers quickly from shocks or illnesses, and you cannot be resilient *to* anything. Note also the spelling, in *-ent*.

resonate This technical term from physics has recently become a frequent vogue word of indeterminate meaning. For example, the editor of a collection of academic articles has recently written, in his introduction, that one author's paper 'resonates with' several others in the collection. Apparently he wants us to believe that there are interesting points of contact among the papers, even though he himself is unable to identify any of these. So used, the word is at best flabby and at worst dishonest. Don't use it.

respective, respectively These somewhat formal words show that two sequences should be interpreted as consisting of paired items. For example, *Jan and Larry drank whisky and brandy, respectively* means that Jan drank whisky while Larry drank brandy.

It is, of course, necessary to have the same number of items in each list. Consider the following mess: **Alice, Susan and Brenda are respectively divorced and separated.* This is gibberish, since a list of three is linked to a list of two, and the reader has no chance of figuring out what the writer is trying to say.

These words are very frequently used pointlessly, when no ambiguity is possible, as in the example **Henman and Kafelnikov won their respective matches.* It is inconceivable that the two players could win each other's matches, or win somebody else's matches, and so that *respective* should not be there: write *Henman and Kafelnikov won their matches.*

In the same vein, it is hardly necessary to write the following: *??After the meeting broke up, the delegates returned to their respective homes.* Just write *. . . returned to their homes*, or, better still, *. . . returned home*. Who will suspect the delegates of returning to one another's homes?

responsible Here we have an instance of flat-out disagreement among the authorities. Traditionally, responsibility can be assigned only to people and their actions, as in *His inflammatory speeches were responsible for the riot*. Recently, however, journalists have been applying *responsible* with great freedom to states of affairs, especially to natural phenomena. Consider an example: ??*The thick fog was responsible for the accident.* What do you think of this? Some authorities condemn it outright, while others endorse it as now an accepted part of standard English. Since many careful writers object to such uses, I advise you to avoid this use of *responsible*. Write instead *The thick fog was the cause of the accident.*

A different case, and this time wrong beyond dispute, is illustrated by this example: **The year 1919 was responsible for the greatest scandal in baseball history*. It is perfectly absurd to blame the year for the scandal: it was the players who misbehaved, and those who drove them to misbehaviour, who were responsible for the scandal.

restaurateur The owner of a restaurant is a *restaurateur*, with no N, and the spelling *restauranteur is wrong.

resurrect Note the spelling: one S, two Rs.

retronym A *retronym* is a word which is obliged to expand its form because its original sense has been usurped by another sense. For example, the players of the medieval game of tennis have been forced to give it a new name, *real tennis*, because its original name has been taken over by the game Martina Hingis plays. Such linguistic developments are often unavoidable, but some of them are nevertheless regrettable.

When I was young, the word *guitar* denoted the traditional wooden instrument played by performers ranging from Andrés Segovia to Gene Autry. Today, however, the word is understood by most young people as applying to a strung piece of metal or plastic which produces little sound unless it is connected to a huge amplifier, and the original article must now be called an *acoustic guitar*.

In Britain, at least, it is both legal and customary to apply the name *ice cream* to a kind of glop manufactured from such delicacies as overripe fish and cattle rectums, and any frozen dessert which has managed to spend the customary time in the vicinity of a cow before going on sale is now called *dairy ice cream* – or, just to drive the point home, *traditional Cornish dairy ice cream, made with real cream*. By the way, *real cream* is another retronym. (Any reader who doesn't believe my account of British ice cream is invited to consult pages 176–181 of David Bodanis's 1986 book *The Secret House*, from Sidgwick.)

Retronyms are often not amusing to those of us old enough to remember when the world was different, but there is little we can do about them.

The term *retronym* was invented by Frank Mankiewicz, the president of National Public Radio in the USA.

revenge See **avenge**.

revise This is the only possible spelling in all varieties of English: the spelling *revize* is never acceptable. In all kinds of English, the word can mean 'modify', 'alter': *The Bank of England has revised its predictions*. In British English, it can also mean 'study (material) in preparation for an examination'; the American equivalent here is *review*.

Rheims, Reims Both spellings are acceptable in English, and opinion is divided as to which should be preferred. The recommended pronunciation is 'reams'.

rhinoceros This Greek word is spelled in English with the Greek ending *-os*, and the spelling *rhinocerus* is wrong. The plural is *rhinoceroses* or sometimes *rhinoceros*; don't even think about the ghastly *rhinoceri*.

rhyme, rime The historical spelling is *rime*, but today, as a result of contamination from *rhythm*, the form *rhyme* predominates and is recommended for the poetic device, though *rime* is preferred as a technical term in certain types of linguistic analysis. However, the unusual word *rime* 'frost' is always so spelled.

right-node raising This is the technical term for the construction illustrated by the next two examples. *Lisa prepared, and Siobhan served, the cucumber sandwiches. She is a very clever, though sometimes careless, student*. In each case, the final item is grammatically linked to each of the two preceding sequences. This construction is confined to formal writing, where it may be appropriate.

However, the construction should be used sparingly, since it requires an exceptional amount of mental processing from your reader. Rather than my second example, you might consider writing *She is a very clever student, though sometimes a careless one*. This second version is easier to read.

If you do use this construction, make sure you punctuate it correctly: it requires a *pair* of commas setting off the second of the two sequences which are grammatically linked to the final item. The common error here is to omit the second of the two required commas: *She is a very clever, though sometimes careless student*. Such careless punctuation forces your reader to do even more work in trying to decipher your meaning.

Many writers are excessively fond of right-node raising, which they seem to believe automatically adds a measure of elegance to their writing. Wrong. It merely makes that writing harder to read. Moreover, most such writers cannot punctuate the construction, and constantly produce distressing things like *Most, but not all of the Cabinet support this policy*. Make that *Most, but not all, of the Cabinet* . . .

See also **missing preposition** for a further example of the dangers of right-node raising.

rob, steal You *steal* valuables by taking them away illegally. But you *rob* people and places by taking valuables from them illegally. So, if I steal your money, then I have robbed you, but I have not robbed your money.

role The preferred spelling is *role*. The variant *rôle* is now old-fashioned and best avoided.

Romania, Rumania, Roumania The official spelling of the name in the country itself is *Romania*, and this is the form you should use. The other two English variant spellings are best avoided, especially the last, which is decidedly old-fashioned.

rosary, rosery A *rosary* is a string of beads used by Roman Catholics in praying. The Spanish female name *Rosa* is often short for *Rosario*, from the Spanish word for *rosary*. But a *rosery* is a rose garden or a rosebed. The second word is rare.

RP See **Received Pronunciation**.

ruination There is rarely any reason to prefer this long word to the shorter *ruin*.

Rumania See **Romania**.

Russian names A Russian personal name consists of a given name followed by a patronymic followed by a surname, where the patronymic merely indicates 'son' or 'daughter' of the named father. For example, the playwright *Anton Pavlovich Chekhov* is the son of a Mr *Chekhov*, whose first name was *Pavel*. In English, the patronymic is rarely used, except in the full names entered in reference books, though readers of nineteenth-century Russian novels will be familiar with it.

Men and women use different forms of their surname. Mr *Pavlov*'s son is also called *Pavlov*, but his daughter is called *Pavlova*.

Russian is not written in the roman alphabet, and so Russian names must be rewritten in our alphabet when we cite them in English. It is customary to base the English version on the Russian spelling, and not on the Russian pronunciation, which is why we write *Gorbachev* (following the Russian spelling), rather than *Gorbachov* (which represents the Russian pronunciation better). But we sometimes depart from this policy when the Russian spelling is highly misleading; for example, we usually write *Fyodor* for 'Theodore' and *Pyotr* for 'Peter', rather than *Fedor* and *Petr*, which conform more closely to the Russian spelling.

There is a notable inconsistency in representing the Russian consonant which sounds like our CH. For example, we write *Anton Chekhov*, not *Tchekhov*, and yet we write *Pyotr Tchaikovsky*, and not *Chaikovsky*. There is no particular reason for this.

saccharin, saccharine The artificial sweetener is *saccharin*; the adjective meaning 'sugary', 'excessively sweet' is *saccharine*.

sacrilegious The word is so spelled, and *＊sacreligious* is wrong. The word is not related to *religious*, and is not spelled like it: instead, it is derived from *sacrilege*.

said, the The wording *the said* should be avoided. It is not proper to write *＊Nearly a thousand languages are spoken in New Guinea, and the said languages fall into more than sixty families*. Write instead *. . . and these languages*.

salacious This word means 'bawdy' or 'erotic'. Hence a *salacious* story is one which is sexually crude or sexually arousing. The word should not be applied to merely sensational or irresponsible gossip.

salutary The adjective meaning 'having a wholesome or beneficial effect' is *salutary*. There is no such word as *＊salutory*.

same The following examples illustrate a usage which is frequent in informal English: *＊Susie has the same colour hair as Natalie*; *＊I need the same size spanner as that one*. This informal style is too awkward for formal writing, and it should be avoided. Write instead *Susie has the same colour of hair as Natalie* (or, much better, *Susie's hair is the same colour as Natalie's*) and *I need a spanner the same size as that one*.

sans This is now merely a joke word. Don't use it. Write *without*.

sans serif, sanserif Both forms are in use, but the first is more usual and is recommended.

sari, saree, sarong A *sari* is a long body-covering worn by a Hindu woman. The variant spelling *saree* is also found but is not recommended. A *sarong* is a long skirt worn by both men and women in southeast Asia and the Pacific.

sat Colloquial British English allows sentences like *∗She was sat next to the host*. This must be avoided in formal writing: write instead *She was sitting next to the host* or *She was seated next to the host*.

savanna, savannah See **grasslands**.

savant Originally, a *savant* was a man of great learning, and this sense is still current. This French word is expressly masculine, and *savante* can be used of a woman. Today, however, *savant* is most commonly applied to a person who is mentally subnormal in most respects but who has one astounding gift, such as the ability to multiply huge numbers in his head almost instantly, or to copy any piece of music perfectly after hearing it once. The earlier term here was *idiot savant*, but this is now regarded as insulting, and it is no longer used.

say The problem with this word is not so much an error as a grave infelicity of style. All too often, a student writing an account of an intellectual debate repeats this word endlessly: *∗Austin says A, but Searle says B. However, Grice says C, while Sperber and Wilson say D*. Such constant repetition of *say* is childish and wearisome, and the problem becomes even worse when the past tense *said* is used. Be careful to avoid this tedious practice by making free use of other verbs, such as *suggest, propose, argue, conclude, observe* and *point out*. English is rich in such verbs: use them.

Scandinavia There is variation in the use of this geographical label. It always includes Norway, Sweden and Denmark. For some people, this is all it includes, while for others it also includes Finland and Iceland, and occasionally even the Faeroe Islands. For those preferring the narrower use, the larger grouping is *the Nordic countries*.

scare quotes See under **quotation marks**.

scarlet See **crimson**.

scenario This technical term from the stage and film business has become something of a vogue word for a possible or hypothetical sequence of events. But it is often used as meaningless padding: for example, *∗a nightmare scenario* is not different from *a nightmare*, and the last word should be deleted.

sceptic, skeptic, septic A person who is not inclined to believe things readily is a *sceptic* in British English but a *skeptic* in American English; these two spellings represent the same pronunciation. The derived adjectives are likewise *sceptical* and *skeptical*. But *septic* is a medical term meaning 'infected', as in *a septic toe*. The common error here is writing *sceptic* where *septic* is intended. See also **cynic**.

schizophrenic *Schizophrenia* is a recognized medical condition, usually a very grave one. Like all medical terms, *schizophrenic* should not be tossed around loosely, and it certainly should not be used frivolously to mean no more than 'divided' or 'exhibiting contradictory tendencies'. The current government's policies may seem to be inconsistent, but they are not schizophrenic.

school In Britain, a *school* is an educational institution below university level. In the US, a school is an educational institution at any level, including university level. Americans should be careful with this word, since Britons are offended when their universities are referred to as 'schools'.

science It is very common for newspapers to begin a sentence by writing *Science says that . . .* or *Scientists say that . . .* This is no good. To begin with, science is an enterprise, a way of looking into things, and it doesn't say anything. The second version is not much better. Anything that all scientists agree on is unlikely to be news. If a few scientists have made a discovery, or proposed something controversial, then by all means identify these scientists accurately, instead of imputing their position vaguely to the entire scientific profession.

scientific terms Most scientific terms have very precise meanings. If you venture to use a scientific term, make sure you use it correctly – something which may not be easy unless you have a grasp of the science involved. For example, I recently ran across a reference to *✽computer and space science*. There is no such discipline, and the writer was doing no more than exposing his incomprehending awe of modern science. If you don't know what a scientific term means, then either find out or refrain from using it.

Scot, Scots, Scottish, scotch A person from Scotland is a *Scot*, and the adjective meaning 'pertaining to (or coming from) Scotland' is *Scottish*. The word *scotch* is only appropriate as a label for Scottish whisky and in a few fixed expressions like *scotch broth* (a kind of hearty soup). You should not write *✽Scotch* when you mean *Scottish*.

The word *Scots* denotes the kind of regional English spoken in Scotland: we may write that 'ilk' or 'dreich' is a *Scots* word.

Scottish and Irish names The only real problem with these names is the prefix meaning 'son of', which may be written *Mac* or *Mc* or sometimes *Mack* or even *M'*; it may be written solid or followed by a white space; when it is written solid the following letter may or may not be capitalized. The variation may be exhibited by a few examples: the US actress *Shirley McLaine* but the Scottish writer *Alistair Maclean*; the Scottish inventor *Charles Macintosh*, but the Scottish architect *Charles Rennie Mackintosh* and the New Zealand opera singer *Sir Donald McIntyre*. When in doubt, consult a good reference book.

This variation causes problems when we are putting names into alphabetical order. Often, though not invariably, *Mc* is treated like *Mac*, so that, for example, *John McEnroe* comes before *James MacGillivray* and before *Ernst Mach*.

The Irish prefix meaning 'descendant of' causes few problems, since it is almost always written in the form illustrated by the name of the Irish writer *Edna O'Brien*.

sea change This is a **cliché**, and one of the most overused ones in the language. Some writers appear to believe that *sea change* is the ordinary English word for 'change'. Don't use it.

seafaring, seafarer Each of these is always written as a single word, as shown; it is wrong to write *✳sea faring* or *✳sea farer*.

second largest This and similar expressions are often misused. It is wrong to write *✳India has the world's second largest population after China*. In fact, India has the world's *largest* population after China, or, to put it differently, India has the world's second largest population.

secret, secretive A *secretive* person is one who keeps his affairs to himself and doesn't tell people what he's up to. A secretive organization is one which operates in secrecy, allowing no public scrutiny of its activities. Only a person or an organization can be secretive, and it is an error to use *secretive* when *secret* is intended: write *a secret wedding*, not *✳a secretive wedding*.

But don't overuse *secret*. Journalists very often use this word when it is not appropriate. For example, if the British prime minister has a quiet meeting with the leaders of Sinn Fein, then that meeting is *secret* only if both sides have taken active steps to keep anyone from finding out about it. If they have merely declined to tell anybody about it, then it is *private* or *confidential*, but it is not secret.

self-destruct See **destruct**.

semantic meaning A meaning is semantic by definition, since semantics is the domain of meaning. Accordingly, *✳semantic meaning* is a **pleonasm**, and should be avoided. Write *meaning* instead, or, in a linguistic context, perhaps *semantic content*.

semantics Semantics is the scholarly study of meaning, and this discipline has a distinguished history among philosophers, linguists and literary scholars. Today the field is not only respectable but flourishing. It is poor style to use *semantics* as a lazy term of abuse for any kind of deception involving words. Write something more explicit or more precise, such as *hair-splitting, quibbling, misrepresentation* or *pettifogging*. And it is intellectually disgraceful to shrug off criticisms of your position as 'semantics'.

semicolon The *semicolon* (;) has only one important function. It serves to connect *two complete sentences* when these sentences meet the following conditions: (1) they are felt to be too closely connected to be separated by a full stop (a period); (2) they are not joined by a connecting word which would require a comma, such as *and, or, but, while* or *yet*; (3) they do not meet the requirements for a colon. The next sentence is an example. *Women's conversation is cooperative; men's is competitive.* Here is another example. *Tolkien published* The Hobbit *in 1937; the first volume of* The Lord of the Rings *followed in 1954.*

The semicolon cannot be used if what precedes or follows it is not a complete sentence. Here is an example of wrong use. *✳I don't like him; not at all.* The semicolon here should be replaced by a comma. And here is another faulty example. *✳In 1991 the music world was shaken by a tragic event; the death of Freddy Mercury.* This time the required punctuation is a colon.

Many people have badly confused the semicolon with the colon, and they routinely write a semicolon where a colon is required. There follows an example. *✳The minority languages of Spain are as follows; Catalan, Basque and Galician.* That semicolon is impossible, and it must be replaced by a colon.

For more on semicolons, see chapter 4 of the *Penguin Guide to Punctuation*.

senior The central meaning of this adjective is 'higher in rank', as in the example *Mr Higgins is senior to me*. When used without a standard of comparison, it means 'highest in rank', as in *Eisenhower was the senior Allied commander in Europe* (there was no other Allied commander of equal or higher rank). Today, however, it is very common to see this word used to mean only 'high-ranking', producing phrases like *✳very senior* and *✳most senior*. Such usages will annoy many readers, and they are best avoided. In place of

*_very senior_, write (_very_) _high-ranking_, and, in place of *_most senior_, write
senior or _highest-ranking_. In place of *_third most senior official_, write _third-ranking official_.

sensual, sensuous These are not always easy to distinguish. However, on
the whole, _sensuous_ is the more neutral term, meaning only 'satisfying
to the senses'. For example, we may write of _the sensuous feel of fine
leather_, meaning that fine leather feels nice. But _sensual_ usually implies
gratification of the senses or of the bodily appetites, and especially of sexual
desire.

sentence This is always so spelled: the spelling *_sentance_ is wrong. Perhaps
you might bear in mind the derivatives _sententious_ 'pompous' and the
technical linguistic term _sentential_ 'pertaining to sentences'.

sentence fragments A _sentence fragment_ is a piece of a sentence punctuated as though it were a complete sentence. Used judiciously, sentence
fragments can be effective in less formal kinds of writing. Example: _Can
England win the World Cup? Probably not._ Here _Probably not_ is a sentence
fragment. But fragments are usually out of place in formal writing, and,
when they occur, they are usually mistakes. Here is an example. _Northern
Italians see southerners as idle and dishonest._ *_While southerners see northerners
as cold-hearted money-grubbers._ Here the portion starting with _while_ is a
fragment which is wrong in any style of writing. This portion is only a
subordinate clause, and it should be joined to the preceding sentence:
_Northern Italians see southerners as idle and dishonest, while southerners see
northerners as cold-hearted money-grubbers._ This is perfect.

separate This is always spelled as shown, with an A in the middle. Do not
write *_seperate_. If you have trouble with this, try the following mnemonic:
You can't sepARATe A RAT from muck.

sequel The word is so spelled; avoid the misspelling *_sequal_. The word is
not spelled like _equal_.

serendipity _Serendipity_ is finding something nice entirely by accident, and
such a discovery is _serendipitous_. A discovery is not serendipitous merely
because it is pleasant; it must also be accidental.

serviette See **napkin**.

sexism It is beyond the scope of this book to treat sexist language at length,
but a few points may usefully be made.
  Some instances of sexism are blatant and inexcusable: they have nothing

to do with the structure of English, and merely express sexist attitudes. Here are two genuine examples: *He attacked his next-door neighbour's wife* (the woman was also his neighbour, unless she was living apart from her husband); *The pioneers trekked across the prairies with their animals, their seed corn and their wives* (the wives were only there to cook, clean, raise the children and have dinner on the table when their husbands got home from a hard day of pioneering). If you can't refrain from writing things like these, you need more help than I can provide.

But other cases are more difficult, since they involve English grammar and vocabulary. A familiar example is the generic use of *man*. It is now widely regarded as inappropriate to use *man*, or *men*, to label people generally. Instead of ✳*Men first reached the Americas about 13,000 years ago*, many careful writers would now prefer *Human beings first reached . . .* But there remain all those words like *chairman, fireman, postman, manhole, man-eating tiger* and *to man a position*. For some of these, adequate replacements have been pressed into service: *chair, firefighter, letter carrier*. But others are more refractory, and elegant solutions may be elusive.

If you can see a simple and clear way of avoiding an obviously sexist term, then take it. But, if you can find no elegant alternative to, say, *man-eating tiger*, then use the existing phrase without fear.

For a well-known special case, see **they**. See also **feminism**.

Shakespeare Though the playwright himself spelled his name in several ways, the version *Shakespeare* is now universally accepted as the standard spelling. Using other spellings, like ✳*Shakspere*, is now pretentious and silly. The derived adjective is usually *Shakespearean*, which is recommended. The variant *Shakespearian* is not wrong, but it is less usual.

shall, will Over the years, these two words have called forth torrents of ink, not all of which has been well spilled. But the only rule you need is a simple one: if one word or the other feels completely natural, then use it without hesitation. Just forget what you think you may have read in some usage manual. What that manual said was very likely wrong anyway, or else it was painstakingly describing the sort of English spoken fifty years ago in another country.

In speech, both words are very often replaced by *'ll* anyway, as in *This'll do the trick*. Like all contractions, this one should be used sparingly in careful writing, and not at all in very formal writing.

In American English, *shall* has almost completely disappeared, except in the kind of question illustrated by *Shall I open the window?* ('Would you like me to open the window?'). Some (not all) Americans also retain the word in one or two fossilized expressions: *A certain writer, who shall remain nameless . . .* The negative form *shan't* is entirely dead in the US.

British English seems to be going the same way, though *shall* is still vigorous in some circles, and *shan't* still finds some use.

There is a traditional textbook ruling that runs as follows. For simple futurity, you use *shall* after *I* or *we* but *will* after everything else, while, to express determination or command, you use *will* after *I* or *we* but *shall* after everything else. By these rules, the required forms are *We shall finish tonight* (simple statement) versus *We will finish tonight* (expressing determination), but *They will finish tonight* (simple statement) versus *They shall finish tonight* (an order).

As grammarians never tire of pointing out, these bizarre rules do not accurately describe the real usage of careful speakers at any time or in any place in the history of English, and they are little more than a fantastic invention. If you are one of that handful of speakers for whom these rules now seem completely natural, then by all means go ahead and follow them. But, if you are not, just forget about them, and use your natural forms.

However, in Britain, the very formal written English used in drafting laws and regulations requires the use of *shall* with a third-person subject for stating requirements. Example: *An average of 40% shall be deemed a pass at Honours level.* Britons engaged in doing such writing must fall into line here. But note that this use is not normal in the US, and may not even be acceptable there.

Do not try to use *shall* if the word does not feel entirely natural, and especially don't try to use it merely in the hope of sounding more elegant. Doing so will probably produce something which is acceptable to no one. A very common error in the student essays that I mark is using *shall* for *will* in cases like the following: *This shall be discussed later in the essay.* This is wrong, since *this shall* is only possible in stating laws, rules and commands.

share (with) Only this morning, the electronic question list on language to whose panel I belong received a question from a young American woman, who asked us 'Could you share with me your thoughts on this matter?' This eccentric use of *share* is still predominantly American, though perhaps not unknown elsewhere. It sounds silly, and it should be avoided. Prefer a blunter verb, such as *tell* or *advise*. Our correspondent would have been wiser to write 'Can you tell me what you think about this?'

sheriff The word is always so spelled; do not write *sherriff, *sherrif or *sherif.

shew See **show**.

shine The past tense is usually *shone*: *The sun shone brightly*; *We shone a light*. However, when it means 'polished', the form is *shined*: *He shined his shoes*.

show, shew Except in quotations and in certain legal contexts, the spelling *shew* for *show* is now obsolete and should not be used. The past tense of *show* is always *showed*: *She showed me her photographs*. The past participle may be either *shown* or *showed* in most circumstances: *She has often shown me her photos* or *She has often showed me her photos*, as you prefer. However, in the passive only *shown* is possible: write *The house is being shown to prospective buyers*, not **. . . is being showed*. Don't ask me why.

shrink This verb has the parts *shrink, shrank, shrunk* in standard English. The past tense is *shrank*, as in *My jeans shrank when I washed them*, and the film title **Honey, I Shrunk the Kids* does not represent standard English for most of us, though a few American commentators are prepared to accept this as a legitimate variant.

sic This, the Latin word for 'thus', has only one function in English. When you are quoting a passage written by someone else which contains a mistake, and you want to explain to your readers that the mistake is in the original and has not been introduced by you, then you place the word *sic*, enclosed in square brackets, immediately after the error. Here is an example, which is meant to be a quotation: *The All Blacks won the match with a fortuitous* [sic] *try in the last minute*. The reason for the *sic* is that the original writer, being quoted here, has wrongly written *fortuitous* where *fortunate* was intended.

    The word *sic* is not properly used for emphasis, nor is it properly used merely to identify something as a quotation: that's what quotation marks are for. Nor is it properly used to convey irony, or to poke fun at the form or content of the passage being quoted.

sick, ill The adjective *sick* formerly meant 'ill', 'in bad health', and it still does in American English. In British English, however, *sick* is now commonly restricted to the senses of 'experiencing nausea' and 'mentally disturbed', and *ill* is preferred as the everyday word. However, the older sense of *sick* survives in Britain in such expressions as *sick pay* and *sick leave*, and also in the locution *He's a sick man*.

siege The word is so spelled; avoid the common error *seige.

sieve The word is so spelled; avoid the misspelling *seive.

significant, significantly These words have become vogue words, and they are heavily overused. If you find yourself writing one of them for the twenty-fifth time that day, stop and think whether some other word might serve your purpose, such as *important(ly)*, *substantial(ly)* or *appreciable, -bly*.

In fact, go a little further, and think whether you need a word there at all, especially with *significantly*, and especially when you find yourself writing this word at the beginning of a sentence. Quite often the word has no function other than making the following sentence look more important than it is.

silicon, silicone These are not identical. The chemical element is *silicon*, which is abundant on the earth and present in sand, in glass and in quartz and other minerals. But a *silicone* is any of certain chemical compounds of silicon. Silicones are useful as lubricants, as adhesives, and of course as breast implants.

silken, silky A *silken* cord is a cord made of silk, while a *silky* cord is a cord which looks like silk, but very likely is not. A cat may have *a silky coat*, but not *∗a silken coat*. However, the word *silken* is now somewhat old-fashioned, and today we normally use *silk* to label something made of silk: *a silk tie*, not *∗a silken tie*.

simplistic This is not a fancy word for *simple*. It is a term of abuse, meaning 'oversimplified', 'ill-thought-out'. Since the word already contains the sense of 'too much', you should not extend it to something like *∗overly simplistic*: nothing can be simplistic to a satisfactory degree.

Sindbad The character in *The Arabian Nights* is *Sindbad*; *∗Sinbad* is wrong, even though this form is used in one or two Hollywood movies.

single-handed This is an adverb as well as an adjective. While *??He did it single-handedly* is not wrong, *He did it single-handed* is shorter and recommended.

single most This is unnecessary. Write *She was the most important person in my life*, not *∗. . . the single most important person*.

singular versus plural See **agreement**.

Sir, Dame Americans and others may not be aware of the proper use of these British titles, which are male and female equivalents. The linguist *Sir John Lyons* and the actress *Dame Peggy Ashcroft* may be referred to in full, as here, or without their surnames, as in *Sir John* and *Dame Peggy*. But it is wrong to use one of these titles with surname alone: *_Sir Lyons_ and *_Dame Ashcroft_ are not acceptable.

situated knowledges This is another of those expressions which seem to occur nowhere but in bad writing. The general idea is that the knowledge we possess is strongly determined by the circumstances in which we have acquired it, and hence that people in different circumstances acquire different knowledge. This is fine with things like etiquette and finding food in the Kalahari. However, the people who use this expression almost invariably go on to suggest that knowledge of things like physics and chemistry is just as 'situated' as knowledge of etiquette, and hence that the Schrödinger wave equation would be different if it had been discovered by somebody other than a white European male who grew up in imperial Vienna. This is absurd to the point of insanity.

Anybody who believes that knowing that the moon is a huge rocky body orbiting the earth is just as 'situated', and hence just as valid, as 'knowing' that the moon is a glowing pumpkin hovering just above the treetops has a serious problem with reality, and should probably not operate machinery until this condition wears off. Oddly, this form of dementia appears to afflict nobody but academics in certain disciplines, while the rest of the population remains immune.

situation This word should not normally occur modified by a preceding noun, since in this position it contributes no meaning at all. That is, *_a crisis situation_ is no different from _a crisis_, *_a combat situation_ is no different from _combat_, and *_the unemployment situation_ is often no different from _unemployment_. Even when explicit reference to a degree or a state of affairs is required, it is usually better to choose a more explicit word than the rather vague _situation_: write _the level of unemployment_, not *_the unemployment situation_, and write _in the heat of combat_, not *_in a combat situation_. The constant use of a pointless or inexplicit _situation_ will make your writing appear wordy, tiresome and childish.

skeptic See **sceptic**, **cynic**.

skiing Write the word like this; the old spelling *_ski-ing_ is now archaic.

slander See **libel**.

slattern, slut, **sloven** Historically, a _slattern_ or a _slut_ is a dirty and unkempt woman, while a _sloven_ is a dirty and unkempt man or woman. Today, however, the word _sloven_ has virtually dropped out of the language, while _slut_ has become specialized to mean a lewd or promiscuous woman, and only *slattern* remains to serve the original sense. The adjectives are *slatternly* 'dirty and unkempt' (of a woman), *sluttish* 'promiscuous' (of a woman) and *slovenly* 'dirty' (of anyone).

slay The parts of this verb are *slay, slew, slain*. Today this ancient English verb is more frequent in American English than in British English, though it remains a favourite of headline-writers everywhere. If you use it, write *They slew him*, and not *☀They slayed him*, and *He was slain*, not *☀He was slayed*. The form *slayed* is permissible only in British English and only in informal transferred senses, as in *The stand-up comic slayed his audience* ('reduced them to helpless laughter').

sleight of hand This term, denoting the manual trickery practised by conjurors, is so spelled, and *☀slight of hand* is not acceptable.

sloven See **slattern**.

slut See **slattern**.

small capitals Small capitals are normally used for writing the abbreviations B.C., A.D., B.C.E., C.E. and B.P.; see **A.D.** In American English, they are also commonly used for writing A.M. and P.M. (of the clock). This is not usual in British English; see **a.m.**

smite, smitten The old verb *smite* has now dropped out of the language, except in jocular use, and except in the expression *be smitten* 'be infatuated', as in *Carl is smitten with one of his classmates*.

Smithsonian Institution The American museum complex is so named, and *☀Smithsonian Institute* is wrong. The complex can be called the *Smithsonian* for short.

smoky The word is so spelled, and *☀smokey* is wrong.

snicker, snigger The American form is *snicker*; the British form is *snigger*.

sometime, some time, sometimes Of these three, *sometimes* is easy. It means 'now and again', and it is always written as one word: *My wife and I sometimes play Scrabble*. The other two are more difficult, and usage varies. When *some* is unstressed, the form is *some time*: *We'll need some time to consider this*. When the sense is 'an indefinite length of time', it is usual to write *some time*: *She arrived some time after dinner*. But some people write *sometime* here, and this style cannot be considered wrong. When the sense is 'at an indefinite time in the future', *sometime* is usual: *We'll talk about this* *sometime next week*. But the adjective meaning 'occasional' or 'former' is always *sometime*: *his sometime colleague*.

somewhat of This wording is always wrong. Write *This is something of a misnomer*, not *This is somewhat of a misnomer*. You can only use *somewhat* with a following adjective or adverb, as in *Her writing is somewhat breathless*.

sort See **kind**.

sorta See **kinda**.

sort out The colloquial expression *sort out*, in the sense of 'deal with', 'solve', is too informal to be used in formal writing.

South America, Latin America These names are not interchangeable. The label *Latin America* is applied to all the territory lying south of the USA, from Mexico onward. In contrast, the continent of South America begins just to the south of the Republic of Panama. Mexico and the seven small countries of Central America are definitely part of North America, not of South America. You can easily give offence by writing *South America* when you mean *Latin America*: many Mexicans are very annoyed at being described as 'South Americans'.

soy, soya The American form is *soybean*; the British form is *soya bean*. But all varieties prefer *soy sauce* to *soya sauce*.

Spanish names A Spaniard normally has two surnames, the father's first surname followed by the mother's first surname (a Spanish woman does not normally take her husband's surname). Very often in Spain, and usually in English, the first surname alone is used in referring to someone. So, for example, *Luis Aznar González* is referred to as *Sr Aznar*, and not as *Sr González*. But there exist exceptions, two famous ones being the poet *Federico García Lorca* and the painter *Pablo Ruiz Picasso*.

The two surnames are occasionally separated by *y* 'and', and either surname may be preceded by *de* 'of'. These particles are ignored in English. So, the great Spanish Basque linguist *Resurrección María de Azkue* is *Azkue*, and not *de Azkue*.

Spaniards who work in the wider world not infrequently join their two surnames with a hyphen. Many academics do this when publishing in English, in order to avoid being listed wrongly by their second surnames, but the most familiar example is the tennis player *Arantxa Sanchez-Vicario*.

In Spanish America, the Spanish custom is sometimes followed but sometimes not. For example, *Fidel Castro Ruz* rarely uses his second surname.

In both Spain and Spanish America, sportsmen, especially football players, sometimes prefer to be known by a single name. This may be a first name, a surname or a nickname. An example is the Spanish footballer *Kiko*.

spatial Even though the noun is *space*, the derived adjective is *spatial*, not *⁎spacial*.

speciality, specialty These words have different spellings and different pronunciations, and so you might reasonably expect them to have different meanings as well. But they don't. Grammarians have searched hard for evidence that the two are regarded as different, but all there is to report is an occasional observation, such as the conclusion that the finest dish offered in a restaurant is *the specialty of the house* in the USA but *the speciality of the house* in the UK. Use whichever form you prefer, and don't worry about it.

specially See **especially**.

spectrum A *spectrum* is by definition a one-dimensional continuum, in which each value shades imperceptibly into the next. The most familiar spectrum is, of course, the visible spectrum, as seen in a rainbow. It is fine to use this word metaphorically when the 'continuum' sense is kept in mind. But the word should not be used thoughtlessly when a simpler word would be more appropriate, such as *range* or *variety*, and it should not be used at all for a discontinuous collection of things.

sped, speeded The past tense and past participle of the verb *speed* are *sped* when the verb means 'hurry': *She sped to the scene*. But it is *speeded* when the meaning is 'drive too fast': *She got a ticket because she had speeded*.

spellcheckers These days, almost all word processors are equipped with spellcheckers. Most of these have to be called up before they will do anything, but some of the newer ones can monitor your work while you're writing it and discreetly flag any words that are not recognized. Spellcheckers can be valuable in catching typos, especially if you find it difficult to spot them when you proofread your work. But a spellchecker is not a substitute for good spelling, and you can't rely on a spellchecker to ensure that your writing is free of spelling errors.

First, all a spellchecker can do is to check whether a particular word is present in its dictionary. It has no way of knowing whether the word on the screen is the one that should be there. Such common errors as writing *there* for *their*, or *proceed* for *precede*, will go unnoticed by the program, and they will make it into your finished document unless you are capable of spotting them yourself.

Second, spellcheckers carry only a limited number of proper names in their dictionaries. All unrecognized proper names will be queried, but this is not much help if you don't know how to spell the names. It doesn't matter whether you write *Solzhenitsyn* (correctly) or *Solzhenytsin* (incorrectly): the machine will flag it regardless, and you still don't know whether your spelling is right or wrong. Of course, for those names you use frequently, you can look up their correct spellings and type them into your spellchecker's dictionary, but this is no help with the much larger number of names you use only rarely.

Third, spellchecker dictionaries do not carry many technical terms. If you do a good deal of technical writing in a specialist subject, such as molecular biology or linguistics, you are likely to find yourself using hundreds of technical terms which are absent from your program's dictionary. If you have trouble spelling some of these, then again you can type them all into your spellchecker, but doing so will probably take about as much time as learning to spell them in the first place. And, of course, when you buy a new word processor, you'll have to go through the whole routine again.

Finally, if you often have to write words or longer expressions from foreign languages, or even from earlier stages of English, then your spellchecker will merely have a nervous breakdown: it will fill your text with pointless red blotches. In fact, almost any sort of writing on language will produce a similar result. Even a dictionary of English contains passages like this one: '*tree*, from Old English *treo*, related to Old Frisian and Old Norse *tre*, Gothic *triu*, Greek *drus*'. With writing like this, your spellchecker will fill the page with so many red blotches that any genuine typos will probably go unnoticed.

Using a spellchecker is no substitute for learning to spell.

See also **grammar checkers**, **style checkers**.

spelling English spelling is notoriously complex, irregular and eccentric, more so than in almost any other written language on earth. For example, the verbs *read* and *lead* rhyme, as do their past tenses *read* and *led*, but the spelling changes only in the second verb. At the same time, the name of the metal *lead* is spelled like *lead* but sounds like *led*. We have mysterious things like *mood*, *good*, *blood* and *door*, like *put*, *cut* and *putt*, like *or*, *ore* and *oar*, like *plain* and *plane*, and thousands more. Few people are sure whether to write *adviser* or *advisor*, *descendent* or *descendant*, *ukelele* or *ukulele*, *sacrilegious* or *sacreligious*, and words like *connoisseur*, *asthma* and *February* drive many of us to tears, as do our apparently mysterious apostrophes.

Our complex spelling requires years of effort to master, and very few people ever master it completely. Most people never acquire more than a moderate command of it. This is why so much of this book is given over to noting the commonest spelling errors, and why many people consult dictionaries more often to check spellings than to look up meanings. Our devilish spelling system is a prominent and often painful part of our lives, and yet mastery of it is essential for anyone who wants to be regarded as literate. If you can't spell words in the accepted manner, then many readers will dismiss your work as obviously not worth reading.

A few people have reacted to this state of affairs by protesting that spelling is over-valued, and that we should learn to accept a range of spellings for each word. After all, they argue, it is content that matters, not spelling, and we should not blink or complain when we encounter unfamiliar spellings that we can none the less decipher with little difficulty. But these people are wrong. Fluent readers do not work through a text word by word, deciphering one word at a time. Instead, their eyes skip quickly along the line, taking in entire words and even entire short phrases at a single glance – providing those words and phrases are instantly familiar. When these readers encounter something they don't immediately recognize, they are brought up short. If this happens repeatedly, they quickly begin to lose the thread of the content altogether, as they are forced to stop and identify one unfamiliar written form after another. Try an example, the opening lines of a book, in which I have altered the spellings but thoughtfully maintained the correct punctuation:

Mathmaticle lores underpin the fabbrick of hour unavers – not just attoms, but galexsies, stars and peple. The proppartys of attoms – there sizez and masses, how meny difarent kinds their are, and the fauces linking them togethre – ditermin the kemastrie of hour every day wurld.

Not much fun to read, is it? What do you suppose it would be like reading this stuff for page after page, through an entire book? Do you suppose you would manage to take in much of the writer's content? Do you suppose you'd even bother to finish the book at all? And, if I had also ruined the punctuation, as well as the spelling, would you even be confident that you could decipher the writer's intended meaning at all? I'm afraid mastery of the established spelling really is essential to communication: it is not merely a pointless and wasteful social convention.

Many other people have adopted a different line. They argue that we should reform our spelling so as to bring it into line with the pronunciation. Well, such spelling reforms have at times been carried out successfully for other languages, such as Spanish, French and German, but could we do the same for English? Probably not.

First, there are severe practical problems. There already exists a vast body of English, both on paper and in electronic form, written in our established spelling, and the volume of this material grows every day. If we changed our spelling substantially, this material would become much harder for future generations to read. Today, we can still read Shakespeare in the original, even though we probably could not understand Shakespeare's speech if we could hear it, because Shakespeare's spellings are still largely our own. Changing our spelling would cut us off from much of our past.

Moreover, people who have spent years toiling to acquire standard spelling would in many cases protest in outrage if they were told that they must forget everything they have so painfully learned in favour of silly-looking new spellings, such as – perhaps – *dore* for *door*, *hite* for *height*, *flem* for *phlegm* and *krooshul* for *crucial*.

Yet another drawback to a spelling system modelled on pronunciation would be the loss of similar spellings for related words. Related words like *photograph* and *photography*, *gelatine* and *gelatinous*, *nation* and *national*, *sane* and *sanity*, *create* and *creation*, would no longer have related spellings in such a system.

But, all this aside, there is one overwhelming reason why we can't change our spelling to match our pronunciation: we don't all pronounce the language in the same way. For example, consider the following pairs of words. For each pair, the two words are pronounced identically by some native speakers of English but differently by other native speakers:

farther and *father*
whine and *wine*
cot and *caught*
caught and *court*
horse and *hoarse*
poor and *pour*
dew and *do*
pull and *pool*

balm and *bomb*
stir and *stare*
hire and *higher*
threw and *through*
pore and *paw*
toe and *tow*
buck and *book*
three and *free*
harm and *arm*

And so on. It may surprise you to learn that some speakers make a distinction you don't make, or fail to make a distinction you do make, but facts are facts. We can even find triplets: some speakers pronounce the words *marry*, *merry* and *Mary* all differently, while others pronounce them all the same, and still others pronounce two of them identically but the third differently. And there are many other pairs which rhyme for some speakers but not for others: *tomato* and *potato*, *finger* and *singer*, *harass* and *embarrass*, *vase* and *base*, *often* and *soften*, *granary* and *tannery*, *miscellany* and *felony*, *vagaries* and *fairies*, and so on, and so on.

So, a reformed spelling that matched my pronunciation well would not match yours at all. The British journalist who argued that we should respell *thought* as *thort* because 'that's the way it's pronounced' was blissfully unaware that, for the majority of the world's English-speakers, *thought* does not remotely rhyme with *short* – as it did for her – and that, for all these others, *thort* would be a much crazier spelling of *thought* than is the existing one.

It appears, therefore, that we are stuck with our established spelling, with all its drawbacks. Moreover, as our pronunciation continues to change – and it is certainly continuing to change – it must inevitably move even further away from the spelling. In fact, English appears to be drifting towards a system like that of Chinese, in which the written form of a word has nothing to do with its pronunciation: instead, each word is represented on paper by a set of arbitrary but conventional marks, and becoming literate means learning to recognize and produce the arbitrary marks attached to each spoken word. Well, it works for the Chinese, so no doubt it will work for us, too.

spiritual This word is grossly overused, and often used in a meaningless way. You should not use the term as a coy code-word for *religious*: if you mean *religious*, then write *religious*, and stop pussyfooting. For example, don't write *I didn't want to deprive my child of a spiritual heritage* if what you mean is *I didn't want to deprive my child of a religious upbringing.* If all you mean is *awe* or *a sense of wonder*, then say so, and refrain from vapourings like *a spiritual experience.* And, for heaven's sake, steer clear of grandiose verbiage like *the spiritual side of life.* If you have nothing more specific to say than this, then you probably have nothing to say at all, and you should stop wasting the readers' time.

spit The past tense of the verb meaning 'expel saliva' is either *spat* or *spit*, though *spat* is more usual and is recommended: *They spat at me.*

split infinitive In all of English grammar, there is perhaps no other topic which inflames passions so strongly for so little reason as the construction wrongly called the *split infinitive.* This construction is illustrated by the examples *She decided to never touch another cigarette* and *She decided to gradually get rid of her teddy bears*, in which the sequences *to never touch* and *to gradually get rid of* are the 'split infinitives'.

First of all, this traditional term is a misnomer, since, in this construction, nothing is split, least of all the infinitive, which is a single word: *touch* and *get* in my examples. A sequence like *to touch* or *to get* is not a single verb-form, nor indeed a grammatical unit of any kind, and it should not be treated as a unit. As can easily be shown, the sequence *to touch another cigarette* (for example) consists of an introductory particle *to* followed by a single grammatical unit, the verb phrase *touch another cigarette.* Accordingly, there is a break in structure between *to* and the following verb, and this break is often the most natural position to place an adverb.

Nevertheless, apparently because of a badly confused comparison with the grammar of Latin (which has nothing corresponding to English *to*), a minority of people have for generations allowed themselves to be persuaded that it is unacceptable to place an adverb, or anything else, between *to* and its following verb. I have no sympathy whatever with this view, which I consider ignorant, wrong-headed, foolish and contrary to the facts.

Still, this view persists, and there exist people with more self-confidence than knowledge who will proclaim loudly that 'split infinitives' are 'ungrammatical'. Assuming you are not one of these unfortunates, you have three choices. First, you can put your adverbs where they seem most natural and appropriate, and resign yourself to the inevitable howls of objection. Second, you can avoid 'splitting' where this is easily done, but 'split' where no good alternative exists. Third, you can scrupulously avoid ever putting anything between *to* and a following verb, in which case you will very likely wind up writing some pretty awful and sometimes ambiguous English.

Don't believe me? Consider an example: *She decided to gradually get rid of the teddy bears she had collected*. The pettifoggers will object to the 'split infinitive' here, and demand that the adverb *gradually* should be moved. But to where? If you write *She decided gradually to get rid* . . ., you are implying, wrongly, that it is the decision which is gradual, rather than the disposal. And moving the adverb to the end is no better: writing . . . *the teddy bears she had collected gradually* implies, again wrongly, that it is the collection which is gradual. And, of course, ✻*She decided to get gradually rid of* . . . is not even grammatical. The adverb *gradually* belongs, logically and naturally, next to the verb *get rid of*, and that is where speakers and writers normally put it, unless they have been intimidated by the noisy opponents of good English style.

Desperate attempts at avoiding 'split infinitives' often produce English which is not only tortured and unnatural but even ambiguous and misleading. Consider a genuine example: ✻*Our monitoring system has failed adequately to provide the required information*. Now, it is possible to *fail badly* or to *fail completely*, but it is hardly possible to ✻*fail adequately*, and the hapless readers of this piece of pseudo-English are forced to wade through it two or three times in order to decipher the writer's intended meaning. In this case, you should write *has failed to adequately provide*, and ignore the complaints.

So, if the grammar checker on your word processor flags a 'split infinitive', my advice is to turn off your grammar checker: it's only a dumb program, and it knows nothing about good English style.

Finally, I may note that a few people have become so carried away with the ridiculous campaign against 'split infinitives' that they even object to the placing of adverbs between two verbs, as in *This will have to be carefully examined* and *They will immediately evacuate the building*. This position is too insane to deserve discussion.

spoonful See **cupful**.

sports scores In Britain, when the final score of a match in a team game is reported, the *home* team is always named first, regardless of who has won: for example, *Arsenal 1 Liverpool 2*. In the US, in great contrast, it is always the *winning* team which is named first, regardless of where the game was played. If you cross the Atlantic, you must get used to this. It certainly bewilders Americans to see a baseball score reported as *Detroit 3 Baltimore 6*.

square brackets See **brackets**.

stadium The established plural is *stadiums*, while ✻*stadia* is pretentious.

stalactite, stalagmite In a cave, *stalagmites* stick up while *stalactites* hang down. If you have trouble with this, think of ants in the pants: the mites go up, and the tights go down.

stammer, stutter A *stammer* is an abnormally hesitant and broken manner of speaking, resulting from a speech defect or from strong emotion. The related verb is also *stammer*: *Terrified at being thrust up on stage, he managed to stammer out only a few words*. But a *stutter* is involuntary repetition of sounds, especially word-initial consonants, and the related verb is also *stutter*. Porky Pig stutters, but he does not stammer.

standard English As the Introduction explains, English is used in countless different varieties. We apply the label *standard English* to just one of those forms – or, more accurately, to a small set of closely related forms. Why is standard English not uniquely specified?

For one thing, the spoken standard is slightly different from the written standard. For example, *Much research has been done* is normal in writing but hardly in speech, while *A lot of research has been done* is normal in speech but often regarded as unacceptable in careful writing. And, of course, written English makes heavier use of long sentences and of complex constructions than does speech. For instance, *The Visigoths waged relentless war against, but were never able to subdue, the Basques* might occur in writing but is unlikely in speech.

For a second thing, Standard English exists in two slightly different versions: the British version and the American version. The differences are not great, but they are real, and mixing features from the two versions produces a result which is acceptable to no one.

For a third thing, standard English, like every variety of every living language, is constantly changing. Words, forms and usages which were accepted as part of standard English in the recent past are constantly falling into disuse and disappearing, while others are coming into use and becoming accepted as part of the standard. As a result, there is at any moment a measure of uncertainty about which forms should be accepted as part of standard English, and informed commentators may differ in their judgements. Many of the entries in this book are devoted to offering advice about just these doubtful cases.

In spite of all these complications, there is enormous agreement today about what is, or is not, standard English. Everyone agrees that *He did it* is standard English, while the more widespread form *He done it* is not. Everyone agrees that *if he had done that* is standard English, while *if he'd've done that* and *if he would have done that* are not. Everyone agrees that *precede* is the standard spelling, while *preceed* is unacceptable. Most of the rest of the entries in this book are devoted to laying down the law about such matters when they cause difficulties.

Standard English is not more beautiful or more logical than other varieties of English. There is nothing logical about accepting *he won't* into the standard language while rejecting *he don't*, and nothing logical or beautiful about rejecting the widespread English form *He didn't do nothing* and insisting upon the comparatively unnatural form *He didn't do anything*.

The point of all these arbitrary decisions is a simple one: convenience. It is simply *convenient* to have a standard form of the language which is agreed on by everybody. If all of us, wherever we were born, learn and use standard English, then we can all speak and write to one another with practically no uncertainty, confusion or misunderstanding. Without an agreed standard, we would all just have to struggle along as best we could in our own local varieties of English, hoping desperately that our intended meaning might get through – with unpredictable consequences. For example, it is at present agreed that *I doubt it's going to rain* is standard English, and that it means 'I suspect it's not going to rain.' But, in the vernacular English of much of Scotland and northern England, *I doubt it's going to rain* means 'I suspect it's going to rain'. You can see the advantage of an agreed standard.

Like a standard electrical plug, like a standard videotape, like a standard size for car tyres, standard English is valuable because it *is* standardized. We cannot stop standard English from changing, but we should be in no hurry to help that change along: in maintaining a standard, a little inertia is a good thing. After all, you would not be amused if manufacturers changed the size of electrical plugs every few years, or the standards required to record and play a videotape.

There is another respect in which standard English is uniquely valuable: it is *elaborated*. That is, recognized varieties of standard English have been developed for every purpose to which anyone might want to put it: writing scientific articles, writing criticism of works of art, writing the minutes of business meetings, and so on. No other variety of English has been developed to do all these various things. From the impersonal passive of scientific research reports to the *shall normally* construction of British university regulations, standard English provides the tools for almost every conceivable job. Other varieties of English have their value, and they may be irreplaceable for such purposes as maintaining warm relations with family and friends, but no other variety of English can do what standard English can do.

Standard English is international: it is the property of no single country, nor is it even the property of just two countries, in spite of the conventional names for its two slightly different versions. Not everyone realizes this. Not long ago, the Department for Education and Science in Britain posted a website containing a glossary of linguistic terms, and that site explicitly contrasted 'standard English' with 'other sorts of English, such as American English and Australian English'. Only after months of pressure from professional linguists and other linguistically informed people was the offending entry finally replaced.

Standard English is the property of anyone who cares to learn it and to use it. Few people learn standard spoken English as their mother tongue – I certainly did not – and all of us must learn the written standard through education. But anyone who wants to can do this. I have met Germans and Swedes whose command of standard English was superior to that of most of my British students.

stationary, stationery The adjective *stationary* means 'not moving': *a stationary van* is a van which is not moving. The noun *stationery* means 'writing materials', such as paper and ink: *a stationery van* is a van which delivers stationery. Do not confuse the two.

steal See **rob**.

steppe See **grasslands**.

stimulant, stimulus A *stimulant* is a drug which (technically) increases physiological activity or (informally) makes you more alert. Caffeine is a good example. But a *stimulus* is anything – though hardly ever a drug – which encourages you to undertake or to pursue an action. The plural of *stimulus* is *stimuli*.

stood Regional British English uses the following construction: *✱He was stood in the doorway*. This is not acceptable in standard English, which requires *He was standing in the doorway*.

straightforward This adjective is always written as a single word: the spellings *✱straight forward* and *✱straight-forward* are never acceptable, except in the rare case when you are combining the two adverbs *straight* and *forward*, as in *I want you to walk straight forward*.

strait, straits A *strait* is a narrow channel of sea connecting two larger bodies of sea. The word is used in the singular, and not in the plural. So, write *the Strait of Dover*, not *the Straits of Dover*, and likewise *the Strait of Gibraltar*, not *the Straits of Gibraltar*.

straitjacket This is the only acceptable spelling: the word has nothing to do with *straight*, and the spelling *straightjacket* should be avoided, even though it is now recognized by some dictionaries.

strait-laced This is the correct spelling of the word meaning 'prudish', 'puritanical'. The mistaken spelling *straight-laced* is now so frequent that it is recognized by most dictionaries, but you should avoid it.

stricken See **struck**.

stride The past tense is *strode*: *He strode into the room*. The past participle is historically *stridden*, but this form is close to non-existent today, and best avoided.

strive The past tense is either *strove* or *strived*. On the whole, British English favours *strove*, while American English perhaps somewhat favours *strived*. The past participle is either *striven* or *strived*. Again, British English favours *striven*, while American English somewhat favours *strived*. So, we can have *She strove/strived to do her best* and *She has striven/strived to do her best*. All are standard.

struck, stricken The past participle of *strike* is normally *struck*: *This has often struck me as curious*; *He was struck by her beauty*. The form *stricken* is now normally an adjective: *a stricken look*, *a stricken cry*. However, *stricken* can be used with names of diseases: *He was stricken with polio*.

student, pupil In the USA, a *student* is a person studying in an educational institution of any kind: a university, a high school, even an elementary school. In Britain, a *student* is traditionally found only in a university, and *pupil* is preferred for a person studying at any lower level. However, the American usage has recently been creeping into British English. British writers may now use it at their own risk: many readers will still object to it.

stupefy This is the only possible spelling, and *stupify* is wrong. The same goes for the derivatives *stupefied* and *stupefaction*.

stutter See **stammer**.

style checkers Of all aspects of written English, good style is by far the hardest one to put into a computer program. We know good style when we see it, but there are many ways of writing English with good style, and there is probably no way of pinning down the common ground among the biologist Stephen Jay Gould, the baseball essayist Roger Angell and the historian Barbara Tuchman, all of whom write exceedingly well. Accordingly, our style checkers are wooden affairs; they can do no more than to count the number of passives or the length of sentences. Obeying the advice of your style checker might perhaps rescue you from a few outrages, but it won't give you good style. Of all the electronic props you can buy in the hope of improving your writing, style checkers are the least useful.

sub- This is a prefix, and it must always be written as one: *subcommittee*, *subcontractor*, *subnormal*, and so on. A hyphen is necessary only before a capital letter, as in *sub-Roman*, or when the result would otherwise be hard on the eye, as in *sub-breed*.

subject-verb agreement See **agreement**.

subjunctive The ancient English subjunctive survives today only in fragments, though those fragments are much more vigorous in American English than in British English. Distinct subjunctive forms exist now only for *be* and in the third-person singular of other verbs. American English still makes a consistent distinction between *He insisted that they were locked up* ('He asserted strongly that they were already in jail') and *He insisted that they be locked up* ('He demanded that they should be put into jail'). Even moderately formal British English commonly uses only *He insisted that they were locked up* in both senses – a use which bewilders Americans. A British writer who feels a need for an overt subjunctive form is more likely to resort to *He insisted that they should be locked up*, rather than to the plain *be*.

In American English, certain verbs must be followed by the subjunctive: *I recommend that she take the job*. Again, British English usually has *I recommend that she takes the job*.

However, the distinct subjunctive form remains available in Britain, and it is often found in very formal writing, such as in official minutes. But note a complication with the negative. American English uses *We recommend that this not be done*, whereas formal British English prefers *We recommend that this be not done*, though the American form is not unknown in Britain.

Formal varieties of both British and American English require *were*, not *was*, in counterfactual conditions: *if Poland were in the EU*; *if she were my daughter*; *if this were my decision*. Vernacular English prefers *was* here, but using *was* in writing will annoy many readers. But the use of *be* in open conditions is now dead: write *if this is what you want*, not *∗if this be what you want*. The second form sounds comical today.

substitute, replace Suppose the football player Shearer is forced to leave the match with an injury, and Owen comes off the bench to take his place. Clearly a substitution has occurred, but who has been substituted?

In standard English, the player who has been substituted is Owen, not Shearer: Shearer has *been replaced* (by Owen), while Owen has *been substituted* (for Shearer). In football commentators' English, it is usual to say that Shearer *has been substituted, or that he *has been substituted by Owen, but these colloquial usages are never acceptable in formal writing. In standard English, neither *substitute(d) with nor *substitute(d) by is ever acceptable.

subsume This verb means 'include', 'incorporate', usually as a special case of something more general: *In modern biological thinking, humans are subsumed under apes.* The word does not mean 'dominate', 'overpower', 'reduce to subordinate status', and it should not be so used.

such as When you use these words, you are indicating that what follows is only a list of representative examples, and not an exhaustive list. It is accordingly a **pleonasm** to follow the list with some continuation like *and so forth* or, still worse, *etc.*, since these do the same job as *such as*. It is atrocious English to write *Japanese has contributed a number of words to English, such as 'sumo', 'geisha', 'karaoke', 'sushi', etc. Write instead *Japanese has contributed a number of words to English, such as 'sumo', 'geisha', 'karaoke' and 'sushi'.*

A further problem is illustrated by the following example: *This phenomenon is found in languages such as Finnish. Here *such as* does no work, since no class of languages illustrated by Finnish has been identified. Write . . . *in Finnish* or . . . *in Finnish and other languages.*

suchlike This word is typical of informal English, and it should never be used in formal writing.

Sudan See *the* **in names of countries**.

suffix A *suffix* is an element which cannot stand alone to make a word but which can be added to the end of an existing word, either to make a different word or merely to provide a grammatical inflection of the same word. Among the many suffixes which produce new words are *-ful* (as in *powerful*), *-ish* (as in *bluish*), *-ly* (as in *slowly*), *-dom* (as in *freedom*), *-wise* (as in *otherwise*), *-ness* (as in *happiness*) and *-al* (as in *comical*). Among those which merely inflect words for grammatical purposes are the plural *-s* (as in *dogs*), the comparative *-er* (as in *bigger*), the past-tense *-ed* (as in *walked*) and the verbal suffix *-ing* (as in *sleeping*). Compare **prefix**, and note that a **combining form**, like *-logy*, is not really a suffix.

sulphur, sulfur Even though the word derives from Latin *sulfur*, and not from Greek, the accepted British spelling is *sulphur*, while the American one is *sulfur*.

Super Bowl The American football championship game is the *Super Bowl*, not the *Superbowl.

supersede This is always so spelled; the spelling *supercede is wrong.

supplement The word is so spelled, with an E in the middle, and *suppliment is wrong.

suppress, depress, oppress I recently read this account of a cricketer: **His recent loss of form has suppressed his average*. (Baseball fans may read this as *His recent slump* . . .) What the writer intended, of course, was *depressed*. These three verbs all have quite different meanings, but they are sometimes confused.

To *suppress* something is to stop it, to prohibit it, to prevent it from becoming public or widespread. You can suppress a smile, a political movement or a book, for example. To *depress* something is to make it lower: you can depress a batting average, the share price of a stock, or a person's spirits. To *oppress* people is to treat them harshly when you have power over them: only people can be oppressed.

surprise The word is so spelled, with two Rs, and *suprise is wrong.

suspicious, suspect If you have a dark feeling that some stranger is up to no good, then you are *suspicious* (of the stranger, and of his behaviour), while his behaviour may be described either as *suspicious* or as *suspect*. All these represent standard use, but you might do well to remember *suspect* and to use it when you can, since an expression like *a suspicious visitor* is potentially ambiguous: is it the visitor who suspects something, or is it someone else who suspects the visitor?

swap, swop This informal verb is out of place in most formal writing, where *exchange* should be used. However, if you do use it, spell it *swap*: the British variant *swop* is frowned on by most authorities.

symmetry The words *symmetry*, *symmetric*, *asymmetry* and *asymmetric* are all spelled with one S and two Ms. Avoid common errors like *assymetric.

syndrome A *syndrome* is not a disease but a collection of symptoms which appear together and which point to the presence of a particular illness.

synergy This technical term denotes a result obtained by joint effort which is greater than could be achieved by adding together the results of the individual components acting separately. But it is frequently used as an empty and foolish term meaning no more than 'cooperation' or 'collaboration'. Don't do this.

syntactic, syntactical In linguistics, the adjective meaning 'pertaining to syntax' was once *syntactical*, but today the preferred form is *syntactic* and *syntactical* sounds dreadfully old-fashioned. Noam Chomsky called his famous 1957 book *Syntactic Structures*.

systematic, systemic The word *systematic* means 'orderly and thorough', as in *a systematic search*. But *systemic* means 'pertaining to a system', as in *systemic poison*, a poison which affects the entire body.

table (verb) In British English, when you *table* a document, you add it to the agenda for a meeting, usually by placing copies on the table at the beginning of the meeting because it was not ready in time to be sent out with the printed agenda. In American English, however, when you table a document, you remove it indefinitely from the agenda. Writers on both sides of the Atlantic should be aware of this possible source of confusion.

talisman A *talisman* is an object believed to bring good luck to its owner. The plural is *talismans*, not **talismen*.

tandem Two people or things which are *in tandem* are lined up one in front of the other, as for example on a tandem bicycle. The expression does not mean merely 'together', and you should not write that two people are working *in tandem* if all you mean is that they are working together.

Taoiseach The title of the Irish prime minister is so spelled.

target A much overused word. Before writing it, think whether *goal* or *objective* might not serve your purpose, or perhaps even something like *ambition* or *aspiration*. If you do write *target*, note that it is not possible to 'achieve' a target, or to 'obtain' a target, and that it is certainly not possible to 'fight for' a target: all of these usages reduce the metaphor to gibberish. And be very careful about using *target* as a verb.

tartan See **plaid**.

tartar, Tartar In all senses, these words are spelled *tartar* and *Tartar*, with two As. There is no such English word as *Tarter, and no such word as *tarter* except in the rare sense of 'more tart'.

task force A *task force* is a temporary grouping of military units formed to undertake a specific mission. But these days macho politicians, businessmen, administrators and even academics seem unable to resist the temptation to apply the term to every committee, commission or working party put together for any purpose at all. Avoid the expression, except in its military sense.

team names Names of sports teams are treated differently in British and American English. First, in British English, such a name always takes plural agreement: *Arsenal have signed a new midfielder*. American English, in contrast, requires singular agreement unless the name is plural in form: hence Americans write (with reference to the Buffalo Bills, an American football team) *Buffalo has signed a new tight end* but *The Bills have signed a new tight end*. Moreover, in Britain, such a name does not take the article *the*, while in the USA it does. So, the Welsh ice-hockey team is *Cardiff Devils*, while the American baseball team is *the Chicago Cubs*, not *Chicago Cubs.

tendency The word is so spelled, with two Es, and *tendancy is wrong.

tend to This expression is usually flabby and inexplicit. Consider an example: *??Question words in English tend to begin with WH-*. This is poor, because there is no tendency about it. Apart from *how*, all the English question words really do begin with *WH-*: *who, whose, whom, which, why, where* and *when*. Prefer something more direct, like *Question words in English usually begin with WH-* or *Most question words in English begin with WH-*.

tennis Once, the name *tennis* denoted a game played on an enclosed court with obstacles; this is the game now called *real tennis*. But, for some decades now, *tennis* has been understood by everybody as the game played by Pete Sampras and Martina Hingis. It is foolish and pretentious to insist on calling this game *lawn tennis*: this older name is now obsolete except in a few very formal contexts, such as in the name of the *Lawn Tennis Association*.

tense English has only two tenses, the past tense and the other one, which is commonly called the 'present' tense, but which might better be called the 'non-past' or the 'present/future' tense. We have no future tense. We have many forms for talking about future time, but not one of them can reasonably be called a future tense: all of them are 'present' tense. Note how the numerous English verb-forms fall into pairs, one 'present' and one past, except that a few forms have no partner; the form in brackets is the functional partner, though not the formal partner, of the form beside it:

Present	Past
She dances.	*She danced.*
She is dancing.	*She was dancing.*
She has danced.	*She had danced.*
[*She dances.*]	*She used to dance.*
She has been dancing.	*She had been dancing.*
She is to dance.	*She was to dance.*
She keeps (on) dancing.	*She kept (on) dancing.*
She will dance.	*She would dance.*
She will be dancing.	*She would be dancing.*
She must dance.	
She ought to dance.	
She can dance.	*She could dance.*
She may dance.	*She might dance.*
She may be dancing.	*She might be dancing.*
She may have been dancing.	*She might have been dancing.*
She will have danced.	*She would have danced.*
She wants to dance.	*She wanted to dance.*

And so on. (There are more.) If these pairings are not clear, note how the present-tense forms naturally follow *She says that . . .*, while the past-tense forms naturally follow *She said that . . .*

This book is not the place to pursue the English tense-system further, but there are two points of usage to be noted. First, the choice of tense in a text must be consistent. Once you have decided which tense you want to use, you must stick to it, unless there are clear reasons for using the other one. Unlike some other European languages, English does not permit the mixing of tenses in a single text.

The second point is more subtle. If you are writing an account of an intellectual debate, which tense do you use? The answer is simple in principle. In reporting all work which you are presenting as relevant to the current debate, you must use the present tense, even when citing authors long dead. You use the past tense only when you mean to imply that the work being reported is now purely a matter of history and no longer of any relevance.

Suppose you are writing an account of the famous debate between the philosophers Bertrand Russell and Peter Strawson, which took place quite a few decades ago. If you mean to present this debate as still relevant to the issues you are discussing, you must write *Russell concludes . . .* and *Strawson denies . . .* , and so on. However, if your view is that this debate is now of historical interest only, and no longer a part of current thinking, then you write *Russell concluded . . .* and *Strawson denied . . .*

The common mistake here is to use the past tense when the work reported is meant to be presented as currently relevant.

terminal See **computer**.

than Informal spoken English requires a non-subject pronoun after· *than*: we say *She is older than me*, not ??*She is older than I*. However, many readers find *She is older than me* distasteful in formal writing, while many others consider ??*She is older than I* to be stilted and affected. Avoid the problem by writing *She is older than I am*.

thankfully There is no problem with using this word as a simple adverb meaning 'with thanks': *She accepted the drink thankfully*. However, like **hopefully**, the word has recently come to be used as a sentence adverb meaning 'we may be thankful that'. Example: *Thankfully, no one was hurt in the crash*. Just as with *hopefully*, this use has attracted severe criticism, even though it is now very familiar. The authorities are divided on this, with some now accepting it as fully standard, but others rejecting it as not yet standard. Caution is advisable, but you will be in good company if you use it. However, unlike *hopefully*, *thankfully* can easily be ambiguous. You should try to avoid writing things like *Thankfully she left the room*, which can easily be misunderstood.

that, which, who A relative clause may often be introduced either with *that* or with *which* (for things) or *who* (for people). So, you may write either *the topic that I want to consider* or *the topic which I want to consider* (or, in a more informal style, *the topic I want to consider*). However, it is impossible to use *that* if the relative clause is non-restrictive – that is, if it does not serve to identify the thing under discussion, but only serves to provide more information about that thing. So, you must write *the Suez Canal, which was opened in 1869*, and you cannot write *the Suez Canal, that was opened in 1869*.

Note in particular that a noun denoting a group of people takes *which*, not *who*. You cannot write *the battalion who had captured the fortress* because a battalion, though composed of people, is not itself a person: write *the battalion which had captured the fortress*.

It is possible to use *that* with people, but the result is often rather clumsy. While *the linguists that are working on this problem* is not quite wrong, it doesn't sound as good as *the linguists who are working on this problem*. Prefer *who* with people.

***the* in names of countries** Today, the only country names which take *the* in English are those which are plural in form, such as *the United States*, *the Netherlands* and *the Philippines*, plus a few others whose name logically requires the article, such as *the United Kingdom* and *the Ivory Coast* (though the authorities in the second have been making strenuous efforts to persuade the English-speaking world to accept the French form *Côte d'Ivoire*). Other country names which formerly took the article now usually occur without it, such as *Lebanon*, *Sudan*, *Gambia* and *Ukraine*. Citizens of some of these countries may find the use of the article rather offensive.

their See **there**.

theism See **deism**.

theory In scientific work, the word *theory* has a rather precise sense. It denotes an integrated set of hypotheses related by mathematics or logic, designed to explain a range of phenomena which, according to the theory, are related. As a rule, a proposal counts as a theory only if it can successfully predict some observations and only if it can be linked to other theories in a principled manner. Typical examples are the theory of evolution and the theory of relativity. A theory differs from a *hypothesis*, which is merely a proposal subject to evaluation, and from a *conjecture*, which is no more than a guess. If you are writing about science, you should refrain from the vulgar tendency to write *theory* when you mean no more than 'hypothesis' or 'conjecture'.

If I propose that life exists below the crust of Jupiter's moon Europa, this might count as a hypothesis if I have hard data confirming that life might be possible there. Otherwise, it is no more than a conjecture. It is certainly not a theory, and it should not be called one.

Finally, it is only the scientifically illiterate who fall into the egregious error of dismissing, say, evolution as 'just a theory'. This ignorant blunder results from a failure to understand the meaning of the word *theory*.

See also **prove**.

there, their, they're These three are often confused, but confusing them will give your writing a dreadful smell of illiteracy. The word *there* means 'in that place', and it is the partner of *here*. We also use *there* to introduce sentences of this kind: *There's a wasp on your back*; *There were no people in New Zealand before the Maoris arrived*. In contrast, *their* is the possessive form corresponding to *they*: *They have kept their word*. Finally, *they're*, as the apostrophe suggests, is a contraction of *they are*: *They're at it again*. If you find this three-way distinction difficult, then you must work at it.

thereof Words like *thereof, therefrom* and *therewith* are stilted and pompous. Choose *of it, from it* and *with it* instead, or *of them* and so on with a plural form.

they English has the pronouns *he* (male), *she* (female) and *it* (everything else), but it has no third-singular pronoun which is not marked for sex. This lack is an infuriating nuisance, since we very often want to use a singular pronoun without any sex-marking. When my students are leaving the classroom, and I notice an unclaimed umbrella, I may call out *Somebody has forgotten ____ umbrella* – but what goes into the blank? These days, many people find *his* intolerably sexist, while *her* must be regarded as equally sexist, and *his or her* is so unbearably clumsy as to be comical. What most of us say in practice, of course, is *their*: *Somebody has forgotten their umbrella*.

This brief and elegant solution is now the norm in most people's speech. However, it is strongly, even violently, disliked by a number of conservative speakers, who regard it as intolerably clumsy to combine the overtly plural form *they* with an overtly singular form like *somebody*. And the jarring effect is even worse when that *they* is referring to somebody more specific than *somebody*: *??Even if your boss is wrong, they are still your boss*; *??If you and your partner are having trouble, tell them about your worries*. Even though such usages have been recorded among good writers for centuries, and even though many usage handbooks now pronounce them established in standard English, it is a blunt fact that many of your readers will find them repellent. Do you really want to upset your readers with your style?

If you don't, then there is only one way round the problem: rewrite the troublesome sentences. Unlike speech, which is usually spontaneous and unplanned, formal writing is planned: you can not only plan your sentences ahead, but edit them after you've written them, before they reach any readers. The awkward examples above might be rewritten as follows: *Even if your boss is wrong, your boss is still your boss*; *If you and your partner are having trouble, you should tell each other about your worries*. Most such troublesome sentences can be safely rewritten, with a little thought, so that the awkward singular *they* disappears, and the result will offend nobody.

In a longer text in which this problem arises constantly, and rewriting seems to be out of the question, a possible solution is to use *he* arbitrarily on one occasion and *she* arbitrarily on the next. Or perhaps you can even find some convenient pattern. A recent book on linguistics, one which refers frequently to arbitrary speakers and hearers, adopts the convention of using *she* for any speaker but *he* for any hearer.

they're See **there**.

tho, tho' These informal spellings of *though* should never be used in careful writing.

threshold The word is so spelled, with one H.

thrive I am astonished that I need to include an entry for this word. But, recently, in an application for a university position, I saw the following: *I always thrive for perfection*. What the applicant meant, of course, was *strive*: the word *thrive* means 'flourish, prosper'.

through The word is so spelled, and the joke spelling *thru* is never acceptable in careful writing, except in proper names in which it is official, as with the *New York State Thruway*, a highway.

thusly There is no such word in standard English: write *thus*, not *thusly*.

till See **until**.

timpani This is the name for the *set* of kettledrums played by the timpanist in an orchestra. The word is plural in Italian, and it is treated as a plural in English: write *these timpani*, not *this timpani*. A single kettledrum cannot be called *a timpani*. The Italian singular *timpano* is not used in English; call one of these drums a *kettledrum*.

title character In a work of fiction or drama, the *title character* is the character in it who has the same name as the work. It is legitimate to write *Isabelle Huppert played the title character in the 1991 film* Madame Bovary if she played the part of Madame Bovary in that film. But *title character* does not mean merely 'protagonist', 'most important character': it is an absurd error to write *Clint Eastwood played the title character in the film* A Fistful of Dollars.

titles in *the* and *a* Just as we would never write *Shakespeare's the last play*, we cannot write *Shakespeare's The Tempest*. The required form is illustrated by *Shakespeare's* Tempest, *Homer's* Iliad, *Anthony Burgess's* Clockwork Orange, and *Rumer Godden's* Episode of Sparrows. If another word intervenes, however, then the article must be retained: *Shakespeare's play* The Tempest, *Godden's wonderful novel* An Episode of Sparrows.

to, too, two It seems surprising that these everyday little words can be confused, but they are, as my students' essays reveal.

The preposition is *to*: *Give it to me*; *I'm flying to Australia*. The marker that sometimes precedes an infinitive verb is also *to*: *I want to go home*; *She persuaded us to continue*.

The word meaning 'also' is *too*: *You too must come along*; *This occurs in Japan, too*. The word meaning 'excessively' is also *too*: *This is too much*; *She drives too slowly*.

The number-name is *two*: *I have two brothers*; *The other two are on their way*.

Note, by the way, that *to*, like any preposition, must always be followed by the object form of a pronoun (*me, us, him, her, them*). Standard English requires *This is familiar to us linguists*, and *This is familiar to we linguists* is wrong.

today, tomorrow Write the words like this; the old spellings *to-day and *to-morrow are now archaic.

Tolkien The famous fantasy writer is *J. R. R. Tolkien*, and the spelling *Tolkein is wrong.

tongue Except in the term *mother tongue*, which means 'native language', the word *tongue* is archaic or highly literary in the sense of 'language'. Don't use it in this sense.

too See **to**.

top The preposed modifier *top*, meaning 'high-ranking', 'important' or merely 'famous', as in *top model*, *top team* and *top executive*, is a feature of journalistic prose best avoided in careful writing.

to plus gerund The following example illustrates a common error: *The Austrian advance had given no thought to secure their flank*. The problem here is that the noun *thought* must be followed by the preposition *to*, not by the infinitival *to*, and so the correct form is . . . *no thought to securing their flank*, in which *to* is followed by the gerund *securing*, not by the infinitive *secure*. If in doubt, you can check for this. If an occurrence of *to* can be followed by a simple noun, then the gerund is required: . . . *no thought to security on their flank*. The same error occurs in the following example: *Ford is reinforcing its commitment to become a leader in electronic commerce*. Make that *to becoming*.

toward, towards Both are correct. On the whole, British English favours *towards*, while American English prefers *toward*.

trade names Trade names should be carefully capitalized. Manufacturers are deeply protective of their trade names, and they may protest, or even prosecute you, if they think you have used their trade name without acknowledging it as such. So, for example, the board game is *Scrabble*, a vacuum cleaner from a particular manufacturer is a *Hoover*, and the most familiar brand of sticky tape is *Sellotape* in Britain, *Scotch Tape* in the US, and *Durex* in Australia.

transferred epithet This is the usual name for the curious English construction in which an adjective is understood as modifying, not the noun following it, but somebody or something else. Example: *She was smoking a pensive cigarette*. Here it is not the cigarette which is pensive but the woman smoking it. This construction is fully acceptable in standard English, and it can be used to great effect. But don't do it every third sentence. See **headline adjective**.

transgress This rare verb means 'break (a law)' or 'overstep (a limit)'. The word is extremely formal and is best avoided in all but the most frostily formal writing. Recently, however, this word has been somewhat mischievously appropriated by the post-modernist brigade as an everyday term meaning something like 'challenge (the accepted order)', 'reject (accepted boundaries or established authority)'. In this sense, transgression is commonly presented as noble or heroic, even though, historically, transgression is illegal, sinful or merely foolish. This ironic extension might be forgivable in principle, but, in practice, those who use it at all often overuse it to the point of tedium. My advice is to steer clear of the word.

In any case, the derived noun is spelled *transgressor*, not *transgresser*.

transitivity Hundreds of English verbs can be used either intransitively or transitively. An example is *sink*: *The ship sank*; *The sub sank the ship*. More verbs enter this class every year, but not all verbs belong to it, at least not in standard English, and you should be careful not to use an intransitive verb with an object, or in the passive. Here are a few faulty examples I have encountered recently: *We've migrated about half the university* (the intended sense is 'changed over (to the new system)'); *Uranus's orbit is deviated by Neptune* (the intended sense is 'perturbed'); *The fabric had been deteriorated by the rain* (the intended sense is 'corroded'). If in doubt about the proper use of a verb, check a good dictionary: don't just charge ahead and hope. Dictionaries of English written for advanced foreign learners are often particularly informative here.

transpire The verb *transpire* means 'come to light', 'become known', as in *It transpired that the councillors had been fiddling their expenses* ('We discovered that the councillors had been fiddling their expenses'). The word does not mean 'happen', 'occur', and it should not be so used. It is wrong to write *We don't know what will transpire if what you mean is We don't know what will happen*. This is a good example of the dangers of using fancy-looking but poorly understood Latinate words in place of everyday words.

trivia Unlike **agenda**, the Latin plural *trivia* remains plural in English. Write *These trivia don't bother me*, not *This trivia doesn't bother me*. The Latin singular *trivium* is almost never used in English. If you require a singular form to label just one trivial thing, use *trifle*.

Trivial Pursuit The name of the famous board game is *Trivial Pursuit*, and not, as often written, *Trivial Pursuits*.

troop, troupe A *troop* is a group of soldiers or Scouts; a *troupe* is a group of actors, dancers or other performers.

trooper, trouper A *trooper* was once a cavalryman – hence the expression 'swear like a trooper'. A trooper is also a troop-carrying ship. In the US, a trooper is a state policeman. A *trouper* is a member of a theatrical company, or, by extension, anyone who is a cooperative member of a group.

truck See **lorry**.

try and Informal English permits the construction illustrated by *try and find it*. But this is too informal for careful writing: use *try to find it*.

tsar, czar Both forms are acceptable. However, the more accurate version *tsar* is recommended for the former Russian emperor, while *czar* is usual, especially in American English, in the extended sense of a powerful or despotic leader: *Judge Landis was the czar of baseball for twenty-four years*.

Tunis, Tunisia The country in north Africa is *Tunisia*, and its capital city is *Tunis*. But *Tunis* was also the name of the Barbary state occupying roughly the same territory in the eighteenth and early nineteenth centuries.

Turkish names Before the 1920s, Turks had no surnames, and they used the traditional Islamic style of given names sometimes accompanied by titles. Since the 1920s, Turks have used surnames of the familiar western kind. These names cause few problems, except that the Turkish alphabet makes heavy use of diacritics, which may be difficult to reproduce. Turkish also has both a small I with no dot, and a capital I with a dot, which few word processors can produce.

The Turks of Cyprus still do not use surnames, with some exceptions. In place of a surname, we find the father's given name. For example, the son of *Orhan Ali* is *Mehmet Orhan*, and his son is *Bülent Mehmet*.

two See **to**.

two-way mirror This bizarrely illogical name now seems to be established, but perhaps it is not too late for us to abandon it in favour of something more sensible. The artefact in question is a plate of glass placed within an interior wall which functions as a window from one side but merely as a mirror from the other side. Its function is to allow people on one side to look through the window without being seen in return by people on the other side. Accordingly, the object is not a two-way mirror in any coherent sense at all: rather, it is a one-way window. The fact that the non-window side of the object is a mirror is an accident: we do not at present have the technology to build a one-way window whose other side looks like a piece of blank wall. But *one-way window* is still a far more sensible name for this gadget.

-type Expressions like **Chinese-type food* and **a Watergate-type situation* are at best clumsy and at worst childish. Prefer something more explicit, such as *food in the Chinese style* and *a state of affairs reminiscent of Watergate*. Brevity is desirable, but not at the cost of explicitness.

Ukraine See *the* **in names of countries**.

Ukrainian names Before the collapse of the Soviet Union, it was customary to convert Ukrainian names into Russian before then converting them into English. With Ukrainian independence, there is no longer any reason to do this, and you are advised to render the Ukrainian forms as directly as you can. This sometimes has unexpected results: for example, the Ukrainian personal names corresponding to Russian *Olga* and *Vladimir* are *Olha* and *Volodymyr*. Most place names also come out different, but, for those which already have established English forms based on the Russian forms, it is probably best to retain the traditional forms. The most famous of these is perhaps *Chernobyl* for Ukrainian *Chornobil*, but note also *Kiev* for Ukrainian *Kiv* and *Odessa* for Ukrainian *Odesa*. Ukrainians may dislike these forms, but they are about as well established in English as *Rome* for Italian *Roma* and *Moscow* for Russian *Moskva*.

ukulele The word is so spelled, and the erroneous spelling ✳*ukelele* should be avoided, even though it is now recognized by one or two dictionaries.

Ulster *Ulster* is the name of one of the four provinces of Ireland. The present-day political unit of Northern Ireland, brought into being by the Boundary Commission of 1927, occupies six of the nine counties of this province. In Britain, it has become commonplace to use *Ulster* as a synonym for *Northern Ireland*. But you should be aware that this usage is disliked in the Republic of Ireland, where *Ulster* continues to be used to refer to the whole province.

umlaut Strictly speaking, *umlaut* is a phenomenon in the Germanic languages in which the vowel of a stem is changed for grammatical purposes. English examples include *foot/feet* and *mouse/mice*, and, less obviously, *sit/set* and *lie/lay*. In German, in which umlaut is far more prominent than in English, the umlaut is usually marked in the spelling by putting two dots over the umlauted vowel, as in *Mann* 'man', *Männer* 'men'. As a result, the label *umlaut* is sometimes applied to the two dots. However, in English, we never represent umlaut with two dots, and it is wrong to use this name for the two dots which we use in cases like *Zoë* and *Brontë* and sometimes in cases like *naïve*. These two dots are properly called the *diaeresis* (US *dieresis*).

un- See **in-**.

unattached modifier See **dangling modifier**.

uncertainty principle Heisenberg's uncertainty principle is one of the cornerstones of modern physics. This principle states that certain pairs of physical quantities, such as position and momentum, are related in the following way: the more accurately one of them is measured for a given particle, the less accurately the other can be measured at the same time. The relationship is precisely stated in the form of an exact inequality. This well-corroborated and well-understood principle causes physicists to lose no sleep. However, because of its perhaps unfortunate name, this principle, or rather its name, is brandished constantly by New Age charlatans who no more understand it than they understand the mathematical theory of quaternions. These frauds want their readers to believe that Heisenberg's great achievement somehow licenses and justifies whatever brand of content-free mumbo-jumbo they happen to be peddling. If you can't state Heisenberg's inequality and explain exactly what all the symbols stand for, then you don't understand the principle and you have no business pretending that you do.

under way This is the traditional and recommended form of the phrase meaning 'in progress'. The one-word form *underway* is now widely accepted in the USA and is gaining ground in Britain, but British writers would be wise to avoid it. A third variant, *under weigh*, results from a misunderstanding and is now rarely seen; you should not use it.

undoubtedly See **doubtless**.

unequivocal There are no such words as *unequivocable* and *unequivocably*. The correct forms are *unequivocal* and *unequivocally*.

unique If something is *unique*, it is the only one of its kind. Consequently, there cannot be degrees of uniqueness: either something is unique, or it is not. Accordingly, locutions like *very unique* and *most unique* are out of order. If you find it necessary to use a degree word like *very* or *most*, choose another adjective, such as *unusual* or *distinctive*. It is, however, proper to describe something as *unique in several respects*.

United States This name is grammatically singular: write *The United States is prepared to negotiate*, not *The United States are* . . . But the plural use was official before the American Civil War, and it is retained in the fossilized American expression *in these United States* – though nowhere else.

unsatisfied See **dissatisfied**.

until, till Both of these are perfectly acceptable, but standard English does not accept any of *til*, *'til* or *'till*. And you should avoid the overly wordy *until such time as*: use *until* instead.

untimely death This pointless expression is used far too often: when was a death ever timely? If you must qualify *his death*, use some more explicit wording: *his early death*, *his sudden death*, *his unexpected death*, or whatever.

unusual plurals English nouns denoting things that cannot be counted, such as *wine*, *coffee* and *intelligence*, do not easily form plurals in their central senses. Some of them, however, can be pluralized when they have transferred senses, such as varieties (*Rhone wines*), measures (*four coffees*) or embodiments (*alien intelligences*). You should not overuse such unusual plurals, however, since they can easily become pretentious, as they do in all those silly high-street signs announcing *ice creams* and *fine beers*.

A more serious problem arises in the writing of the cultural relativists, in which unusual plurals are used as a rhetorical device. An example is the use of *scientific knowledges*, in place of the normal *scientific knowledge*, by a writer intent on insisting that there is no such thing as scientific objectivity, but that instead we have only a disparate collection of scientists all brandishing their own 'socially constructed' interpretations of a reality that probably doesn't exist anyway. If you regard this as acceptable, then you have bigger problems than I can help you with. See also **energy** for a particularly flagrant abuse of this kind.

unwieldy The word is so spelled, and *unwieldly* is wrong.

upwards of The phrase *upwards of £1 million* means 'somewhat more than £1 million', and not, as is sometimes thought, 'almost £1 million'. There is no need to use this informal and possibly misleading expression: prefer *more than £1 million* or *almost £1 million*, as required.

used to, be used to Write *I used to dance*, not *I use to dance*. The negative is either *I didn't use to dance* (informal) or *I used not to dance* (formal).

Do not confuse *used to* with *be used to*. Write *I am used to snow* and *I am used to getting up early*. Note the difference between *I used to get up early* (in the past, I always got up early) and *I am used to getting up early* (getting up early doesn't bother me). There is no such form as *I am used to get up early*.

utilize This is not just a fancy word for *use*, and you should not write things like *Computers can be utilized for a number of purposes*. The word means 'put to a useful purpose (something which would otherwise be wasted)'. For example, oil companies used to throw away petrol (gasoline), until the invention of the internal-combustion engine meant that it could finally be utilized.

vacuum The word is so spelled, and *vacum* and *vaccuum* are wrong. The plural is *vacua* in scientific contexts, but *vacuums* in everyday English.

Vandyke, Van Dyck The Flemish painter originally wrote his surname *Van Dyck*, but, after settling in England, he altered this to *Vandyke*. Either form is acceptable, but the one-word form is more usual, and this is required in derivatives like *a Vandyke beard*.

venal, venial The word *venal* means 'corrupt', 'easy to bribe'. But the rare word *venial* means 'easy to overlook or to forgive, trifling (of an offence)'.

vender, vendor The preferred British spelling is *vendor*, while American English favours *vender*.

vendetta Originally, a *vendetta* was a prolonged feud between two families. Today the word is often used to denote a sustained and unpleasant attack on a person or a group, as in *He accused the tabloids of waging a vendetta against him.* This use is acceptable. However, a vendetta is *pursued* (or *waged*) against someone. It is not good style to write *He had a vendetta against the company.* The word does not mean 'grudge'.

vengeance The word is so spelled, and *vengence is wrong.

Venusian, Venerean Strictly, the adjective meaning 'pertaining to the planet Venus' should be *Venerean*, just as we use *Martian* for 'pertaining to Mars' and *Jovian* for 'pertaining to Jupiter'. Some years ago, however, the astronomers astonishingly voted to make *Venusian* their official term. If you are writing a scientific work, then, you must fall into line with *Venusian*. In other contexts, though, you may choose the more literate *Venerean*. The official decision is preposterous: it is as though physicians had voted that sexually transmitted diseases should be called *venusial diseases.

verbal See **oral**.

verbal noun See **gerund**.

verbs ending in -*ie* The few verbs of this form all show the same irregularity in spelling their *-ing* forms: *die, dies, died, dying; lie, lies, lay, lying; tie, ties, tied, tying.* A partial exception is the rare verb *hie*, for which *hieing* is more frequent than *hying*.

verbs ending in -*y* Most regular verbs ending in *-y* preceded by a vowel letter are perfectly normal in their written forms: *plays, played, playing; conveys, conveyed, conveying; enjoys, enjoyed, enjoying.* The only exceptions are *lay, lays, laid, laying; pay, pays, paid, paying;* and *say, says, said, saying.* But regular verbs ending in *-y* preceded by a consonant letter all show the same irregularities of spelling: *try, tries, tried, trying; spy, spies, spied, spying; copy, copies, copied, copying, copier.*

very In standard English, *very* can modify only an adjective or an adverb: *She is very clever; She did it very carefully.* The word should not be used to modify a preposition: things like *Graham Greene was very against divorce* are unacceptable in careful writing. Write instead *Graham Greene was very much against divorce*, or, much better, *Graham Greene was strongly opposed to divorce.*

You should also be careful about using *very* with participles. Write *Her paintings are much admired*, not *Her paintings are very admired.* But a few participles are now accepted as adjectives, and you can safely use *very* with these: *very interested*, *very concerned*, and some others. If in doubt, avoid *very*: write *She is deeply involved with drug addicts*, not *She is very involved . . .

very real This curious collocation is almost always inappropriate and waffly. After all, *the very real issues* can hardly denote anything different from *the real issues*, which in turn is unlikely to mean anything more than *the issues*. Who would suspect you of having non-existent issues in mind, or issues that are only slightly real?

vexatious The word is so spelled, and *vexacious* is wrong.

viable Overused and often misused. The word does not mean 'plausible', 'workable' or 'feasible'; it means 'capable of normal growth and development', 'capable of independent existence'. It is fine to write *A fetus is not viable before 28 weeks*, meaning that the fetus cannot survive outside its mother's body before this time. But it is wrong to write *a viable product* if all you mean is a product which can be successfully sold.

vial See **phial**.

vice, vise British English uses *vice* in all senses. American English requires *vise* for the clamping tool, but *vice* in all other senses.

vice- This, meaning 'deputy', is a prefix, and it must always be written as one, and never as a separate word. It is almost always hyphenated: *vice-chair*, *vice-president*, and so on.

vice-versa This Latin phrase means 'the other way round', and it is often misused. Here is an example of acceptable use: *The Indians have accused the Pakistanis of artillery strikes and vice-versa*. This, of course, means that the Pakistanis have also accused the Indians of artillery strikes, though it might be better style to write *The Indians and the Pakistanis have accused each other of artillery strikes*. But here is an example of faulty use: *The USA has expelled a number of Russian diplomats and vice-versa*. Presumably what the writer means is that Russia has expelled a number of American diplomats, but what he has written appears to mean that a number of Russian diplomats have expelled the USA, which is gibberish.

vicious, viscous The adjective *vicious* means 'very nasty, violent', while *viscous* means 'very thick and slow-running'. Thugs are vicious, but honey is viscous.

Vietnamese names In a Vietnamese name, unlike in a Chinese name, the surname comes last. So, for example, *Nguyen Cao Ky* is *Ky* or *Mr Ky* at a later mention.

vilify The word, which is distantly related to *vile*, is so spelled, and *✳villify* is wrong.

violoncello This now rare word is so spelled, with three Os, and *✳violincello* is wrong: the word is not spelled like *violin*. In practice, the instrument is almost always called a *cello*. See **cello**.

viscous See **vicious**.

vise See **vice**.

vital See **crucial**.

viz. This Latin abbreviation means 'namely', and it should not be used. Write *namely* instead.

vocal cords The muscular bands in the throat which allow us to speak are *vocal cords*, or, in technical use, *vocal folds*. The spelling *✳vocal chords* is wrong.

volcano, vulcanism A mountain which explodes is a *volcano*, and the derived adjective is *volcanic*. However, volcanic activity is *vulcanism*, and a scientist who studies volcanoes is a *vulcanologist*. Why the difference? The forms with O are derived from Italian, while those with U are derived from Latin.

vowel Vowels are speech sounds, not letters. Native speakers of English may use anywhere from about fourteen to about twenty vowels, depending on the accent. For example, most of the words 'peat', 'pit', 'pate', 'pet', 'pared', 'pat', 'plight', 'part', 'pawed', 'pot', 'putt', 'put', 'pert', 'pout' and 'point' will have different vowels for you, regardless of your accent, though possibly not all of them will. But our roman alphabet provides only the five letters A E I O U for spelling all these vowels, with a little half-hearted assistance from Y and occasionally from other letters. The letters A E I O U can be called *vowel letters*, but calling them *vowels* is loose and misleading. See also **consonant**.

wacky, whacky Both spellings are in use, though most sources prefer *wacky*.

Washington The name *Washington* is given both to the American capital city and to one of the states of the USA. If there is any possibility of misunderstanding, American practice is to write *Washington, DC* for the city (never ✳*Washington City*) and *Washington State* for the state. (The *DC* here stands for *District of Columbia*, the small federal territory containing the city.) Writers elsewhere are advised to follow suit, though *Washington* may be written alone whenever there is no possibility of misunderstanding.

waste, wastage The word *wastage* is not a fancy equivalent for *waste*, and you should not write things like this: ✳*Low-flow toilets reduce wastage of water*. *Waste* is failure to use something which could easily be used. But *wastage* is loss resulting from unavoidable natural causes, such as evaporation.

Waste Land, The T. S. Eliot's poem is *The Waste Land*, not ✳*The Wasteland*.

watershed A *watershed* is literally a dividing line between rivers flowing into one sea and rivers flowing into another. For example, in the USA the Continental Divide is the watershed separating rivers flowing to the Pacific from those flowing to the Atlantic. For many years, the word has been used metaphorically to mean 'turning point', 'crucial event', as in this example: *The case of* Brown vs. Board of Education *was a watershed in American race relations*. Only a handful of conservatives still object to this figurative sense, and you should feel free to use it, if you like. However, the word is not properly used to mean 'area in which something happens'.

weave English has two unrelated verbs of the form *weave*, derived from different historical sources. The one pertaining to cloth has the past tense *wove* and the participle *woven*. But the one pertaining to movement is regular, with past tense and participle *weaved*. So, you should write *She wove this rug herself* but *She weaved her way through the crowd*, not ✳*She wove her way through the crowd*.

Wednesday The pronunciation of this word has strayed so far from the spelling that we have little choice but to memorize the now mysterious spelling.

weird This word is always so spelled, and ✳*wierd* is an error.

Welsh names Modern Welsh names pose few problems. However, figures from the past sometimes have established English forms of their names which are different from the Welsh forms, a good example being *Owen Glendower* for Welsh *Owain Glyndwr*. In such a case, it is best to use the established English form, though the Welsh form should perhaps be added at first mention.

Welsh rabbit, Welsh rarebit The conventional name for cheese on toast is *Welsh rabbit*, which is admittedly a snide joke. The strangely altered form *Welsh rarebit* sounds pretentious; it is now generally acceptable, but I think people who use it should be ashamed of themselves.

whacky See **wacky**.

whence The word *whence* means 'from where' or 'from which', and so you should never write *✱from whence*, which is a **pleonasm**. You can write *the villages whence the refugees are fleeing* or *the plant whence this new drug is derived*, but these usages are now old-fashioned, or at best frostily formal: it is more usual to write *the villages from where the refugees are fleeing* and *the plant from which this new drug is derived*. In contemporary English, *whence* is usual only as a logical connective, as in *The Basque village of Axpe, whose name means 'under the crag', nestles beneath a towering crag, whence its name*.

which See **that**.

while, whilst British English permits both *while* and *whilst*, but American English recognizes only *while*.

whisky, whiskey In Scotland, England and Canada the preferred spelling is *whisky*. In Ireland and the USA *whiskey* is preferred. If you like to show off your erudition, you may write *Scotch whisky* and *Canadian whisky* but *Irish whiskey*.

whither This is an archaic word for 'where to?'. You should not use it.

who See **that**.

wholesome See **healthy**.

whom In spite of the outraged howls of traditionalists, the word *whom* is all but dead in English, even in formal written English. There is just one circumstance in which *whom* is still usual in formal writing, and that is as the object of a preposition which immediately precedes it. Informal English uses *the woman I was living with* and *Who did you give it to?*, while formal written English may use instead *the woman with whom I was living* and *To whom did you give it?* But this is the only case in which *whom* is normal and proper.

The American newspaper columnist who chided George Bush for his slogan *Who do you trust?* and demanded instead *✱Whom do you trust?* must have spent several generations living in a cave. Things like *✱Whom do you* *trust?* are not English, and have not been English for a very long time. Don't even think about trying to use them.

The form *whom* is now probably not native to any English-speakers at all, and most people find it utterly mysterious. Many people, having dimly gathered that there is something desirable about *whom*, make desperate but wholly misguided efforts to introduce it into their speech and writing. As a result, they produce monstrosities which are not acceptable in any variety of English, not even the most frostily formal. A good example is this, which I recently found in a serious newspaper: *a friend whom she thought was perfect*. Well, unless you think that *She thought him was perfect* is good English, you will quickly see the nonsense here. This writer clearly had no understanding of *whom* but had allowed herself to be persuaded that there was something good about sticking it into her writing, and so stick it in she did – disastrously. Another example of the same error is the classic line, in answering the phone: *Whom shall I say is speaking?* To this there can be only one answer: *You can say me is speaking.*

Almost as bad is the next example: *the young man whom she had been playing with*. You can write the normal *the young man* (*who*) *she had been playing with*, or you can write the very formal *the young man with whom she had been playing*, but tangling them up like this is inexcusable: it represents just one more pathetic attempt at shoving *whom* in where it doesn't belong, from a misplaced sense of guilt.

Very different, but also wholly unacceptable, is the error illustrated by this example: *We were talking about whom should be invited*. Here, at first glance, you might think *whom* was acceptable, since it is immediately preceded by the preposition *about*. But it is not. The problem is that *who* here is not the object of *about*. Instead, the object of the preposition is the entire sequence *who should be invited*. And even the most confused speaker of English is probably not going to suspect that *Whom should be invited?* is English.

Unless you are certain that you know how to use *whom* properly, it is safest not to use it at all.

whose Contrary to certain opinions, there is no difficulty at all in using *whose* with reference to things. It is perfectly normal in standard English to write sentences like the following: *The plane, whose pilot had safely ejected, crashed into the woods*; *The* Guardian, *whose typos are legendary, has published a collection of some of its funniest typos*; *Standard Basque, in whose construction Luis Michelena was deeply involved, has now gained general acceptance*. Of course, you should always consider whether the alternative *of which* might give you a more elegant result. In my examples it would not: *the pilot of which* is clumsy, *in the construction of which* is worse, and ✱*the typos of which* is not even English.

wife, the There are few more offensive expressions in the language than ✱*the wife*. Referring to your wife as ✱*the wife* implies strongly that she belongs to a set of collectibles including *the house, the car, the dog* and *the wife*, possibly more or less in that order.

will See **shall**.

-wise Only a handful of adverbs ending in *-wise* are established in standard English, notably *otherwise, clockwise, lengthwise* and *likewise*. The numerous recent formations like *clotheswise, healthwise* and *moneywise* should be avoided in careful writing, as should *ad hoc* formations like *population-resource-wise*, which represent nothing more than a failure to construct an English sentence.

withhold The word is so spelled, with two Hs.

wordiness A very common failing is the writing of three or six words where one or two will do. It is impossible to list all the examples I have encountered recently, but here are a few of the most frequent cases, with suggested replacements:

Avoid	Write
as to whether	*whether*
at the present time	*now*
at this moment in time	*at present* or *now*
because of the fact that	*because*
by virtue of the fact that	*because*
due to the fact that	*because*
has a tendency to	*tends to*
in the absence of	*without*
in the event that	*if*
in the near future	*soon*
in the not too distant future	*eventually*
prior to	*before*
subsequent to	*after*
the question as to whether	*whether*

See also **omissible phrases**.

word processor This is properly written as two words, as shown; though now frequent, the variant *wordprocessor is hard on the eye and should be avoided.

worth while A tricky one. Originally, this expression was clearly two words, as it still plainly is in cases like *This task is not worth your while*. However, when no other word intervenes, opinion differs. Should we write *This is not worth while* or *This is not worthwhile*? In American English, the matter is settled, and the solid form *worthwhile* is the only possibility. In British English, some authorities still recommend the two-word form *worth while*, but in practice the one-word form now predominates in use, just as in the USA, and most authorities have bowed to reality and now recommend *worthwhile*, which is also the form preferred by recent British dictionaries. In another generation, *worthwhile* will be the only possibility in Britain, just as it already is in the USA. Meanwhile, you may still write *worth while* in British English if you prefer it, but it is beginning to look decidedly old-fashioned.

However, when this expression precedes the noun it is modifying, then it *must* be written as one word in all varieties of English, though writers who prefer *worth while* elsewhere may choose to hyphenate the preposed form: *a worthwhile investment* or *a worth-while investment*.

wrack See **rack**.

writing system See **language**.

-y, -ey The suffix making adjectives from nouns, and occasionally from other words, is *-y*, not *-ey*. Examples: *dirty, foggy, dusty, smelly, sunny*. A final E is lost: *icy, spicy, stony, smoky, wiry*. But there are exceptions. A word ending in UE keeps its E: *gluey*. The word *hole* makes *holey*, in order to distinguish the result from *holy*. If the source word ends in Y, the ending is *-ey*, as in *clayey* and the rare *skyey*. A few such words have two forms: *gam(e)y, hom(e)y, mous(e)y, nos(e)y, stag(e)y*. With these, you may use whichever spelling you prefer. Note also the unusual case of **fiery**. If the source word ends in C, this is replaced by CK: *garlic, garlicky; panic, panicky*.

year-old Write *a fifteen-year-old boy*, and not *a fifteen-years-old boy*.

years You may write any of the following: *The war went on from 1939 to 1945*; *The war went on between 1939 and 1945*; *The war went on 1939–1945*. But do not tangle these up. All the following are hopelessly wrong: *The war went on from 1939–1945*; *The war went on between 1939 to 1945*; *The war went on between 1939–1945*.

yogurt, yoghurt, **yoghourt** Though this word has been in the language for over a century, its spelling has not yet settled down, and all three of these spellings are in use, though *yoghourt* is now much the rarest and seemingly on the way out. I recommend *yogurt*: this is much the simplest spelling, and it also happens to be the spelling used in Turkish, the language from which the word is taken.

yours This is the correct spelling, and both *your's and *yours' are wrong.

yo-yo All sources agree that the hyphenated version is the only acceptable spelling. This is odd, since it is hard to see what is wrong with the simpler *yoyo, but nobody seems willing to accept this spelling.

-yze, -yse British English permits only *-yse* in the words *analyse*, *catalyse* and *paralyse*. American English permits only *-yze*, and hence has *analyze*, *catalyze* and *paralyze*. But the related nouns are spelled *analysis*, *catalysis* and *paralysis* in all varieties of English.

See also **-ize**, **-ise**.

Annotated Bibliography

I have consulted all of the handbooks listed below in preparing my own handbook. All have their good points, though some have notable short-comings. Naturally, I find myself occasionally disagreeing with the advice offered in almost every one of them.

Allen, R. E., *Oxford Writers' Dictionary* (Oxford: Oxford University Press, 1981).

Every publisher has a house style summarized in a guidebook. The Oxford University Press has published its stylebook, which, like every such book, presents the style used in its own publications, without attempting anything more. This one is unusually detailed, but, like every house stylebook, it contains a few choices I find surprising.

Amis, Kingsley, *The King's English* (London: HarperCollins, 1997).

Not a handbook at all, but merely a collection of Mr Amis's opinions. Some-times fun.

Burchfield, R. W., *The New Fowler's Modern English Usage* (Oxford: Oxford University Press, 1996).

A new edition of Fowler's classic *Modern English Usage* of 1926, required because accumulated changes have left Fowler's great book now somewhat out of date. Huge and comprehensive, and brilliantly done. Just about the only usage handbook I never disagree with.

The Economist Style Guide: Books, 1998).

Another style guide. Brief but good.

Greenbaum, Sidney, and Janet Whitcut, *Longman Guide to English Usage*
(London: Longman, 1988).

One of the best guides to British English, with comments on American usage.

Howard, Godfrey, *The Good English Guide* (London: Macmillan, 1993).

Contemporary, refreshing, a little idiosyncratic.

Inman, Colin, *The Financial Times Style Guide* (London: Financial Times/
Prentice Hall, 1994).

This is another style guide, this time for the *FT*.

King, Graham, *Collins Wordpower: Word Check* (Glasgow: HarperCollins,
2000).

Brief and engagingly written. Unfortunately, the text of the book contains a
number of errors in English.

Partridge, Eric, *Usage and Abusage*, 3rd edition, revised by Janet Whitcut
(London: Penguin, 1999).

An updated version of a classic work.

Wilson, Kenneth G., *The Columbia Guide to Standard American English*
(New York: Columbia University Press, 1993).

Possibly the best guide to standard American English, though it also mentions
British usage where this differs significantly.